The Original

Summer Bridge Activities™

P9-DME-296

Preschool to Kindergarten

SBA was created by
Michele D. Van Leeuwen

written by
Julia Ann Hobbs
Carla Dawn Fisher

illustrations by
Magen Mitchell
Amanda Sorensen

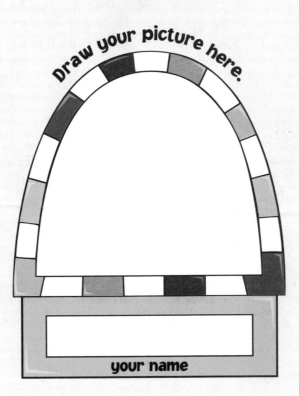

Draw your picture here.

your name

Summer Learning Staff
Clareen Arnold, Lori Davis, Melody Feist, Aimee Hansen, Christopher Kugler,
Kristina Kugler, Molly McMahon, Paul Rawlins, Liza Richards, Linda Swain

Design
Andy Carlson, Robyn Funk

Cover Art
Karen Maizel

ISBN: 978-1-59441-725-2

20 19 18 17 16 15 14 13 12 11

Dear Parents,

The summer months are a perfect time to reconnect with your child on many levels after a long school year. Your personal involvement is so important to your child's immediate and long-term academic success. No matter how wonderful your child's classroom experience is, your involvement outside the classroom will make it that much better!

Summer Bridge Activities™ is the original summer workbook developed to help parents support their children academically while away from school, and we strive to improve the content, the activities, and the resources to give you the highest quality summer learning materials available. Ten years ago, we introduced **Summer Bridge Activities™** to a small group of teachers and parents after I had successfully used it to help my first grader prepare for the new school year. It was a hit then, and it continues to be a hit now! Many other summer workbooks have been introduced since, but **Summer Bridge Activities™** continues to be the one that both teachers and parents ask for most. We take our responsibility as the leader in summer education seriously and are always looking for new ways to make summer learning more fun, more motivating, and more effective to help make your child's transition to the new school year enjoyable and successful!

We are now excited to offer you even more bonus summer learning materials online at www.**SummerBridgeActivities**.com! This site has great resources for both parents and kids to use on their own and together. An expanded summer reading program where kids can post their own book reviews, writing and reading contests with great prizes, assessment tests, travel packs, and even games are just a few of the additional resources that you and your child will have access to with the included **Summer Bridge Activities™** Online Pass Code.

Summer Learning has come a long way over the last 10 years, and we are glad that you have chosen to use **Summer Bridge Activities™** to help your children continue to discover the world around them by using the classroom skills they worked so hard to obtain!

Have a wonderful summer!

Michele Van Leeuwen and the Summer Learning Staff!

Hey Kids!

We bet you had a great school year!
Congratulations on all your hard work! We just want to say
that we're proud of the great things you did this year, and we're excited
to have you spend time with us over the summer. Have fun with your
Summer Bridge Activities™ workbook, and visit us online at
www.**SummerBridgeActivities**.com for more fun, cool, and exciting stuff!

Have a great summer!

The T. O. C. (Table of Contents)

Official Pass Code

dl6474c

Log on to **www.SummerBridgeActivities.com** and join!

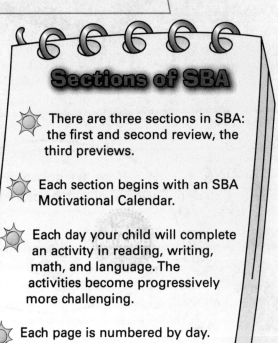

Sections of SBA

- There are three sections in SBA: the first and second review, the third previews.

- Each section begins with an SBA Motivational Calendar.

- Each day your child will complete an activity in reading, writing, math, and language. The activities become progressively more challenging.

- Each page is numbered by day.

Here's what you will find inside

Summer Bridge Activities™

Exercises in **Summer Bridge Activities™** (SBA) are easy to understand and presented in fun and creative ways that motivate children to review familiar skills while being progressively challenged. In addition to basic skills in reading, writing, math, and language arts, SBA contains activities that challenge and reinforce reading comprehension, phonemic awareness, and letter, word, and number recognition for young learners.

Daily exercises review and preview skills in reading, writing, math, and language arts. Activities are divided into three sections to correlate with traditional summer vacation.

Bonus Super Summer Science pages provide hands-on science activities.

A Summer Reading List introduces kids to some of today's popular titles as well as the classics. Kids can rate books they read and log on to www.**SummerBridgeActivities**.com to post reviews, find more great titles, and participate in national reading and writing contests!

Motivational Calendars begin each section and help kids achieve all summer long.

Discover Something New lists offer fun and creative activities that teach kids with their hands and get them active and learning.

Grade-specific flashcards provide a great way to reinforce basic skills in addition to the written exercises.

Removable Answer Pages ensure that parents know as much as their kids!

A Certificate of Completion for parents to sign congratulates kids for their work and welcomes them to the grade ahead.

A grade-appropriate, official Summer Fun pass code gives kids and parents online access to more bonus games, contests, and resources at www.**SummerBridgeActivities**.com.

Here are some groups who say our books are great!

Mr. Fredrickson

10 Ways to Maximize
The Original Summer Bridge Activities™

1 First, let your child explore the book. Flip through the pages and look at the activities with your child to help him become familiar with the book.

2 Help select a good time for reading or working on the activities. Suggest a time before your child has played outside and becomes too tired to do the work.

3 Provide any necessary materials. A pencil, ruler, eraser, and crayons are all that are required.

4 Offer positive guidance. Remember, the activities are not meant to be tests. You want to create a relaxed and positive attitude toward learning. Work through at least one example on each page with your child. "Think aloud" and show your child how to solve problems.

5 Give your child plenty of time to think. You may be surprised by how much children can do on their own.

6 Stretch your child's thinking beyond the page. If you are reading a book, you might ask, "What do you think will happen next?" or "What would you do if this happened to you?" Encourage your child to talk about her interests and observations about the world around her.

7 Reread stories and occasionally flip through completed pages. Completed pages and books will be a source of pride to your child and will help show how much he accomplished over the summer.

8 Read and work on activities while outside. Take the workbook out in the backyard or on a family campout. It can be fun wherever you are!

9 Encourage siblings, relatives, and neighborhood friends to help with reading and activities. Other children are often perfect for providing the one-on-one attention necessary to reinforce reading skills.

10 Give plenty of approval! Stickers and stamps are effective for recognizing a job well done. At the end of the summer, your child can feel proud of her accomplishments and will be eager for school to start.

Helping Your Child Learn

As a parent, you are eager for your child to learn and to achieve some of the skills needed in order to succeed in school. The best way for you to help your child is to create a living and learning environment in which your child will want to explore, learn new concepts, and practice new skills.

Here are some ideas for activities and materials that will enhance the learning experiences that you can provide for your child.

Parent:

Exercises for these skills can be found inside **Summer Bridge Activities**™ and can be used for extra practice.

Language Arts and Reading

The single most important skill that a child needs for success in school, and later in life, is to be "literate." In other words, your child must learn how to read. You can do many things to encourage literacy.

1. Read to your child every day. This often becomes a favorite time of the day for the child and parent.
   - Talk about the pictures.
   - Ask questions.
   - Ask your child to guess what is going to happen next.
   - Encourage your child to retell favorite stories or favorite parts of a story.
   - Have your child make up a new ending for a story.
   - Encourage "pretend" reading. This is when children look at the pictures and make up what they think the words say.

2. Encourage letter recognition. Preschoolers can begin developing an interest in reading and phonics by making observations of how we use written language.
   - Point out letters in the environment, such as on cereal boxes, in your child's name, and on billboards.
   - Find ways to help your child learn to match letters.
   - Play listening games. Have your child identify words that begin with the same sound.

3. Provide language arts materials. Fill your child's environment with literacy materials. Here is a suggested selection:
   • Magnetic letters
   • Books, magazines, newspapers, and catalogs
   • Paper, pencils, crayons, and paints (Encourage children to experiment with making circles, squiggles, and lines.)
   • CDs of children's music and recorded children's stories

Math and Science

Many toys and puzzles provide young children with early math and science learning experiences. Remember to point out all the ways we use numbers and science in our daily lives.

1. Cook or garden together. Not only is this a special activity for families to do together but the learning experiences themselves are infinite. Children can gain these valuable skills:
   • Measuring
   • Numbers and counting ("Stir 10 times" or "Add 1 cup water")
   • Increased vocabulary development (hot, cold, wet, dry, sticky, and so on)
   • Increased observation skills

2. Provide math and science materials and activities. Here is a suggested list:
   • Magnifying glass
   • Blocks and other building materials
   • Magnets and magnetic numerals
   • Scales (concepts of heavier and lighter)
   • Pouring liquids
   • Sink and float objects for the bath or for sink water play
   • Calculators and toy cash registers
   • Puzzles
   • Sorting, matching, and classifying games
   • Trips to science and children's museums
   • Taking walks and observing nature

Summertime = Reading Time!

We all know how important reading is, but this summer show kids how GREAT the adventures of reading really are! Summer learning and summer reading go hand-in-hand, so here are a few ideas to get you up and going:

Encourage your child to read out loud to you and make a theatrical performance out of even the smallest and simplest read. Have fun with reading and impress the family at the campsite next to you at the same time!

Establish a time to read together each day. Make sure and ask each other about what you are reading and try to relate it to something that may be going on within the family.

Show off! Let your child see you reading for enjoyment and talk about the great things that you are discovering from what you read. Laugh out loud, stamp your feet—it's summertime!

Sit down with your child and establish a summer reading program. Use our cool Summer Reading List and Summer Reading Program at www.**SummerBridgeActivities**.com, or visit your local bookstore and, of course, your local library. Encourage your child to select books on topics he is interested in and on his reading level. A rule of thumb for selecting books at the appropriate reading level is to choose a page and have your child read it out loud. If he doesn't know five or more of the words on the page, the book may be too difficult.

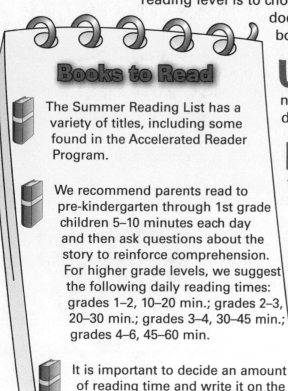

Books to Read

The Summer Reading List has a variety of titles, including some found in the Accelerated Reader Program.

We recommend parents read to pre-kindergarten through 1st grade children 5–10 minutes each day and then ask questions about the story to reinforce comprehension. For higher grade levels, we suggest the following daily reading times: grades 1–2, 10–20 min.; grades 2–3, 20–30 min.; grades 3–4, 30–45 min.; grades 4–6, 45–60 min.

It is important to decide an amount of reading time and write it on the SBA Motivational Calendar.

Use your surroundings (wherever you are) to show your child how important reading is on a daily basis. Read newspaper articles, magazines, stories, and road maps during the family vacation...just don't get lost!

Find books that tie into your child's experiences. If you are going fishing or boating, find a book on the subject to share. This will help your child learn and develop interests in new things.

Get library cards! Set a regular time to visit the library and encourage your child to have her books read and ready to return so she is ready for the next adventure! Let your child choose her own books. It will encourage her to read and pursue her own interests.

Make up your own stories! This is great fun and can be done almost anywhere—in the car, on camping trips, in a canoe, on a plane! Encourage your child to tell the story with a beginning, middle, AND end! To really challenge each other, start with the end, then middle, and then the beginning— yikes!

Summer Bridge Activities™

Summer Reading List

Fill in the stars and rate your favorite (and not so favorite) books here and online at www.SummerBridgeActivities.com!

1 = I struggled to finish this book.
2 = I thought this book was pretty good.
3 = I thought this book rocked!
4 = I want to read this book again and again!

Madeline
Bemelmans, Ludwig ☆☆☆☆

Goldilocks and the Three Bears
Brett, Jan ☆☆☆☆

Moo, Baa, La La La!
Boynton, Sandra ☆☆☆☆

Clifford, the Big Red Dog
Bridwell, Norman ☆☆☆☆

Goodnight, Moon
Brown, Margaret W. ☆☆☆☆

Cross-Country Cat
Calhoun, Mary ☆☆☆☆

The Very Hungry Caterpillar
Carle, Eric ☆☆☆☆

Click, Clack, Quackity-Quack
Cronin, Doreen ☆☆☆☆

Bark, George
Feiffer, Jules ☆☆☆☆

Corduroy
Freeman, Don ☆☆☆☆

Is Your Mama a Llama?
Guarino, Deborah ☆☆☆☆

Angelina Ballerina
Holabird, Katharine ☆☆☆☆

The Snowy Day
Keats, Ezra Jack ☆☆☆☆

There's a Nightmare in My Closet
Mayer, Mercer ☆☆☆☆

Make Way for Ducklings

McCloskey, Robert ☆☆☆☆☆

Train Leaves the Station

Merriam, Eve ☆☆☆☆

The Little Engine that Could

Piper, Watty ☆☆☆☆

The Tale of Peter Rabbit

Potter, Beatrix ☆☆☆☆

Curious George

Rey, H.A. ☆☆☆☆

Little Pea

Rosenthal, Amy Krouse ☆☆☆☆

When was the last time your mother told you, "Make sure you eat all your candy at dinner, or there will be no spinach for dessert…"?

Heavy is a Hippopotamus

Schlein, Miriam ☆☆☆☆

Sheep in a Jeep ☆☆☆☆

Shaw, Nancy E.

Take five sheep and one red jeep, put them all together on a hill that's steep… There's bound to be trouble.

A Mouse in the House!

Wagner, Gerda ☆☆☆☆

Mike and the Bike

Ward, Michael ☆☆☆☆

Mike takes off on an adventure around the world with his best friend—his bike.

Don't Let the Pigeon Drive the Bus!

Willems, Mo ☆☆☆☆

Join the SBA Kids Summer Reading Club!

Quick! Get Mom or Dad to help you log on and join the SBA Kids Summer Reading Club. You can find more great books, tell your friends about your favorite titles, and even win cool prizes! Log on to www.SummerBridgeActivities.com and sign up today.

Summer Bridge Activities™

Motivational Calendar

Month _____

My parents and I decided that if I complete
15 days of **Summer Bridge Activities™** and
read _____ minutes a day, my incentive/reward will be:

_____

Child's Signature _____ Parent's Signature _____

Day 1	☆	📖	____	**Day 9**	☆	📖	____
Day 2	☆	📖	____	**Day 10**	☆	📖	____
Day 3	☆	📖	____	**Day 11**	☆	📖	____
Day 4	☆	📖	____	**Day 12**	☆	📖	____
Day 5	☆	📖	____	**Day 13**	☆	📖	____
Day 6	☆	📖	____	**Day 14**	☆	📖	____
Day 7	☆	📖	____	**Day 15**	☆	📖	____
Day 8	☆	📖	____				

Child: Color the ☆ for daily activities completed.
Color the 📖 for daily reading completed.

Parent: Initial the ____ when all activities are complete.

Discover Something New!

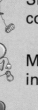

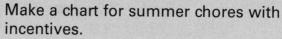

1 Sign up for summer classes through the community or local parks.

2 Make a chart for summer chores with incentives.

3 Write to a relative about your summer plans.

4 Check the library for free children's programs.

5 Boost reading—make labels for household objects.

6 Start a journal of summer fun.

Fun Activity Ideas to Go Along with the First Section!

7 Make up a story at dinner. Each person adds a new paragraph.

8 Enjoy the summer solstice. Time the sunrise and sunset.

9 Have some bubble fun: one-third cup liquid dishwashing soap, plus two quarts water. Use cans or pipe cleaners for dippers.

10 Have a zoo contest—find the most African animals.

11 Shop together—use a calculator to compare prices.

12 Tune up those bikes. Wash 'em, too.

13 Play flashlight tag.

14 Check out a science book—try some experiments.

15 Arrange photo albums.

Triceratops

Trace the dotted lines.

3

 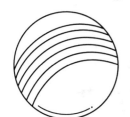 Color the first picture and all the others in each row that are the same.

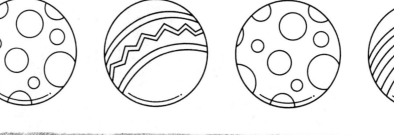

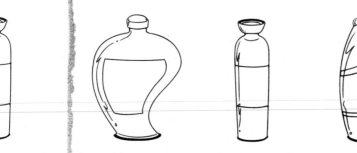

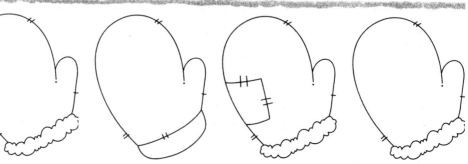

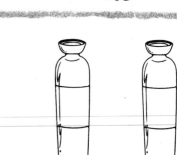

Diplodocus

Trace the dotted lines.

5

© **Summer Bridge Activities**™ Pre–K

Color all the squares on the page.

This is a square.

Pteranodon

Trace the dotted lines.

11

Find all the rectangles and put an "X" on them.

This is a rectangle.

X

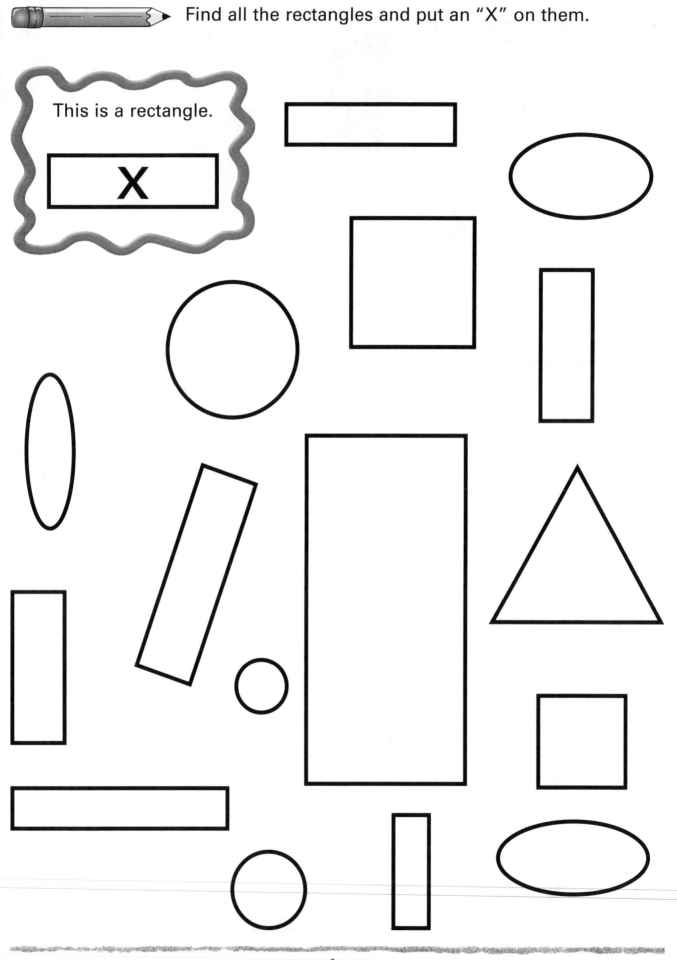

Trachodon

Trace the dotted lines.

13

An egg has an oval shape. Color all the ovals.

This is an oval.

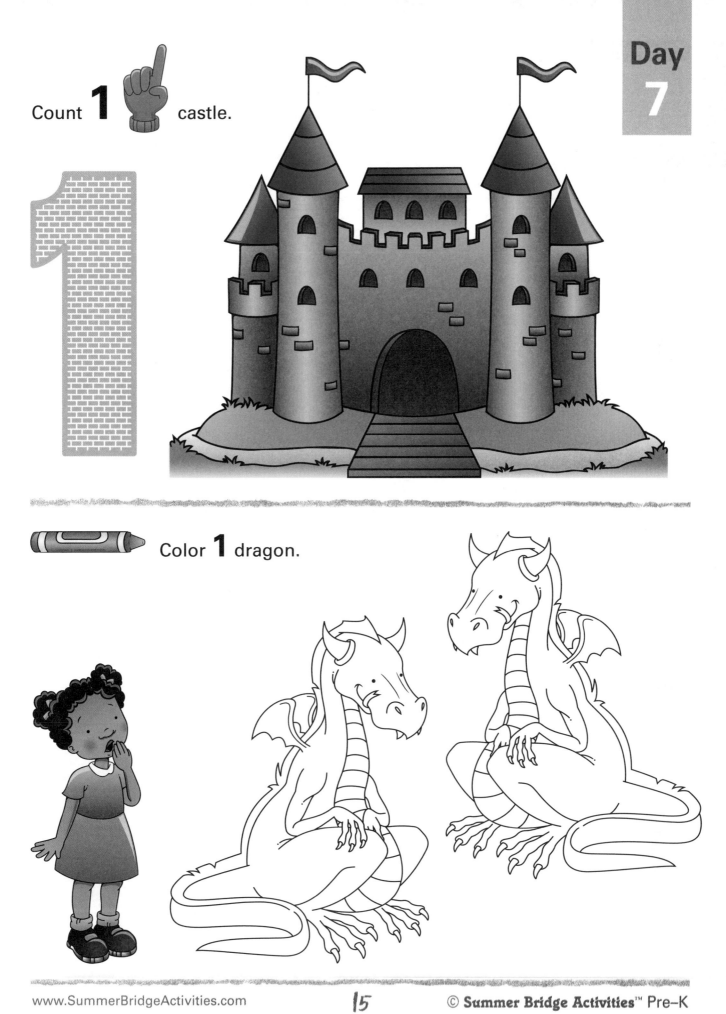

Count **1** castle.

1

Color **1** dragon.

15

Trace these lines. Begin at the star ★.

Count **2** garages.

Color **2** automobiles.

17

A kite has a diamond shape. Draw lines from the big purple diamond to all the diamond shapes.

This is a diamond.

Count **3** flags.

Color **3** classroom items.

19

Hearts stand for love. Color this heart doll.

This is a heart.

Count **4**  singers.

Color **4** musical instruments.

21

Sometimes we make a wish on a star. Count all the stars and color them yellow. I counted _____ stars.

This is a star.

Draw lines to match the big and little shapes that are the same.

Color.

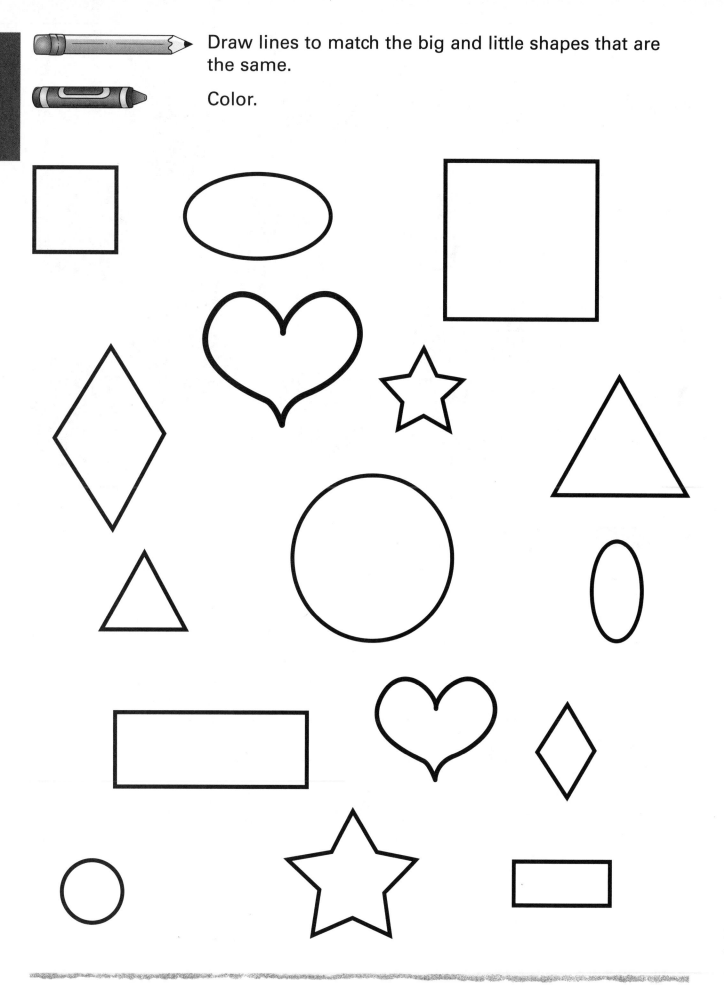

Count **8** leaves.

Color **8** apples.

 Circle and color the objects that are the same size.

EXAMPLE:

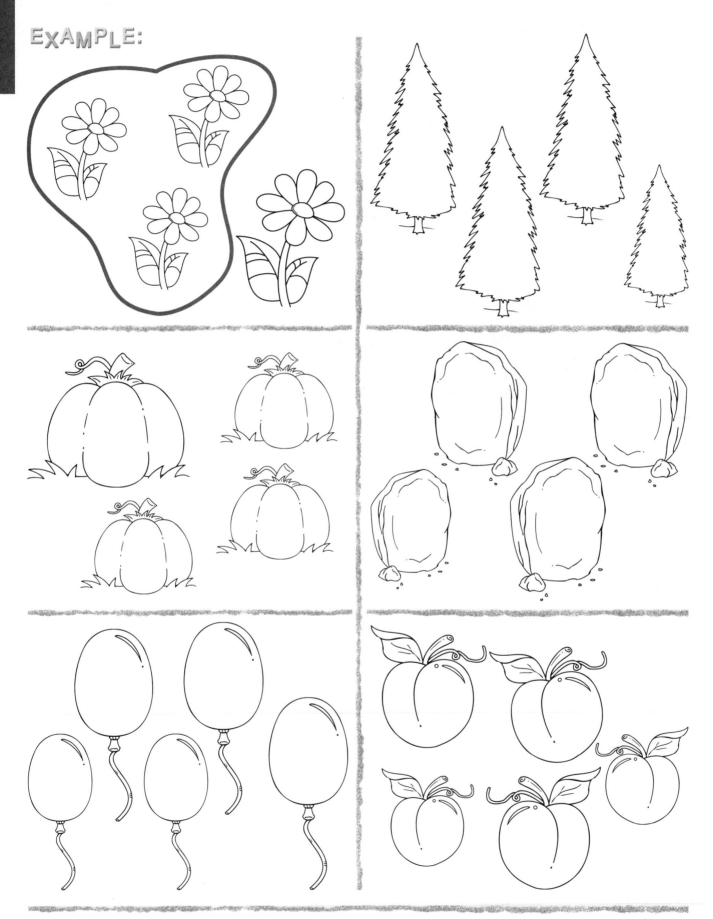

Count **7** clouds.

Color **7** umbrellas.

© **Summer Bridge Activities**™ Pre–K

Count and circle the correct number for each row.
Color.

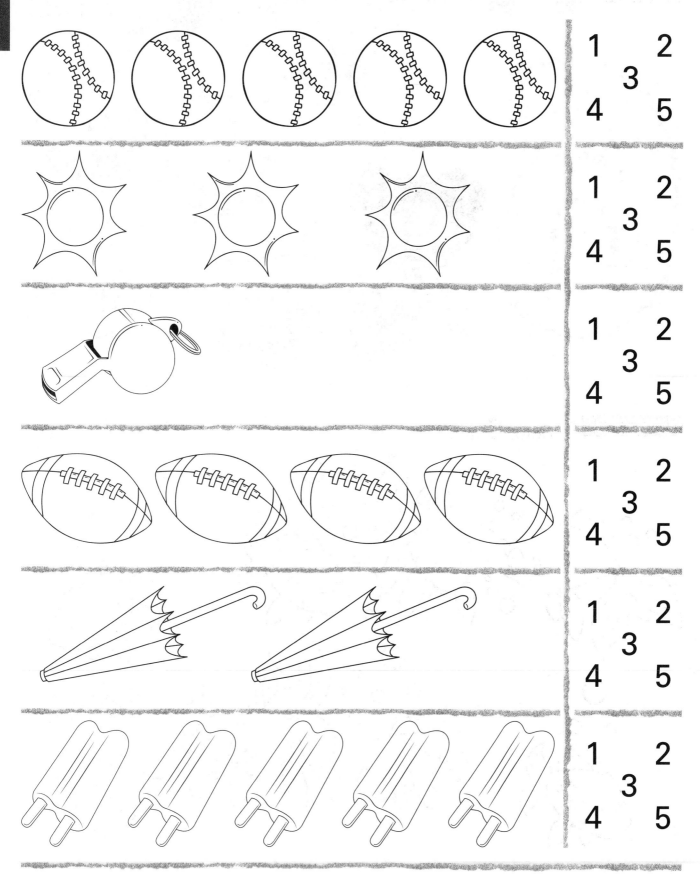

Count **6** fish bowls.

Color **6** fish.

Put a square ☐ around the objects that are shaped like circles ◯.

Color them.

Count **5** pots.

Color **5** flowers.

23

Count **9** sandwiches.

Color **9** glasses of juice.

31

 Find and outline each shape with a different color.

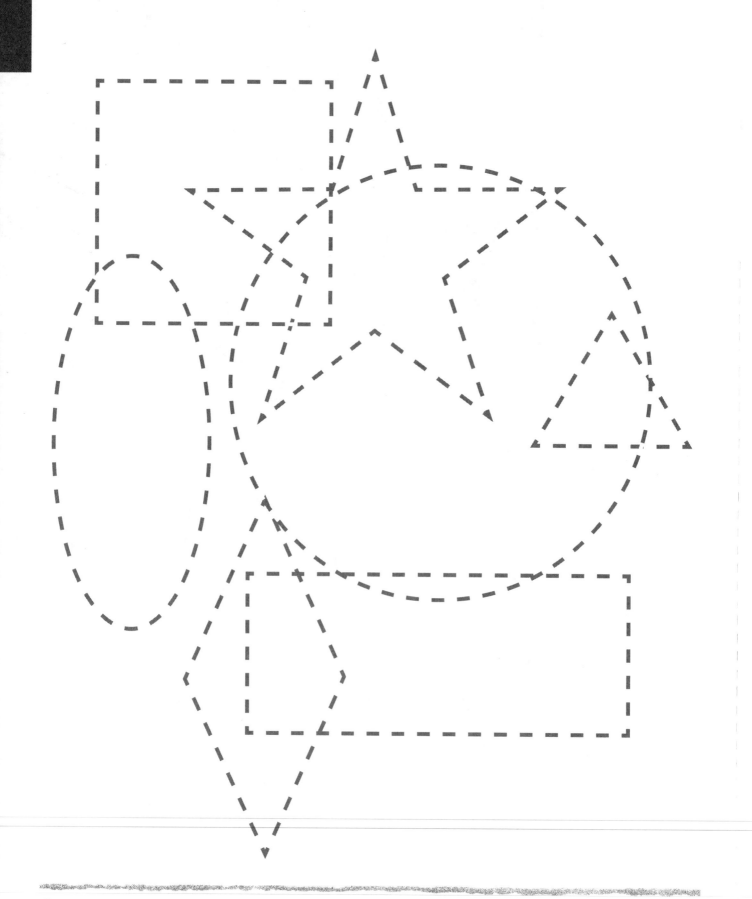

Summer Bridge Activities™

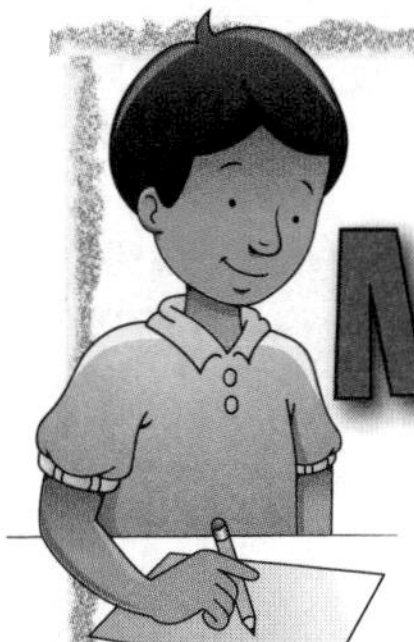

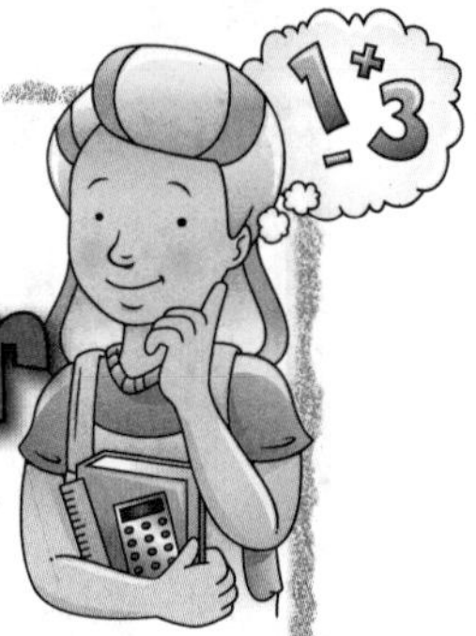

Motivational Calendar

Month ______________________

My parents and I decided that if I complete 20 days of **Summer Bridge Activities™** and read _____ minutes a day, my incentive/reward will be:

____

Child's Signature ____________________ Parent's Signature____________________

Day 1	☆	📖	_____	**Day 11**	☆	📖	_____
Day 2	☆	📖	_____	**Day 12**	☆	📖	_____
Day 3	☆	📖	_____	**Day 13**	☆	📖	_____
Day 4	☆	📖	_____	**Day 14**	☆	📖	_____
Day 5	☆	📖	_____	**Day 15**	☆	📖	_____
Day 6	☆	📖	_____	**Day 16**	☆	📖	_____
Day 7	☆	📖	_____	**Day 17**	☆	📖	_____
Day 8	☆	📖	_____	**Day 18**	☆	📖	_____
Day 9	☆	📖	_____	**Day 19**	☆	📖	_____
Day 10	☆	📖	_____	**Day 20**	☆	📖	_____

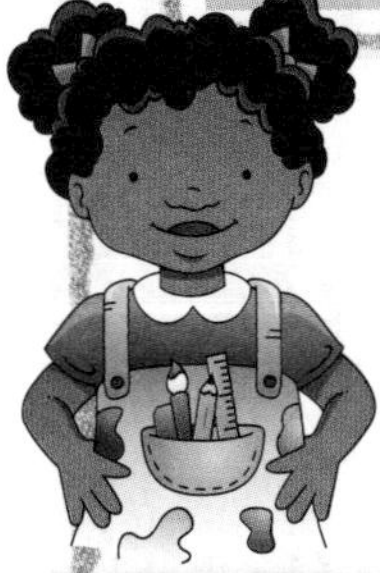

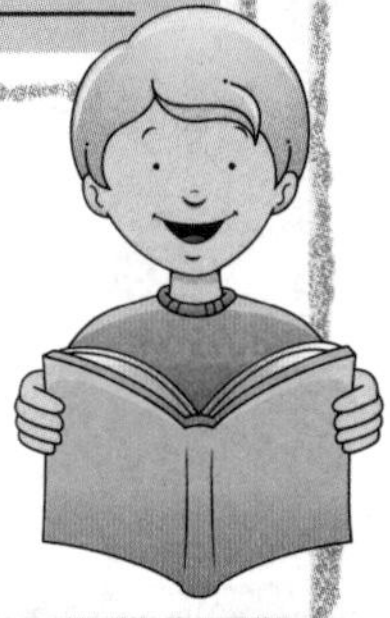

Child: Color the ☆ for daily activities completed.
Color the 📖 for daily reading completed.

Parent: Initial the ____ when all activities are complete.

Discover Something New!

1. Make a cereal treat.

2. Read a story.

3. Catch a butterfly.

4. Take a tour of the local hospital.

5. Check on how your garden is doing.

6. Organize your toys.

7. Go on a bike ride.

8. Run through the sprinklers.

Fun Activity Ideas to Go Along with the Second Section!

9. Go to the local zoo.

10. Create a family symphony with bottles, pans, and rubber bands.

11. Color noodles with food coloring. String them for a necklace or glue a design on paper.

12. Get the neighborhood together and play hide-and-seek.

13. Decorate your bike. Have a neighborhood parade.

14. Collect sticks and mud. Build a bird's nest.

15. Help plan your family grocery list.

16. Go swimming with a friend.

17. Clean your bedroom and closet.

18. In the early morning, listen to the birds sing.

19. Lie down on the grass and find shapes in the clouds.

20. Make snow cones with crushed ice and punch.

Count **10** paint cans.

10

Color **10** paintbrushes.

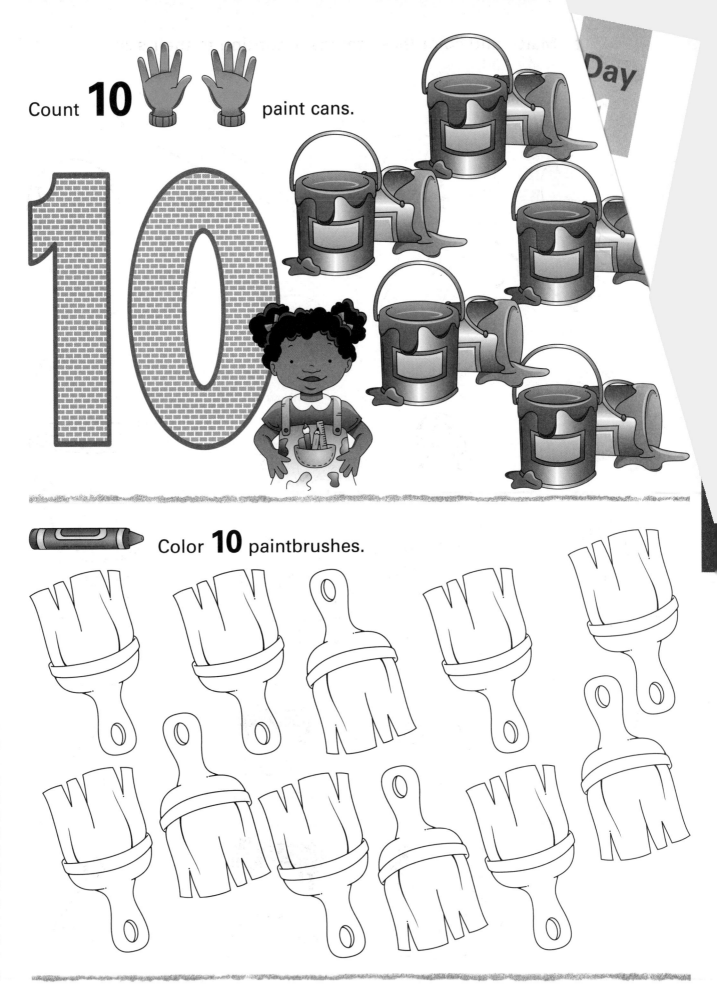

Match and color these things according to their size.

Count **11** balls.

Color **11** caps.

37

 Color the first shape and all the others in each row that are the same.

Count **12** moons.

Day 3

Color **12** stars.

 Draw lines to match the numbers to the boxes.

 Color the squares.

EXAMPLE:

1

2

3

4

5

Aa

apple

Write.

Color. These pictures begin like 🍎 .

ambulance

alligator

astronaut

ant

 Draw lines to match the numbers to the boxes.

 Color the squares.

EXAMPLE:

6

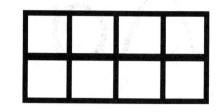

7

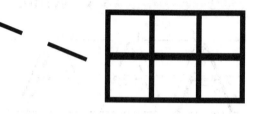

8

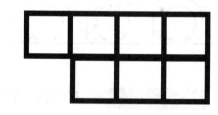

9

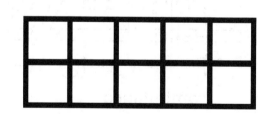

10

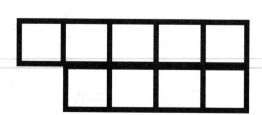

B b

balloon

Write.

B B B

b b b

Color. These pictures begin like 🎈.

bird

ball

bee

bike

Yellow

is the color of sunflowers.

Color all these pictures yellow.

duck

corn

pear

sunflower

bananas

sun

Cc

cup

Write.

Color. These pictures begin like .

can

cake

car

clown

Orange

is both a color and a kind of fruit.

Color all these pictures orange.

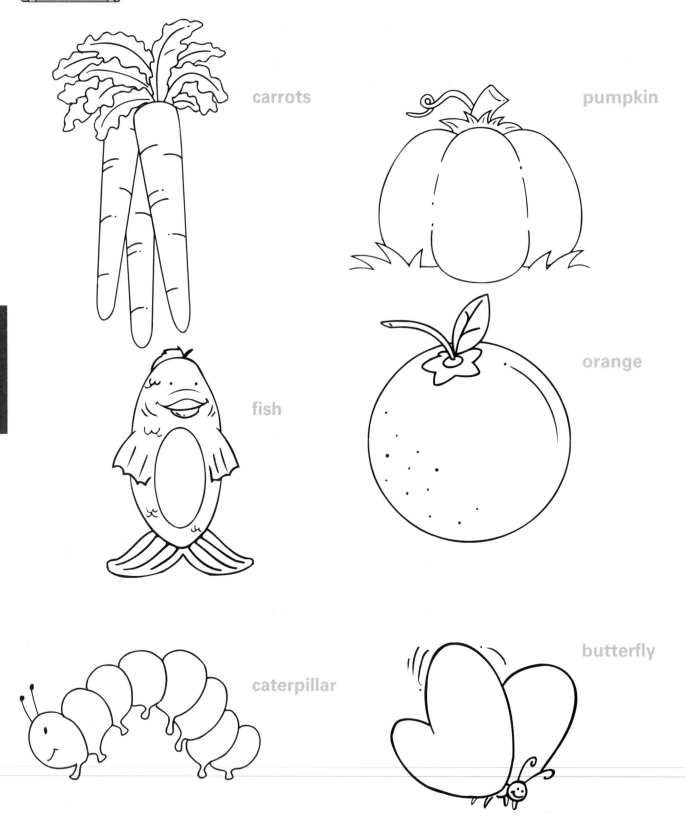

carrots

pumpkin

fish

orange

caterpillar

butterfly

Dd

dog

Write.

D D D D _____

d d d _____

Color. These pictures begin like  .

dinosaur

deer

dart

dress

Blue is the color of the sky.

Color all these pictures blue.

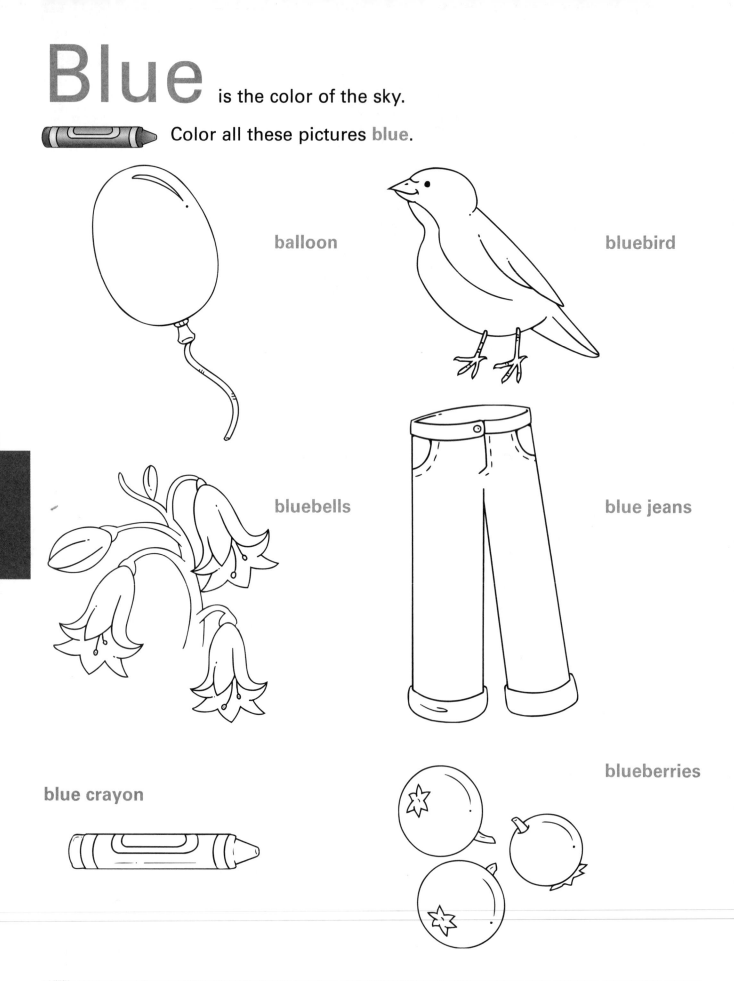

balloon

bluebird

bluebells

blue jeans

blueberries

blue crayon

E e

egg

Write.

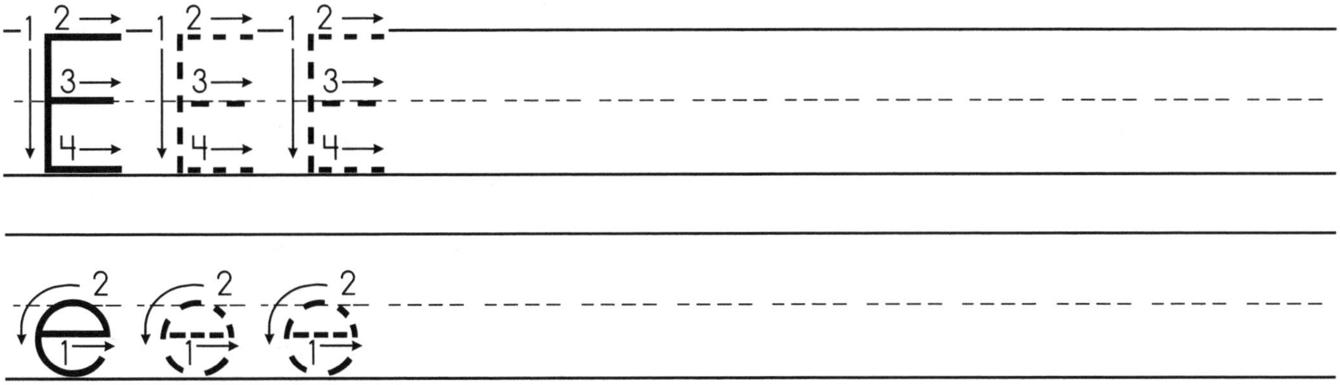

Color. These pictures begin like 🥚.

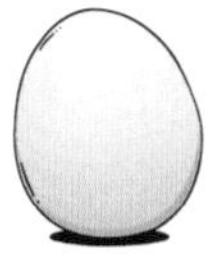

elephant

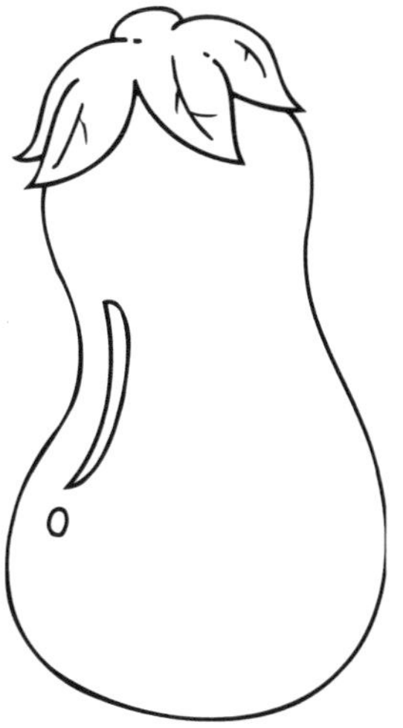

eggplant

elf

envelope

RBP

Green

grass is fun to play on in the summer.

Color all these pictures green.

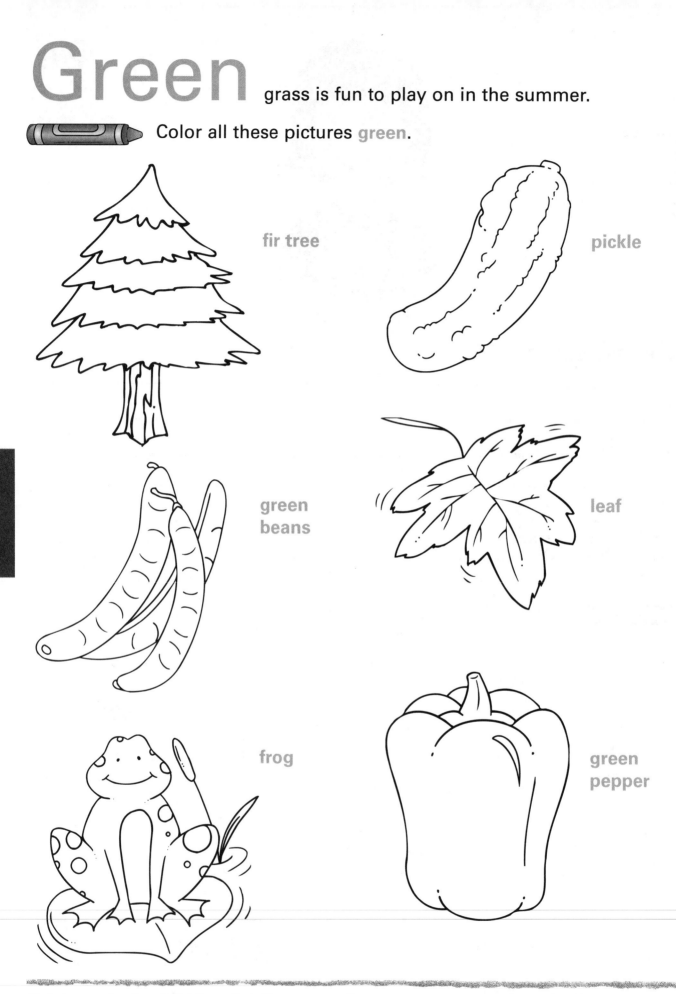

fir tree

pickle

green beans

leaf

frog

green pepper

F f

fish

Write.

Color. These pictures begin like 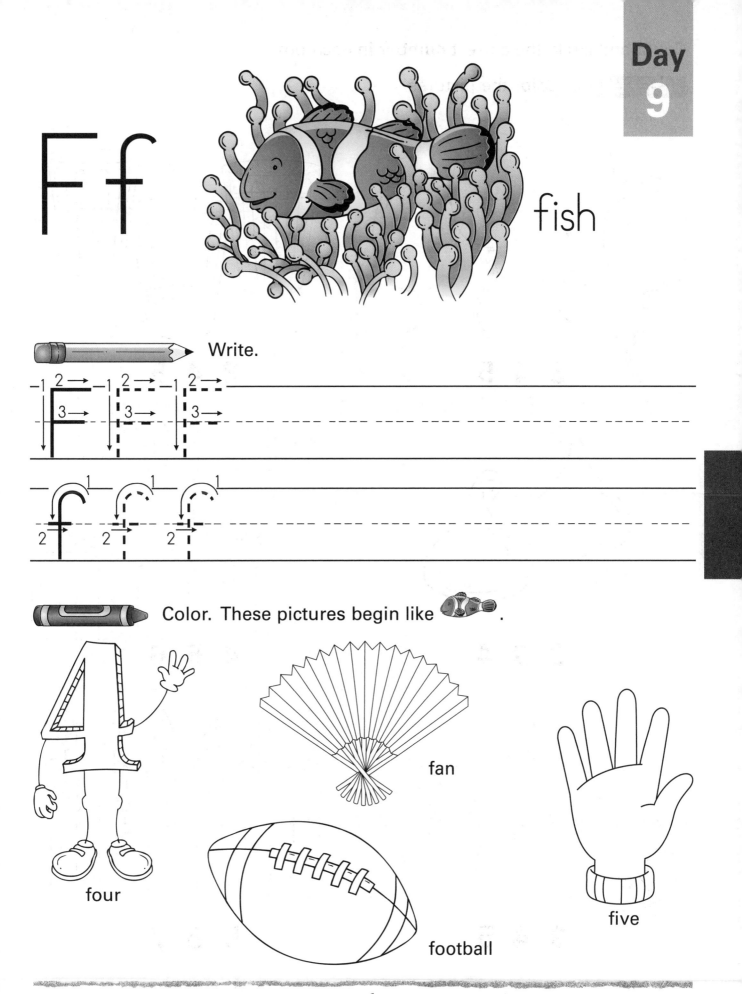.

four

fan

football

five

Count and circle the correct number in each box.

 Color the pictures.

3 4 5

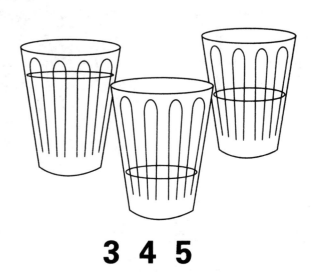

3 4 5

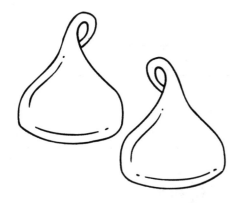

2 3 4

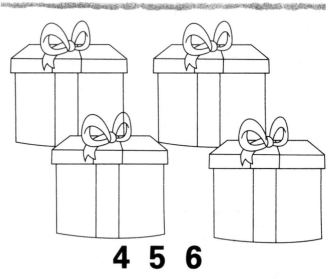

4 5 6

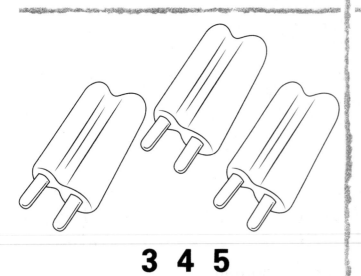

3 4 5

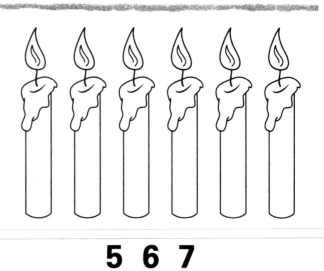

5 6 7

Gg

guitar

Write.

Color. These pictures begin like 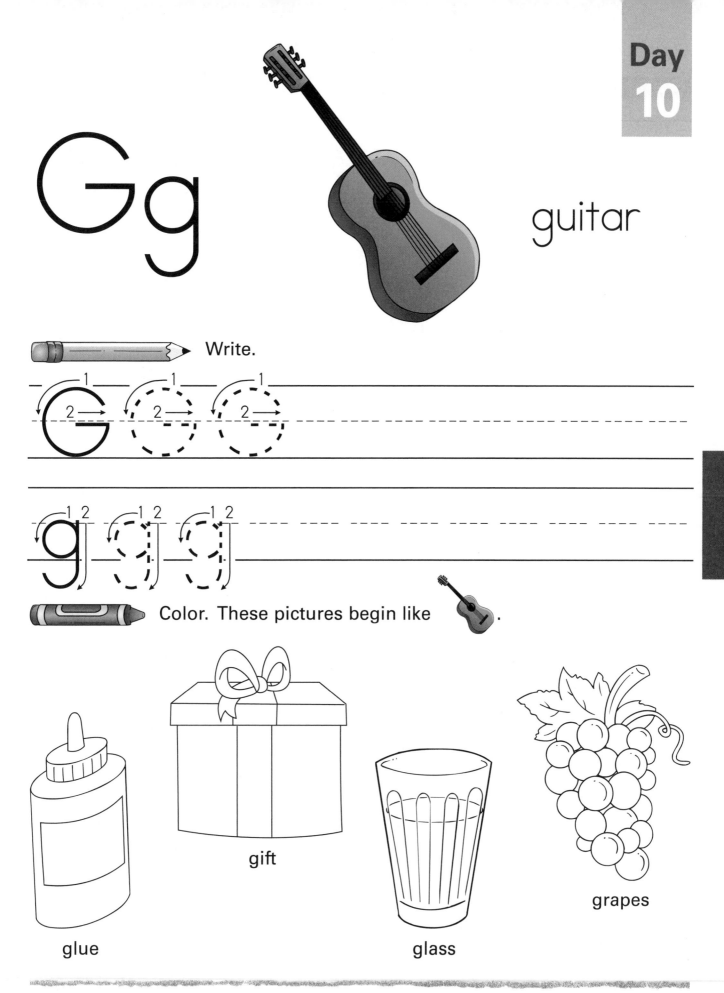.

glue

gift

glass

grapes

Count and circle the correct number in each box.

 Color the pictures.

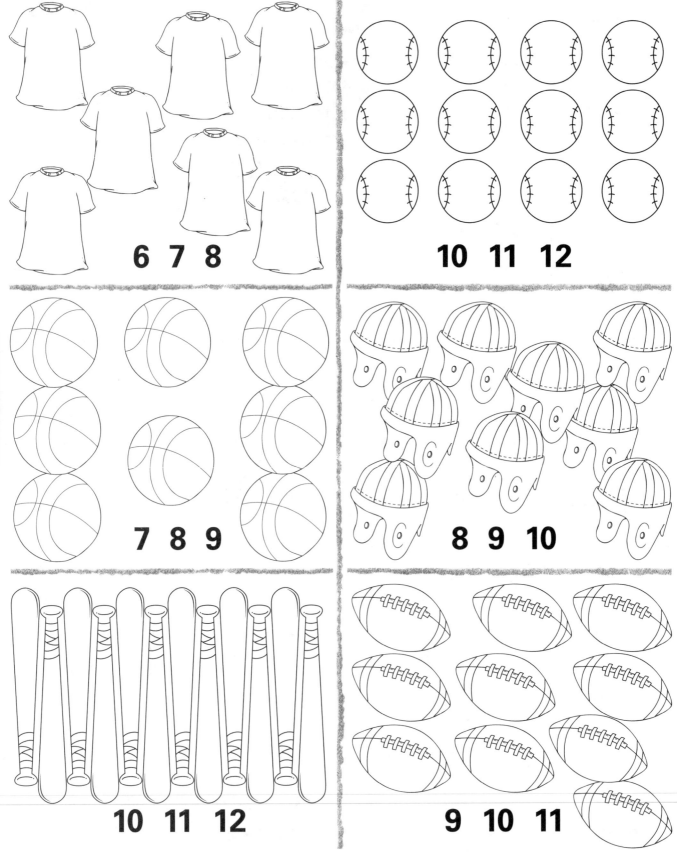

6 7 8

10 11 12

7 8 9

8 9 10

10 11 12

9 10 11

Hh

heart

Write.

Color. These pictures begin like 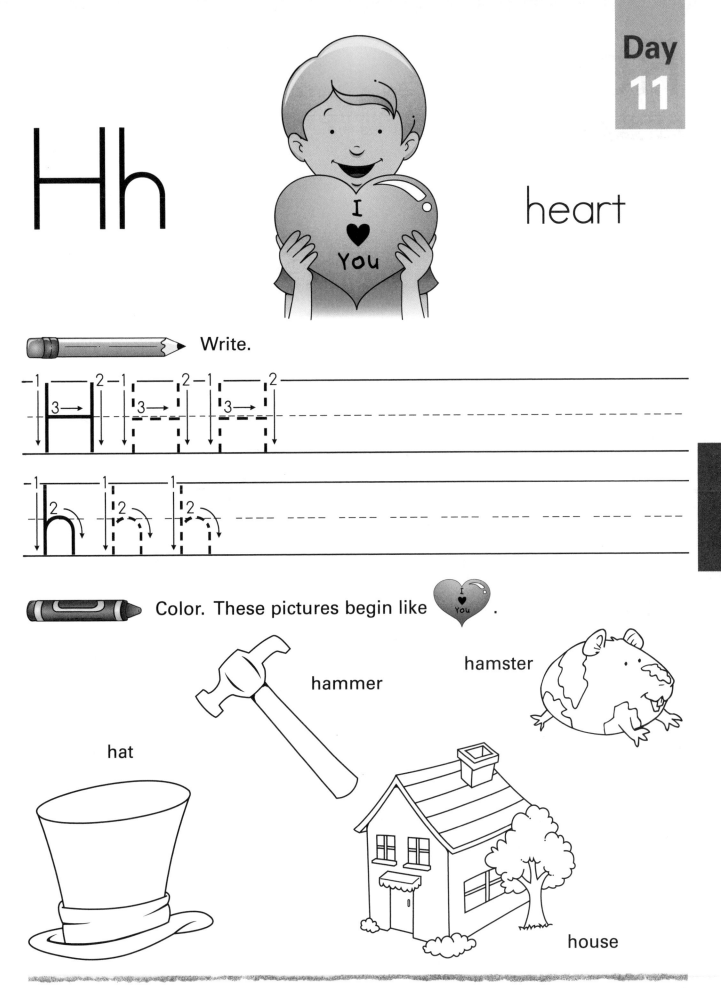.

hammer

hamster

hat

house

Red

is the color of Santa Claus's suit.

Color all these pictures **red**.

tulip

stop sign

fire engine

apple

cherries

cardinal

I i

igloo

✏️ Write.

2→ 1↓ 3→   2→ 1↓ 3→   2→ 1↓ 3→

1• ↓   1• ↓   1• ↓

🖍️ Color. These pictures begin like 🏠 .

inch

iguana

ink

instrument

Black is the color of shadows.

 Color all these pictures **black**.

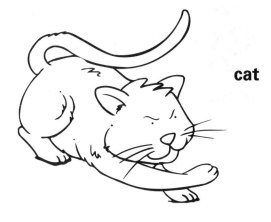 cat

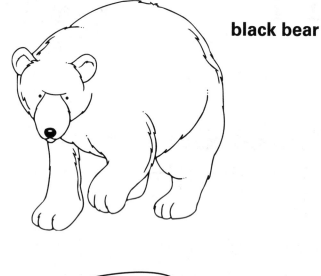 black bear

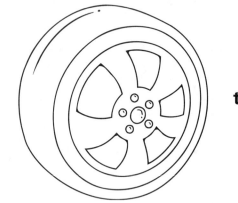 tire

 hat

 kettle

 crow

J j

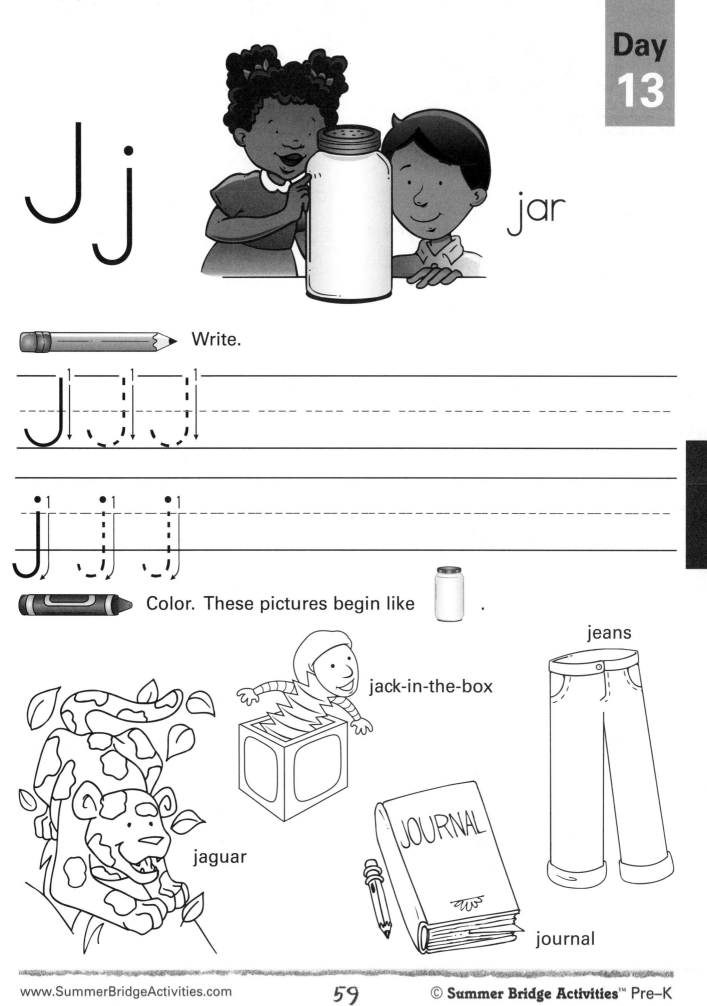

jar

Write.

J J J J

j j j j

Color. These pictures begin like ⬜ .

jaguar

jack-in-the-box

JOURNAL

journal

jeans

Purple
is the last color of the rainbow.

 Color all these pictures **purple**.

grapes

hat

purple
crayon

pansy

plum

eggplant

Kk

king

Write.

Color. These pictures begin like [king].

keys

kangaroo

kettle

kite

61

Brown is the color of chocolate.

Color all these pictures **brown**.

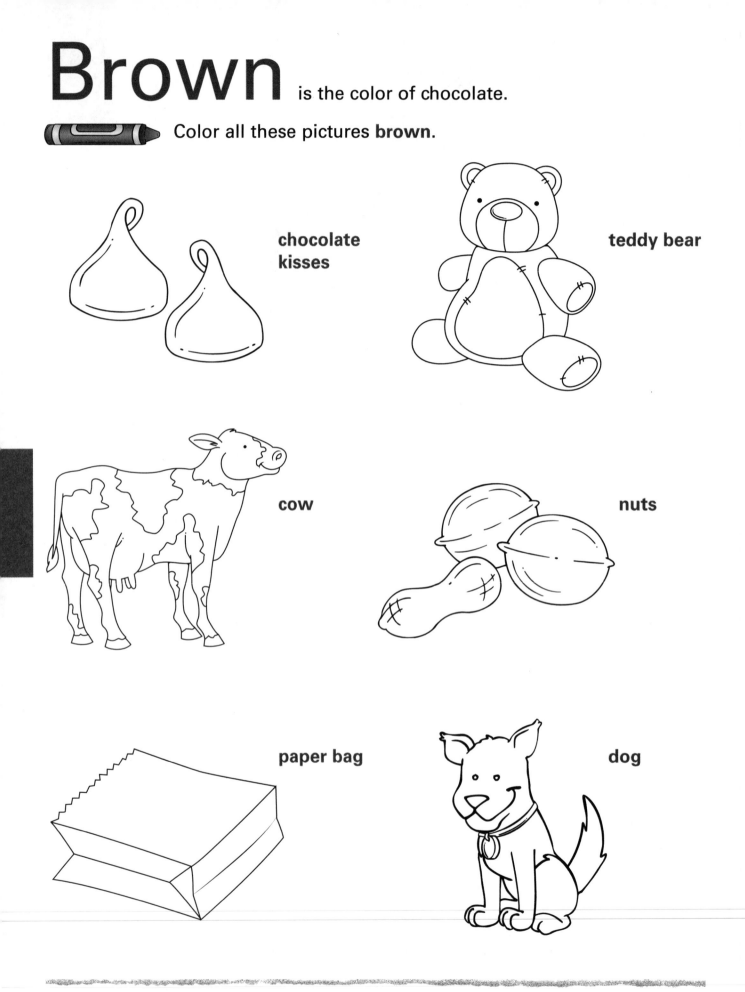

chocolate
kisses

teddy bear

cow

nuts

paper bag

dog

Nn

nail

Write.

-1 3 -2 -1 3 -2 -1 3 -2
N N N N

1 2 1 2 1 2
n n n

Color. These pictures begin like 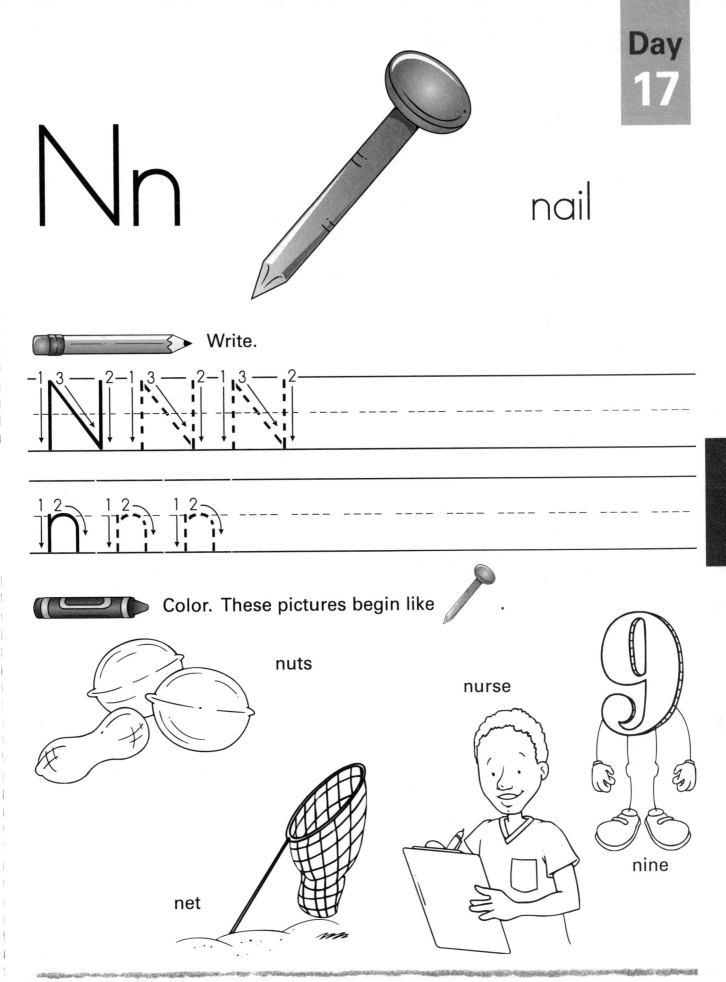 .

nuts

nurse

nine

net

Count and color.

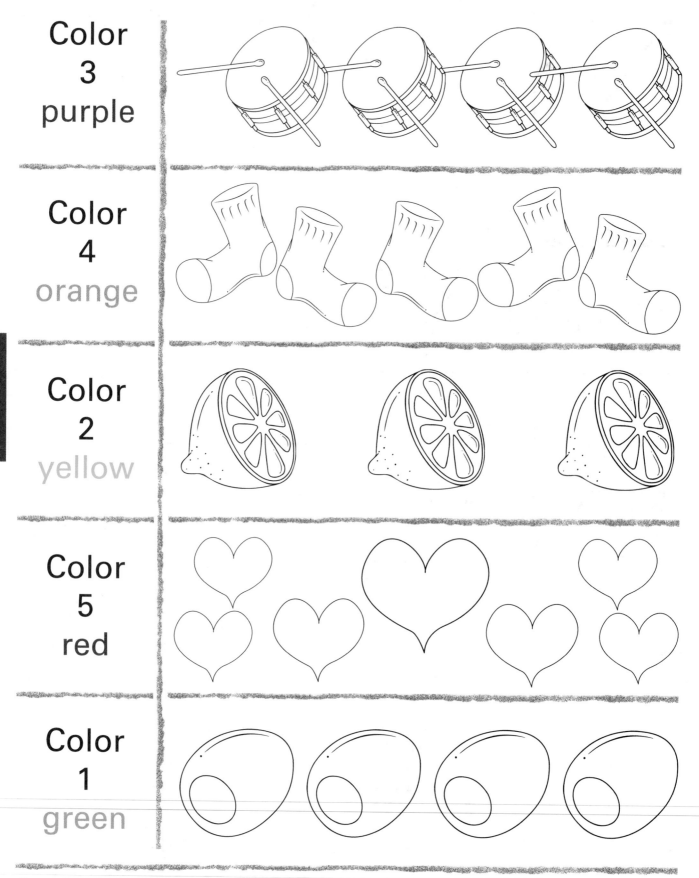

Color
3
purple

Color
4
orange

Color
2
yellow

Color
5
red

Color
1
green

ostrich

🖍 Write.

Color. These pictures begin like 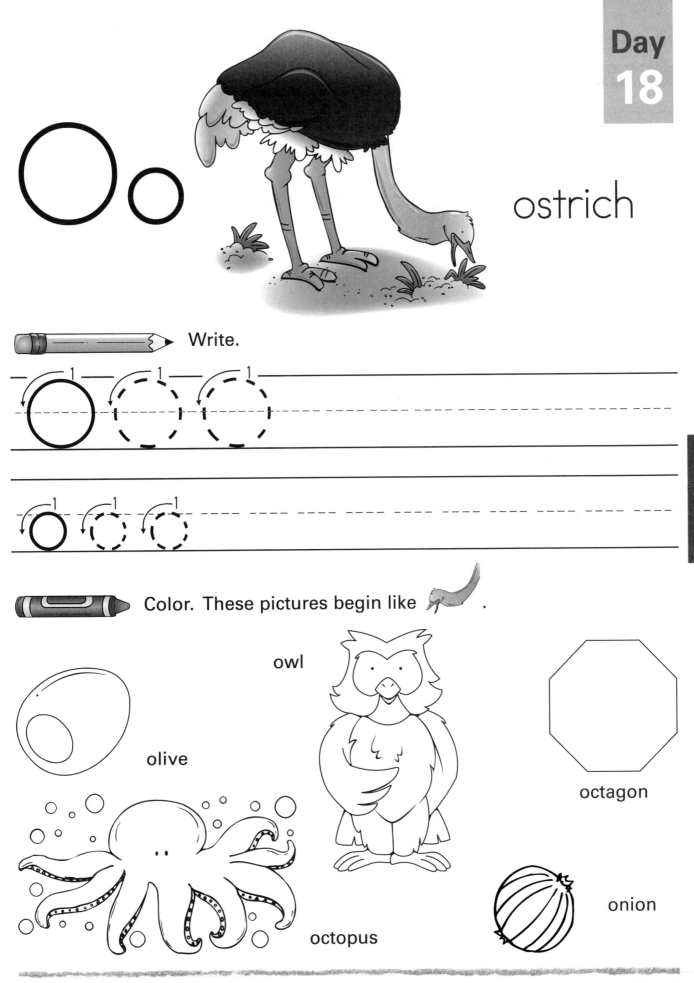 .

owl

olive

octagon

octopus

onion

Count the shapes and circle the correct number.

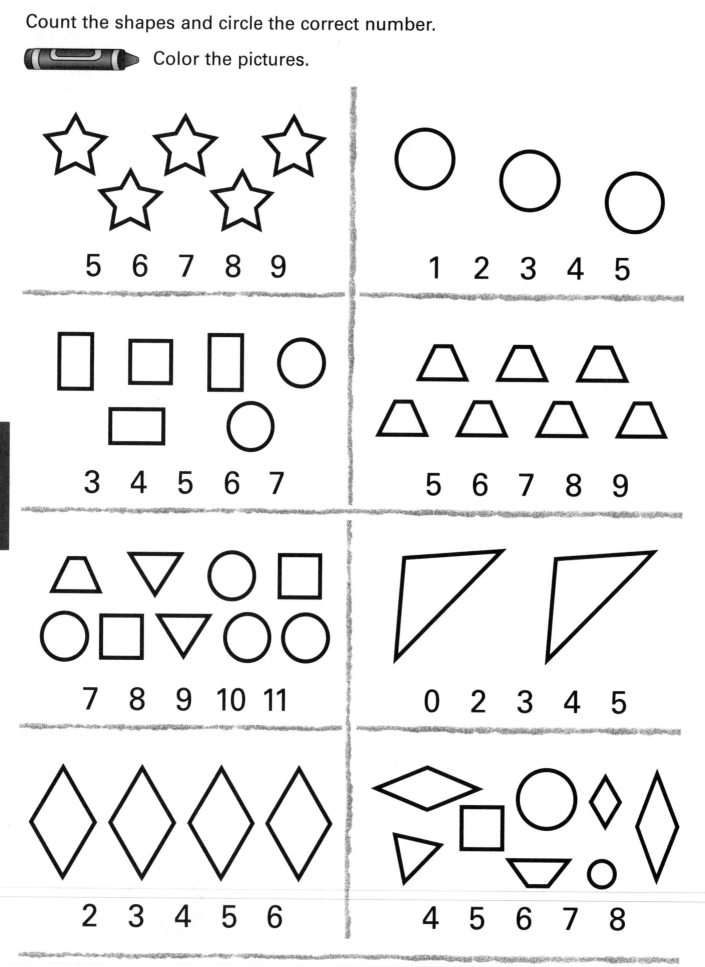

Color the pictures.

5   6   7   8   9   1   2   3   4   5

3   4   5   6   7   5   6   7   8   9

7   8   9   10   11   0   2   3   4   5

2   3   4   5   6   4   5   6   7   8

P p

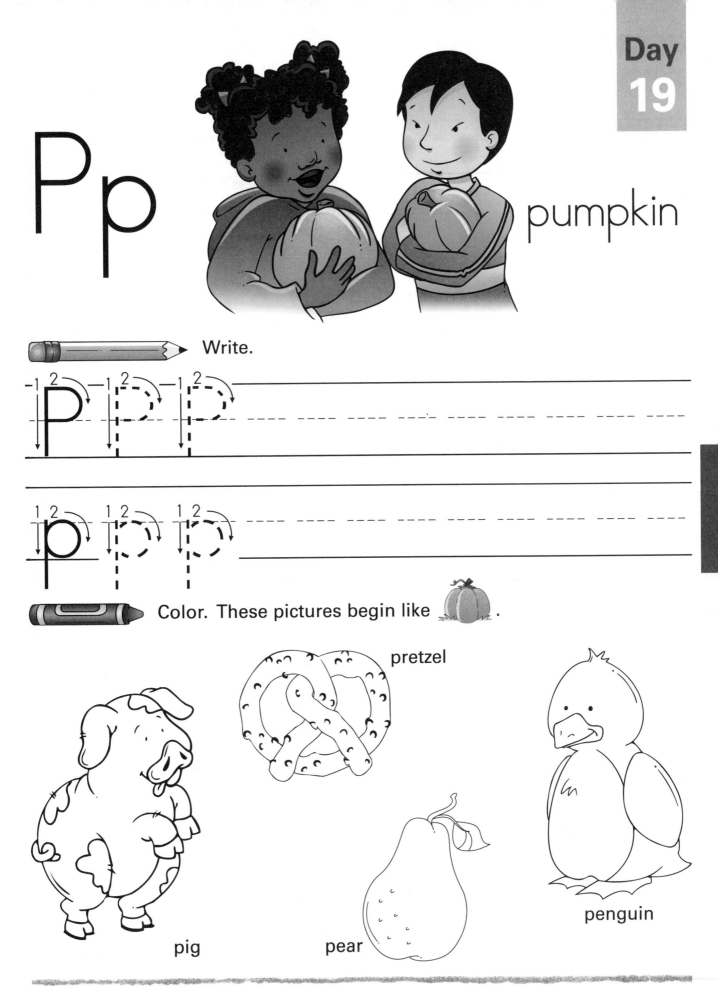

pumpkin

Write.

P P P

p p p

Color. These pictures begin like 🎃 .

pretzel

pig

pear

penguin

O - Orange   G - Green   R - Red   B - Blue   Y - Yellow

Qq

queen

Write.

Q Q Q

q q q

Color. These pictures begin like  .

? question

quail

quarter

quilt

Draw the shapes that come next to finish the pattern.

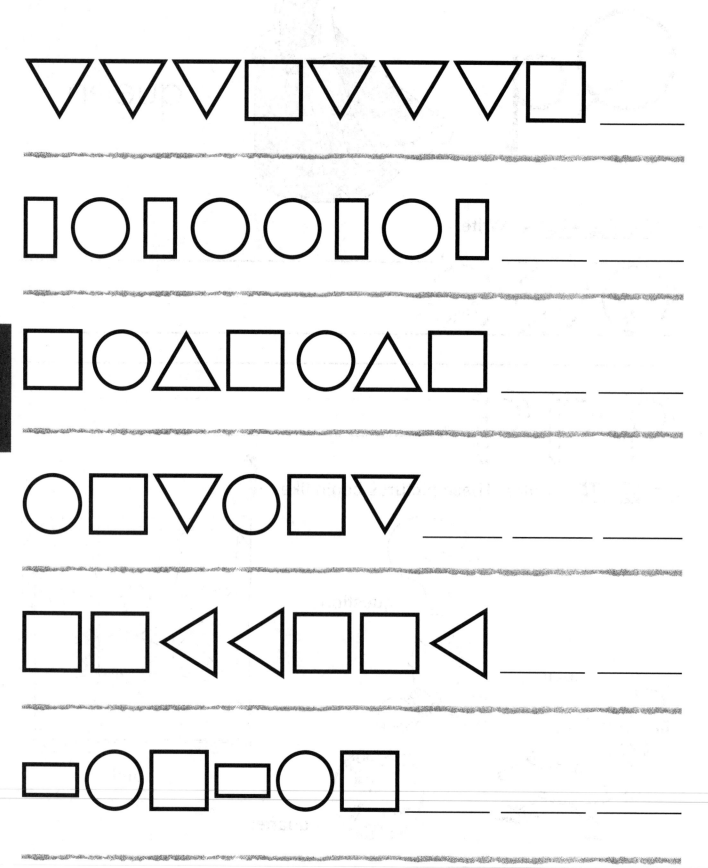

Summer Bridge Activities™

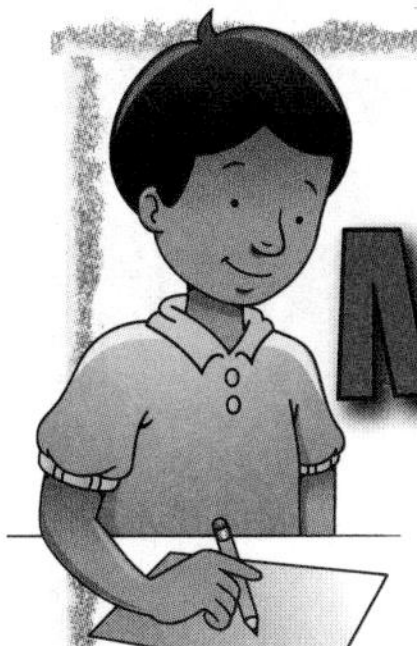

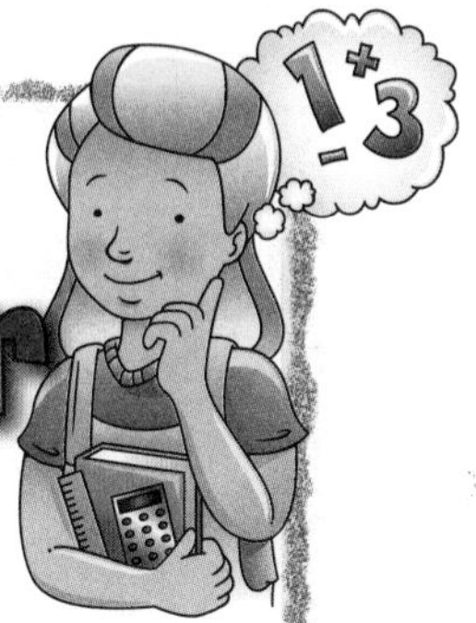

Motivational Calendar

Month ______________________

My parents and I decided that if I complete
15 days of **Summer Bridge Activities™** and
read _____ minutes a day, my incentive/reward will be:

____

Child's Signature ____________________ Parent's Signature ____________________

Day 1	☆	📖	_____	**Day 9**	☆	📖	_____
Day 2	☆	📖	_____	**Day 10**	☆	📖	_____
Day 3	☆	📖	_____	**Day 11**	☆	📖	_____
Day 4	☆	📖	_____	**Day 12**	☆	📖	_____
Day 5	☆	📖	_____	**Day 13**	☆	📖	_____
Day 6	☆	📖	_____	**Day 14**	☆	📖	_____
Day 7	☆	📖	_____	**Day 15**	☆	📖	_____
Day 8	☆	📖	_____				

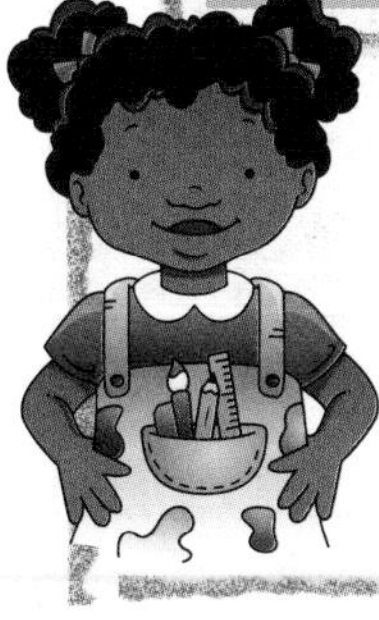

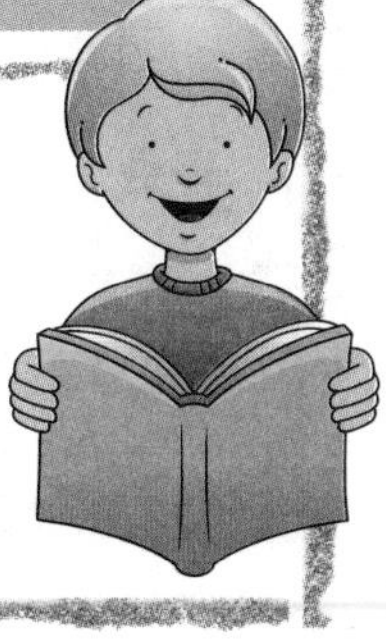

Child: Color the ☆ for daily activities completed.
Color the 📖 for daily reading completed.

Parent: Initial the ____ when all activities are complete.

Discover Something New!

Fun Activity Ideas to Go Along with the Third Section!

1. Play hopscotch, marbles, or jump rope.

2. Visit a fire station.

3. Take a walk around your neighborhood.

4. Name all of the trees and flowers you can.

5. Make up a song.

6. Make a hut out of blankets and chairs.

7. Put a note in a helium balloon and let it go.

8. Start a journal. Write about your favorite vacation memories.

9. Make 3-D nature art. Glue leaves, twigs, dirt, grass, and rocks on paper.

10. Find an ant colony. Spill some food and see what happens.

11. Play charades.

12. Make up a story by drawing pictures.

13. Do something to help the environment. Clean up an area near your house.

14. Weed a row in the garden. Mom will love it!

15. Take a trip to a park.

16. Learn about different road signs.

R r

rocket

Write.

R R R

r r r

Color. These pictures begin like 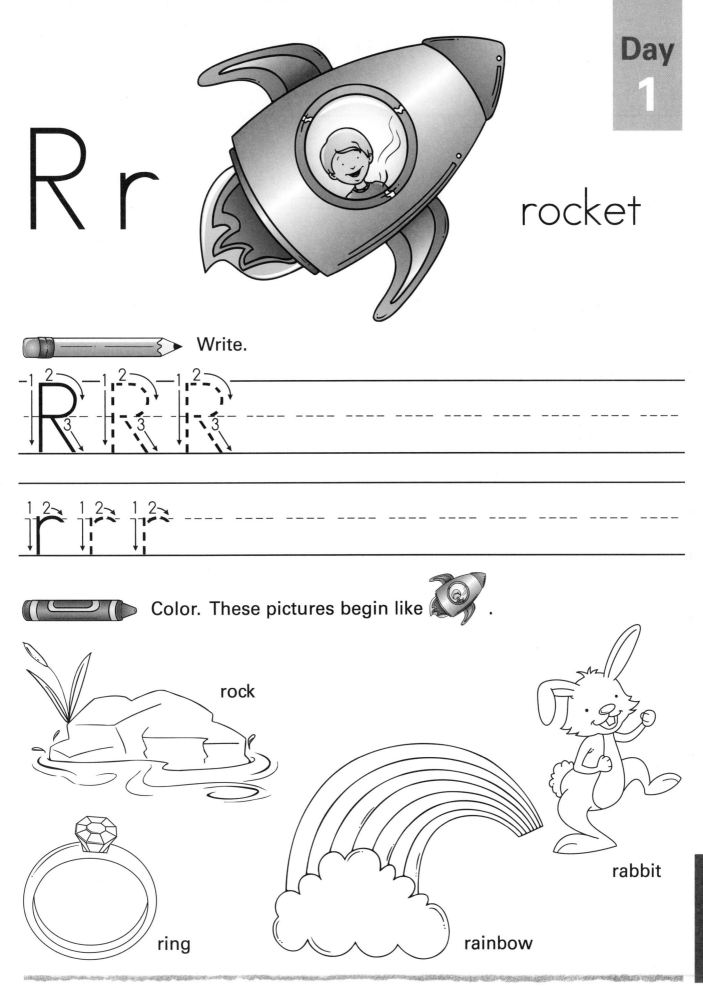.

rock

ring

rainbow

rabbit

77

Draw the correct number of circles in each box.

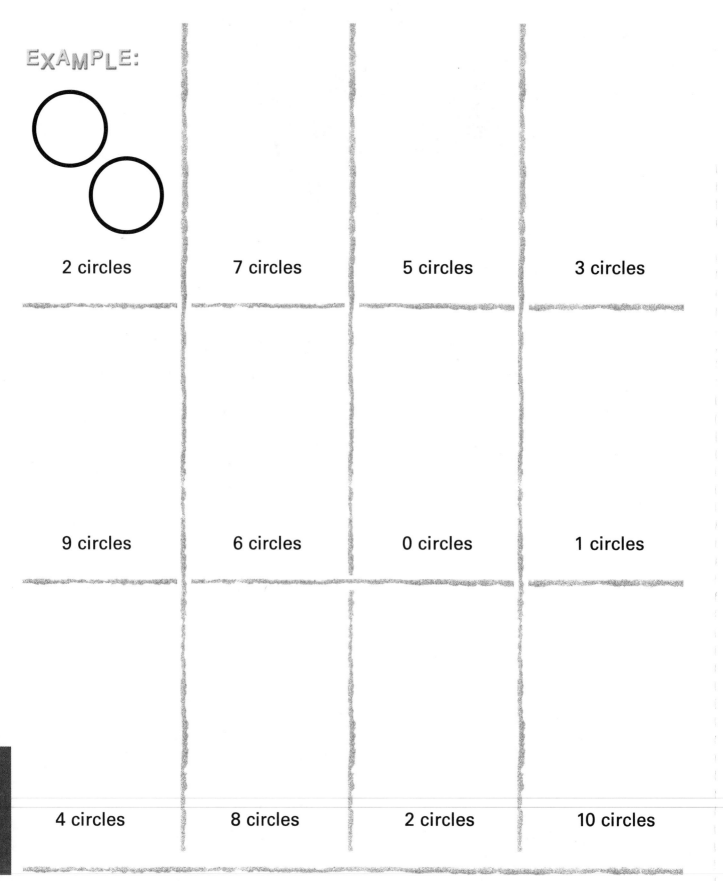

EXAMPLE:

2 circles

7 circles

5 circles

3 circles

9 circles

6 circles

0 circles

1 circles

4 circles

8 circles

2 circles

10 circles

S s

sun

✏️ Write.

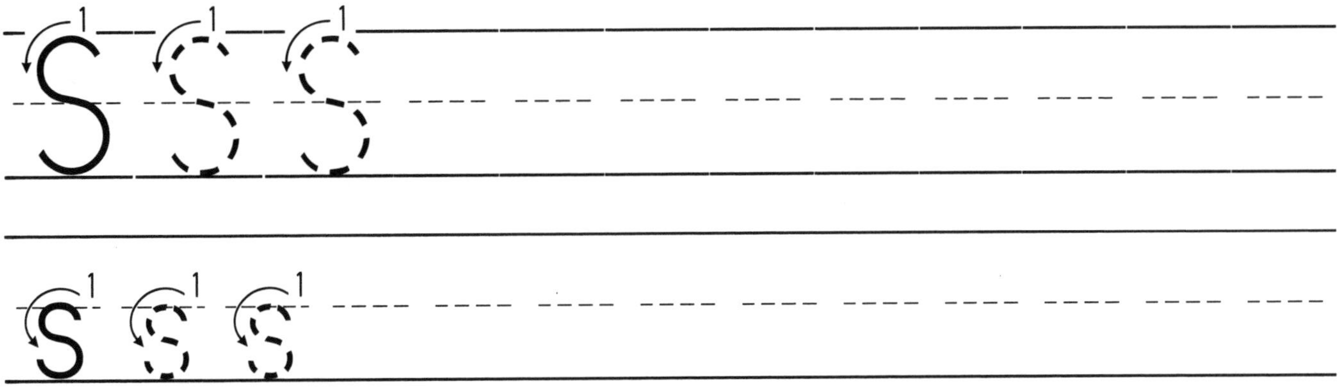

S S S

s s s

🖍️ Color. These pictures begin like ☀️ .

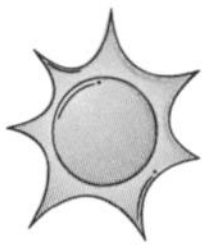

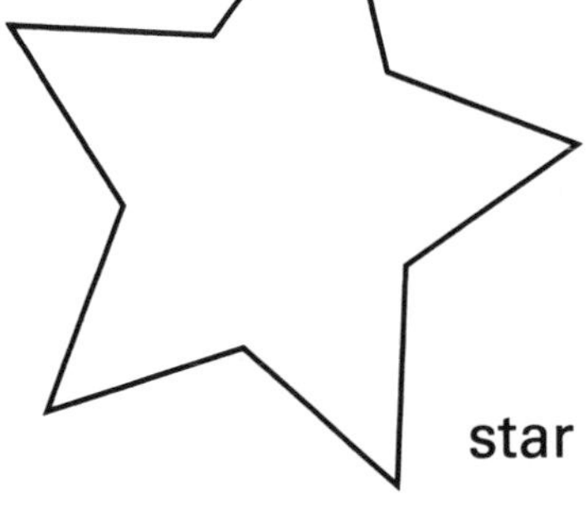

six

star

seal

sock

Color all the living things.

bird

fish

flower

popsicle

puppet

television

turtle

dog

T t

teeter-totter

Write.

Color. These pictures begin like ⟨teeter-totter⟩.

two

teddy bear

tape

toast

81

 Color all of the things that are not alive.

bike

butterfly

book

pig

mug

house

van

fish

box

Uu

umbrella

Write.

U U U

u u u

Color. These pictures begin like .

undershirt

unhappy

up

umpire

Bonus Section

107

 Match each word to the correct picture.

Color.

EXAMPLE:

sun
dog
bat
pin
jug
hen

Match the animal to its home.

Color.

Match each word to the correct picture.

Color.

EXAMPLE:

gum

egg

tub

nut

ant

log

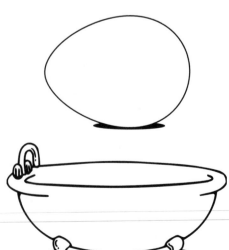

Draw a square ☐ around the things you find **inside**.

Draw a circle ◯ around the things you find **outside**.

Color them.

Circle the word that goes with the picture.

Color.

EXAMPLE:

cap (van) rat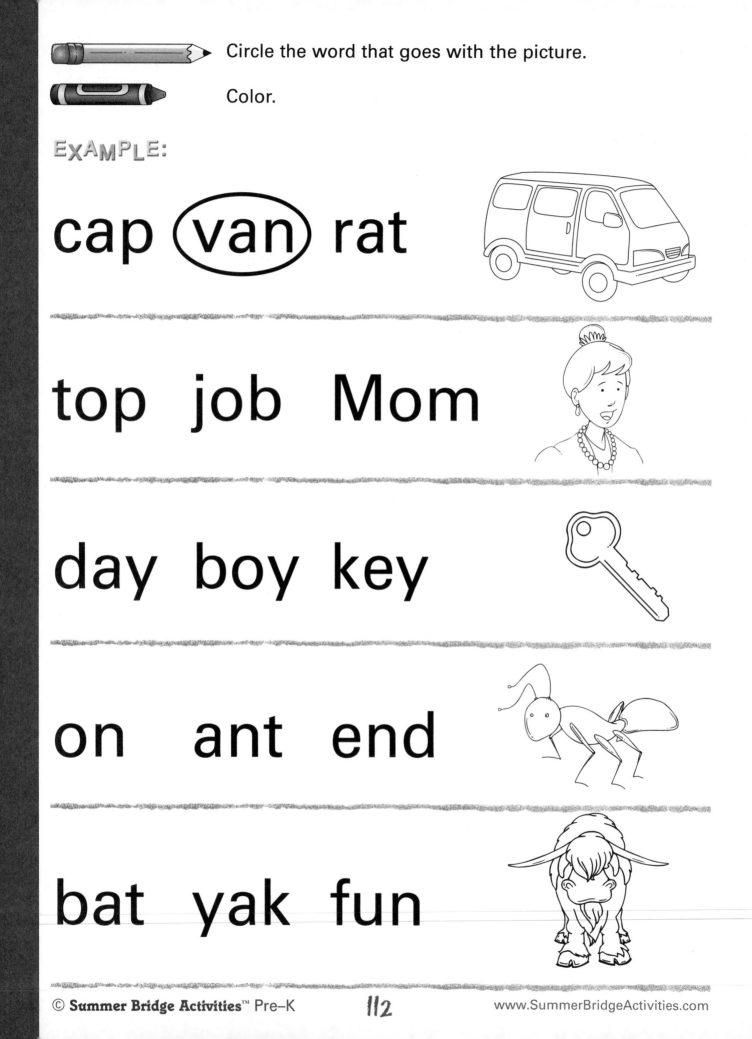

top job Mom

day boy key

on ant end

bat yak fun

 **Color the things you can see.**

Color the things you can hear.

Ding Dong

 Draw a line to match the things that go together.

Color.

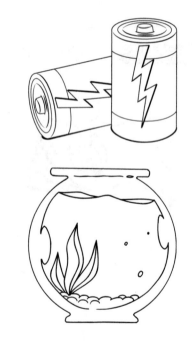

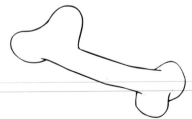

 Color the things you can **taste**.

Color the things you can **smell**.

Color the things you can **touch**.

Circle the word that goes with the picture.

Color.

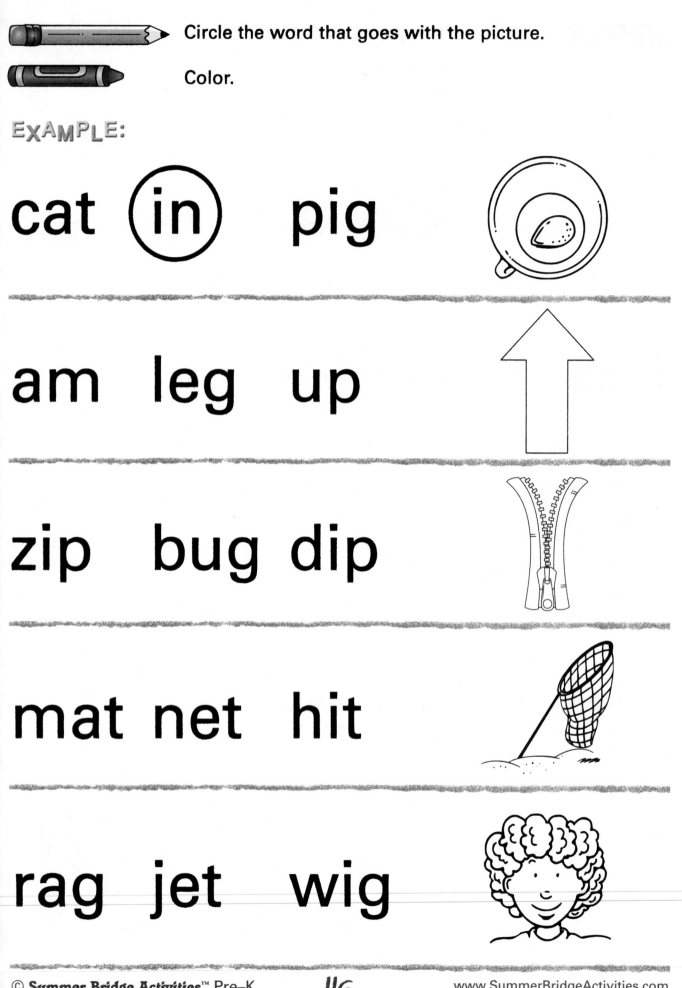

cat (in) pig

am   leg   up

zip   bug   dip

mat   net   hit

rag   jet   wig

Circle ◯ the thing that happened **first**.

Draw a square ☐ around the thing that happened **last**.

117 © **Summer Bridge Activities**™ Pre–K

Circle ◯ the thing that has **more**.

Draw a square ☐ around the thing that has **less**.

 Practice writing below.

A

a

B

b

C

c

D

d

 Practice writing below.

E

e

F

f

G

g

H

h

 Practice writing below.

I

i

J

j

K

k

L

I

M

m

N

n

O

o

P

p

Q

q

R

r

S

s

T

t

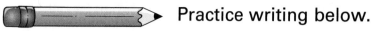 Practice writing below.

U

u

V

v

W

W

X

X

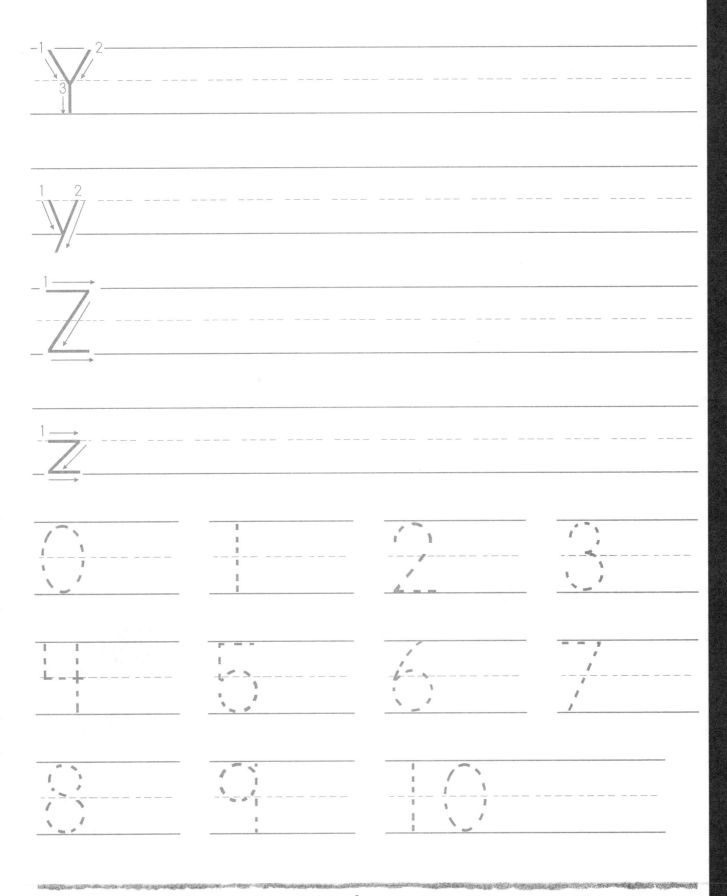

Trace each lowercase letter of the alphabet; then write it on your own.

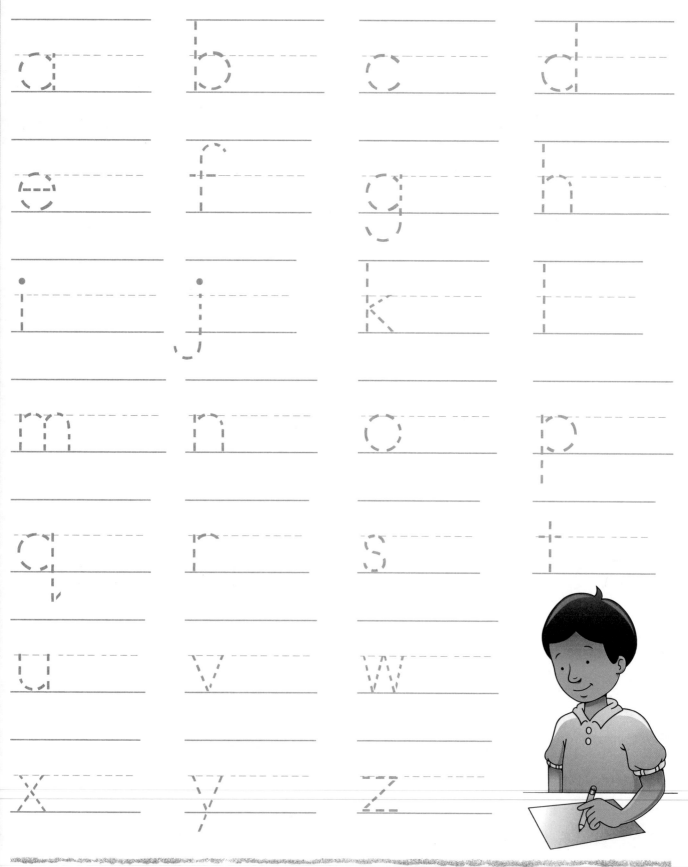

Better Bodies

Better Behavior

Up until now, **Summer Bridge Activities**™ has been all about your mind...

But the other parts of you—who you are, how you act, and how you feel—are important too. These pages are all about helping build a better you this summer.

Keeping your body strong and healthy helps you live better, learn better, and feel better. To keep your body healthy, you need to do things like eat right, get enough sleep, and exercise. The Physical Fitness pages of Building Better Bodies will teach you about good eating habits and the importance of proper exercise. You can even train for a Presidential Fitness Award over the summer.

The Character pages are all about building a better you on the inside. They've got fun activities for you and your family to do together. The activities will help you develop important values and habits you'll need as you grow up.

After a summer of Building Better Bodies and Behavior and **Summer Bridge Activities**™, there may be a whole new you ready for school in the fall!

For Parents: Introduction to Character Education

Character education is simply giving your child clear messages about the values you and your family consider important. Many studies have shown that a basic core of values is universal. You will find certain values reflected in the laws of every country and incorporated in the teachings of religious, ethical, and other belief systems throughout the world.

The character activities included here are designed to span the entire summer. Each week your child will be introduced to a new value, with a quote and two activities that illustrate it. Research has shown that character education is most effective when parents reinforce the values in their child's daily routine; therefore, we encourage parents to be involved as their child completes the lessons.

Here are some suggestions on how to maximize these lessons.
- Read through the lesson yourself. Then set aside a block of time for you and your child to discuss the value.
- Plan a block of time to work on the suggested activities.
- Discuss the meaning of the quote with your child. Ask, "What do you think the quote means?" Have your child ask other members of the family the same question. If possible, include grandparents, aunts, uncles, and cousins.
- Use the quote as often as you can during the week. You'll be pleasantly surprised to learn that both you and your child will have it memorized by the end of the week.

- For extra motivation, you can set a reward for completing each week's activities.
- Point out to your child other people who are actively displaying a value. Example: "See how John is helping Mrs. Olsen by raking her leaves."
- Be sure to praise your child each time he or she practices a value: "Mary, it was very courteous of you to wait until I finished speaking."
- Find time in your day to talk about values. Turn off the radio in the car and chat with your children; take a walk in the evening as a family; read a story about the weekly value at bedtime; or give a back rub while you talk about what makes your child happy or sad.
- Finally, model the values you want your child to acquire. Remember, children will do as you do, not as you say.

Name _____   Date _____

How I Measure Up!

You will be filling in this page twice—once now and once at the end of the summer to see how you have grown. Have an adult help you measure yourself to fill in the blanks below.

around the neck __ / __

smile __ / __

neck to belly button __ / __

around the wrist __ / __

around the waist __ / __

waist to ankle __ / __

around the ankle __ / __

shoulder to elbow __ / __

elbow to wrist __ / __

length of longest finger __ / __

around the knee __ / __

foot length __ / __

around the neck __ / __

smile __ / __

neck to belly button __ / __

around the waist __ / __

waist to ankle __ / __

around the ankle __ / __

foot length __ / __

shoulder to elbow __ / __

elbow to wrist __ / __

around the wrist __ / __

length of longest finger __ / __

around the knee __ / __

Nutrition

The food you eat helps your body grow. It gives you energy to work and play. Some foods give you protein or fats. Other foods provide vitamins, minerals, or carbohydrates. These are all things your body needs. Eating a variety of good foods each day will help you stay healthy. How much and what foods you need depends on many things, including whether you're a girl or boy, how active you are, and how old you are. To figure out the right amount of food for you, go to http://www.mypyramid.gov/ mypyramid/index.aspx and use the Pyramid Plan Calculator. In the meantime, here are some general guidelines.

Your body needs nutrients from each food group every day.

Grains	Vegetables	Fruits	Oils	Milk	Meat & Beans
4 to 5 ounce equivalents each day (an ounce might be a slice of bread, a packet of oatmeal, or a bowl of cereal)	1 1/2 cups each day	1 to 1 1/2 cups each day		1 to 2 cups of milk (or other calcium-rich food) each day	3 to 5 ounce equivalents each day

Put a ☐ around the four foods from the Grains Group.

Put a △ around the two foods from the Meat and Beans Group.

Put a ◇ around the three foods from the Milk Group.

Put a ◯ around the two foods from the Fruits Group.

Put a ☐ around the four foods from the Vegetables Group.

Foods I Need Each Day

Plan out three balanced meals for one day. Arrange your meals so that by the end of the day, you will have had all the recommended amounts of food from each food group listed on the food pyramid.

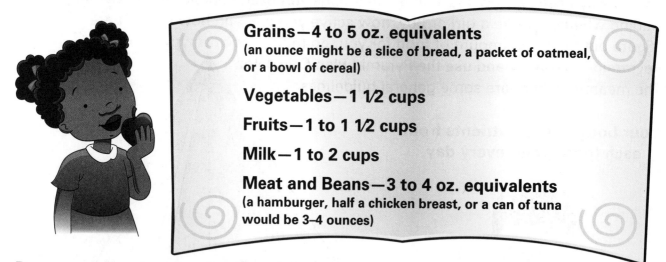

Grains—4 to 5 oz. equivalents
(an ounce might be a slice of bread, a packet of oatmeal, or a bowl of cereal)

Vegetables—1 1/2 cups

Fruits—1 to 1 1/2 cups

Milk—1 to 2 cups

Meat and Beans—3 to 4 oz. equivalents
(a hamburger, half a chicken breast, or a can of tuna would be 3–4 ounces)

Draw or cut and paste pictures of the types of food you need each day.

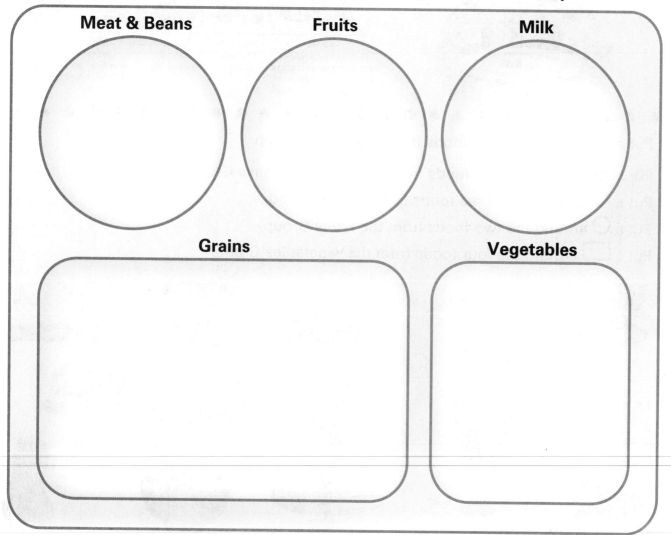

Meal Tracker

Use these charts to record the amount of food you eat from each food group for one or two weeks. Have another family member keep track, too, and compare.

	Grains	Milk	Meat & Beans	Fruits	Vegetables	Oils
Monday						
Tuesday						
Wednesday						
Thursday						
Friday						
Saturday						
Sunday						

	Grains	Milk	Meat & Beans	Fruits	Vegetables	Oils
Monday						
Tuesday						
Wednesday						
Thursday						
Friday						
Saturday						
Sunday						

Get Moving!

Did you know that getting no exercise can be almost as bad for you as smoking? So get moving this summer!

Summer is the perfect time to get out and get in shape. Your fitness program should include three parts:

- Get 30 minutes of aerobic exercise per day, three to five days a week.

- Exercise your muscles to improve strength and flexibility.

- Make it FUN! Do things that you like to do. Include your friends and family.

Couch Potato Quiz

1. Name three things you do each day that get you moving.

2. Name three things you do a few times a week that are good exercise.

3. How many hours do you spend each week playing outside or exercising?

4. How much TV do you watch each day?

5. How much time do you spend playing computer or video games?

If the time you spend on activities 4 and 5 adds up to more than you spend on 1–3, you could be headed for a spud's life!

You can find information on fitness at www.fitness.gov or www.kidshealth.org

Activity Pyramid

The Activity Pyramid works like the Food Pyramid. You can use the Activity Pyramid to help plan your summer exercise program. Fill in the blanks below.

List 1 thing that isn't good exercise that you could do less of this summer.

1._____

List 3 fun activities you enjoy that get you moving and are good exercise.

1._____

2._____

3._____

List 3 exercises you could do to build strength and flexibility this summer.

1._____

2._____

3._____

List 3 activities you would like to do for aerobic exercise this summer.

1._____

2._____

3._____

List 2 sports you would like to participate in this summer.

1._____

2._____

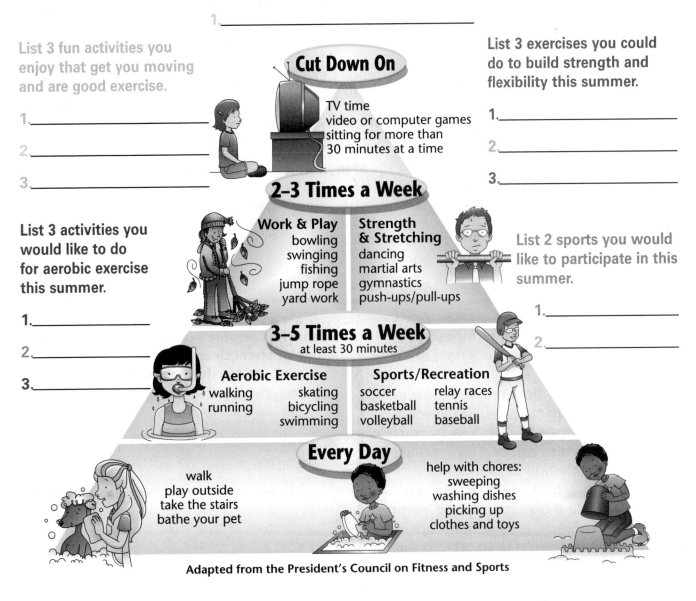

Cut Down On
TV time
video or computer games
sitting for more than
30 minutes at a time

2–3 Times a Week

Work & Play
bowling
swinging
fishing
jump rope
yard work

Strength & Stretching
dancing
martial arts
gymnastics
push-ups/pull-ups

3–5 Times a Week
at least 30 minutes

Aerobic Exercise
walking   skating
running   bicycling
swimming

Sports/Recreation
soccer   relay races
basketball   tennis
volleyball   baseball

Every Day
walk
play outside
take the stairs
bathe your pet

help with chores:
sweeping
washing dishes
picking up
clothes and toys

Adapted from the President's Council on Fitness and Sports

List 5 everyday things you can do to get moving more often.

1._____

2._____

3._____

4._____

5._____

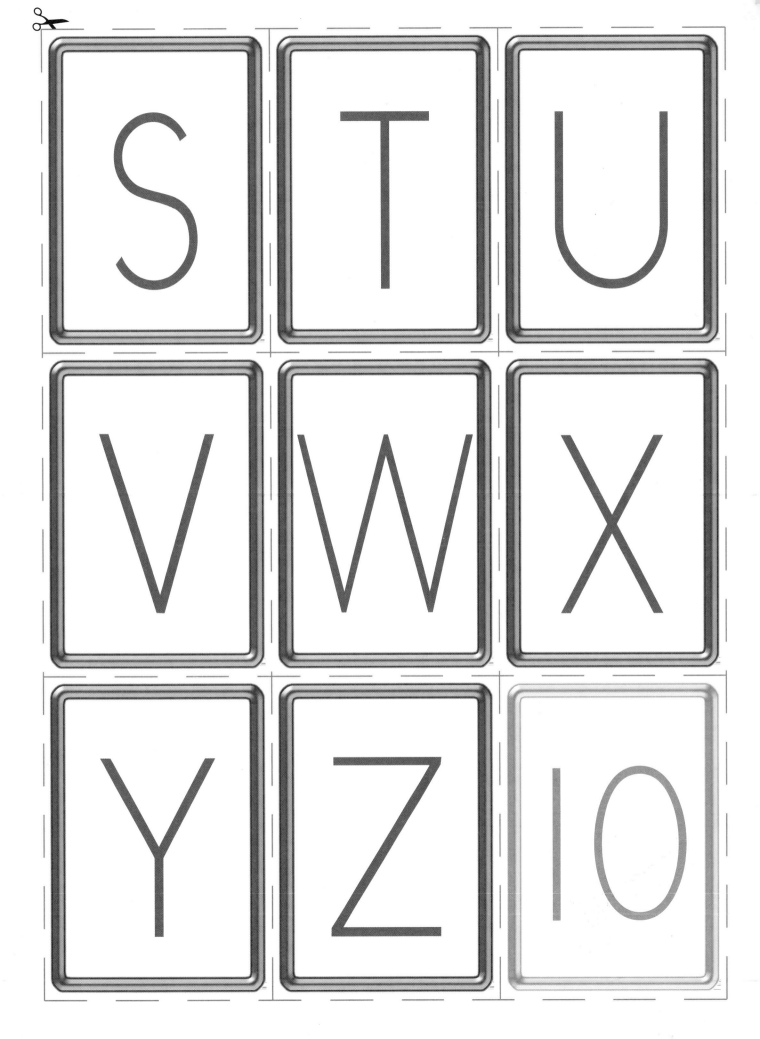

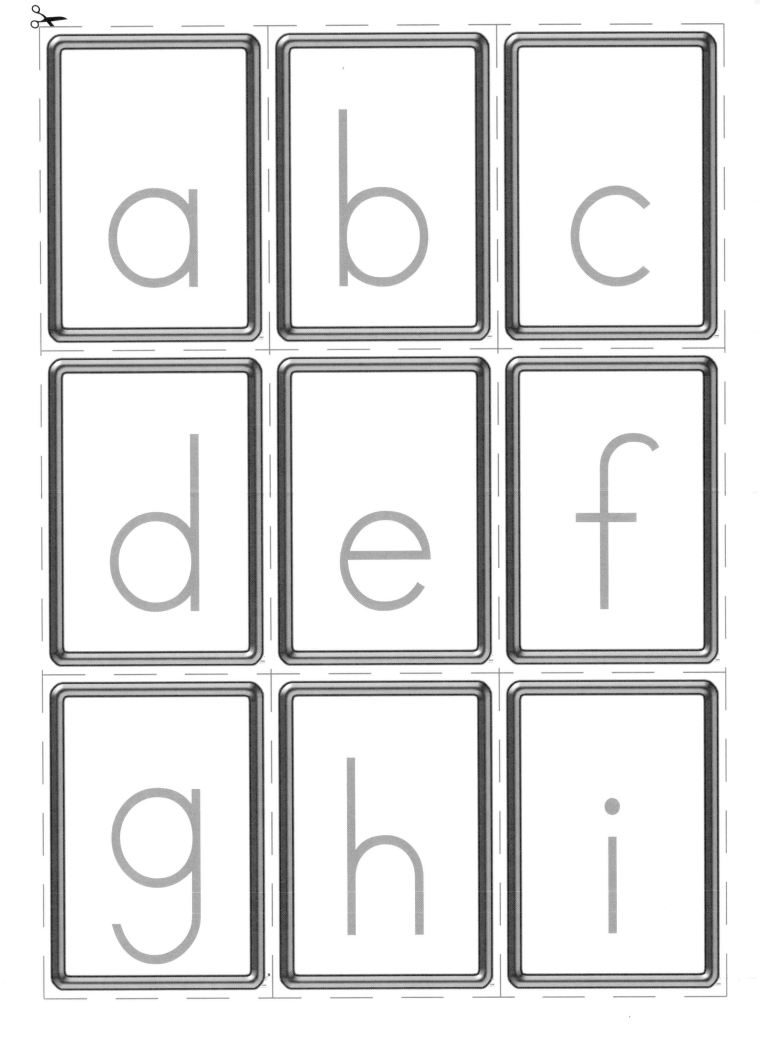

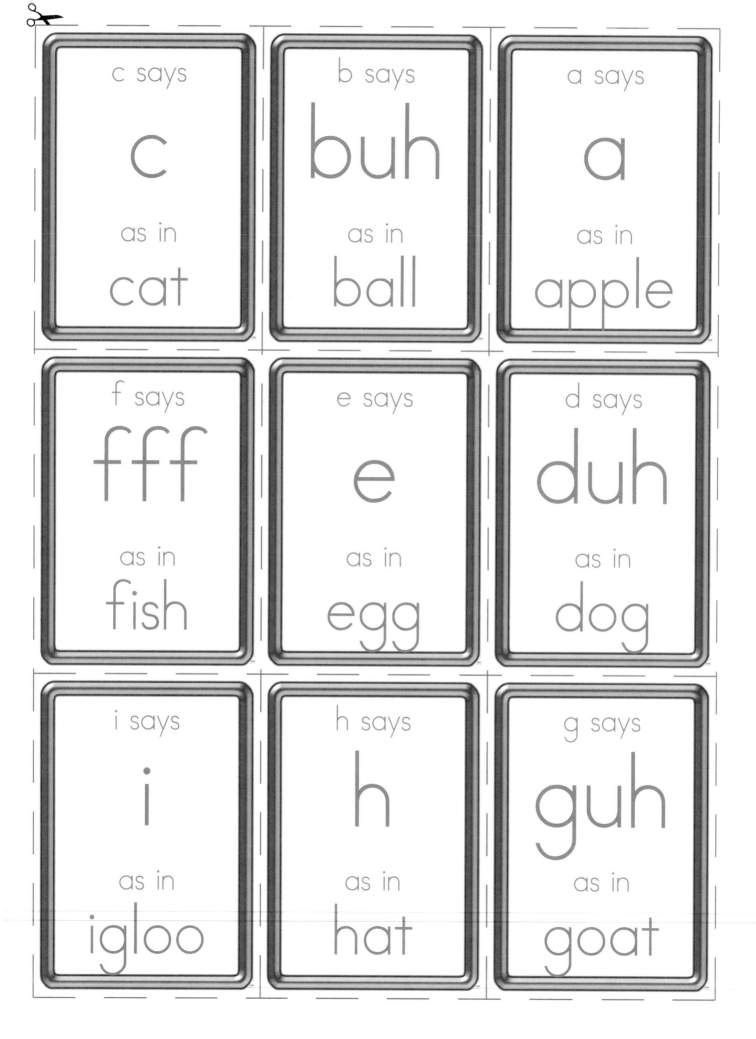

Why Is the Concept of Culture Important?

This chapter examines in greater detail the concept of culture, one of the most influential ideas that anthropologists have developed. We survey different ways that anthropologists have used the culture concept to expose the fallacies of biological determinism. We also discuss the reasons why some anthropologists believe that continuing to use the culture concept today may be a problem.

Anthropologists have long argued that the human condition is distinguished from the condition of other living species by *culture*. Other living species learn, but the extent to which human beings depend on learning is unique in the animal kingdom. Because our brains are capable of open symbolic thought and our hands are capable of manipulating matter powerfully or delicately, we interact with the wider world in a way that is distinct from that of any other species.

How Do Anthropologists Define Culture?

In chapter 1, we defined **culture** as patterns of learned behavior and ideas acquired by people as members of society. Culture is not reinvented by each generation; rather, we learn it from other members of the social groups we belong to, although we may later modify this heritage in some way. Therefore, culture is *shared* as well as *learned*. Many things we learn, such as table manners and what is good to eat and where people are supposed to sleep, are never explicitly taught but rather are absorbed in the course of daily practical living. This kind of cultural learning is sometimes called *habitus*. The cultural practices shared within social groups always encompass the varied knowledge and skills of many different individuals. For example, space flight is part of North American culture, and yet no individual North American could build a space shuttle from scratch.

Human cultures also appear *patterned*; that is, related cultural beliefs and practices show up repeatedly in different areas of social life. For example, in North America individualism is highly valued, and its influence can be seen in child-rearing practices (babies are expected to sleep alone, and children are reared with the expectation that they will be independent at the age of 18), economic practices (individuals are urged to get a job, to save their money, and not to count on other people or institutions to take care of them; many people would prefer to be in business for themselves; far more people commute to work by themselves in their own cars than carpool), and religious practices (the Christian emphasis on personal salvation and individual accountability before God). Cultural patterns can be traced through time: That

English and Spanish are widely spoken in North America, whereas Fulfulde (a language spoken in West Africa) is not, is connected to the colonial conquest and domination of North America by speakers of English and Spanish in past centuries. Cultural patterns also vary across space: In the United States, for example, the English of New York City differs from the English of Mississippi in style, rhythm, and vocabulary ("What? You expect me to schlep this around all day? Forget about it!" is more likely to be heard in the former than the latter!).

It is this patterned cultural variation that allows anthropologists (and others) to distinguish different "cultural traditions" from one another. But separate cultural traditions are often hard to delineate. That is because, in addition to any unique elements of their own, all contain contradictory elements, and they also share elements with other traditions. First, customs in one domain of culture may contradict customs in another domain, as when religion tells us to share with others and economics tells us to look out for ourselves alone. Second, people have always borrowed cultural elements from their neighbors, and many increasingly refuse to be limited in the present by cultural practices of the past. Why, for example, should literacy not be seen as part of Ju/'hoansi culture once the children of illiterate Ju/'hoansi foragers learn to read and write (see EthnoProfile 11.1: Ju/'hoansi)? Thus, cultural patterns can be useful as a kind of shorthand, but it is important to remember that the boundaries between cultural traditions are always fuzzy. Ultimately, they rest on someone's judgment about how different one set of customs is from another set of customs. As we will see shortly, these kinds of contradictions and challenges are not uncommon, leading some anthropologists to think of culture not in terms of specific customs but in terms of rules that become "established ways of bringing ideas from different domains together" (Strathern 1992, 3).

So far we have seen that culture is learned, shared, and patterned. Cultural traditions are also reconstructed and enriched, generation after generation, primarily because human biological survival depends on culture. Thus, culture is also *adaptive*. Human newborns are not born with "instincts" that would enable them to survive on their own. On the contrary, they depend utterly on support and nurturance from adults and other members of the group in which they live. It is by learning the cultural practices of those around them that human beings come to master appropriate ways of thinking and acting that promote their own survival as biological organisms (Figure 2.1). Culture allows us both to adapt to and to transform the environments in which we live.

Finally, culture is *symbolic*. A **symbol** is something that stands for something else. The letters of an alphabet, for example, symbolize the sounds of a spoken language.

---

culture Sets of learned behaviors and ideas that humans acquire as members of society. Humans use culture to adapt to and transform the world in which they live.

symbol Something that stands for something else.

In Their Own Words

The Paradox of Ethnocentrism

Ethnocentrism is usually described in thoroughly negative terms. As Ivan Karp points out, however, ethnocentrism is a more complex phenomenon than we might expect.

Anthropologists usually argue that ethnocentrism is both wrong and harmful, especially when it is tied to racial, cultural, and social prejudices. Ideas and feelings about the inferiority of blacks, the cupidity of Jews, or the lack of cultural sophistication of farmers are surely to be condemned. But can we do without ethnocentrism? If we stopped to examine every custom and practice in our cultural repertoire, how would we get on? For example, if we always regarded marriage as something that can vary from society to society, would we be concerned about filling out the proper marriage documents, or would we even get married at all? Most of the time we suspend a quizzical stance toward our own customs and simply live life.

Yet many of our own practices are peculiar when viewed through the lenses of other cultures. Periodically, for over fifteen years, I have worked with and lived among an African people. They are as amazed at our marriage customs as my students are at theirs. Both American students and the Iteso of Kenya find it difficult to imagine how the other culture survives with the bizarre, exotic practices that are part of their respective marriage customs. Ethnocentrism works both ways. It can be practiced as much by other cultures as by our own.

Paradoxically, ethnographic literature combats ethnocentrism by showing that the practices of cultures (including our own) are "natural" in their own setting. What appears natural in one setting appears so because it was constructed in that setting—made and produced by human beings who could have done it some other way. Ethnography is a means of recording the range of human creativity and of demonstrating how universally shared capacities can produce cultural and social differences.

This anthropological way of looking at other cultures—and, by implication, at ourselves—constitutes a major reason for reading ethnography. The anthropological lens teaches us to question what we assume to be unquestionable. Ethnography teaches us that human potentiality provides alternative means of organizing our lives and alternative modes of experiencing the world. Reading ethnographies trains us to question the received wisdom of our society and makes us receptive to change. In this sense, anthropology might be called the subversive science. We read ethnographies in order to learn about how other peoples produce their world and about how we might change our own patterns of production.

Source: Karp 1990, 74–75.

There is no necessary connection between the shape of a particular letter and the speech sound it represents. Indeed, the same or similar sounds are represented symbolically by very different letters in the Latin, Cyrillic, Hebrew, Arabic, and Greek alphabets, to name but five. Even the sounds of spoken language are symbols for meanings a speaker tries to express. The fact that we can translate from one language to another suggests that the same or similar meanings can be expressed by different symbols in different languages. But language is not the only domain of culture that depends on symbols. Everything we do in society has a symbolic dimension, from how we conduct ourselves at the dinner table to how we bury the dead. It is our heavy dependence on symbolic learning that sets human culture apart from the apparently nonsymbolic learning on which other species rely.

Human culture, then, is *learned, shared, patterned, adaptive,* and *symbolic.* And the contemporary human capacity for culture has also evolved, over millions of years. Culture's beginnings can perhaps be glimpsed among Japanese macaque monkeys who invented the custom of washing sweet potatoes and among wild chimpanzees who invented different grooming postures or techniques to crack open nuts or to gain access to termites or water (Boesch-Ackerman and Boesch 1994; Wolfe 1995, 162–63). Our apelike ancestors surely shared similar aptitudes when they started walking on two legs some 6 million years ago. By 2.5 million years ago, their descendants were making stone tools. Thereafter, our hominin lineage gave birth to a number of additional species, all of whom depended on culture more than their ancestors had. Thus, culture is not something that appeared suddenly, with the arrival of *Homo sapiens.* By the time *Homo sapiens* appeared some 200,000 years ago, a heavy dependence on culture had long been a part of our evolutionary heritage.

Thus, as Rick Potts puts it, "an evolutionary bridge exists between the human and animal realms of behavior.

FIGURE 2.1 Of all living organisms, humans are the most dependent on learning for their survival. From a young age, girls in northern Cameroon learn to carry heavy loads on their heads and also learn to get water for their families.

. . . Culture represents continuity" (1996, 197). Potts proposes that modern human symbolic culture, and the social institutions that depend on it, rest on other, more basic abilities that emerged at different times in our evolutionary past (Figure 2.2). Monkeys and apes possess many of these abilities to varying degrees, which is why they may be said to possess simple cultural traditions. Certainly our earliest hominin ancestors were no different.

Apes apparently also possess a rudimentary capacity for *symbolic coding*, or symbolic representation, something our ancestors undoubtedly possessed as well. But new species can evolve new capacities not found in their ancestors. This occurred in the human past when our ancestors first developed a capacity for *complex symbolic representation*, including the ability to communicate freely about the past, the future, and the invisible. This ability distinguishes human symbolic language, for example, from the vocal communication systems of apes (see chapter 5). Biological anthropologist Terrence Deacon argues that evolution produced in *Homo sapiens* a brain "that has been significantly overbuilt for learning symbolic associations" such that "we cannot help but see the world in symbolic categories" (1997, 413, 416). Complex symbolic representation apparently was of great adaptive value for our ancestors. It created selective pressures that increased human symbolic capacities over time. Put another way, culture and the human brain *coevolved*, each furnishing key features of the environment to which the other needed to adapt (Deacon 1997, 44; Odling-Smee 1994). We have used our complex symbolic abilities, moreover, to create *institutions*—complex, variable and enduring forms of cultural practice that organize social life, also unique to our species. As a result, for *Homo sapiens*, culture has become "the predominant manner in which human groups vary from one another . . . it *swamps* the biological differences among populations" (Marks 1995, 200). We are truly biocultural organisms.

Culture, History, and Human Agency

The human condition is rooted in time and shaped by history. As part of the human condition, culture is also historical, being worked out and reconstructed in every generation. Culture is also part of our biological heritage. Indeed, our *biocultural* heritage has produced a living species that uses culture to surmount biological and individual limitations and is even capable of studying itself and its own biocultural evolution.

This realization, however, raises another question: Just how free from limitations are humans? Opinion in Western societies often polarizes around one of two extremes: Either we have *free will* and may do just as we please, or our behavior is completely determined by forces beyond our control. Many social scientists, however, are convinced that a more realistic description of human freedom was offered by Karl Marx, who wrote, "Men make their own history, but they do not make it just

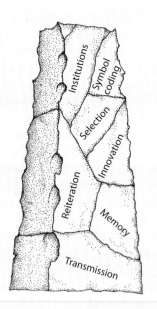

FIGURE 2.2 The modern human capacity for culture did not appear all at once; rather, the various pieces that make it up were added at different times in our evolutionary past.

In Their Own Words

Culture and Freedom

Finding a way to fit human agency into a scientific account of culture has never been easy. Hoyt Alverson describes some of the issues involved.

One's assumptions concerning the existence of structure in culture, or the existence of freedom in human action, determine whether one believes that there can be a science of culture or not. Note that the possibility of developing a science of culture has nothing to do with the use of mathematics, the precision of one's assertions, or the elegance of one's models. If a phenomenon actually has structure, then a science of that phenomenon is at least conceivable. If a phenomenon exhibits freedom and is not ordered, then a science of that phenomenon is inconceivable. The human sciences, including anthropology, have been debating the issue of structure versus freedom in human cultural behavior for the past two hundred years, and no resolution or even consensus has emerged.

Some persuasive models of culture, and of particular cultures, have been proposed, both by those working with scientific, universalist assumptions, and by those working with phenomenological, relativistic assumptions.

To decide which of these approaches is to be preferred, we must have a specific set of criteria for evaluation. Faced with good evidence for the existence of both structure and freedom in human culture, no coherent set of criteria for comparing the success of these alternative models is conceivable. The prediction of future action, for example, is a good criterion for measuring the success of a model that purports to represent structure: it must be irrelevant to measuring the success or failure of a model that purports to describe freedom. For the foreseeable future, and maybe for the rest of time, we may have to be content with models that simply permit us to muddle through.

Source: Alverson 1990, 42–43

as they please; they do not make it under circumstances chosen by themselves, but under circumstances directly encountered, given and transmitted by the past" (1963, 15). That is, people regularly struggle, often against great odds, to exercise some control over their lives. Human beings active in this way are called *agents* (Figure 2.3). Human agents cannot escape from the cultural and historical context within which they act. However, they must frequently select a course of action when the "correct" choice is unclear and the outcome uncertain. Some anthropologists even liken human existence to a mine field that we must painstakingly try to cross without blowing ourselves up. It is in such contexts, with their ragged edges, that human beings exercise their **human agency** by making interpretations, formulating goals, and setting out in pursuit of them.

Many anthropologists insist that it is possible to develop a view of human beings that finds room for culture, history, and human agency. The anthropological point of view called *holism* assumes that no sharp boundaries separate mind from body, body from environment, individual from society, my ideas from our ideas, or their traditions from our traditions. Rather, holism assumes that mind and body, body and environment, and so on, interpenetrate each other and even define each other. From a holistic perspective, attempts to divide reality into mind and matter are unsuccessful because of the complex nature of reality which resists isolation and dissection. Anthropologists who have struggled to develop this holistic perspective on the human condition have made a contribution of unique and lasting value. Holism holds great appeal for those who seek a theory of human nature that is rich enough to do justice to its complex subject matter.

In anthropology, **holism** is traditionally understood as a perspective on the human condition in which the whole (for example, a human being, a society, a cultural tradition) is understood to be greater than the sum of its parts. For example, from a holistic perspective, human beings are complex, dynamic living entities shaped by genes and culture and experience into entities whose properties cannot be reduced to the materials out of which they were constructed. To be sure, human organisms are closed off from the wider world in some ways by how our cells, tissues, and organs are bound into a single body. At the same time, like all living organisms, human beings are open to the world in other ways: we breathe, eat, harbor colonies of intestinal bacteria to aid

human agency The exercise of at least some control over their lives by human beings.

holism Perspective on the human condition in which the whole is understood to be greater than the sum of its parts.

FIGURE 2.3 People regularly struggle, often against great odds, to exercise some control over their lives. During the "Dirty War" in Argentina in the 1970s and early 1980s, women whose children had been disappeared by secret right-wing death squads began, at great personal risk, to stand every Thursday in the Plaza de Mayo, the central square of Buenos Aires, with photographs of their missing children. Called the Mothers of Plaza de Mayo, they continue their weekly vigil today. They were a powerful rebuke to the dictatorship and to subsequent governments that were not forthcoming about providing information about the disappeared.

our digestion, excrete waste products, and learn from experience (Deacon 2003, 296–97). Similarly, a society is not just the sum of its individual members; people in groups develop dynamic relationships that facilitate collective actions impossible for individuals to bring about on their own. And cultural traditions are not just a list of beliefs, values, and practices; rather, different dimensions of cultural activity, such as economics and politics and religion, are knotted together in complex ways. To understand any human community requires untangling those cultural threads in order to reveal the full range of factors that shape particular cultural practices in that community.

Human beings who develop and live together in groups shaped by cultural patterns are deeply affected by shared cultural experiences. They become different from what they would have been had they matured in isolation; they also become different from other people who have been shaped by different social and cultural patterns. Social scientists have long known that human beings who grow up isolated from meaningful social

interactions with others do not behave in ways that appear recognizably human. As anthropologist Clifford Geertz observed long ago, such human beings would be neither failed apes nor "natural" people stripped of their veneer of culture; they would be "mental basket cases" (1973, 40). Social living and cultural sharing are necessary for individual human beings to develop what we recognize as a *human* nature.

One useful way of thinking about the relationships among the parts that make up a whole is in terms of **coevolution**. A coevolutionary approach to the human condition emphasizes that human organisms, their physical environments, and their symbolic practices *co-determine* one another; with the passage of time, they can also *coevolve* with one another. A coevolutionary view of the human condition also sees human beings as organisms whose bodies, brains, actions, and thoughts are equally involved in shaping what they become. Co-evolution produces a human nature connected to a wider world and profoundly shaped by culture. These connections make us vulnerable over the courses of our lives to influences that our ancestors never experienced. The open, symbolic, meaning-making properties of human culture make it possible for us to respond to those influences in ways that our ancestors could not have anticipated.

Why Do Cultural Differences Matter?

The same objects, actions, or events frequently mean different things to people with different cultures. In fact, what counts as an object or event in one tradition may not be recognized as such in another. This powerful lesson of anthropology was illustrated by the experience of some Peace Corps volunteers working in southern Africa.

In the early 1970s, the Peace Corps office in Botswana was concerned by the number of volunteers who seemed to be "burned out," failing in their assignments, leaving the assigned villages, and increasingly hostile to their Tswana hosts. (See Figure 2.4 and EthnoProfile 2.1: Tswana.) The Peace Corps asked American anthropologist Hoyt Alverson, who was familiar with Tswana culture and society, for advice. Alverson (1977) discovered that one major problem the Peace Corps volunteers were having involved exactly this issue of similar actions having very different meanings. The volunteers complained that the Tswana would never leave them

coevolution The dialectical relationship between biological processes and symbolic cultural processes, in which each makes up an important part of the environment to which the other must adapt.

In Their Own Words

Human-Rights Law and the Demonization of Culture

Sally Engle Merry is professor of anthropology at New York University.

Why is the idea of cultural relativism anathema to many human-rights activists? Is it related to the way international human-rights lawyers and journalists think about culture? Does this affect how they think about anthropology? I think one explanation for the tension between anthropology and human-rights activists is the very different conceptions of culture that these two groups hold. An incident demonstrated this for me vividly a few months ago. I received a phone call from a prominent radio show asking if I would be willing to talk about the recent incident in Pakistan that resulted in the gang rape of a young woman, an assault apparently authorized by a local tribal council. Since I am working on human rights and violence against women, I was happy to explain my position that this was an inexcusable act, that many Pakistani feminists condemned the rape, but that it was probably connected to local political struggles and class differences. It should not be seen as an expression of Pakistani "culture." In fact, it was the local Islamic religious leader who first made the incident known to the world, according to news stories I had read.

The interviewer was distressed. She wanted me to defend the value of respecting Pakistani culture at all costs, despite the tribal council's imposition of a sentence of rape. When I told her that I could not do that, she wanted to know if I knew of any other anthropologists who would. I could think of none, but I began to wonder what she thought about anthropologists.

Anthropologists, apparently, made no moral judgments about "cultures" and failed to recognize the contestation and changes taking place within contemporary local communities around the world. This also led me to wonder how she imagined anthropologists thought about culture. She seemed to assume that anthropologists viewed culture as a coherent, static, and unchanging set of values. Apparently cultures have no contact with the expansion of capitalism, the arming of various groups by transnational superpowers using them for proxy wars, or the cultural possibilities of human rights as an emancipatory discourse. I found this interviewer's view of culture wrongheaded and her opinion of anthropology discouraging. But perhaps it was just one journalist, I thought.

However, the recent article "From Skepticism to Embrace: Human Rights and the American Anthropological Association" by Karen Engle in *Human Rights Quarterly* (23: 536–60) paints another odd portrait of anthropology

and its understanding of culture. In this piece, a law professor talks about the continuing "embarrassment" of anthropologists about the 1947 statement of the AAA Executive Board, which raised concerns about the Universal Declaration of Human Rights. Engle claims that the statement has caused the AAA "great shame" over the last fifty years (p. 542). Anthropologists are embarrassed, she argues, because the statement asserted tolerance without limits. While many anthropologists now embrace human rights, they do so primarily in terms of the protection of culture (citing 1999 AAA Statement on Human Rights at www.aaanet.org). Tensions over how to be a cultural relativist and still make overt political judgments that the 1947 Board confronted remain. She does acknowledge that not all anthropologists think about culture this way. But relativism, as she describes it, is primarily about tolerance for difference and is incompatible with making moral judgments about other societies.

But this incompatibility depends on how one theorizes culture. If culture is homogenous, integrated and consensual, it must be accepted as a whole. But anthropology has developed a far more complex way of understanding culture over the last two decades, focusing on its historical production, its porosity to outside influences and pressures, and its incorporation of competing repertoires of meaning and action. Were this conception more widely recognized within popular culture as well as among journalists and human-rights activitists, it could shift the terms of the intractable debate between universalism and relativism. Instead, culture is increasingly understood as a barrier to the realization of human rights by activists and a tool for legitimating noncompliance with human rights by conservatives.

One manifestation of the understanding of culture prevalent in human-rights law is the concept of harmful traditional practices. Originally developed to describe female genital mutilation or cutting, this term describes practices that have some cultural legitimacy yet are designated harmful to women, particularly to their health. In 1990, the committee monitoring the Convention on the Elimination of All Forms of Discrimination Against Women (CEDAW), an international convention ratified by most of the nations of the world, said that they were gravely concerned "that there are continuing cultural, traditional and economic pressures which help to perpetuate harmful

(continued on next page)

In Their Own Words

Human–Rights Law and the Demonization of Culture

(continued)

practices, such as female circumcision," and adopted General Recommendation 14, which suggested that state parties should take measures to eradicate the practice of female circumcision. Culture equals tradition and is juxtaposed to women's human rights to equality. It is not surprising, given this evolving understanding of culture within human-rights discourse, that cultural relativism is seen in such a negative light. The tendency for national elites to defend practices oppressive to women in the name of culture exacerbates this negative view of culture.

Human-rights activists and journalists have misinterpreted anthropology's position about relativism and difference because they misunderstand anthropology's position about culture. Claims to cultural relativism appear to be defenses of holistic and static entities. This conception of culture comes from older anthropological usages, such as the separation of values and social action advocated in the 1950s by Talcott Parsons. Since "culture" was defined only as values, it was considered inappropriate to judge one ethical system by another one. For Melville Herskovits, the leader of the AAA's relativist criticism of the Universal Declaration of Human Rights in 1947, cultural relativism meant protecting the holistic cultures of small communities from colonial intrusion (AAA 1947 Statement, AA 49: 539–43).

If culture is understood this way, it is not surprising that cultural relativism appears to be a retrograde position to human-rights lawyers. Nor is it puzzling that they find anthropology irrelevant. As human-rights law demonizes culture, it misunderstands anthropology as well.

The holistic conception of culture provides no space for change, contestation or the analysis of the links between power, practices and values. Instead, it becomes a barrier to the reformist project of universal human rights. From the legal perspective on human rights, it is the texts, the documents and compliance that matter. Universalism is essential while relativism is bad. There is a sense of moral certainty which taking account of culture disrupts. This means, however, that the moral principle of tolerance for difference is lost.

When corporate executives in the U.S. steal millions of dollars through accounting fraud, we do not criticize American culture as a whole. We recognize that these actions come from the greed of a few along with sloppy institutional arrangements that allow them to get away with it. Similarly, the actions of a single tribal council in Pakistan should not indict the entire culture, as if it were a homogeneous entity. Although Pakistan and many of its communities have practices and laws that subordinate women, these are neither homogeneous nor ancient. Pakistan as a "culture" can be indicted by this particular council's encouragement to rape only if culture is understood as a homogenous entity whose rules evoke universal compliance. Adopting a more sophisticated and dynamic understanding of culture not only promotes human-rights activism, but also relocates anthropological theorizing to the center of these issues rather than to the margins, where it has been banished.

Source: Merry 2003.

---

alone. Whenever they tried to get away and sit by themselves for a few minutes to have some private time, one or more Tswana would quickly join them. This made the Americans angry. From their perspective, everyone is entitled to a certain amount of privacy and time alone. To the Tswana, however, human life is social life; the only people who want to be alone are witches and the insane. Because these young Americans did not seem to be either, the Tswana who saw them sitting alone naturally assumed that there had been a breakdown in hospitality and that the volunteers would welcome some company. Here, one behavior—a person walking out into a field and sitting by himself or herself—had two very different meanings (Figure 2.5).

From this example we can see that human experience is inherently ambiguous. Even within a single cultural tradition, the meaning of an object or an action may differ, depending on the context. Quoting philosopher Gilbert Ryle, anthropologist Clifford Geertz (1973, 6) noted that there is a world of difference between a wink and a blink, as anyone who has ever mistaken one for the other has undoubtedly learned. To resolve the ambiguity, experience must be interpreted, and human beings regularly turn to their own cultural traditions in search of an interpretation that makes sense. They do this daily as they go about life among others with whom they share traditions. Serious misunderstandings may arise, however, when individuals confront the same ambiguous situation without realizing that their cultural ground rules differ.

What Is Ethnocentrism?

Ethnocentrism is the term anthropologists use to describe the opinion that one's own way of life is natural or correct, indeed the only way of being fully human. Ethnocentrism is one solution to the inevitable tension when people with different cultural backgrounds come into contact. It reduces the other way of life to a version of one's own. Sometimes we correctly identify meaningful areas of cultural overlap. But other times, we are shocked by the differences we encounter. We may conclude that if our way is right, then their way can only be wrong. (Of course, from their perspective, our way of life may seem to be a distortion of theirs.)

The members of one society may go beyond merely interpreting another way of life in ethnocentric terms. They may decide to do something about the discrepancies they observe. They may conclude that the other way of life is wrong but not fundamentally evil and that the members of the other group need to be converted to their own way of doing things. If the others are unwilling to change their ways, however, the failed attempt at conversion may

EthnoProfile 2.1

Tswana

Region: Southern Africa

Nation: Botswana

Population: 1,200,000 (also 1,500,000 in South Africa)

Environment: Savanna to desert

Livelihood: Cattle raising, farming

Political organization: Traditionally, chiefs and headmen; today, part of a modern nation-state

For more information: Comaroff, Jean. 1985. *Body of power, spirit of resistance: The culture history of a South African people.* Chicago: University of Chicago Press.

enlarge into an active dualism: us versus them, civilization versus savagery, good versus evil. The ultimate result may be war and *genocide*—the deliberate attempt to exterminate an entire group based on race, religion, national origin, or other cultural features.

Is It Possible to Avoid Ethnocentric Bias?

One way to address this question is to view relationships between individuals with different cultural backgrounds as not being fundamentally different from relationships between individuals with very similar cultural backgrounds. Even people with little in common can learn to get along, even if it is not always easy. Like all human relationships, they affect all parties involved in the encounter, changing them as they learn about each other. People with a cultural background very different from your own may help you see possibilities for belief and action that are drastically at odds with everything your tradition considers possible. By becoming aware of these unsuspected possibilities, you become a different person. People from cultural backgrounds different from yours are likely to be affected in the same way.

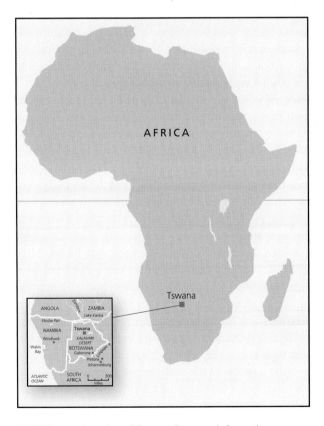

FIGURE 2.4 Location of Tswana. For more information, see EthnoProfile 2.1.

ethnocentrism The opinion that one's own way of life is natural or correct and, indeed, the only true way of being fully human.

FIGURE 2.5 For Tswana, human life is social life. It was difficult for Peace Corps volunteers from the United States accustomed to having "private time" to adjust to Tswana practices.

Learning about other cultures is at once enormously hopeful and immensely threatening; once it occurs, we can no longer claim that any single culture has a monopoly on truth. Although this does not mean that the traditions in question must therefore be based entirely on illusion or falsehood, it does mean that the truth embodied in any cultural tradition is bound to be partial, approximate, and open to further insight and growth.

What Is Cultural Relativism?

Anthropologists must come to terms with the tensions produced by cultural differences as they do their fieldwork. One result has been the formulation of the concept of cultural relativism. Definitions of cultural relativism have varied as different anthropologists have tried to

---

cultural relativism Understanding another culture in its own terms sympathetically enough so that the culture appears to be a coherent and meaningful design for living.

---

draw conclusions based on their own experience of other ways of life. For example, **cultural relativism** can be defined as "understanding another culture in its own terms sympathetically enough so that the culture appears to be a coherent and meaningful design for living" (Greenwood and Stini 1977, 182). According to this holistic definition, the goal of cultural relativism is to promote understanding of cultural practices, particularly of those that an outsider finds puzzling, incoherent, or morally troubling. These practices range from trivial (like eating insects) to horrifying (like genocide), but most are likely to be located somewhere between these extremes.

How Can Cultural Relativity Improve Our Understanding of Controversial Cultural Practices?

Rituals initiating girls and boys into adulthood are widely practiced throughout the world. In some parts of Africa, this ritual includes genital cutting (Figure 2.6). For example, ritual experts may cut off the foreskins of the penises of adolescent boys, who are expected to endure this operation without showing fear or pain. In the case of girls, ritual cutting may involve little more than nicking the clitoris with a knife blade to draw blood. In other cases, however, the surgery is more extreme. The clitoris itself may be cut off (or *excised*), a procedure called *clitoridectomy*. In some parts of eastern Africa, however, the surgery is even more extreme: The labia are excised along with the clitoris, and remaining skin is fastened together, forming scar tissue that partially closes the vaginal opening. This version is often called *pharaonic circumcision* or *infibulation*. When young women who have undergone this operation marry, they may require further surgery to widen the vaginal opening. Surgery may be necessary again to widen the vaginal opening when a woman gives birth; and after she has delivered her child, she may expect to be closed up again. Many women who have undergone these procedures repeatedly can develop serious medical complications involving the bladder and colon later in life.

The removal of the male foreskin—or *circumcision*— has long been a familiar practice in Western societies, not only among observant Jews, who perform it for religious reasons, but also among physicians, who have encouraged circumcision of male newborns as a hygienic measure. The ritual practice of female genital cutting, by contrast, has been unfamiliar to most people in Western societies until recently.

Genital Cutting, Gender, and Human Rights

In 1978, radical feminist Mary Daly grouped "African female genital mutilation" together with practices such as foot binding in China and witch burning in medieval Europe and labeled all these practices patriarchal "Sado-Rituals" that destroy "the Self-affirming be-ing of women" (1978, 111). Feminists and other cultural critics in Western societies spoke out against such practices in the 1980s. In 1992, African American novelist Alice Walker published a best-selling novel *Possessing the Secret of Joy*, in which the heroine is an African woman who undergoes the operation, suffers psychologically and physically, and eventually pursues the female elder who performed the ritual on her. Walker also made a film, called *Warrior Marks*, that condemned female genital cutting. While many Western readers continue to regard the positions taken by Daly and Walker as formidable and necessary feminist assertions of women's resistance against patriarchal oppression, other readers—particularly women from societies in which female genital cutting is an ongoing practice—have responded with far less enthusiasm.

Does this mean that these women are in favor of female genital cutting? Not necessarily; in fact, many of them are actively working to discourage the practice in their own societies. But they find that when outsiders publicly condemn traditional African rituals like clitoridectomy and infibulation, their efforts may do more harm than good. Women anthropologists who come from African societies where female genital cutting is traditional point out that Western women who want to help are likely to be more effective if they pay closer attention to what the African women themselves have to say about the meaning of these customs: "Careful listening to women helps us to recognize them as political actors forging their own communities of resistance. It also helps us to learn how and when to provide strategic support that would be welcomed by women who are struggling to challenge such traditions within their own cultures" (Abusharaf 2000).

A better understanding of female genital cutting is badly needed in places like the United States and the European Union, where some immigrants and refugees from Africa have brought traditions of female genital cutting with them. Since the mid-1990s, growing awareness and public condemnation of the practice has led to the passage of laws that criminalize female genital cutting in 15 African states and 10 industrialized nations, including the United States and Canada (http://www.crlp.org/pub_fac _fgmicpd.html). Nonprofit legal advocacy organizations

FIGURE 2.6   Among many East African people, including the Maasai, female genital cutting is an important part of the transformation of girls into women. These young women are recovering from the operation. Maasai women are proud of their new status as adults.

such as the Center for Reproductive and Legal Rights consider female genital cutting (which they call *female genital mutilation*, or FGM) to be a human rights violation. They acknowledge: "Although FGM is not undertaken with the intention of inflicting harm, its damaging physical, sexual, and psychological effects make it an act of violence against women and children" (http://www.crlp .org/pub_fac_fgmicpd.html). Some women have been able successfully to claim asylum or have avoided deportation by claiming that they have fled their home countries to avoid the operation. However, efforts to protect women and girls may backfire badly when immigrant or refugee mothers in the United States who seek to have their daughters ritually cut are stigmatized in the media as "mutilators" or "child abusers" and find that this practice is considered a felony punishable by up to five years in prison (Abusharaf 2000). Indeed, such efforts can backfire even when members of the receiving society attempt to be culturally sensitive.

Genital Cutting as a Valued Ritual

Female genital cutting is clearly a controversial practice about which many people have already made up their minds. In such circumstances, is there any role to be played by anthropologists? Abusharaf thinks there is. She writes: "Debates swirling around circumcision must be restructured in ways that are neither condemnatory nor demeaning, but that foster perceptions illuminated by careful study of the nuanced complexities of culture" (Abusharaf 2000, 17).

One ethnographic study that aims to achieve these goals has been written by Janice Boddy, a cultural anthropologist who has carried out field research since 1976 in the Muslim village of Hofriyat in rural northern Sudan, where female genital surgery is traditionally performed in childhood. She writes that "nothing . . . had adequately prepared me for what I was to witness" when she first observed the operation; nevertheless, "as time passed in the village and understanding deepened I came to regard this form of female circumcision in a very different light" (1997, 309). Circumcisions in Hofriyat were traditionally performed on both boys and girls, but the ritual had a different meaning for boys than it did for girls. Once circumcised, a boy takes a step toward manhood, but a girl will not become a woman until she marries. Female circumcision is required, however, to make a girl marriageable, making it possible for her "to use her one great gift, fertility" (1997, 310).

In Hofriyat, female circumcision traditionally involved infibulation, the most extreme version of genital cutting. Among the justifications offered for infibulation, Boddy found that preserving chastity and curbing female sexual desire made the most sense in rural northern Sudan, where women's sexual conduct is the symbol of family honor. In practical terms, infibulation ensures "that a girl is a virgin when she marries for the first time" (313). Women who undergo the procedure do indeed suffer a lot, not only at the time of circumcision, but whenever they engage in sexual intercourse, whenever they give birth, and, over time, as they become subject to recurring urinary infections and difficulties with menstruation. What cultural explanation could make all this suffering meaningful to women?

The answer lies in the connection rural northern Sudanese villagers make between the infibulated female body and female fertility. Boddy believes that the women she knew equated the category of "virgin" more with fertility than with lack of sexual experience and believed that a woman's virginity and her fertility could be renewed and protected by the act of reinfibulation after giving birth. Women she knew described infibulated female bodies as clean and smooth and pure (313). Boddy concluded that the ritual was best understood as a way of socializing female fertility "by dramatically de-emphasizing their inherent sexuality" and turning infibulated women into potential "mothers of men." This means they are eligible, with their husbands, to found a new lineage section by giving birth to sons. Women who become "mothers of men" are more than mere sexual partners or servants of their husbands and may attain high status, their name remembered in village genealogies (314).

Boddy discovered that the purity, cleanliness, and smoothness associated with the infibulated female body is also associated with other activities, concepts, and objects in everyday village customs. For example, Boddy discovered that "clean" water birds, "clean food" like eggs, ostrich eggshells, and gourds shaped like ostrich eggshells were associated with female fertility. Indeed, "the shape of an ostrich egg, with its tiny orifice, corresponds to the idealized shape of the circumcised woman's womb" (317). Fetching water is traditionally considered women's work, and the ability of an object to retain moisture is likened to its ability to retain fertility. A dried egg-shaped gourd with seeds that rattle inside it is like the womb of an infibulated woman that contains and mixes her husband's semen with her own blood. The traditional house in Hofriyat itself seems to be a symbol for the womb, which is called the "house of childbirth" (321). In the same way that the household enclosure "protects a man's descendants, so the enclosed womb protects a woman's fertility . . . the womb of an infibulated woman is an oasis, the locus of appropriate human fertility" (321).

Evidence like this leads Boddy to insist that, for the women of Hofriyat, pharaonic circumcision is "an assertive symbolic act." The experience of infibulation, as well as other traditional curing practices teach girls to associate pure female bodies with heat and pain, making them meaningful. Such experiences become associated with the chief purpose women strive for—to become mothers of men—and the lesson is taught them repeatedly in a variety of ways when they look at waterbirds or eggs or make food or move around the village. Boddy's relativistic account demonstrates how the meanings associated with female infibulation are reinforced by so many different aspects of everyday life that girls who grow up, marry, and bear children in Hofriyat come to consider the operation a dangerous but profoundly necessary and justifiable procedure that enables them to help sustain all that is most valued in their own world.

Culture and Moral Reasoning

A relativistic understanding of female genital cutting, therefore, accomplishes several things. It makes the practice comprehensible and even coherent. It reveals how a physically dangerous procedure can appear perfectly acceptable—even indispensable—when placed in a particular context of meaning. It can help us see how some of the cultural practices that we take for granted, such as the promotion of weight loss and cosmetic surgery among women in our own society, are equally dangerous—from "Victorian clitoridectomy" (Sheehan 1997) to twenty-first century cosmetic surgery. In the March 1, 2007, issue of the *New York Times*, for example, reporter Natasha Singer observes, "Before braces, crooked teeth were the norm. Is wrinkle removal the new orthodontics?" (Singer 2007, 3). Media and marketing pressure for cosmetic treatments that stop the visible signs of aging bombard middle-aged women. People are living longer, and treatments like Botox injections are becoming more easily available, with the result that "the way pop culture perceives the aging face" is changing, leaving women "grappling with the idea of what 60 looks like" (2007, E3). Moreover, pressure to undergo antiaging treatments, including plastic surgery, is not simply a matter of vanity. "At the very least, wrinkles are being repositioned as the new gray hair—another means to judge attractiveness, romantic viability, professional competitiveness and social status" (2007, E3). Singer quotes a 33-year-old real estate broker who has had Botox injections, chemical peels, and laser treatments who said, "If you want to sell a million-dollar house, you have to look good . . . and you have to have confidence that you look good" (2007, E3). In Sudan, people say that virgins are "made, not born" (Boddy 1997, 313); perhaps in the United States, youth is also "made, not born." In the United States today, the media message to women is that success in life requires not an infibulated body, but a face that never ages. In both cases, cultural practices recommend surgical intervention in the female life cycle to render permanent certain aspects of youthful female bodies that are otherwise transient (fertility and unlined faces, respectively).

Did Their Culture Make Them Do It?

Do these examples imply that women support "irrational" and harmful practices simply because "their culture makes them do it?" For some people, this kind of explanation is plausible, even preferable, to alternative explanations, because it absolves individual people of blame. How can one justify accusing immigrant African women of being mutilators or abusers of children and throw them into prison if they had no choice in the matter, if their cultures conditioned them into believing that female circumcision was necessary and proper and they are powerless to resist?

Nevertheless, such an explanation is too simplistic to account for the continued practice of infibulation in Hofriyat. First, the villages of northern Sudan are not sealed off from a wider, more diverse world. Northern Sudan has experienced a lively and often violent history as different groups of outsiders, including the British, have struggled to control the land. Boddy describes the way rural men regularly leave the village as migrant workers and mix with people whose customs—including sexual customs—are very different from the ones they left behind; and outsiders, like anthropologists, also may come to the village and establish long-lasting relationships with those

whom they meet. Second, Boddy's account makes clear that the culture of Hofriyat allows people more than one way to interpret their experiences. For example, she notes that although men in Sudan and Egypt are supposed to enjoy sexual intercourse with infibulated women more than with noninfibulated women, in fact these men regularly visit brothels where they encounter prostitutes who have not undergone the surgery.

Third and perhaps most significantly, Boddy observes that a less radical form of the operation began to gain acceptance after 1969, and "men are now marrying—and what is more, saying that they prefer to marry—women who have been less severely mutilated," at least in part because they find sexual relations to be more satisfying (312). Finally, as these observations all show, Boddy's account emphatically rejects the view that women or men in Hofriyat are passive beings, helpless to resist cultural indoctrination. As Abusharaf would wish, Boddy listened to women in Hofriyat and recognized them "as political actors forging their own communities of resistance." Specifically, Boddy showed how increasing numbers of women (and men) continued to connect female genital cutting with properly socialized female fertility—but they no longer believed that infibulation was the only procedure capable of achieving that goal.

Understanding something is not the same as approving of it or excusing it. People everywhere may be repelled by unfamiliar cultural practices when they first encounter them. Sometimes when they understand these practices better, they change their minds. They may conclude that the practices in question are more suitable for the people who employ them than their own practices would be. They might even recommend incorporating practices from other cultures into their own society. But the opposite may also be the case. It is possible to understand perfectly the cultural rationale behind such practices as slavery, infanticide, headhunting, and genocide—and still refuse to approve of these practices. Insiders and outsiders alike may not be persuaded by the reasons offered to justify these practices, or they may be aware of alternative arrangements that could achieve the desired outcome via less drastic methods. In fact, changing practices of female circumcision in Hofriyat seem to be based precisely on the realization that less extreme forms of surgery can achieve the same valued cultural goals. This should not surprise us: It is likely that any cultural practice with far-reaching consequences for human life will have critics as well as supporters within the society where it is practiced. This is certainly the case in the United States, where abortion and capital punishment remain controversial issues.

A sensitive ethnographic account of a controversial cultural practice, like Boddy's account of infibulation in Hofriyat, will address both the meaningful dimensions of the practice and the contradictions it involves. As Boddy concludes,

> Those who work to eradicate female circumcision must, I assert, cultivate an awareness of the custom's local significances and of how much they are asking people to relinquish as well as gain. The stakes are high and it is hardly surprising that efforts to date have met with little success. It is, however, ironic that a practice that—at least in Hofriyat—emphasizes female fertility at a cultural level can be so destructive of it physiologically and so damaging to women's health overall. That paradox has analogies elsewhere, in a world considered "civilized," seemingly far removed from the "barbarous East." Here too, in the west from where I speak, feminine selfhood is often attained at the expense of female well-being. In parallels like these there lies the germ of an enlightened approach to the problem (322).

Cultural relativism makes moral reasoning more complex. It does not, however, require us to abandon every value our own society has taught us. Every cultural tradition offers more than one way of evaluating experience. Exposure to the interpretations of an unfamiliar culture forces us to reconsider the possibilities our own tradition recognizes in a new light and to search for areas of intersection as well as areas of disagreement. What cultural relativism does discourage is the easy solution of refusing to consider alternatives from the outset. It also does not free us from sometimes facing difficult choices between alternatives whose rightness or wrongness is less than clear-cut. In this sense, "cultural relativism is a 'toughminded' philosophy" (Herskovits 1973, 37).

Does Culture Explain Everything?

We believe that our view of the concept of culture as presented in this chapter is widely shared among contemporary cultural anthropologists. Nevertheless, in recent years the concept of culture has been critically reexamined as patterns of human life have undergone major dislocations and configurations. The issues are complex and are more fully explored in later chapters, but we offer here a brief account to provide some historical context.

For at least the past 50 years, many anthropologists have distinguished between Culture (with a capital C) and cultures (plural with a lowercase c). *Culture* has been used to describe an attribute of the human species as a whole—its members' ability, in the absence of highly specific genetic programming, to create and to imitate patterned, symbolically mediated ideas and activities that promote the survival of our species. By contrast, the term *cultures* has been used to refer to particular, learned *ways of life* belonging to specific groups of human beings. Given this distinction, the human species as a whole can be said to have Culture as a defining attribute, but actual human beings would only have access to particular human cultures—either their own or other people's.

It is the plural use of cultures with a lowercase c that has been challenged. The challenge may seem puzzling, however, because many anthropologists have viewed the plural use of the culture concept not only as analytically helpful but as politically progressive. Their view reflects a struggle that developed in nineteenth-century Europe: Supporters of the supposedly progressive, universal civilization of the Enlightenment, inaugurated by the French Revolution and spread by Napoleonic conquest, were challenged by inhabitants of other European nations, who resisted both Napoleon and the Enlightenment in what has been called the Romantic Counter-Enlightenment. Romantic intellectuals in nations like Germany rejected what they considered to be the imposition of "artificial" Enlightenment *civilization* on the "natural" spiritual traditions of their own distinct national *cultures* (Kuper 1999; Crehan 2002).

This political dynamic, which pits a steamroller civilization against vulnerable local cultures, carried over into the usage that later developed in anthropology, particularly in North America. The decades surrounding the turn of the twentieth century marked the period of expanding European colonial empires as well as westward expansion and consolidation of control in North America by European settlers. At that time, the social sciences were becoming established in universities, and different fields were assigned different tasks. Anthropology was allocated what Michel-Rolph Trouillot (1991) has called "the savage slot"—that is, the so-called "primitive" world that was the target of colonization. Anthropologists thus became the official academic experts on societies whose members suffered racist denigration as "primitives" and whose ways of life were being undermined by contact with Western colonial "civilization."

Anthropologists were determined to denounce these practices and to demonstrate that the "primitive" stereotype was false. Some found inspiration in the work of English anthropologist E. B. Tylor, who, in 1871, had defined "culture or civilization" as "that complex whole which includes knowledge, belief, art, morals, law, custom, and any other capabilities and habits acquired by man as a member of society" (1958 [1871]:1). This definition had the virtue of blurring the difference between "civilization" and "culture," and it encouraged the view that even "primitives" possessed "capabilities and habits" that merited respect. Thus, in response to stereotypes of "primitives" as irrational, disorganized, insensitive, or promiscuous, anthropologists like Franz Boas and Bronislaw Malinowski were able to show that, on the contrary, so-called "primitives" possessed "cultures" that were reasonable, orderly, artistically developed, and morally disciplined. The plural use of culture allowed them to argue that, in their own ways, "primitives" were as fully human as "civilized" people.

By the end of the twentieth century, however, some anthropologists became concerned about the way the plural concept of culture was being used. That is, the boundary that was once thought to protect vulnerability was starting to look more like a prison wall, condemning those within it to live according to "their" culture, just as their ancestors had done, like exhibits in a living museum, whether they wanted to or not. But if some group members criticize a practice, such as female genital cutting, that is part of their cultural tradition, does this mean that the critics are no longer "authentic" members of their own culture? To come to such a conclusion overlooks the possibility that alternatives to a controversial practice might already exist *within* the cultural tradition and that followers of that tradition may *themselves* decide that some alternatives make more sense than others in today's world. The issue then becomes not just which traditions have been inherited from the past—as if "authentic" cultures were monolithic and unchanging—but, rather, which traditional practices *ought* to continue in a contemporary world—and who is entitled to make that decision.

Culture Change and Cultural Authenticity

It is no secret that colonizing states have regularly attempted to determine the cultural priorities of those whom they conquered. Sending missionaries to convert colonized peoples to Christianity is one of the best-known practices of Western cultural imperialism. In North America in the 1860s, for example, escalating struggles between settlers and Native American groups led federal policymakers to place federal Indian policy in the hands of Christian reformers "who would embrace the hard work of transforming Indians and resist the lure of getting rich off the system's spoils" (Lassiter et al. 2002, 22). And although missionaries were initially resisted, eventually they made many converts, and Christianity remains strong among indigenous groups like the Comanches and Kiowas today. But how should this religious conversion be understood?

Doesn't the fact that Kiowas are Christians today show that federal officials and missionaries succeeded in their policies of Western Christian cultural imperialism? Maybe not: "Taking the 'Jesus Way' is not necessarily the story of

how one set of beliefs replace another one wholesale, or of the incompatibility of Kiowa practices with Christian ones. Rather, it is a more complex encounter in which both sides make concessions" (Lassiter et al. 2002,19). True, missionaries arrived as the buffalo were disappearing and Kiowa people were being confined to reservations, and in 1890 the U.S. government used military force to put an end to the Kiowa Sun Dance, the centerpiece of Kiowa ceremonies. And yet, Lassiter tells us, "For many Kiowas—as for Indian people generally—Christianity has been, and remains, a crucially important element in their lives as Native people. Its concern for community needs, its emphasis on shared beliefs, and its promise of salvation have helped to mediate life in a region long buffeted by limited economic development, geographic isolation, and cultural stress" (Lassiter et al. 2002, 18).

One reason it succeeded was that missionaries did not insist that the Kiowa give up all traditional ways (2002, 53). Prominent Kiowa individuals adopted Christianity, and Kiowa converts were trained to become missionaries and ministers, which proved attractive (2002, 57; Figure 2.7). Especially persuasive were women missionaries who "lived in the Kiowa camps, ate their food, and endured the privations of life on the plains with impressive strength" (2002, 59). Missionaries, in turn, actively

FIGURE 2.7 Among the Kiowa, prominent individuals, like Chief Lone Wolf, adopted Christianity and invited missionaries to train Kiowa ministers.

sought to adapt Christian practices to traditional Kiowa ways. For example, "Missions were historically located in and around established camps and communities," with the result that "churches were the natural extension of traditional Kiowa camps" and eventually took their place at the center of Kiowa life (2002, 61). "People would often camp on the grounds or stay with relatives for weeks at a time. . . . Services with Kiowa hymns and special prayers often extended into the evening" (2002, 62).

It might be as accurate to say that the Kiowa "kiowanized" Christianity, therefore, as it would be to say that missionaries "Christianized" the Kiowa. One of Lassiter's Kiowa collaborators, Vincent Bointy, insists that Christianity is not the same as "the white man's way" and explains that "the elders didn't say 'Christian.' . . . They said 'this is the way of God'" (Lassiter et al. 2002, 63). Kiowa identity and Christian values are so closely intertwined for Bointy that "he believes that he can express the power of Christianity better in Kiowa than in English." And this is why Kiowa hymns are so important. Unlike other Kiowa songs, Kiowa hymns are sung in the Kiowa language, which is spoken less and less in other settings. Kiowa hymns "give life to a unique Kiowa experience, preserve the language, and affirm an ongoing (and continually unfolding) Kiowa spirituality. Indeed, Kiowa Indian hymns are as much Kiowa (if not more) as they are "Christian" (Lassiter 2004, 205).

The way in which Kiowa Christians have been able to transform what began as cultural imperialism into a reaffirmation of traditional Kiowa values challenges the presumption that "authentic cultures" never change. Such an inflexible concept of culture can accommodate neither the agency of Kiowa Christians nor the validity of the "ongoing" and "continually unfolding" cultural traditions they produce.

Today, a variety of groups, from indigenous activists in Amazonia to immigrant activists in Europe, have incorporated the plural use of culture into their own self-definitions, and in some cases anthropologists defend

this move as valuable and progressive. In addition, scholarly disciplines outside anthropology, from cultural studies to cognitive science, have incorporated "culture" into their own technical vocabularies. On the one hand, this can be seen (perhaps ironically) as a measure of the success of earlier generations of anthropologists in demonstrating the value of the culture concept. On the other hand, it means that today, "culture" is sometimes used in ways that anthropologists find objectionable but that they cannot control.

Attempts by anthropologists to deal with these complications are a focus in future chapters, especially in our discussions of anthropological approaches to ethnicity and nationalism (chapter 13) and globalization and multiculturalism (chapter 14).

The Promise of the Anthropological Perspective

The anthropological perspective on the human condition is not easy to maintain. It forces us to question the commonsense assumptions with which we are most comfortable. It only increases the difficulty we encounter when faced with moral and political decisions. It does not allow us an easy retreat, for once we are exposed to the kinds of experience that the anthropological undertaking makes possible, we are changed. We cannot easily pretend that these new experiences never happened to us. There is no going back to ethnocentrism when the going gets rough, except in bad faith. So anthropology is guaranteed to complicate your life. Nevertheless, the anthropological perspective can give you a broader understanding of human nature and the wider world, of society, culture, and history, and thus help you construct more realistic and authentic ways of coping with those complications.

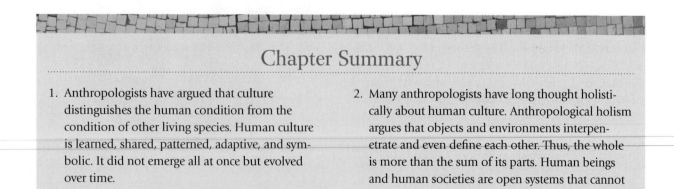

Chapter Summary

1. Anthropologists have argued that culture distinguishes the human condition from the condition of other living species. Human culture is learned, shared, patterned, adaptive, and symbolic. It did not emerge all at once but evolved over time.

2. Many anthropologists have long thought holistically about human culture. Anthropological holism argues that objects and environments interpenetrate and even define each other. Thus, the whole is more than the sum of its parts. Human beings and human societies are open systems that cannot

be reduced to the parts that make them up. The parts and the whole mutually define, or codetermine, each other and coevolve. This book adopts a coevolutionary approach to human nature, human society, and the human past. Human beings depend on symbolic cultural understandings to help them resolve the ambiguities inherent in everyday human experience.

3. Anthropologists believe that ethnocentrism can be countered by a commitment to cultural relativism, an attempt to understand the cultural underpinnings of behavior. Cultural relativism does not require us to abandon every value our society has taught us; however, it does discourage the easy solution of refusing to consider alternatives from the outset. Cultural relativism makes moral decisions more difficult because it requires us to take many things into account before we make up our minds.

4. Human history is an essential aspect of the human story. Culture is worked out over time and passed on from one generation to the next. The cultural beliefs and practices we inherit from the past or borrow from other people in the present make some things easier for us and other things more difficult. At the same time, culture provides resources human beings can make use of in the pursuit of their own goals. Thus, the anthropological understanding of human life recognizes the importance of human agency.

5. Many anthropologists have criticized using the term *cultures* to refer to particular, learned ways of life belonging to specific groups of human beings. Critics argue that this way of talking about culture seems to endorse a kind of oppressive cultural determinism. Supporters, however, argue that in some cases this version of the culture concept can be used to defend vulnerable social groups against exploitation and oppression by outsiders.

For Review

1. What are the five aspects of culture that are highlighted in this chapter?
2. What are complex symbolic representation and institutions, and why are they important to human culture?
3. Describe human agency. Why is it important?
4. Define holism as it is used in the text.
5. Describe the problems Peace Corps volunteers were having in Botswana and the explanation that was provided by anthropologist Hoyt Alverson.
6. Explain ethnocentrism and cultural relativism.
7. Summarize in your own words how cultural relativity can improve our understanding of female genital cutting.
8. Distinguish between Culture (with a capital C) and culture(s) (with a lowercase c).
9. Summarize the case study on Kiowa Christianity.

Key Terms

culture	human agency	coevolution	cultural relativism
symbol	holism	ethnocentrism	

Suggested Readings

Gamst, Frederick, and Edward Norbeck. 1976. *Ideas of culture: Sources and uses*. New York: Holt, Rinehart & Winston. A useful collection of important classic articles about culture. The articles are arranged according to different basic approaches to culture.

Geertz, Clifford. 1973. Thick description: Towards an interpretive theory of culture *and* The impact of the concept of culture on the concept of man. In *The interpretation of cultures*. New York: Basic Books. Two classic discussions of culture from a major figure in American anthropology. These works have done much to shape the discourse about culture in anthropology.

Kuper, Adam. 1999. *Culture: The anthropologists' account*. Cambridge, MA: Harvard University Press. A critical history of the use of the culture concept in anthropology, which traces its links to earlier Western ideas about culture and analyzes the work of several late twentieth-century anthropologists who made the concept central to their scholarship. Based on his experience with the abuse of the culture concept in apartheid South Africa, Kuper recommends that anthropologists drop the term entirely from their professional vocabulary.

Fieldwork

One of the hallmarks of cultural anthropology is close, first-hand knowledge of the ways of life of people all over the world. This chapter describes how cultural anthropologists become familiar with other ways of life by engaging in participant-observation in the course of ethnographic fieldwork. It also considers some of the effects of the fieldwork experience on anthropologists, the people they work with, and the discipline of anthropology itself.

Roger Lancaster is an anthropologist who carried out intensive research in a Nicaraguan working-class neighborhood during the 1980s (Figure 3.1; see Ethno-Profile 3.1: Managua). In June 1985, he went to Don Pablo's *tienda popular* (a "popular store" that carried government-subsidized food basics) to buy a chicken. On his way into the store, he was stopped by a drunken old man who wanted to talk. They exchanged greetings in Spanish and then the old man "uttered a string of vowels and consonants that proved entirely unintelligible." Lancaster explained in Spanish that he did not understand what the man was saying and then entered the store to buy chicken. He relates the rest of the encounter:

> I was trying to decide how large the chicken should be when the drunk old man appeared in the door-way, waving his arms and raving that he had caught an agent of the CIA trying to spy on Nicaragua. "¡La CIA!" he kept shouting. I turned and realized he was talking about me. . . .
>
> Now it was Don Pablo's turn to speak. "Now what makes you think this *joven* [youth] is CIA?" "Because," replied the old man with a flourish of cunning, "I spoke to him in English, and he pretended that he didn't understand what I was saying! Now why else would he do that unless he were trying to conceal his nationality? And why would he conceal his nationality unless he were trying to hide something? He must be CIA. Arrest him!"
>
> I was growing concerned because the old man was now blocking the doorway, and it would scarcely have been appropriate for me to push my way past him. I was trying to figure out how to prevent this from becoming an even more unpleasant scene when Don Pablo's wife

EthnoProfile 3.1

Managua

Region: Central America

Nation: Nicaragua

Population: 1,000,000 (1995 est.)

Environment: Tropical city

Livelihood: Modern stratified city

Political organization: City in modern nation-state

For more information: Lancaster, Roger. 1992. *Life is hard: Machismo, danger, and the intimacy of power in Nicaragua.* Berkeley: University of California Press.

walked over to the meatbox, pulled out a chicken, and asked me if it were acceptable. I said that it was, and she put it on the scales. "Two and a half pounds," she observed, and then turned to address the old man. With an air of authority, she announced, "Listen, compañero, this isn't a spy from the CIA. This is Róger Lancaster, a friend of Nicaragua from the United States. He's an anthropology student at the University of California at Berkeley—not Los Angeles, there's another one in Berkeley, which doesn't have a basketball team. He's working on his doctoral dissertation, and he's here studying the

FIGURE 3.1 A shopkeeper in a neighborhood store in Managua, Nicaragua, in 1986.

role of religion in our revolution, especially the Popular Church. When he goes back, he's going to tell the truth about Nicaragua, and our revolution, and it will be good for us."

I listened with amazement. I had never been inside the popular store before, and I didn't even know either the proprietor or his wife by their names. I had seen them only in passing, and we had never been introduced. Yet here was Doña Carmen, accurately describing my credentials and my research topic. Gossip moves quietly but quickly on the streets of the neighborhoods. (Lancaster 1992, 76)

Like Lancaster, many anthropologists have encountered both suspicion about their motives and surprisingly accurate knowledge about their reasons for being in the community where they were working. Almost always, they have been able to reassure community members that they are not spies, but the accusation makes clear that ethnographic research is not carried out in a vacuum. People's understanding of world politics at a particular moment in history can determine whether they welcome or are suspicious of ethnographers from the United States or elsewhere who suddenly appear in their midst.

Even when they do not suspect the ethnographer of covert activities, however, many people around the world find something unusual about ethnographic fieldwork. Here is someone who shows up in the community, plans to be there for a year or more, claims to be interested in their way of life, and then spends all of his or her time observing, talking to people, and taking notes! In this chapter we will consider why anthropologists put themselves into these situations, as well as the effect field research has on anthropologists and the people whose lives they study.

Why Do Fieldwork?

Ethnographic **fieldwork** is an extended period of close involvement with the people whose way of life interests the anthropologist. This is the period in which anthropologists collect most of their data. Fieldwork deliberately brings together people from different cultural backgrounds, an encounter that makes misunderstandings, understandings, and surprises likely. It is nevertheless through such encounters that fieldwork generates much of what anthropologists come to know about people in other societies.

Gathering data while living for an extended period in close contact with members of another social group is called **participant-observation**. Cultural anthropologists also gather data by conducting interviews and administering surveys as well as by consulting archives and previously published literature relevant to their research. But participant-observation, which relies on face-to-face contact with people as they go about their daily lives, was pioneered by cultural anthropologists and remains characteristic of anthropology as a discipline. Participant-observation allows anthropologists to interpret what people say and do in terms of cultural beliefs and values, social interactions, and the wider political context within which people live. Sometimes anthropologists administer questionnaires and psychological tests as part of their fieldwork, but they would never rely solely on such methods. Participant-observation is perhaps the best method available to scholars who seek a holistic understanding of culture and the human condition.

The Fieldwork Experience

For most cultural anthropologists, ethnographic fieldwork is the experience that characterizes the discipline. Anthropologists sometimes gain field experience as undergraduates or early in their graduate studies by working on research projects or in field schools run by established anthropologists. An extended period of fieldwork is the final phase of formal anthropological training, but most anthropologists hope to incorporate additional periods of field research into their subsequent careers.

Beginning anthropologists usually decide during graduate school where and on what topic they wish to do their research. Success depends on being able to obtain both official permission to work in a particular place and the funds to support one's research. Getting grants from private or government agencies involves, among other things, persuading them that your work will focus on a topic of current interest within anthropology and is connected to their funding priorities. As a result, "field sites end up being defined by the crosshatched intersection of visa and clearance procedures, the interests of funding agencies, and intellectual debates within the discipline and its subfields" (Gupta and Ferguson 1997, 11). Because there is a great demand for grants, not all topics of current interest can be funded, and so some anthropologists pay for their research themselves by getting a job in

---

fieldwork An extended period of close involvement with the people in whose language or way of life an anthropologist is interested, during which anthropologists ordinarily collect most of their data.

participant-observation The method anthropologists use to gather information by living as closely as possible to the people whose culture they are studying while participating in their lives as much as possible.

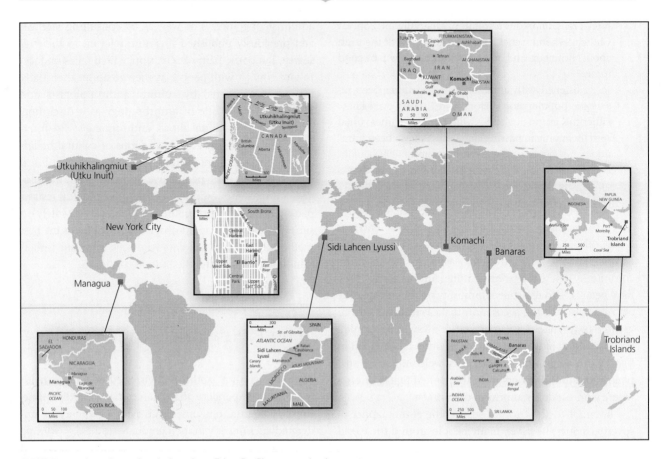

FIGURE 3.2   Locations of societies whose EthnoProfiles appear in chapter 3.

the area where they want to do fieldwork or by supplementing small grants out of their own pockets.

Classic anthropological fieldwork emphasized working "abroad"—that is, doing fieldwork in societies that were culturally and geographically distant from that of the ethnographer. This orientation bears undeniable traces of its origins under European colonialism, but it continues to be a valuable means of drawing attention to ways of life and parts of the world that elite groups in powerful Western nations have traditionally dismissed and marginalized. It also forces the fieldworker to recognize differences that might not be so obvious at home.

More recent discussions of anthropological fieldwork have drawn attention to the significance of working "at home"—including paying attention to the forms of social differentiation and marginalization present in the society to which the ethnographer belongs. This orientation has the virtue of emphasizing ethnographers' ethical and political accountability to those among whom they work, especially when the anthropologists are themselves members of the groups they study. Such an orientation incorporates traditions of anthropological research that have developed in countries like Mexico, Brazil, India, and Russia, where fieldwork at home has long been the norm. At the beginning of the twenty-first century, these

developments are helping to create an anthropology that will be enriched by varied contributions of anthropologists trained in different traditions, working at home and abroad, who seek to forge "links between *different* knowledges that are possible from different locations" (Gupta and Ferguson 1997, 35, 38).

As virtual worlds—World of Warcraft or Second Life, for example—have become increasingly popular around the world, anthropologists have been trying to figure out ways to study them. One of the most successful studies is Tom Boellstorff's *Coming of Age in Second Life*. Boellstorff argues that Second Life, and virtual worlds in general, are sites of human culture and can be studied the same way a cultural anthropologist studies any other cultural site: through participant observation. As Boellstorff puts it,

> Not only did I create the avatar Tom Bukowski; I shopped for clothes for my avatar in the same stores as any Second Life resident. I bought land with the help of a real estate agent and learned how to use Second Life's building tools. I then created a home and office for my research named "Ethnographia," purchasing items like textures, furniture, and artwork. I learned games created and played inside Second Life, like "Tringo" (a combination of Tetris and Bingo) and "primtionary" (a variant of Pictionary). I wandered across the Second Life

landscape, flying, teleporting, or floating along in my hot air balloon, stopping to investigate events, buildings, or people I happened to encounter. I also used the "events" list and notices in Second Life publications to learn of interesting places to visit. In turn, many people stumbled upon my house, either during leisurely explorations of their own or to attend an event I was hosting. I joined many Second Life groups and participated in a range of activities, from impromptu relationship counseling to larger-scale events like a community fair. (Boellstorff 2008, 70)

One could hardly ask for a better description of participant-observation in any kind of world!

A Meeting of Cultural Traditions

Living conditions in the field can provide major insights into the culture under study. This is powerfully illustrated by the experiences of Charles and Bettylou Valentine, whose field site was a poor neighborhood they called *Blackston*, located in a large city in the northern United States (see EthnoProfile 3.2: Blackston). The Valentines lived for the last field year on one-quarter of their regular income; during the final six months, they matched their income to that of welfare families:

> For five years we inhabited the same decrepit rat- and roach-infested buildings as everyone else, lived on the same poor quality food at inflated prices, trusted our health and our son's schooling to the same inferior institutions, suffered the same brutality and intimidation from the police, and like others made the best of it by some combination of endurance, escapism, and fighting back. Like the dwellings of our neighbors, our home went up in flames several times, including one disaster caused by the carelessness or ill will of the city's "firefighters." For several cold months we lived and worked in one room without heat other than what a cooking stove could provide, without hot water or windows, and with only one light bulb. (C. Valentine 1978, 5)

Not all field sites offer such a stark contrast to the middle-class backgrounds of many fieldworkers, and indeed some can be almost luxurious. But physical and mental dislocation and stress can be expected anywhere. People from temperate climates who find themselves in the tropics have to adjust to the heat; fieldworkers in the Arctic have to adjust to the cold. In hot climates especially, many anthropologists encounter plants, animals, insects, and diseases with which they have had no previous experience. In any climate, fieldworkers need to adjust to local water and food.

In addition, there are the cultural differences—which is why the fieldworkers came. Yet the immensity of what they will encounter is difficult for them to anticipate.

EthnoProfile 3.2

Blackston

Region: North America

Nation: United States

Population: 100,000

Environment: Urban ghetto

Livelihood: Low-paying full-time and temporary jobs, welfare

Political organization: Lowest level in a modern nation-state

For more information: Valentine, Bettylou. 1978. *Hustling and other hard work.* New York: The Free Press.

Initially, just getting through the day—finding a place to stay and food to eat—may seem an enormous accomplishment; but there are also data to gather, research to do!

Sometimes, however, the research questions never become separate from the living arrangements. Philippe Bourgois, who studied drug dealers in East Harlem in New York City, had to learn to deal not only with the violence of the drug dealers but also with the hostility and brutality that white police officers directed toward him, a white man living in *El Barrio* (see EthnoProfile 3.3: *El Barrio*; Figure 3.3). His experiences on the street pressed him to consider how the situation he was studying was a form of what he calls "inner-city apartheid" in the United States (Bourgois 1995, 32).

Early in their stay, it is not uncommon for fieldworkers to feel overwhelmed. With time, however, they discover that the great process of human survival begins to assert itself: They begin to adapt. The rhythms of daily activity become familiar. Their use of the local language improves. Faces of the local inhabitants become the faces of neighbors. They are participating and observing—and doing a lot of writing as well. It seems as though fieldworkers always have a notebook somewhere handy and, whenever possible, jot down notes on what they are seeing, hearing, doing, or wondering. These days, laptops, digital cameras, video cameras, and digital recorders are usually considered essential to the accurate recording of field data. We cannot really trust our memories to keep track of the extraordinary range of information that comes at us in the field. But note taking is not sufficient. The quickly jotted scrawls in notebooks must be turned into field notes; as a result, anthropologists spend a lot of their time in front of their computers, writing as complete and coherent a set of notes as possible. Most ethnographers try to write up field notes on a daily basis, and they also try to code the

EthnoProfile 3.3

El Barrio

Region: North America

Nation: United States (New York City)

Population: 110,000 (1990 census)

Environment: Urban ghetto

Livelihood: Low-paying full-time and temporary jobs, selling drugs, welfare

Political organization: Lowest level in a modern nation-state

For more information:
Bourgois, Philippe. 1995. *In search of respect: Selling crack in El Barrio.* New York: Cambridge University Press.

information so that they can find it later. There are very useful field manuals for neophyte ethnographers to consult to assist them in developing workable and straightforward coding systems (e.g., Bernard 2006; DeWalt and DeWalt 2002). As fieldworkers type up their notes, places for further inquiry become plain and a back-and-forth process begins. The ethnographer collects information, writes it down, thinks about, analyzes it, and then takes new questions and interpretations back to the people with whom he or she is working to see if these questions and interpretations are more accurate than the previous ones.

It is important to realize that even the best field notes, however, are not **ethnographies**, published books or articles based on anthropological fieldwork. Writing about the cultural practices one has learned is not as straightforward as it may seem to nonanthropologists. Over the last century, anthropologists' ideas about what ethnographies ought to look like—how long they ought to be, how much and what kinds of details they should contain, whether they should be addressed to audiences of other professionals or to popular audiences or to members of the societies being studied—have undergone revision. Contemporary ethnographers try to be explicit about who they are and how they came to do their research and try to take into account who the various intended (and unintended) readers of their work might be. They search for

sensitive and insightful ways to include multiple points of view besides their own in their texts. When the topics of their research are socially or politically sensitive and could put vulnerable people at risk, they need to be vigilant about their disclosures in order to protect the identity of those with whom they worked.

Ethnographic Fieldwork: How Has Anthropologists' Understanding Changed?

When anthropology began to take on its own identity as an intellectual discipline during the nineteenth century, it aspired to be scientific. Anthropology still aims to be scientific in its study of human nature, human society, and human history. For several decades, however, scientists, philosophers, historians and increasing numbers of social scientists have been reexamining some deeply rooted assumptions about what science is and how it works. This research effort has challenged many popular understandings about science. One outcome of this work has been the demonstration that the so-called hard sciences (such as physics, chemistry, and biology) and the so-called soft sciences (such as psychology, sociology, and anthropology) actually have more in common with each other than previously recognized (e.g., Barad 1999; Pickering 1995). Another outcome has been to show that instead of a single Scientific Method, there are actually a variety of different scientific methods that have been developed to produce reliable knowledge in different scientific disciplines that focus on different aspects of the world (e.g., Knorr Cetina 2000). Anthropologists have joined in this effort to reconsider what science is all about. Sarah Franklin, a pioneer in this effort, writes: "Anthropology is a science and has the tools to understand science as a form of culture" (1995, 165).

Cultural anthropologists have made many efforts over the years to understand the scientific status of the data gathered during participant-observation–based fieldwork. This research strategy came into its own in the early decades of the twentieth century, in the work of such pioneer ethnographers as Bronislaw Malinowski (who, it is often said, invented long-term participant-observation–based fieldwork), Franz Boas, and Boas's best-known student, Margaret Mead. Since that time, the conditions within which fieldwork has been carried out have changed, and with these changed conditions, anthropologists have been prompted to rethink and revise their basic views about fieldwork, both in terms of its scientific status and as a

---

ethnography An anthropologist's written or filmed description of a particular culture.

FIGURE 3.3   *El Barrio*, the part of New York City in which Philippe Bourgois did his research, is a socially complex, dynamic urban neighborhood.

form of human interaction (Figure 3.4). We will briefly review three approaches to ethnographic fieldwork that have developed over the last hundred years: the positivist approach, the reflexive approach, and multisited fieldwork.

The Positivist Approach

The traditional method of the physical sciences, which early social scientists tried to imitate, is now often called *positivistic science*. Its proponents based their view of science on a set of principles most fully set out in the writings of a group of influential thinkers known as positivists, who were active in the late nineteenth and early twentieth centuries. Today, **positivism** has become a label for a particular way of looking at and studying the world scientifically.

Positivism aims to explain how the material world works, and in terms of material causes and processes that we can detect using our five senses (sight, smell, touch, hearing, and taste). Second, to achieve this goal, positivists also are committed to a scientific methodology that separates facts from values. This separation is justified on the grounds that facts relate to the nature of physical, material reality—what *is*—whereas, in their view, values

are based on speculation about what *ought to be*. To the positivist, scientific research is concerned only with what is. As a result, all valid scientific inquiry, from subatomic structure, to genetic engineering, to in vitro fertilization, or human sexual response should be understood as different aspects of a single, disinterested quest for knowledge, a quest that cannot be compromised simply because it offends some people's moral or political sensibilities. Truth remains the truth, whether people like it or not, whether it conforms to their idea of what is good and proper or not. These examples point to a third feature of positivism: the conviction that a single scientific method can be used to investigate any domain of reality, from planetary motion to chemical reactions to human life. The most ambitious positivists are convinced that all scientific knowledge will ultimately be unified in a "theory of everything." Based on these commitments, the traditional goal of the positivist program has been to

positivism The view that there is a reality "out there" that can be known through the senses and that there is a single, appropriate set of scientific methods for investigating that reality.

Participant-observation has characterized cultural anthropology from its earliest days, although "fieldwear" may have changed between Malinowski's day (top) and Wolf Schiefenhövel's in the 1990s (below). There are other important differences as well in how fieldwork is carried out.

produce **objective knowledge**, knowledge about reality that is true for all people in all times and places.

Anthropologists were encouraged by the enormous successes achieved by physical scientists committed to positivist methods. However, the prototypical scientific research scenario involves a physical scientist working in a laboratory, not an ethnographer doing participant observation in a natural setting. Some early cultural anthropologists tried to find ways to get around this limitation. In the 1930s, for example, Margaret Mead carried out research in four different societies in an attempt to discover the range and causes of gender roles. She used a method called *controlled comparison*, which aimed to turn the field into a "living laboratory" by carefully selecting

four different field sites that exhibited naturally the kind of variation that a laboratory scientist could create artificially. Since Mead's day, ethnography inspired by positivist principles has produced systematic and accurate accounts of the ways of life of many peoples. But anthropologists increasingly found themselves confronting a troubling paradox. They were, after all, studying human beings who belonged to the same species (and sometimes even the same society) as they did. Yet positivist ethnography required them to write about human subjects as if they were no different from rocks or molecules. Although anthropologists regularly developed close personal ties to people among whom they worked, defending their full humanity to outsiders and sometimes intervening on their behalf with the government, none of this showed up in their ethnographies. Instead, they wrote as if they had been invisible observers recording

objective knowledge Knowledge about reality that is absolute and true.

objective facts about a way of life in which they were not personally involved.

Questioning the Positivist Approach

The 1960s and 1970s mark a turning point in anthropological understandings of fieldwork. This was a period of social and political turmoil throughout the world, as struggles for civil rights, women's rights, and independence from colonial control called into question many assumptions about the way the world worked. This included questioning the nature of science. Anthropologists began to reconsider the ethics and politics of positivist science in general and of participant-observation in particular. In the 1970s and 1980s anthropologists began to write ethnographies highlighting the ways their own involvement with others in the field had contributed to the growth of cross-cultural knowledge. They were able to show how different observers, working from different assumptions, often produce different knowledge about the same society. At the same time, differently situated fieldworkers also sometimes draw similar conclusions, which allows them to link up their work in productive ways.

Consider the fieldwork of Annette Weiner in the Trobriand Islands carried out in the 1970s, nearly 60 years after Bronislaw Malinowski did his original and celebrated fieldwork there. Weiner and Malinowski were anthropologists of different nationalities and different genders working in different villages with different informants during different historical periods. Weiner made an important contribution to our understanding of Trobriand life by describing and explaining activities involving Trobriand women's "wealth" that were absolutely central to the continued healthy functioning of Trobriand life—but about which Malinowski had written nothing (see chapter 10). Weiner might have published her findings by declaring that Malinowski had got it wrong. But this route did not appeal to her, primarily because, as she put it, he got so very much right. Malinowski's own preoccupations led him to write about aspects of Trobriand life different from those that interested Weiner. As a result, he left behind a portrait of Trobriand society that Weiner later felt obliged to supplement. Nevertheless, Weiner found that much of Malinowski's work remained valid and insightful in her day. She quoted long passages from his ethnographies in her own writings about the Trobriands, in tribute to him (see Weiner 1976, 1988; see also EthnoProfile 3.4: Trobriand Islanders).

But the reconsideration of fieldwork looked not only at the way the backgrounds of ethnographers shaped their fieldwork. It also began to pay closer attention to the ethical and political dimensions of the relationships that anthropologists develop with the people whose way of life

EthnoProfile 3.4

Trobriand Islanders

Region: Oceania

Nation: Papua New Guinea

Population: 8,500 (1970s)

Environment: Tropical island

Livelihood: Yam growing

Political organization:
Traditionally, chiefs and others of rank; today, part of a modern nation-state

For more information:
Weiner, Annette. 1988. *The Trobrianders of Papua New Guinea.* New York: Holt, Rinehart and Winston.

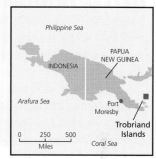

they study, usually referred to as **informants**. Anthropologists in the 1960s and 1970s began to reexamine the laboratory model of fieldwork. In geology and chemistry, for example, it is fairly easy to justify a hierarchy elevating the inquiring intelligence of the scientists over their subject matter. It seems difficult to imagine ethical obligations that the geologist might have to a mineral, or the political differences that might complicate chemists' relationships with the molecules in their test tubes.

But matters are otherwise when the subject matter of science is other human beings. Anthropologists wanting to do scientific fieldwork cannot avoid the realization that they share crucial commonalities with their subject matter that geologists and chemists do not share with theirs. Human beings *do* have ethical obligations to other human beings; political factors *can* complicate the relationships ethnographers are able to develop with their informants. Scientific accuracy therefore requires that anthropologists regard their informants as full human beings. Their subjects may be as eager to learn about the anthropologist as the anthropologist is to learn about them, and they may have their own motives for engaging in ethnographic fieldwork. Anthropologists must also see themselves as full human beings, not as impersonal recording machines, and acknowledge that human involvement

informants People in a particular culture who work with anthropologists and provide them with insights about their way of life. Also called teachers or friends.

with their informants is central to cross-cultural under-standing. This is why, for example, many contemporary ethnographers no longer use the word *informant* to refer to those with whom they work, preferring a term like *consultants, guides, advisors,* or, more generally, *the people with whom I work.*

But these requirements for scientific fieldwork mean that anthropologists can no longer accept the basic assumptions of positivist research without question. Such questioning of positivist science is not taken lightly, especially by other scientists committed to it. Often those who question positivist methods are accused of abandoning scientific discipline entirely, allowing material facts to be obscured by their own, individual *subjective* values and preferences. This is a serious charge. Does the rejection of positivism turn fieldwork into just one person's subjective impressions of other people?

Most anthropologists would answer with a firm "no," because the fieldwork is a *dialogue* between ethnographers and their informants. The fact that ethnographer and informant are both human beings means that scientist and subject matter *both* possess inquiring intelligences. Ethnographers engage in real, literal, conversations with their informants in order to learn about their informants' way of life. These dialogues are often patient and painstaking collaborative attempts to sort things out, to piece things together. When successful, the outcome is a new understanding of the world that both anthropologist and informant can share. This means that field data are not subjective, but *intersubjective:* They are the product of long dialogues between researcher and informant. The focus of fieldwork is the range of **intersubjective meanings** that informants share. Fieldworkers can come to understand these meanings by sharing activities and conversations with their informants. This is what participant-observation is all about.

The Reflexive Approach

The intersubjective meanings on which informants rely are public, not private. Informants take them for granted, but they may not be obvious to an outsider. In order to make these meanings explicit, anthropologist and informant together must occasionally step back from the ordinary flow of daily life and examine them critically. They must think about the way members of the culture normally think about their lives. This thinking about

thinking is known as **reflexivity**; thus, fieldwork in cultural anthropology is a reflexive experience. Reflexive fieldwork retains a respect for detailed, accurate information gathering (Figure 3.5), but it also pays explicit attention to the ethical and political context of research, the background of researchers, the full partnership of informants, and the collaborative relationships that produce anthropological knowledge.

Reflexive fieldwork takes into consideration a broader range of contextual information than does positivistic fieldwork. But consideration of these factors is seen to be essential in order to produce knowledge about human beings that is scientifically valid. Ethnographers have come to recognize that the reliability of their knowledge of other cultures depends on explicit recognition of the ethical and political dimensions of fieldwork, and acknowledgement of how these may have shaped that knowledge. Thus, ethnographic knowledge, shaped by the reflexivity of the ethnographer, has to be understood as *situated knowledge* (Haraway 1991). The "situating" to which Donna Haraway refers involves making explicit exactly who you are as an ethnographer, i.e., your nationality, your class background, your gender, your ethnic background, your educational background, your political preferences, why you undertook this research project, and so forth.

While it might seem that these factors are irrelevant to science and ought to be suppressed, Haraway and others stress that it is precisely these kinds of factors that will shape the kinds of interactions ethnographers will be able to enter into with their informants. In some societies, being a male ethnographer may bar you from studying certain social activities that are seen as inappropriate for men. If these activities are central to the ongoing viability

FIGURE 3.5 Anthropologists use different technologies for different research purposes. Anthropologist Ryan Cook videotapes spectators and ritual performers at the Popocatepetl volcano in Mexico.

intersubjective meanings The shared, public symbolic systems of a culture.

reflexivity Critically thinking about the way one thinks; reflecting on one's own experience.

In Their Own Words

Who's Studying Whom?

Anthony Seeger is an anthropologist who has carried out multiyear research on music in Amazonian Brazil among the Suyá. Seeger, the nephew of legendary folk musician Pete Seeger, and his wife are both accomplished musicians who brought their instruments—guitar and banjo—to the field with them. This led Seeger to deep insight into the process of ethnographic research.

The first time we played and sang in an Indian village, my whole perception of our roles as fieldworkers in the Xingu region was changed. We were invited to record some flute music in the village of the Yawalapiti, near Posto Leonardo Villas Boas. When we finished recording, the men asked us to return and play some of our own music. So the next day we went back with our instruments. The men were finishing an afternoon of singing themselves, and were covered with red body paint, brightly colored head ornaments, and feather arm bands. In the lengthening shadows we sat down by the flute house and tuned up our banjo and guitar. As we started to play, a Yawalapiti man, painted and ornamented like the others but wearing dark glasses and carrying a Sony tape recorder, walked over to us and started recording our music!

Who was studying whom? What was a tape recorder doing in the middle of the jungle? Our astonishment quickly gave way to a clearer understanding of the situation in which we were working. In the Xingu, different societies were confronting each other with curiosity and some hostility. All of my research would be two-sided. We would be watched, studied, evaluated, and discussed just as I was watching, writing, and discussing. The Indians in the Xingu expected to be treated as equals or superiors. The Suyá once threatened to kill a passing anthropologist who they believed had ordered them to do something. "Here, we tell people what to do," they affirmed. One woman told us the Suyá liked us because we never told them what to do or criticized the way they did something.

What I learned that first day when we were recorded in the Yawalapiti village, and in subsequent months, applies to anthropological research throughout the world. We are not dealing with passive objects, or "subjects." We live in a world in which realignment of power is occurring, and in which a solitary researcher inevitably has to accede to the will of the members of the society with which he or she works or find him or herself quickly removed. If this passage from colonialism to mutual respect and curiosity can be bridged, it will be better for both anthropology and ethnomusicology (to say nothing of the peoples themselves). But it takes some patience on the part of researchers unaccustomed to having their images of themselves questioned.

Increasingly anthropologists are being asked, "What can you do for us?" by the people whose societies they are doing research on. It is sometimes a disturbing question, but generally a healthy one, indicating an end to some forms of colonial domination. The Suyá never asked us this question, partly because they knew what they wanted us for: we could become "their Whites," bring them things they wanted, treat the sick, answer questions they had about our world, and sing for them.

Source: Seeger 2004, 22–23.

---

believe themselves to be related to each other. A trained anthropologist comes to the field with knowledge of a variety of possible forms of social organization in mind. These ideas derive in part from the anthropologist's own experience of social relations, but they will also be based on research and theorizing about social relations by other anthropologists. As the fieldworker begins to ask questions about social relations, he or she may discover that the informants have no word in their language that accurately conveys the range of meaning carried by a term like *kinship* or *ethnic group*. This does not mean that the anthropologist must give up. Rather, the anthropologist must enter into the dialectic process of *interpretation* and *translation*.

The process works something like this. The anthropologist asks about "ethnic groups" using a term in the informants' language that seems close in meaning to the term *ethnic group* in English. Informants then try to interpret the anthropologist's question in a way that makes sense to them. That is, each informant has to be reflexive, thinking about how people in his or her society think about the topic that the anthropologist is addressing. Having formulated an answer, the informant responds in terms he or she thinks the anthropologist will understand. Now it is the anthropologist's turn to interpret this response, to decide if it makes sense and carries the kind of information he or she was looking for.

In the dialectic of fieldwork, both anthropologist and informant are active agents. Each party tries to figure out what the other is trying to say. If there is goodwill on the part of both, each party also tries to provide responses that make sense to the other. As more than one anthropologist has remarked (see, for example, Crick 1976;

Rabinow 1977), anthropological fieldwork is translation, and translation is a complicated and tricky process, full of false starts and misunderstandings. Moreover, the informant is just as actively engaged in translation as the anthropologist.

As time passes and the partners in this effort learn from their mistakes and successes, their ability to communicate increases. Each participant learns more about the other: The anthropologist gains skill at asking questions that make sense to the informant, and the informant becomes more skilled at answering those questions in terms relevant to the anthropologist. The validity of this ongoing translation is anchored in the ongoing cultural activities in which both anthropologist and informant are participant-observers. Out of this mutual activity comes knowledge about the informant's culture that is meaningful to both anthropologist and informant. This is new knowledge, a hybrid product of common understandings that emerges from the collaboration of anthropologist and informant.

Informants are equally involved in this dialogue and may end up learning as much or more about anthropologists as anthropologists learn about them. But it is important to emphasize that in field situations *the dialogue is initiated by anthropologists*. Anthropologists come to the field with their own sets of questions, which are determined not by the field situation but by the discipline of anthropology itself (see Karp and Kendall 1982, 254). Furthermore, when anthropologists are finished with a particular research project, they are often free to break off the dialogue with informants and resume discussions with fellow professionals. The only link between these two sets of dialogues—between particular anthropologists and the people with whom they work and among anthropologists in general—may be the particular anthropologists themselves.

Beyond the Dialectic

Fieldwork regularly involves differences of power and places a heavy burden of responsibility on researchers. They are accountable not only to their informants but also to the discipline of anthropology, which has its own theoretical and practical concerns and ways of reasoning about ethnographic data.

At the same time, anthropologists feel strongly that their informants' identities should be protected, all the more so when they belong to marginal and powerless groups that might suffer retaliation from more powerful members of their society. Some informants, however, wish to express their identity and their ideas openly, and some anthropologists have experimented with forms of ethnographic writing in which they serve primarily as translators and editors of the voices and opinions of individual informants (see, for example, Keesing 1983; Shostak

1981). Anthropologists working in their own societies have written about their fieldwork both as observers of others and as members of the society they are observing (see, for example, Foley 1989; Kumar 1992).

In recent years, members of indigenous societies have begun to speak powerfully on their own behalf, as political advocates for their people, as lawyers, as organizers, and as professional scholars. Nevertheless, it is often the case that the people with whom anthropologists work may encounter linguistic and other barriers that keep them from addressing scholarly audiences on academic topics. They also may not share the interests of professional scholars.

As a result, a number of anthropologists have begun to call for forms of ethnographic research and writing that go beyond the dialectic of fieldwork. Luke Eric Lassiter, for example, observes that "anthropologists and American Indian scholars alike" are searching for collaborative ways to "write texts both responsive and relevant to the public with whom they work" (2001, 139). Lassiter used a collaborative methodology as he wrote and rewrote first the text of his Ph.D. dissertation on Kiowa song and, later, the book based on his dissertation. One of the key issues he faced was how to write about "a felt entity encountered in song called, in Kiowa, *daw* and in English *power* or, more precisely, *Spirit*" (2001, 140). Most academically oriented ethnographers tend to write about such entities "from a position of disbelief," but for Kiowa singers like Ralph Kotay, "Spirit is not a concept. It is a very real and tangible thing" (2001, 140). And so Lassiter struggled in his ethnography

> to shift my focus from situating Spirit within an academic sacred/secular dichotomy (based on distance and disbelief) to that of emphasizing the phenomenological questions about Spirit (based in proximity and belief) emergent in our collaborative conversations. Discussions about the ethnographic text itself powerfully reshaped and redefined the book's evolution and further shifted the authority and control of the text from the ethnographer to the *dialogue* between ethnographer and consultants (2001, 140).

Lassiter's work with Ralph Kotay and other Kiowa consultants raised a further issue as well (Figure 3.7). At one point, Kotay had told him, "I'm always willing to give out information like this. But . . . I don't want anything else said *above* this" (2001, 143). Lassiter suggests that Kotay's comment is not just about the obligation to report Kotay's views accurately but also implies that Lassiter should "draw my interpretation of Kiowa song from his perspective rather than my own, and that I will privilege any public representations of Kiowa song (i.e., in texts, essays, etc.) from that same perspective. For Kotay and many other Kiowa consultants, the issue . . . is truly about who has control and who has the 'last word'" (2001, 143).

In Their Own Words

Japanese Corporate Wives in the United States

Anthropologist Sawa Kurotani writes about the "breakthrough" in her research with Japanese corporate wives living in the United States while their husbands were on assignment there.

The fact that I did not have children was perhaps the most significant factor that made my working relationships with Japanese corporate wives awkward. I was Japanese, I was female, and I came from a family background that was very similar to that of many of the women. However, I did not take the typical path of a woman from such a habitus, namely, to work for a few years after college, marry a man with a stable job, quit my job, have a child or two, and become a full-time wife/mother. Instead, I moved to the United States, went on to graduate school, married a foreigner, and postponed having children. If I were, say, an American woman, they could have attributed all our differences to the difference in sociocultural norms; but with me, that was not an option. I was, in a way, a freak of a middle-class Japanese woman, who turned her back on the respectable life that she was supposed to live; that made my character somewhat questionable. The combination of similarities and differences made it difficult for my female informants to relate to my choices and experiences. Among the mothers with young children, there were also more pragmatic issues with having a childless woman around. They were often afraid that their children would do something to offend those who were not used to having children—often crying, whining, and messy children—around. In fact, many of Kawagoe-san's friends apologized to me every time their children tried to get on my knees, or tugged at my clothes, or even looked in my direction. I repeatedly told them that I liked children (which was true) and that their children were not bothering me at all (which was usually true), but I could see that they found it cumbersome as much as I did to have to worry so much about their children all the time. This went on for a couple of months, until the chicken incident.

One day, I was sitting in Kawagoe-san's living room over take-out Chinese lunch with several other women and their children. Although I was becoming a familiar face at Kawagoe-san's, I felt that most of Kawagoe-san's friends were still somewhat unsure about me. They continued to talk to me in polite language, and they rarely initiated a conversation with me. The only exception was Irie-san, who, on a number of occasions, sat next to me and engaged in conversation about my work and my experience in the United States, That day, too, she and her son Yohei were sitting next to me; suddenly, Yohei grabbed a piece of chicken from his plate and handed it to me. The chicken had been pushed around on his plate for a while, and perhaps was even chewed on a couple of times. I took it anyway and immediately threw it into my mouth. I did so partly because I did not want to disappoint the child and also because, somewhere in my mind, I calculated its effect on the mothers. Irie-san was first to speak.

"You know, my husband won't eat the food from Yohei's plate, let alone from his hands," she said. "Men simply can't do that. After all, they are not like women, they are not mothers."

"That's so true," Kawagoe-san chimed in, "but I can't blame them, either. I couldn't have done that before I had my own kids!"

From the way other women chuckled, it seemed to be the same with their husbands. They went on citing instances of men's inability to deal with the filth and dirt (kitanaimono) generated by children: half-eaten food, spilled drinks on the floor, runny noses, and dirty diapers.

The chicken incident was a critical turning point in two ways. First, it gave me an invaluable insight into the problem of my marginality; second, it became the beginning of our negotiation to establish me, the childless woman, as mother material (if my true potential was untested). Irie-san and other women distinguished between themselves and their husbands by the way they physically related to their children, in particular, through their reaction to the filth and dirt that, in their mind, necessarily came with small children. It suddenly dawned on me that this was, for them, an important criterion of gender categories: those who could handle the filth are (potential) mothers, thus necessarily female. The gender of nonmother females, who could not deal with it, was more ambiguous; it was certainly not the same as that of the mothers. The problem of female academicians, according to these women's stereotype at least, was their lack of motherly ability to take care of the dirty things that children produce and, thus, a fatal flaw in their femininity. The gender category of these (biological) women was left unclear when they could not perform the motherly function. In the eyes of my female Japanese informants, I crossed the threshold into womanhood/motherhood with that gooey piece of chicken in my mouth.

Source: Kurotani 2005, 132–133.

FIGURE 3.7   Anthropologist Luke Eric Lassiter (on the right) and Kiowa collaborator Ralph Kotay.

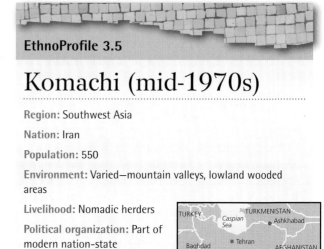

EthnoProfile 3.5

Komachi (mid-1970s)

Region: Southwest Asia

Nation: Iran

Population: 550

Environment: Varied—mountain valleys, lowland wooded areas

Livelihood: Nomadic herders

Political organization: Part of modern nation-state

For more information: Bradburd, Daniel. 1998. *Being there: The necessity of fieldwork.* Washington DC: Smithsonian Institution Press.

To produce collaborative ethnographies of this kind would require anthropologists to resist the deeply rooted Western academic practice of writing texts for which they claimed sole authorship; this could have repercussions in university settings where scholars are expected to publish as individuals. But it would also transform "the role of the so-called informant—where collaborators appear only to inform the production of knowledge—to that of 'consultant,' of 'co-intellectual,'" and would introduce into their ethnographic writings forms of activism that already engage many ethnographers in other contexts (2001, 145).

In a similar fashion, Arjun Appadurai has urged anthropologists to collaborate with colleagues outside the United States, such as grassroots activists, who often lack the kinds of institutional resources and professional experience that scholars in the United States take for granted. With the right support, such colleagues could become equal partners in "a conversation about research" in which they "bring their own ideas of what counts as new knowledge" as well as their own ideas of how to measure the researcher's accountability to those among whom they work (2002, 281).

The Dialectic of Fieldwork: Some Examples

Daniel Bradburd writes about the give and take of cross-cultural learning in his discussion of fieldwork among the Komachi, a nomadic people in Iran with whom he and his wife, Anne Sheedy, lived in the mid-1970s (see Ethno-Profile 3.5: Komachi). Bradburd had gone to Iran to study the process of active decision making among nomadic herding people, and he was therefore quite interested in when and why people would move their camps (Figure 3.8). His first experience with moving was not what he expected. After a month in one place, he started to hear talk about moving. Why? he asked. To be closer to the

village and because the campsite was dirty. When? Soon. When is soon? When Tavakoli comes. This answer made no sense until further questioning revealed that Tavakoli was the son of the leader of the camp.

Eventually their hosts told them that the move would be the next day, but when the next day came, there were no signs of activity in the camp. Finally, when it became clear that they would not be moving that day, Bradburd began asking why they hadn't moved. The answer was "*ruz aqrab.*" When they looked up *aqrab* in the dictionary, the answer made even less sense than the previous one: they weren't moving because it was the day of the scorpion. "As was often the case, we felt as though we had moved one step forward and two steps back. We had an answer, but we hadn't the faintest idea what it meant. We were pretty certain it didn't have anything to do with real scorpions, because we hadn't seen any. We were also pretty certain that we hadn't heard any mention of them. So back we trudged to Qoli's tent, and we started asking more questions. Slowly it became clear. The scorpion was not a real, living one; it was the constellation Scorpio, which Qoli later pointed out to us on the horizon" (Bradburd 1998, 41).

After more questioning and more thinking, Bradburd and Sheedy finally concluded that the Komachi believed it was bad luck to undertake a new activity on days when it appeared that Scorpio would catch the rising moon. On checking back with their informants, they found that their conclusion was correct, but they were still puzzled. On the day that they had been told that the move would be the next day, the Komachi in their camp had been fully aware that Scorpio and the rising moon would be in conjunction the next day. Eventually, Bradburd and Sheedy decided that *ruz aqrab* was a reasonable excuse for not moving, but they never did figure out the real reason for not moving that day. In fact, over the course of many such experiences, Bradburd and Sheedy came to realize that the Komachi didn't have specific reasons for not moving. Rather, they still had one or another thing to do where they were, or the weather was uncertain, or the route to take wasn't clear yet, and so on. As a result of Bradburd's questions and the Komachi's responses, he gradually concluded that the Komachi decision-making process was an attempt to minimize the risks they had to take. Rather than being heroic nomads, masters of their fate, the Komachi made decisions only when they had to.

Nita Kumar is an anthropologist from Delhi, India, who chose to do fieldwork in her own country, but in a region of India very different from the one where she grew up: "Banaras was such a mystery to me when I arrived there in 1981 ironically *because* I was an Indian and expected to have a privileged insight into it. In fact, from Banaras I was *thrice* removed: through my education and upbringing, than which there is no greater molder of attitudes; by language and linguistic culture; and by region and regional culture" (1992, 15) (see EthnoProfile 3.6: Banaras). Although her social connections smoothed the way for her in official circles, she had no special advantage when trying to make contact with the artisans in Banaras whose way of life interested her.

Finding informants and establishing rapport with them has always been seen as an indispensable first step in fieldwork, but there are no foolproof procedures that guarantee success. In her fieldwork memoir, *Friends, Brothers, and Informants* (1992), Kumar shares the four failed attempts she made to contact weavers. The first time, the weavers turned out to have well-established ties to rickshaw pullers and taxi drivers who regularly brought tourists to visit their shop and buy souvenirs. Not wishing to become just another business contact, she left. Her second contact was with the Muslim owner of a weaving establishment whose suspicions of her motives caused her to turn elsewhere. Her third attempt was made through a

EthnoProfile 3.6

Banaras

Region: Southern Asia

Nation: India

Population: 1,000,000

Environment: Tropical monsoon region

Livelihood: Arts, weaving silk, handicrafts; pilgrimage center; urban occupations, education

Political organization: City in a modern nation-state

For more information: Kumar, Nita. 1992. *Friends, brothers, and informants: Fieldwork memories of Banaras.* Berkeley: University of California Press.

sari salesman who took her to a market where silk weavers sold their wares. Unfortunately for her, he would periodically announce to all assembled who she was and invite weavers to come up and speak with her, a procedure she found deeply embarrassing. Her fourth attempt followed the accidental discovery that two members of a family selling firecrackers were also weavers. When she was invited to see one brother's loom, however, she grew "uncomfortable with all the obvious evidence of bachelor existence and their readiness to welcome me into it. . . . I just went away and never came back" (99). On her fifth attempt, she was introduced by a silk-yarn merchant to weavers living in a government-subsidized housing project next to his house. In the home of a weaver named Shaukatullah, surrounded by members of his family, she finally found a setting in which she felt welcome and able to do her work. "In a matter of weeks I was given the status of a daughter

FIGURE 3.8 Daniel Bradburd and Komachi camels packed for moving.

of Shaukatullah" (105). That status of daughter was not only important to Kumar's research, but it was also a congenial status to her, one with which she was familiar.

Ruptures in Communication

Jean Briggs is an anthropologist who was also adopted by a family of informants. Briggs worked among the Utkuhikhalingmiut (Utku, for short), an Inuit group in Alaska (see EthnoProfile 3.7: Utkuhikhalingmiut [Utku Inuit]). There were several steps her informants took in order to figure her out once she took on the role of daughter in the home of her new "father," Inuttiaq, and "mother," Allaq: "From the moment that the adoption was settled, I was 'Inuttiaq's daughter' in the camp. [They] drilled me in the use of kin terms appropriate to my position, just as they drilled [Inuttiaq's] three-year-old daughter, who was learning to speak" (Briggs 1980, 46). The context of their interactions had clearly changed as a result of the adoption, and Briggs's family had new expectations both of Briggs and of themselves: "Allaq, and especially Inuttiaq . . . more and more attempted to assimilate me into a proper adult parent-daughter relationship. I was expected to help with the household work . . . and I was expected to obey unquestioningly when Inuttiaq told me to do something. . . . Inevitably, conflicts, covert but pervasive, developed" (47).

Briggs found herself feeling increasingly uncomfortable and began to analyze her situation. She began to realize that part of the problem had to do with differences between her ideas of how parents ought to relate to their daughters and Utku beliefs on these matters. She also experienced contradictions between her roles as daughter and anthropologist. The dialectic of fieldwork brought sharply to awareness—aided in the construction of—her understanding of the meaning of those roles in her own culture. Moreover, Briggs was not the only person who had to be reflexive. Her Utku informants were forced to reconsider how they had been dealing with her since her arrival. As she was able to reconstruct it, their understanding of her went through three stages. At first, her informants thought she was strange, anomalous. After her adoption, they saw her as educable. But when the communication breakdown occurred, they concluded that she was "uneducable in important ways . . . a defective person" (60–61). Unlike Kumar, Briggs found that assuming the role of daughter was uncomfortable for her personally. While it initially provided her with an opportunity to "fit into" the community she was studying, it also posed challenges to the very continuation of her fieldwork.

Briggs's experience among the Utku also illustrates how, despite strenuous efforts at mutual understanding and translation, the dialectic of fieldwork is not always

EthnoProfile 3.7

Utkuhikhalingmiut (Utku Inuit)

Region: North America

Nation: Canada (Northwest Territories)

Population: 35

Environment: Tundra

Livelihood: Nomadic fishing, hunting, gathering

Political organization: Communal

For more information: Briggs, Jean. 1970. *Never in anger: Portrait of an Eskimo family.* Cambridge, MA: Harvard University Press.

smooth, and how, despite one's best efforts, the ethnographer may fail to perceive how the same behavior in different cultural circumstances can be interpreted differently. Briggs understood from her informants that anger was dangerous and must never be shown. She also became aware of the various ways her informants diverted or diffused angry feelings. Nevertheless, she remained ignorant of the full power of this value in Utku culture until she found herself having seriously violated it.

Beginning a few years before her fieldwork, Briggs relates, sportsmen from the United States and Canada had begun to fly into the inlet where her informants lived during July and August. Once there, they borrowed canoes belonging to the Utku. Although there had at one time been several usable canoes in the community, only two remained when Briggs arrived. That summer some sportsmen borrowed one canoe, but ran it onto a rock. They then asked the Utkus if they could borrow the one remaining canoe, which happened to belong to Briggs's "father," Inuttiaq.

Briggs became the translator for the sportsmen. She was annoyed that their carelessness had led to the ruin of one of the last two good canoes. Because canoes are used for getting food and are not pleasure craft, the loss had serious economic consequences for her informants. When the outsiders asked to use the last canoe afloat, Briggs says, "I exploded." She lectured the sportsmen about their carelessness and insensitivity and explained how important canoes were to the Utku. Then, remembering Inuttiaq's often-repeated admonition never to lend his canoe, she told the sportsmen that the owner of the one remaining canoe did not want to lend it. When Inuttiaq insisted that the canoe be lent, she was not only surprised, she was shocked.

But this was only the beginning. Briggs discovered that, following her outburst, her informants seemed to turn against her rather than against the sportsmen. "I had spoken unbidden and in anger. . . . Punishment was a subtle form of ostracism. . . . I was isolated. It was as though I were not there. . . . But . . . I was still treated with the most impeccable semblance of solicitude" (56–57). Briggs discovered just how much at odds her breaking point was with Utku cultural style. This breach might well have ended her fieldwork if a Westernized Utku friend, Ikayuqtuq, had not come to her rescue. "I had written my version of the story to Ikayuqtuq, had told her about my attempt to protect the Utku from the impositions of the kaplunas [white men] and asked her if she could help to explain my behavior to the Eskimos" (58). Ikayuqtuq did write to Allaq and Inuttiaq, although the letter did not arrive until three months later. During that time, Briggs seemed to be frozen out of Utku society.

Once the letter arrived, everything changed. Briggs's friend had found a way to translate her intentions into terms that Allaq and Inuttiaq could understand. As Briggs recalls, "the effect was magical." Inuttiaq began to tell the others what a dangerous task Briggs had taken on to defend the Utkus against the white men. The ice melted. And Briggs knew that relationships had been restored (and perhaps deepened) when Inuttiaq called her "daughter" once again.

The struggle that ensued when Briggs tried to be a good Utku daughter stems in part from what happens when ethnographers struggle to keep in check the full expression of their own cultural selves, in an effort to avoid offending their informants. The situation is complicated by the fieldworker's imperfect awareness of the sorts of behavior that are likely to offend informants. As a result, the fieldworkers have frequently felt that their motto ought to be "The informant is always right." Many fieldworkers therefore forbid themselves to express anger or disgust or disagreement. But this behavior is likely to cause problems for both them and their informants. After all, what sort of person is always smiling, never angry, without opinions? Anthropologists who refuse to challenge or be challenged by their informants dehumanize both themselves and their informants. Clearly, it takes a good deal of diplomatic skill to walk a fine line between ethnocentrism and depersonalization. Sometimes, as in Briggs' case, this may not be possible, and the fieldwork itself may be put in jeopardy.

Paul Rabinow reflected on the consequences of his own commitment to the fieldworkers' motto in his relations with his informant Ali, who had agreed to take Rabinow to a wedding at some distance from the town where they lived; they were to go in Rabinow's car. Unfortunately, Rabinow was ill the day of the wedding. He did not want to break his promise and perhaps offend Ali and ruin any future chances to attend weddings, but he felt terrible. Ali agreed to stay only a short time at the wedding and then leave. Once they arrived, however, Ali disappeared for long stretches, returning to announce that they would definitely be leaving soon only to wander off again. Rabinow found himself feeling worse, trying to smile at members of the wedding party, and growing angrier and angrier with Ali. At last, many hours after their arrival, Rabinow managed to get Ali into the car and they headed for home. Things did not improve. Rabinow was certain that his annoyance must be obvious to Ali as they drove along, yet Ali kept asking him if he was happy, which was the sign of a pleased guest and a good host. When Rabinow steadfastly refused to answer him, Ali then declared that if Rabinow was unhappy, he, Ali, was insulted and would get out of the car and walk back to town. Rabinow had had enough. He stopped the car to let his companion out and drove on without him.

Rabinow was sure he had sabotaged his fieldwork completely. In retrospect, he acknowledged that this event led him to question seriously whether or not the informant is always right. He said, "If the informant was always right, then by implication the anthropologist had to become a sort of non-person. . . . He had to be willing to enter into any situation as a smiling observer. . . . One had to completely subordinate one's own code of ethics, conduct, and world view, to 'suspend disbelief' . . . and sympathetically and accurately record events" (1977, 46). The quarrel with Ali forced him to drop the anthropologist's all-accepting persona and allow the full force of his personality through. Rabinow chose to be true to himself on this occasion, regardless of the consequences for his fieldwork.

The results could have been disastrous, as they were for Briggs, but Rabinow was lucky. This rupture of communication with Ali was the prelude to Rabinow's experiencing one of his most significant insights into Moroccan culture. After his anger had cooled, he attempted to make up with Ali. To his great surprise, after only a few hours of warm apologies, his relationship with Ali was not only restored but even closer than before! How was this possible? Rabinow had unwittingly behaved toward Ali in the only manner that would impress him, in Moroccan terms. Rabinow learned that Moroccan men test each other all the time to see how far they can assert dominance before their assertions are challenged. In this world, a man who is all-accepting, such as an anthropologist, is not respected or admired but viewed as weak. "There was a fortuitous congruence between my breaking point and Moroccan cultural style. Perhaps in another situation my behavior might have proved irreparable. . . . By standing up to Ali I had communicated to him" (49).

Ruptures of communication between anthropologists and their informants can ultimately lead to a deepening of insight and a broadening of mutual understanding. This is what all fieldworkers hope for—and dread—because, as in Briggs' case, negotiating the rupture can be dangerous, and no positive outcome is ensured. The risks may seem greater when the informants' culture is very different from the anthropologist's, and consequently, it might seem that the resulting insights must also be more startling. Yet Bettylou Valentine discovered that fieldwork in the United States, among African Americans like herself, also held surprises: "At the start of fieldwork I assumed at a subconscious level that my college education . . . would enable me, unlike many ghetto residents, to handle successfully any problem resulting from the impact of the larger society on my family, myself, or any less-skilled ghetto resident I chose to help. This assumption was proved totally wrong many, many times" (1978, 132).

These examples of ethnographic fieldwork illustrate, each in its own way, the effects of reflexive awareness on the production of anthropological knowledge by means of participant-observation rooted in the dialectic of fieldwork. These commitments also affect the kind of ethnography anthropologists write. Unlike earlier ethnographies committed to the positivist approach, in reflexive ethnographies, the presence, the personalities, and the voices of ethnographers and informants alike become vivid elements.

All these accounts highlight the complications and misunderstandings that are a regular part of the dialectic of fieldwork, while Bourgois's, Kumar's, and the Valentines' accounts illustrate the particular opportunities and challenges that arise when doing fieldwork in your own society. In these respects, all these ethnographic accounts would seem to mark a clear advance over positivistic ethnographies in which such matters are never addressed or are ruled out of bounds. As a result, each account can lay claim to strong objectivity.

The Effects of Fieldwork

How Does Fieldwork Affect Informants?

Fieldwork changes both anthropologists and informants. What kinds of effects can the fieldwork experience have on informants? Anthropologists have not always been able to report on this. In some cases, the effects of fieldwork on informants cannot be assessed for many years. In other cases, it becomes clear in the course of fieldwork that the anthropologist's presence and questions have made the informants aware of their own cultural selves in new ways that are both surprising and uncomfortable.

As he reflected on his own fieldwork in Morocco, Rabinow recalled some cases in which his informants' new reflexivity led to unanticipated consequences (Figure 3.9). One key informant, Malik, agreed to help Rabinow compile a list of landholdings and other possessions of the villagers of Sidi Lahcen Lyussi (see EthnoProfile 3.8: Sidi Lahcen Lyussi). As a first step in tracing the economic status of the middle stratum in society, Rabinow suggested that Malik list his own possessions. Malik appeared to be neither rich nor poor; in fact, he considered himself "not well off." "As we began to make a detailed list of his possessions, he became touchy and defensive. . . . It was clear that he was not as impoverished as he had portrayed himself. . . . This was confusing and troubling for him. . . . Malik began to see that there was a disparity between his self-image and my classification system. The emergence of this 'hard' data before his eyes and through his own efforts was highly disconcerting for him" (1977, 117–18).

Malik's easy understanding of himself and his world had been disrupted, and he could not ignore the disruption. He would either have to change his self-image or find some way to assimilate this new information about himself into the old self-image. In the end Malik managed to reaffirm his conclusion that he was not well-off by arguing that wealth lay not in material possessions alone. Although he might be rich in material goods, his son's health was bad, his own father was dead, he was responsible for his mother and unmarried brothers, and he had to be constantly vigilant in order to prevent his uncle from stealing his land (117–19).

Bettylou Valentine was determined from the outset to acknowledge the point of view of her informants in Blackston. Yet before the publication of her ethnography, she discovered that some informants were not pleased with what she had said about them. One woman read in the manuscript about her own illegal attempts to combine work and welfare to better her family's standard of living. Angry, she denied to Valentine that she had ever done such a thing. Valentine talked to her informant at some length about this matter, which was well documented in field notes. It gradually became clear that the woman was concerned that if the data about her illegal activities were published, her friends and neighbors on the block would learn about it. In particular, she was afraid that the book would be sold on corner newsstands. Once Valentine explained how unlikely this was, her informant relaxed considerably: "The exchange made clear how different interests affect one's view. From my point of view, corner newsstand distribution would be excellent because it would mean the possibility of reaching the audience I feel needs to read and ponder the implications of the book. Yet Bernice and Velma [the informant and her friend] specified that they wouldn't mind where else it was distributed, even in Blackston more generally, if it could be kept from people on Paul Street and the surrounding blocks" (B. Valentine 1978, 122).

How Does Fieldwork Affect the Researcher?

What does it feel like to be in the field, trying to figure out the workings of an unfamiliar way of life? What are the consequences of this experience for the fieldworker? Graduate students in anthropology who have not yet been in the field often develop an idealized image of field experience: at first, the fieldworker is a bit disoriented and potential informants are suspicious, but uncertainty soon gives way to understanding and trust as the anthropologist's good intentions are made known and accepted. The fieldworker succeeds in establishing rapport. In fact, the fieldworker becomes so well loved and trusted, so thoroughly accepted, that he or she is accepted as an equal and allowed access to the culture's secrets. Presumably, all this happens as a result of the personal attributes of the fieldworker. If you have what it takes, you will be taken in and treated like one of the family. If this doesn't happen, you are obviously cut out for some other kind of work.

But much more than the anthropologist's personality is responsible for successful fieldwork. Establishing rapport with the people being studied is an achievement of anthropologist and informants together. Acceptance is problematic, rather than ensured, even for the most gifted fieldworkers. After all, fieldworkers are often outsiders with no personal ties to the community in which they will

EthnoProfile 3.8

Sidi Lahcen Lyussi

Region: Northern Africa

Nation: Morocco

Population: 900

Environment: Mountainous terrain

Livelihood: Farming, some livestock raising

Political organization: Village in a modern nation-state

For more information: Rabinow, Paul. 1977. *Reflections on fieldwork in Morocco.* Berkeley: University of California Press.

do their research. According to Karp and Kendall (1982), it is therefore not just naive to think that the locals will accept you as one of them without any difficulty, but it is also bad science.

Rabinow recalled the relationship he formed with his first Moroccan informant, a man called Ibrahim, whom he hired to teach him Arabic. Rabinow and Ibrahim seemed to get along well together, and, because of the language lessons, they saw each other a great deal, leading Rabinow to think of Ibrahim as a friend. When Rabinow planned a trip to another city, Ibrahim offered to go along as a guide and stay with relatives. This only confirmed Ibrahim's

FIGURE 3.9 Paul Rabinow's reflections on his fieldwork experiences in a Moroccan village much like this one led him to reconceptualize the nature of anthropological fieldwork.

friendliness in Rabinow's eyes. But things changed once they arrived at their destination. Ibrahim told Rabinow that the relatives with whom he was to stay did not exist, that he had no money, and that he expected Rabinow to pay for his hotel room. When Rabinow was unable to do so, however, Ibrahim paid for it himself. Rabinow was shocked and hurt by this experience, and his relationship with Ibrahim was forever altered. Rabinow remarks: "Basically I had been conceiving of him as a friend because of the seeming personal relationship we had established. But Ibrahim, a lot less confusedly, had basically conceptualized me as a resource. He was not unjustly situating me with the other Europeans with whom he had dealings" (1977, 29).

Rabinow's experience illustrates what he calls the "shock of otherness." Fieldwork institutionalizes this shock. Having to anticipate **culture shock** at any and every turn, anthropologists sometimes find that fieldwork takes on a tone that is anything but pleasant and sunny. For many anthropologists, what characterizes fieldwork, at least in its early stages, is anxiety—the anxiety of an isolated individual with nothing familiar to turn to, no common sense on which to rely, and no relationships that can be taken for granted. There is a reason anthropologists have reported holing up for weeks at a time reading paperback novels and eating peanut butter sandwiches. One of the authors (EAS) recalls how difficult it was every morning to leave the compound in Guider, Cameroon. Despite the accomplishments of the previous day, she was always convinced that no one would want to talk to her *today* (see EthnoProfile 8.1: Guider).

The move to multisited fieldwork can bring additional anxieties. George Marcus (1995) notes that the special value of single-sited fieldwork comes from its ability to offer insights that can only come from long-term, intense involvement in a single locale, which would seem to suggest that it is not the kind of research strategy best suited to investigating "global" phenomena. But attempting to carry out fieldwork in more than one setting would appear to dilute the intensity of involvement fieldworkers are able to develop with their informants in each site studied, thereby limiting the depth of understanding and insight. As well, some anthropologists are activists who use their ethnography as a way of drawing public attention to the plight of those whose lives they study, and multisited research would seem to undercut or call into question their political commitments to their primary informants.

Marcus recognizes these drawbacks, but does not see them as fatal. Even multisited fieldwork usually is based in one primary site, as in the past; its major innovation involves doing some fieldwork in additional sites and bringing information from all these sites together in a single study that is able to argue for their relationships "on the basis of first-hand ethnographic research" (Marcus 1995, 100). However, concerns about the way multisited ethnography may dilute one's ability to adopt an unequivocal position as defender of a single group is an issue with no easy resolution. Multisited ethnography is a form of fieldwork that highlights the multi-centered, complex conflicts of the contemporary world, in which clear-cut "good guys" and "bad guys" are increasingly hard to identify. When individuals can legitimately claim, or be accorded, multiple identities, some of which conflict, innocent "identity politics" becomes impossible (Haraway 1991, 192). For example, to defend the views of working-class women in a single site is to downplay or ignore the points of view of middle-class women, or unemployed women; it may gloss over differences *among* those women based on class or "race" or ethnicity or religion; and it ignores entirely the points of view of men. Moreover, the spread of industrial capitalism across the globe means that the growth of an urban immigrant workforce in one place is probably connected to a lack of employment somewhere else. A multisited ethnography offers the possibility of juxtaposing more than one place and more than one point of view, thereby bringing to light connections among them that would otherwise remain undetected.

Something like this seems to have inspired Paul Rabinow, who shifted his ethnographic focus from Morocco to study Western scientists at work. His book *Making PCR* (1996) as well as an earlier article, "Reflections on Fieldwork in Alameda" (1993), explores the culture of a private start-up biotechnology firm in the San Francisco Bay area, one of whose members, Kary Mullis, was awarded the Nobel Prize in 1988 for coming up with the technique of polymerase chain reaction (PCR), a technique that enabled biologists to produce vast quantities of genetic material quickly and cheaply. Rabinow's work had a historical dimension, since the key events he was analyzing had ended years earlier. But he was curious about the scientists who worked at the Cetus Corporation during the years when PCR was made. His methodology was to "follow the life" by interviewing key members of the research team about how they came to be scientists and their understandings about how their collaboration in the lab had led to the invention of PCR. Rabinow sees his book as "an experiment in posing the problem of who has the authority—and responsibility—to represent experience and knowledge" (1996, 17). Transcribed interviews—the dialogue of fieldwork in textual form—make up a large part of the book. Multisited ethnography of this kind clearly enabled him to seek in the biographies of scientists the clues

culture shock The feeling, akin to panic, that develops in people living in an unfamiliar society when they cannot understand what is happening around them.

The Relationship between Anthropologists and Informants

Many anthropologists have developed warm, lasting relationships with their informants. However, as Allyn Stearman points out, the nature of the anthropologist–informant relationship is not always unproblematic.

While doing fieldwork among the Ik (pronounced "eek") of Uganda, Africa, anthropologist Colin Turnbull challenged the old anthropological myth that the researcher will like and admire the people he or she is studying. A corollary of this assumption is that to the uninformed outsider who does not "understand" the culture, a group may seem hostile, unresponsive, or stoic, or may have any number of less admirable characteristics; but to the trained observer who truly knows "his or her" people, these attributes are only a façade presented to outsiders. What Turnbull finally had to concede, however, was that overall the Ik were not a very likable people. His portrait of the Ik as selfish, uncaring, and uninterested even in the survival of their own children is understandable when he describes their history of displacement, social disruption, and the constant threat of starvation. Nonetheless, an intellectual understanding of the factors contributing to Ik personality and behavior did not make it any easier for Turnbull to deal emotionally with the day-to-day interactions of fieldwork.

For me, knowing of Turnbull's situation alleviated some of my own anxieties in dealing with the Yuquí. As was Turnbull's, my previous field experiences among other peoples had been very positive. In the anthropologist's terms, this meant that I was accepted quite rapidly as a friend and that my informants were open and cooperative. The Yuquí did not fit any of these patterns. But like Turnbull, I understood something of the Yuquí past and thus on an intellectual level could comprehend that since they

were a hunted, beleaguered people being threatened with extinction I could not expect them to be warm, friendly, and welcoming. Still, on an emotional level it was very difficult to cope with my frequent feelings of anger and resentment at having to put up with their teasing, taunting, and testing on an almost daily basis. My only consolation was that while I was often the brunt of this activity, so were they themselves. I am uncertain whether I finally came to understand the Yuquí, or simply became hardened to their particular way of dealing with the world. By doing favors for people, I incurred their indebtedness, and these debts could be translated into favors owed. How I chose to collect was up to me. As favors mounted, I found that relationships with individual Yuquí were better. Then came the challenges. Could I be easily duped or taken advantage of? At first, I extended kindnesses gratuitously and was mocked. I learned to show my anger and stubbornness, to demand something in return for a tool lent or a service provided. Rather than alienate the Yuquí, this behavior (which I found difficult and distasteful throughout my stay) conferred prestige. The more I provided and then demanded in return, the more the Yuquí were willing to accept me. In the Yuquí world, as in any other, respect must be earned. But unlike many other peoples, for the Yuquí, kindness alone is not enough. In the end it is strength that is valued and that earns respect.

Source: Stearman 1989, 7–10.

---

that might help explain how scientists are made. And this is what he sees as the goal of ethnography: "In my view, the task of the human sciences is neither glorification nor unmasking, nor is it to embody some phantom neutrality. The anthropologically pertinent point is the fashioning of the particularity of practices" (1996, 17)—how people in particular places at particular moments engage with one another and the world.

The Humanizing Effects of Fieldwork

Anthropological knowledge is the fruit of reflexivity produced by the mutual attempts of anthropologist and informant to understand each other. As a result,

anthropological knowledge ought to be able to provide answers to questions about human nature, human society, and the human past. Somehow, good ethnography should not only persuade its readers, on intellectual grounds, that the ethnographer's informants were human beings. It should also allow readers to *experience* the informants' humanity. This privileged position, the extraordinary opportunity to experience "the other" as human beings while learning about their lives, is an experience that comes neither easily nor automatically. It must be cultivated, and it requires cooperation between and effort from one's informants and oneself. We have made an important first step if we can come to recognize, as Paul Rabinow did, that "there is no primitive. There are other [people] living other lives" (1977, 151).

Multisited ethnography can complicate the picture by simultaneously offering rich, fieldwork-based portraits of other people living other lives as variously situated as AIDS patients and corporate managers, and by demonstrating, moreover, that members of these groups share important cultural commitments. In the best ethnographic writing, we can grasp the humanity—the greed, compassion, suffering, pleasure, confusions and ambivalences—of the people who have granted the anthropologist the privilege of living with them for an extended period of time. Because of such experiences, it may also become more natural for us to talk about cultural differences by saying "not 'they', not 'we', not 'you', but some of us are thus and so" (W. Smith 1982, 70).

Where Does Anthropological Knowledge Come From?

The dialectic of fieldwork often involves extended discussions about just what counts as "the facts" that constitute anthropological knowledge. Anthropologist David Hess defines **fact** as a widely accepted observation, a taken-for-granted item of common knowledge (1997, 101–2). Ethnographers' field notebooks will be full of facts collected from different informants, as well as facts based on their own cultural experiences and professional training. But what happens when facts from these various sources contradict one another?

Producing Knowledge

Facts turn out to be complex phenomena. On the one hand, they assert that a particular state of affairs about the world is true. On the other hand, reflexive analysis has taught us that *who* tells us that *x* is a fact is an extremely important thing to know. This is because facts do not speak for themselves. They speak only when they are interpreted and placed in a context of meaning that makes them intelligible. What constitutes a cultural fact is ambiguous. Anthropologists and informants can disagree; anthropologists can disagree among themselves; informants can disagree among themselves. The facts of anthropology exist neither in the culture of the anthropologist nor in the culture of the informant. "Anthropological facts are cross-cultural, because they are made across

cultural boundaries" (Rabinow 1977, 152). In short, facts are not just out there, waiting for someone to come along and pick them up. They are made and remade (1) in the field, (2) when fieldworkers reexamine field notes and reflect on the field experience at a later time, and (3) when the fieldworkers write about their experiences or discuss them with others.

For Daniel Bradburd, fieldwork begins with "being there." But simply being there is not enough. As Bradburd puts it, "my experiences among the Komachi shaped my understanding of them, and that part of field experience consists of a constant process of being brought up short, of having expectations confounded, of being forced to think very hard about what is happening, right now, with me and them, let alone the thinking and rethinking about those experiences when they have—sometimes mercifully—passed" (1998, 161–62). After all, fieldwork is field*work*—there are notes to be taken, interviews to be carried out, observations to make, interpretations to be made. According to Harry Wolcott (1999, 262), it is what ethnographers *do* with data—"making considered generalizations about how members of a group tend to speak and act, warranted generalizations appropriate for collectivities of people rather than the usual shoot-from-the-hip stereotyping adequate for allowing us to achieve our individual purposes"—that makes fieldwork experience different from just experience and turns it into doing ethnography.

Multisited fieldwork elaborates upon and further complicates this experience, because it involves being "here and there." In the course of the movement from site to site, new facts come into view that would otherwise never be known, adding a further layer to the thinking and rethinking that all fieldwork sets in motion. What happens if you find that your activism in support of the urban poor at one site works against the interests of the indigenous people you have supported at a different site? "In conducting multisited research," Marcus says, "one finds oneself with all sorts of cross-cutting commitments" that are not easily resolved. Unlike positivists, however, who might have found "refuge in being a detached anthropological scholar," Marcus suggests that the multisited journey will itself shape the "circumstantial activism" of ethnographers doing fieldwork in a variety of sites. "If that sounds contradictory or ambivalent, it is nevertheless faithful to key features of the contemporary world in which we all live" (Marcus 1995).

Anthropological Knowledge as Open-Ended

We have suggested that there is no such thing as purely objective knowledge and that when human beings are both the subject and object of study, we must speak in terms of reflexivity rather than objectivity. Cultivating

fact A widely accepted observation, a taken-for-granted item of common knowledge. Facts do not speak for themselves; only when they are interpreted and placed in a context of meaning do they become intelligible.

In Their Own Words

The Skills of the Anthropologist

Anthropologists cannot avoid taking their own cultural and theoretical frameworks into the field. However, as Stephen Gudeman observes, fieldwork draws their attention in unanticipated directions, making them aware of new phenomena that constantly challenge those frameworks.

According to the accepted wisdom, poets should be especially facile with language and stretch our vision with freshly cut images. Historians, with their knowledge of past events, offer a wise and sweeping view of human change and continuities. Physical scientists, who have analytical yet creative minds, bring us discoveries and insights about the natural world.

What about anthropologists? Have we any finely honed talents and gifts for the world?

Because anthropology is the study of human life, the anthropologist needs to know a little something about everything—from psychology to legal history to ecology. Our field equipment is primitive, for we rely mainly on the eye, the ear, and the tongue. Because ethnographers carry few tools to the field and the tools they have can hardly capture the totality of the situation, the background and talents of the researcher strongly determine what is "seen" and how it is understood. But the field experience itself has a special impact, too. I studied economic practices in Panama because I was trained to do so, but the field research forced me to alter all the notions I had been taught. Most of them were useless! Anthropologists try to open themselves up to every facet of their field situation and to allow its richness to envelop them. In this, the tasks of the anthropologist are very unlike those of the normal laboratory scientist: the anthropologist can have no predefined hypothesis and testing procedures. The best equipment an ethnographer can possess is a "good ear" and patience to let the "data talk."

This is not all. In the field, anthropologists carry out intense and internal conversations with themselves. Every observation, whether clearly seen or dimly realized, must be brought to consciousness, shuffled about, and questioned. Only by recognizing and acknowledging their own incomprehension can anthropologists generate new questions and lines of inquiry. In the solitude of the field, the anthropologist must try to understand the limits of her or his knowledge, have the courage to live with uncertainty, and retain the ambition to seize on openings to insight.

But field studies constitute only a part of the total research process. Once home, the field notes have to be read and reread, put aside, and then rearranged. The anthropologist is a pattern seeker, believing that within the data human designs are to be found. The task is like solving a puzzle, except that there is no fixed solution and the puzzle's pieces keep changing their shapes! With work and insight, however, a picture—an understanding or an explanation—begins to emerge.

Eventually, the results of all these efforts are conveyed to others, and so anthropologists also need to have expository skills and persuasive powers, for they have to convince others of their picture and their viewpoint about how cultures and social lives are put together.

Source: Gudeman 1990, 458–59.

---

reflexivity allows us to produce less distorted views of human nature and the human condition, and yet we remain human beings interpreting the lives of other human beings. We can never escape from our humanity to some point of view that would allow us to see human existence and human experience from the outside. Instead, we must rely on our common humanity and our interpretive powers to show us the parts of our nature that can be made visible.

If there truly is "no primitive," no subsection of humanity that is radically different in nature or in capacity from the anthropologists who study it, then the ethnographic record of anthropological knowledge is perhaps best understood as a vast commentary on human

possibility. As with all commentaries, it depends on an original text—in this case, human experience. But that experience is ambiguous, speaking with many voices, capable of supporting more than one interpretation. Growth of anthropological knowledge is no different, then, from the growth of human self-understanding in general. It ought to contribute to the domain of human wisdom that concerns who we are as a species, where we have come from, and where we may be going.

Like all commentaries, the ethnographic record is and must be unfinished: Human beings are open systems; human history continues; and problems and their possible solutions change. There is no one true version of human life. For anthropologists, the true version of human life consists of all versions of human life. This is a sobering possibility. It makes it appear that "the anthropologist is condemned to a greater or lesser degree of failure" in even trying to understand another culture (Basham 1978, 299). Informants would equally be condemned to never know fully even their own way of life. And the positivistic orientation resists any admission that the understanding of anything is impossible. But total pessimism does not seem warranted. We may never know everything, but it does not follow that our efforts can teach us nothing. "Two of the fundamental qualities of humanity are the capacity to understand one another and the capacity to be understood. Not fully certainly. Yet not negligibly, certainly. . . . There is no person on earth that I can fully understand. There is and has been no person on earth that I cannot understand at all" (W. Smith 1982, 68–69).

Moreover, as our contact with the other is prolonged we can always learn more. Human beings are open organisms, with a vast ability to learn new things. This is significant, for even if we can never know everything, it does not seem that our capacities for understanding ourselves and others are likely to be exhausted soon. This is not only because we are open to change but also because our culture and our wider environment can change, and all will continue to do so as long as human history continues. The ethnographic enterprise will never be finished, even if all nonindustrial ways of life disappear forever, all people move into cities, and everyone ends up speaking English. Such a superficial homogeneity would mask a vast heterogeneity beneath its bland surface. In any case, given the dynamics of human existence, nothing in human affairs can remain homogeneous for long.

Chapter Summary

1. Anthropological fieldwork traditionally involved participant-observation, extended periods of close contact at a single site with members of another society. Anthropologists were expected to carry out research in societies different from their own, but in recent years increasing numbers have worked in their own societies. Each setting has its own advantages and drawbacks for ethnographers.

2. Early anthropologists who wanted to be scientific tried to remake fieldwork in the image of controlled laboratory research. According to positivist scientists and philosophers, laboratory research was the prototype of scientific investigation. Following this positivist model, anthropologists systematically collected highly accurate data on societies in many parts of the world.

3. When human beings study other human beings, scientific accuracy requires that they relate to one another as human beings. Successful fieldwork involves anthropologists who think about the way they think about other cultures. Informants also must reflect on the way they and others in their society think and they must try to convey their insights to the anthropologist. This is basic to the reflexive approach to fieldwork, which sees participant-observation as a dialogue about the meaning of experience in the informant's culture.

Fieldworkers and informants work together to construct an intersubjective world of meaning.

4. When communication between anthropologist and informant is ruptured, learning about another culture is often greatest. Ruptures occur when current intersubjective understandings prove inadequate to account for experience. A rupture always carries the possibility of bringing research to an end. But when the reasons for the rupture are explored and explanations for it are constructed, great insights are possible.

5. In recent years, a number of anthropologists have begun to carry out fieldwork that takes them to a number of different sites. Such multisited fieldwork is usually the outcome of following cultural phenomena wherever they lead, often crossing local, regional, and national boundaries in the process. Such fieldwork allows anthropologists to understand better many cultural processes that link people, things, metaphors, plots, and lives that are not confined to a single site.

6. Taking part in ethnographic fieldwork has the potential to change informants and researchers in sometimes-unpredictable ways. In some cases, anthropologists have worked with their informants to effect social change, although not all anthropologists agree that this is appropriate. In other cases, anthropologists argue that their main task is

about by social restrictions, and there was no single standard according to which anything could be assigned a value. Capitalism changed all this.

What began as trade contracts with European nations was followed nearly everywhere by European conquest. **Colonialism** refers to a social system in which political conquest by one society of another leads to "cultural domination with enforced social change" (Beidelman 1982, 2). Western conquest of non-Western societies created European colonial empires in two historical phases. The first phase of European colonialism, involving Spain, Portugal, and Holland, required colonies to pay tribute to the empire through trading companies, but the second phase, led by England and France, was based on industrial capitalism (Gledhill 1994, 74). When capitalist practices were imposed on non-Western societies through colonialism, indigenous life was forever altered. To function intelligibly within the capitalist world order, colonized peoples had to begin to see the world as a storehouse of potential commodities. Much of recent world history can usefully be viewed as a narrative of non-Western responses to this new worldview and the practical actions it encouraged and justified. Some people's responses were enthusiastic, others were resentful but accommodating, still others were violent in repudiation or took action to protect themselves.

In western Africa, first the Portuguese and later the Dutch, British, and French found themselves confined for more than 400 years to trading posts built on the coast or on offshore islands. During this period, local peoples living along the coast procured the goods sought by their European trading partners. This long-lasting arrangement shows that western African societies were resilient enough to adapt to the European presence and strong enough to keep Europeans and their commercial interests at arm's length for several centuries. The European presence also reshaped societies of the western African coast, stimulating the growth of hierarchical social forms in some areas where there had been none before. These changes had repercussions farther inland, as the new coastal kingdoms sought trade goods from the people of the African hinterland. Only in the second half of the nineteenth century did this relationship between Europeans and western Africans change.

The situation in southern Africa was different. The Dutch community on the Cape of Good Hope was founded to service Dutch ships on the route to India, but it soon attracted settlers who had moved inland by the late seventeenth century. Their arrival led to the subjugation and destruction of indigenous peoples, both by warfare and by disease. In western Africa, the situation was

often just the reverse; Europeans succumbed to tropical maladies such as malaria to which coastal African populations had greater resistance.

In America, the complex civilizations of Mexico and Peru had been conquered within thirty years of the arrival of Columbus (see Figure 4.2). Indigenous American populations, like those of southern Africa, were laid waste more by European-borne diseases such as measles and smallpox than by armed conflict. They suffered further dislocation after Spanish colonial administration was established. Spain was determined to keep control of the colonies in its own hands, and it checked the attempts of colonists to set themselves up as feudal lords commanding local indigenous groups as their peasants. These efforts, however, were far from successful. Conquered indigenous people were put to work in mines and on plantations. Hard labor further reduced their numbers and fractured their traditional forms of social organization. By the time the worst of these abuses were finally curtailed, in the early seventeenth century, indigenous life in New Spain had been drastically reshaped. Indeed, in the areas of greatest Spanish penetration and control, indigenous groups were reduced to but one component in the complex hierarchy of colonial society.

The Fur Trade in North America

The fur trade had important consequences for indigenous societies in North America. When the Dutch first began to trade with indigenous Americans for furs, they already had trading links to Russia, where fur collecting and fur processing had been established for centuries (Wolf 1982, 158ff.). The fur trade was thus an international phenomenon, and the strong stimulus that indigenous American populations felt to seek fur was shaped by the demand of the fur-processing industry in eastern Europe. The most eagerly sought fur was beaver, used to make felt for cloth and especially hats.

Involvement in the fur trade significantly modified the traditional ways that indigenous North American groups made a living. While the beaver supply lasted, they could obtain many of the material items they needed by exchanging pelts for them at the trading post. This gave them a strong incentive to neglect or even abandon the activities that previously had supplied those items and to devote themselves to fur trapping. Once the beaver were gone, however, people discovered that their highly successful new adaptation had become obsolete. They also discovered that a return to the old ways was impossible, either because those ways had been forgotten or because the new circumstances of life made them impossible to carry out. The result often was severe social dislocation.

---

colonialism Cultural domination with enforced social change.

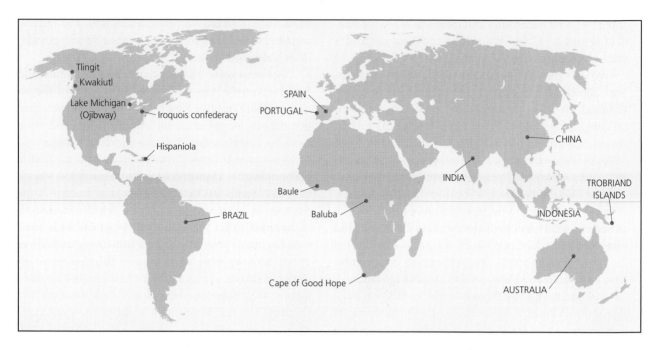

FIGURE 4.1   Locations of societies and places discussed in chapter 4.

Capitalism and Colonialism

By the end of the Middle Ages, centralized monarchies had come into existence in several different European territories. Since the fall of the Roman Empire, Europe had never been politically unified, which meant that, beginning in the fifteenth century, fledgling European states could strike out on their own without being answerable to any central authority (Gledhill 1994, 58–59). At the same time, Europeans were working out a new kind of society with a new kind of economy whose development was aided by trade and conquest—namely, **capitalism**.

The term *capitalism* refers to at least two things: an economic system dominated by the supply-demand-price mechanism called *the market*, and the way of life that grew up in response to and in service to that market. This new way of life changed the face of Europe and transformed other regions as well.

There had been expansive empires before the rise of capitalism, but capitalist exploitation was unique because it derived from a new worldview. In the words of Eric Wolf, "The guiding fiction of this kind of society—one of the key tenets of its ideology—is that land, labor, and wealth are commodities, that is, goods produced not for use, but for sale" (1969, 277). The world is a market, and everything within the world has, or should have, its price.

The genius of capitalism has been the thoroughgoing way in which those committed to the marketing metaphor have been able to convert anything that exists into a commodity; they turn land into real estate and material objects into inventory. They can also attach price tags to ideas (copyright laws) and even to human beings. The

slave in Western society is considered "first and foremost a commodity. He is a chattel, totally in the possession of another person who uses him for private ends" (Miers and Kopytoff 1977, 3). Even human beings who are not slaves are nevertheless reduced to their labor power by the capitalist market and become worth whatever price the laws of supply and demand determine.

To be sure, complex commercial activity was not invented by Western capitalists. In China and India, for example, the use of trade, money, and markets by stratified state societies was highly developed by the time the first representatives of Western capitalism arrived on the scene. Elites in such societies were well prepared to take advantage of new economic opportunities.

However, the consequences of capitalism were often negative for ordinary members of these societies, who lost many traditional socioeconomic supports. Capitalism was even more devastating in small-scale societies existing outside the control of these complex states. Members of these societies saw the land they had always used turned into a commodity for sale on the capitalist market. They experienced the devaluation of their traditional social identities based on descent, alliance, and residence and the erosion of traditional obligations that protected them from poverty. Before the introduction of capitalism, multipurpose money did not exist, exchanges were hedged

capitalism   An economic system dominated by the supply-demand-price mechanism called the market; an entire way of life that grew in response to and in service of that market.

In Their Own Words

The Ecologically Noble Savage?

Part of the stereotype of the "primitive," as Paul Rabinow pointed out, includes the belief that "primitives" live in total harmony with their environment. Kent Redford explores how this stereotype has been recycled in recent years into the image of an idealized "ecologically noble savage."

To live and die with the land is to know its rules. When there is no hospital at the other end of the telephone and no grocery store at the end of the street, when there is no biweekly paycheck nor microwave oven, when there is nothing to fall back on but nature itself, then a society must discover the secrets of the plants and animals. Thus indigenous peoples possess extensive and intensive knowledge of the natural world. In every place where humans have existed, people have received this knowledge from their elders and taught it to their children, along with what has been newly acquired. . . . Writings of several scientists and indigenous rights advocates echo the early chroniclers' assumption that indigenous people lived in "balance" with their environment. Prominent conservationists have stated that in the past, indigenous people "lived in close harmony with their local environment." The rhetoric of Indian spokespersons is even stronger: "In the world of today there are two systems, two different irreconcilable 'ways of life.' The Indian world—collective, communal, human, respectful of nature, and wise—and the western world—greedy, destructive, individualist, and enemy of nature" (from a report to the International NGO Conference on Indigenous Peoples and the Land, 1981). The idealized figure of centuries past had been reborn, as the ecologically noble savage.

The recently accumulated evidence, however, refutes this concept of ecological nobility. Precontact Indians were not "ecosystem men"; they were not just another species of animal, largely incapable of altering the environment, who therefore lived within the "ecological limitations of their home area." Paleobiologists, archaeologists, and botanists are coming to believe that most tropical forests had been severely altered by human activities before European contact. Evidence of vast fires in the northern Amazonian forests and of the apparently anthropogenic origins of large areas of forest in eastern Amazonia suggests that before 1500, humans had tremendously affected the virgin forest, with ensuing impacts on plant and animal species. These people behaved as humans do now: they did whatever they had to to feed themselves and their families.

"Whatever they had to" is the key phrase in understanding the problem of the noble savage myth in its contemporary version. Countless examples make it clear that indigenous people can be either forced, seduced, or tempted into accepting new methods, new crops, and new technologies. No better example exists than the near-universal adoption of firearms for hunting by Indians in the Neotropics. Shotguns or rifles often combined with the use of flashlights and outboard motors, change completely the interaction between human hunters and their prey.

There is no cultural barrier to the Indians' adoption of means to "improve" their lives (i.e., make them more like Western lives), even if the long-term sustainability of the resource base is threatened. These means can include the sale of timber and mining right s to indigenous lands, commercial exploitation of flora and fauna, and invitations to tourists to observe "traditional lifestyles." Indians should not be blamed for engaging in these activities. They can hardly be faulted for failing to live up to Western expectations of the noble savage. They have the same capacities, desires, and perhaps, needs to overexploit their environment as did our European ancestors. Why shouldn't Indians have the same right to dispose of the timber on their land as the international timber companies have to sell theirs? An indigenous group responded to the siren call of the market economy in just this spirit in Brazil in 1989, when Guajajara Indians took prisoners in order to force the government Indian agency, FUNAI, to grant them permission to sell lumber from their lands.

Source: Redford 1993, 11–13.

---

people coping actively with contemporary problems and opportunities, people whose history is also our history. Finally, in spite of everything, human societies around the world continue to generate and retain an impressive variety of cultural forms in response to the changing circumstances under which they live.

Colonial empires no longer exist, but global influences today are having if anything an even more powerful effect on the populations of the world. This means that making sense of the variety of forms of human society that exist across space and time is an ongoing task for anthropologists. One important technique that anthropologists have used in this effort has been to devise a **typology** in order to classify the societies they study according to

typology A classification system based on, in this case, forms of human society.

their similarities and differences. In the rest of the chapter, we will briefly examine some of the most influential typologies that anthropologists have devised. We will also show how the colonial context of ethnographic research shaped the kinds of typologies that became influential in the discipline, and discuss some of the reasons why, eventually, these typologies fell out of favor.

Evolutionary Typologies: The Nineteenth Century

A system of classification reflects the features that its creator believes to be most significant. As a result, different assessments of what is significant can lead to different classifications. In the early years of anthropology, most Westerners who compared non-Western societies with their own were struck by certain features that set apart Europeans from the various peoples they conquered. Westerners identified these differences between themselves and others as *deficiencies*: lack of a state, lack of sophisticated technology, lack of organized religion, and so forth. Perhaps without realizing it, observers took Western industrial capitalist society as the universal standard against which to measure all other human societies. Having done this, they often assumed that the alleged defects of non-Western societies were too obvious to require comment.

This approach to cultural differences was persuasive to nineteenth-century Westerners. It spoke directly to the cross-cultural experience that Western nations were having with the non-Western peoples they had colonized or with whom they traded. A colonial ruler eager to establish a smoothly working administration in New Spain or the operator of a trading post anxious to maximize profits in the fur trade would be most aware of the facets of a people's life that kept him from reaching his goals. How do you successfully collect taxes in a colony that has poor roads, lacks government officials who can read and write, and is populated by subjects who do not speak your language? How do you "pay" for beaver pelts when the "sellers" are not interested in money? Europeans faced with such practical problems were bound to see life outside Europe in terms of a series of deficiencies compared with what they could count on in the home country.

Observers of a more philosophical nature, too, were bound to wonder why there should be such deficiencies in societies outside western Europe (or in the more provincial areas of Europe outside the capital cities). Although their research rarely took them outside their libraries, they studied the reports of travelers and missionaries as well as history. They learned that many of the social and technological patterns they took for granted had not always existed, even in Europe. They became aware of the "advances" that had occurred and were continuing in all areas of European social life since the Middle Ages. It seemed clear that their ancestors too had once lacked the tools and ideas and social forms that made them powerful today. If they went back far enough, perhaps they would discover that their more distant ancestors had lived much as many peoples of America or Africa were living at that time. Indeed, ancient writers such as Julius Caesar had painted a picture of indigenous life in early Europe that resembled the contemporary customs of indigenous Americans and Africans. As archaeology developed, particularly in the nineteenth century, researchers could supplement written records with ancient artifacts presumably made by the primitive ancestors of modern Europeans.

Unilineal Cultural Evolutionism For many nineteenth-century thinkers, the experience of social change, together with historical and archaeological evidence of past social change, was suggestive. Perhaps the ways of life of the non-Western peoples they were reading about were similar to, and even repeats of, the ways of life of European generations long past. That is, perhaps the West had already moved through periods of history in which ways of life had been the same as those of contemporary non-Western societies. According to these scholars, if non-Western societies were left to themselves and given enough time, they would make the same discoveries and change socially the same way that western Europe had.

This way of thinking about social and cultural change has been called **unilineal cultural evolutionism**. It reached its most elaborate development in the nineteenth century, when evolutionary ideas were popular in all areas of Western thought (Figure 4.4). Unilineal cultural evolutionism was one way to explain the widespread cultural diversity that Europeans had been finding since the Age of Exploration. It proposed to account for this diversity by arguing that different kinds of society represented different stages of cultural evolution through which every human society either had passed or would pass, if it survived. Unilineal evolutionists viewed their own late-nineteenth-century European capitalist industrial society as the most advanced stage of cultural evolution yet. Living societies that had not already reached this level were seen as relics of more primitive stages that the West had already left behind.

Today, anthropologists find this approach to the classification of forms of human society to be inadequate—if not totally misleading. Nevertheless, it is a powerful scheme, and its continuing popularity among ordinary members of Western societies is not difficult to understand: It offers a coherent framework for classifying all societies.

---

unilineal cultural evolutionism A nineteenth-century theory that proposed a series of stages through which all societies must go (or had gone) in order to reach civilization.

In Chinese tradition, five elements are said to make up the world: water, fire, wood, metal, and earth. This theory, which dates to the third century b.c.e. was one of the bases of all Chinese scientific thought. These elements were understood not as substances but as *processes*, differentiated by the kinds of changes they underwent. Water was associated with soaking, dripping, and descending. Fire was allied with heating, burning, and ascending. Wood was connected with that which accepted form by submitting to cutting and carving instruments. Metal was affiliated with that which accepted form by molding when in the liquid state and had the capacity to change form by remelting and remolding. Earth was associated with the production of edible vegetation.

In Han times (about 200 b.c.e. to 200 c.e.), the theory achieved a final form, which has been passed down through the ages. According to Colin Ronan and Joseph Needham in their *Shorter Science and Civilisation in China*, "one aspect of the theory, the mutual conquest order, described the series in which each element was supposed to conquer its predecessor. It was based on a logical sequence of ideas that had their basis in everyday scientific facts: for instance, that Wood conquers Earth because, presumably, when in the form of a spade, it can dig up earth. Again, Metal conquers Wood since it can cut and carve it; Fire conquers Metal for it can melt or even vaporize it; Water conquers Fire because it can extinguish it; and, finally, Earth conquers Water because it can dam it and contain it—a very natural metaphor for people to whom irrigation and hydraulic engineering were so important. This order was also considered significant from the political point of view; it was put forward as an explanation for the course of history, with the implication that it would continue to apply in the future and was, therefore, useful for prediction. . . . The Five Elements gradually came to be associated with every conceivable category of things in the universe that it was possible to classify in fives" (1978, 151;153). This included the seasons, the points of the compass, tastes, smells, numbers, kinds of musical notes, heavenly bodies, planets, weather, colors, body parts, sense organs, affective states, and human psychological functions. It also included the periods of dynastic history, the ministries of government, and styles of government, which included relaxed, enlightened, careful, energetic, and quiet, corresponding respectively to wood, fire, earth, metal, and water.

"As we might imagine," Ronan and Needham conclude, "these correlations met with criticism, sometimes severe, because they led to many absurdities. . . . Yet in spite of such criticisms, it seems that in the beginning these correlations were helpful to scientific thought in China. They were certainly no worse than the Greek theory of the elements that dominated European medieval thinking, and

it was only when they became overelaborate and fanciful, too far removed from the observation of Nature, that they were positively harmful" (1978, 156–57).

These observations are relevant to any apt metaphor or good scientific theory. They apply to anthropology as well. Like the Chinese sages, anthropologists began by sorting human cultures into different categories based on what they believed to be their similarities and differences. Over time, the purposes of classification have been questioned, and the categories have been modified or discarded, reflecting changes in the wider world and changing research interests among anthropologists. This chapter considers some of the influential classifications, placing them in the context of the development of anthropology as a discipline within the political and economic influence of the West.

Capitalism, Colonialism, and the Origins of Ethnography

As we mentioned in chapter 2, anthropology became organized as a university discipline in the nineteenth century, at the height of European colonial expansion. In the division of labor between the new social sciences, anthropology specialized in research on societies that either had already been, or soon would become, dominated territories within one or another European empire. In the United States, attention was focused on the indigenous inhabitants of the continent who were being subdued as the country followed its "manifest destiny" to occupy the continent from Atlantic to Pacific.

Writing about the encounter between anthropologists and Native Americans, Peter Whiteley observes that the development of the discipline of anthropology is closely intertwined with the history of European (and Euro-American) imperialism. At the same time, however, Whiteley insists that "in the long run, Native American ethnography has been—by no means always consciously—a principal means of subverting the premises of colonial reason rather than one of its tools. Despite its multiple problems—discursive, ethical, and interpretive—ethnography has been the most powerful contributor to intercultural knowledge and important philosophical complication the world has ever seen" (2004, 460). We think Whiteley is correct, but to make sense of his claims, we need to review key historical developments that made both European expansion and anthropological scholarship possible.

Anthropology, History, and the Explanation of Cultural Diversity

L ike any field of scholarship, anthropology has a history. In this chapter, we look at how cultural anthropology developed in Europe and the United States and how anthropology's explanations of cultural diversity have varied over time. In particular, we highlight the way in which cultural anthropologists and biological anthropologists joined forces in the twentieth century to demonstrate that biological races do not exist and therefore cannot explain why human populations differ from one another.

Chapter Outline

to figure out and explain to others how people in particular places at particular moments engage with one another and with the world.

7. Because cultural meanings are intersubjectively constructed during fieldwork, cultural facts do not speak for themselves. They speak only when they are interpreted and placed in a context of meaning that makes them intelligible. Multisited fieldwork complicates this because it involves the anthropologist in cross-cutting commitments in different contexts, where the same cultural facts may be differently understood or valued.

8. The ethnographic record of anthropological knowledge is perhaps best understood as a vast unfinished commentary on human possibility. We may never learn all there is to know, but we can always learn more.

For Review

1. Explain the basic elements of ethnographic fieldwork.
2. What are the main differences between positivist fieldwork and reflexive fieldwork?
3. Describe multisited fieldwork and explain why many anthropologists undertake it.
4. What is the dialectic of fieldwork, and why is it important for ethnographic research?
5. Discuss collaborative approaches to ethnography.
6. Using the examples in the text, explain how ruptures of communication in fieldwork may turn out to have positive consequences.
7. Explain how fieldwork affects informants.
8. What are some of the ways that fieldwork affects the researcher?
9. What is the importance of "being there" for ethnographic fieldwork?
10. In your view, what are the strengths and weaknesses of ethnographic fieldwork?

Key Terms

fieldwork	positivism	intersubjective meanings	multisited fieldwork
participant-observation	objective knowledge	reflexivity	culture shock
ethnography	informants	dialectic of fieldwork	fact

Suggested Readings

Bigenho, Michelle. 2002. *Sounding indigenous: Authenticity in Bolivian musical performance*. New York: Palgrave Macmillan. A recent multisited ethnography that follows Bolivian and non-Bolivian members of a Bolivian musical ensemble through different settings on more than one continent, chronicling varied understandings of what counts as "indigenous" Bolivian music.

Bradburd, Daniel. 1998. *Being there: The necessity of fieldwork*. Washington, DC: Smithsonian Institution Press. An engaging personal study of how the many seemingly small details of experience during field research add up to anthropological understanding.

Briggs, Jean. 1970. *Never in anger: Portrait of an Eskimo family*. Cambridge, MA: Harvard University Press. A moving, insightful study of fieldwork and of an Utku family.

Faubion, James D. and Geáge E. Marcus, eds. 2009. *Fieldwork is not what it used to be*. Ithaca, NY: Cornell University Press. The authors of the essays in this collection creatively reimagine what ethnographic fieldwork may become in the twenty-first century.

Kumar, Nita. 1992. *Friends, brothers, and informants: Fieldwork memories of Banaras*. Berkeley: University of California Press. A moving and thought-provoking reflection on the experience of fieldwork in the author's own country but in a culture quite different from her own.

Levi-Strauss, Claude. 1974. *Tristes Tropiques*. New York: Pocket Books. Originally published in French in 1955, this book (with an untranslatable title) is considered by some to be the greatest book ever written by an anthropologist (although not necessarily a great anthropology book). This is a multifaceted work about voyaging, fieldwork, self-knowledge, philosophy, and much more. It is a challenging read in some parts but highly rewarding overall.

Rabinow, Paul. 1977. *Reflection on fieldwork in Morocco*. Berkeley: University of California Press. An important, brief, powerfully written reflection on the nature of fieldwork. Very accessible and highly recommended.

Valentine, Bettylou. 1978. *Hustling and other hard work*. New York: Free Press. A classic, innovative, provocative study of African American inner-city life. Reads like a good novel.

FIGURE 4.4   E. B. Tylor (1832–1917), one of the founders of anthropology in Great Britain, was convinced that societies moved through a series of unilineal stages.

For example, unilineal cultural evolutionism provided scholars who worked in museums an analytic framework for organizing artifacts collected from different types of living societies into a sequence based on the discoveries of history and archaeology. Thus, contemporary groups who made a living by gathering, hunting, and fishing were assumed to represent the way of life that had once existed universally, before farming and herding were invented. By the nineteenth century, however, it was clear that agriculture and animal husbandry had been invented only a few thousand years ago, whereas human beings had been around far longer than that. Researchers concluded that contemporary foragers had somehow gotten stuck in the earliest stage of human cultural development, whereas other societies had managed to move upward by domesticating plants and animals. Many of the non-Western groups with which nineteenth-century Europeans and Americans were familiar did farm or herd for a living, however. Their societies were usually larger than those of the foragers and technologically more complex. Farmers usually also built permanent structures and made pottery and woven cloth, goods that were unknown among foragers. Their social patterns too were often more elaborate. These peoples clearly seemed to be a rung above the

foragers. But they were also very different from Europeans. Most did not have writing, and their societies were not organized in anything resembling a European nation-state. For such reasons, this group of societies, midway between the foragers and modern Europeans, were given their own category. They seemed to typify the stage through which gatherers and hunters had to pass—through which Europe's ancestral populations had already passed—before attaining modern civilization.

In this manner, the first important anthropological typology of human social forms emerged. It had three basic categories, corresponding to the preceding distinctions. But the labels given these categories indicated more than objective differences; they also carried moral implications. The foragers—peoples who neither farmed nor herded—were called *savages.* Groups that had domesticated plants and animals but had not yet invented writing or the state were called *barbarians. Civilization* was limited to the early states of the Mediterranean basin and southwestern Asia (such as Mesopotamia and Egypt), their successors (such as Greece and Rome), and certain non-Western societies boasting a similar level of achievement (such as India and China). However, the advances that Europe had experienced since antiquity were seen to be unique, unmatched by social changes in other civilizations, which were understood to be declining. That decline seemed proven when representatives of Western civilization found they could conquer the rulers of such civilizations, as the English had done in India.

As we noted in chapter 1, this way of classifying different societies into stages also involved a classification of the peoples who were members of those societies into different categories called "races." A major disagreement developed in the nineteenth century between those who saw movement from lesser to greater cultural complexity as the result of the efforts of only one or a few "races" and those who believed that all peoples everywhere were equally inventive and might, under favorable circumstances, advance from lower to higher stages of cultural accomplishment. It would not be until the second half of the twentieth century, however, after the establishment of evolutionary theory in biology and the joining of genetics to studies of natural selection, that anthropologists would develop the theoretical and practical tools to demonstrate that biological races do not exist.

Social Structural Typologies: The British Emphasis

As time passed, better and more detailed information on more societies led anthropologists to become dissatisfied with grand generalizations about cultural diversity and cultural change. This change in perspective was the outcome of improved scholarship and better scientific reasoning, but it was also a consequence of the changes taking place in the world itself.

Origins in the Colonial Setting As we have seen, the last quarter of the nineteenth century ushered in the final phase of Western colonialism. Most of Africa and much of Asia, which until then had remained nominally independent, were divided up among European powers. At the same time, the United States assumed a similarly powerful and dominating role in its relationships with the indigenous peoples in its territory and with the former colonies of Spain. Unilineal cultural evolutionism may have justified the global ambitions of Europe and made colonial rule appear inevitable and just. However, it was inadequate for meeting the practical needs of the rulers once they were in power.

Effective administration of subject peoples required accurate information about them. For example, one goal of a colonial administrator in Africa was to keep peace among the various groups over which he ruled. To do so, he needed to know how those people were accustomed to handling disputes. Most colonies included several societies with various customs for dispute resolution. Administrators had to be aware of the similarities and differences among their subjects in order to develop successful government policies. At the same time, colonial officials planned to introduce certain elements of European law and political economy uniformly throughout the colony. Common examples were commercial laws permitting the buying and selling of land on the open market. They also tried to eliminate practices like witchcraft accusations or local punishment for capital crimes. Reaching these goals without totally disrupting life in the colony required first-hand understanding of local practices. The earlier "armchair anthropology" was wholly incapable of providing that understanding.

These changes in the relationships between the West and the rest of the world encouraged the development of a new kind of anthropological research. Under the colonial "peace," anthropologists found that they could carry out long-term fieldwork. Unsettled conditions had made such work difficult in earlier times. Anthropologists also found that colonial governments would support their research when persuaded that it was scientific and could contribute to effective colonial rule. This did not mean that anthropologists who carried out fieldwork under colonial conditions supported colonialism. To the contrary, their sympathies often lay with the colonized peoples with whom they worked. For example, Sir E. E. Evans-Pritchard,

who worked in central Africa for the British government in the 1920s and 1930s, saw himself as an educator of colonial administrators. He tried to convey to them the humanity and rationality of Africans. His goal was to combat the racism and oppression that seemed an inevitable consequence of colonial rule. For these reasons, colonial officials were often wary of anthropologists and distrustful of their motives. It was all too likely that the results of anthropological research might make colonial programs look self-serving and exploitative.

Colonial officials quickly learned that the task of administering their rule would be easier if they could rely on traditional rulers to keep the peace among their traditional subjects through traditional means (Figure 4.5). Thus developed the British policy of *indirect rule*. Colonial officials were at the top of the hierarchy. Under them, the traditional rulers (elders, chiefs, and so on) served as intermediaries with the common people. How could anthropologists contribute to the effectiveness of indirect rule? Perhaps the information they gathered about the traditional political structures of different groups might offer insights into the best way to adapt indirect rule to each group. Anthropologists—especially British ones—developed a new way of classifying forms of human society. Their focus was on the **social structure**, especially the political structure, of groups under colonial rule. That British anthropologists came to call themselves *social anthropologists* reflects these developments.

In 1940, in a classic work on African political systems, Meyer Fortes and E. E. Evans-Pritchard distinguished between state and stateless societies. This distinction is similar to the unilineal evolutionary classifications in terms of lower and higher stages. However, there is a significant difference in the terminology used by Evans-Pritchard and Fortes: It makes no mention of "progress" from "lower" to "higher" forms of society. But the emphasis on contemporary social structures was bringing rich new insights to anthropology. Questions of evolution and social change took a back seat as social anthropologists concerned themselves with figuring out the enduring traditional structures of the societies in which they worked. A detailed knowledge of social structures was supposed to allow the anthropologist to identify the social type of any particular society. These types were treated as unchanging. They were compared for similarities and differences, and out of this comparison emerged a new classification of social forms.

The Classification of Political Structures A contemporary example of a typical social-structural classification of forms of human society is shown in Figure 4.6. Here, the major distinction is between *centralized* and *uncentralized*, or *egalitarian*, political systems. This distinction is similar to the one Evans-Pritchard and Fortes made

---

social structure The enduring aspects of the social forms in a society, including its political and kinship systems.

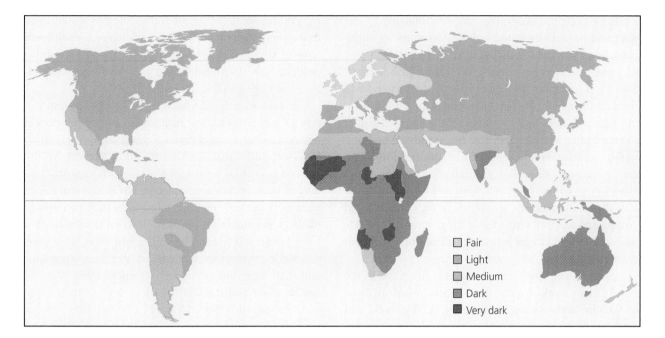

FIGURE 4.8 When the unexposed skin of indigenous people is measured and mapped according to the degree of pigmentation, skin shades tend to grow progressively lighter the farther one moves from the equator.

279). Clinal variation explains why people searching for "races" have never been able to agree on how many there are or how they can be identified. *Clines are not groups.* The only group involved in clinal mapping is the entire human species. Each cline is a map of the distribution of a *single* trait. Biologists might compare the clinal maps of trait A and trait B to see if they overlap and, if so, by how much. But the more clines they superimpose, the more obvious it becomes that the trait distributions they map *do not coincide* in ways that neatly subdivide into distinct human subpopulations. Since the biological concept of race predicts exactly such overlap, the biological concept of race cannot be correct. In other words, *clinal analysis tests the biological concept of race and finds nothing in nature to match it.* And if biological races cannot be found, then the so-called "races" identified over the years can only be symbolic constructs, based on cultural elaboration of a few superficial phenotypic differences—skin color, hair type and quantity, skin folds, lip shape, and the like. In short, early race theorists "weren't extracting races from their set of data, they were imposing races upon it" (Marks 1995, 132).

Many anthropologists hoped that the cultural category of "race" would disappear once its supposed biological underpinnings were exposed as false. During the 1960s and 1970s, anthropologists and others replaced racial explanations for social differences with cultural explanations. In the last 30 years, however, we have witnessed in the United States and elsewhere a resurgence of attempts to explain group differences in terms of race. Sometimes it is the powerful who engage in such practices, in controversial books like *The Bell Curve* (Herrnstein and Murray,

1994). Sometimes it is members of politically and economically marginalized groups who do so, as a calculated move in political struggles with those who dominate them (see chapter 13).

Genetic and other biological evidence alone cannot dismantle oppressive sociopolitical structures, but it can provide an important component in the struggle to eliminate racist practices from our societies. As we show in chapter 13, anthropologists can make a strong case when they combine the lack of biological justification for racial categories with powerful ethnographic evidence to show how racial categories have been socially, culturally, and politically constructed in the course of human history. Of course, to deny the existence of biological race is not to deny the existence of human biological or genetic diversity. It is, rather, to deny that the patterns of human diversity can be usefully sorted into a handful of mutually exclusive categories. As Jonathan Marks reminds us, it was the recognition that human variation did not come in neat divisions called races that "began to convert racial studies into studies of human microevolution" (1995, 117).

Postcolonial Realities

World War II was closely followed by the breakup of European colonial empires in Africa and Asia and by the civil rights movement in the United States. Former colonies were now independent states. Their citizens rejected the traditional Western view of them as savages or barbarians.

Political realities thus created for Westerners new experiences of the non-Western other. These experiences made the pretensions of unilineal evolutionism even less plausible. As well, the leaders of the new states set out to consolidate national consciousness among the supposedly structurally separate societies within their borders. This effort made the structural focus of preindependence social anthropologists seem increasingly misguided, leading many Western anthropologists to acknowledge that the traditional societies they had been studying had not, in fact, been structurally separate even under colonialism. Decolonization allowed anthropologists to pay direct attention to colonialism as a form of political domination that eliminated the autonomy of indigenous social groups and forcibly restructured them into subordinate positions within a larger entity. We will take up this thread again in chapter 14.

At the same time, anthropologists with roots in the non-Western world began to add their voices to those of Western anthropologists (Figure 4.9). They were and continue to be highly critical of the cultural stereotypes institutionalized by unilineal evolutionism and structural-functionalism. But this does not mean that typologies have disappeared altogether in contemporary cultural and social anthropology.

Studying Forms of Human Society Today

Opinions about the importance of classifying forms of human society vary greatly among contemporary anthropologists. Some anthropologists, especially those interested in political and economic issues, continue to find typologies useful. Still, most anthropologists would agree that an emphasis on similarities or differences in different types of society is closely related to the questions anthropologists are investigating and the theoretical assumptions they bring to their research.

For example, let us turn again to Lewellen's classification of social types. How meaningful is it? What does it reflect? Lewellen argues that it is designed to reflect structural, organizational similarities and differences. To defend such criteria, he employs a house metaphor: "Two houses built of different materials but to the same floor plan will obviously be much more alike than two houses of the same materials but very different designs (say, a town house and a ranch house). . . . In short, a house is defined in terms of its organization, not its components, and that organization will be influenced by its physical environment and the level of technology of the people who designed it" (1983, 17).

Because he assumes that structural similarities and differences are both significant and obvious, Lewellen seems to be affiliated with the tradition of British social anthropology. Similarities and differences concerning the materials out of which the houses are made can safely be ignored. For certain purposes, and for certain observers, this may be true. But is a house's organization manifested in its floor plan or in the way the various rooms are *used* regardless of floor plan? Is a bedroom still a bedroom, whether in a town house or a ranch house, when the people living in that house use it to cook in? Does a family's ideas about how living space should properly be used change when the

FIGURE 4.9   At the beginning of the twenty-first century, increasing numbers of anthropologists are coming from regions of the world outside the West. Sri Lankan anthropologist Arjun Guneratne converses with some of his informants in Nepal.

family moves from a thatched hut to an apartment with wooden floors and plaster walls?

Structural similarities and differences that seemed obvious to many political anthropologists in the British tradition led those anthropologists to set off states and chiefdoms sharply from tribes and bands. Would these similarities and differences seem so sharp to an anthropologist interested in classifying the ways different societies make a living? As we shall see, anthropologists interested in making such a classification employ concepts like *subsistence strategy* or *mode of production* to order their typologies, focusing on the strategies and technologies for organizing the production, distribution, and consumption of food, clothing, housing, tools, and other material goods. They therefore define a different domain of relevance, and different domains yield different typologies.

Since the end of colonialism, anthropologists have had to contend with new forms of classification, as the "peoples" of an earlier period were now being turned into citizens of postcolonial states. During the Cold War (between 1948 and 1989), a new set of categories came into existence that classified these states into either the First (or "developed") World, the Second (or "communist") World, or the Third (or "underdeveloped") World. Anthropologists adjusted to this transmuted context; many of them eventually became highly critical of the way "development" and "underdevelopment" were understood and addressed by scholars and government officials alike. With the passing of the Cold War, these distinctions have become even more problematic.

The Comparative Study of Processes

The kinds of typologies we have considered were valued at different times because they promised to allow useful comparisons to be made between different kinds of societies or cultures. But such typologies presume that societies or cultures are clearly defined entities that can be easily placed into distinct categories. If societies or cultures turn out to have contradictory structures or blurry boundaries and fail to fit into the available categories, then the usefulness of classification is called into question. Once anthropologists rejected the idea that social changes are fated to go in one direction only—the presumption of the unilineal evolutionists—it also became clear that typologies offer no logical way of addressing processes of social change. This would seem to suggest that classifying the forms of human societies, and perhaps anthropological comparison itself, is no longer a worthwhile activity for anthropologists.

Sally Falk Moore (2005), however, would disagree. In the early twenty-first century, she says, a new form of anthropological comparison has emerged that focuses on the *comparative study of processes*.

One example of this kind of ethnographic comparison, cited by Moore, is Richard Wilson's collection of articles investigating human rights struggles in different parts of the world. "Human rights" are ordinarily taken to be universal—and universally identifiable—everywhere in the world, but the essays in Wilson's collection show that the task of making universal categories relevant in a local setting in Guatemala may be very different from the challenges encountered in a local setting in Hawaii. The comparative study of processes of human rights implementation, therefore, reveals that "human rights doctrine does get reworked and transformed in different contexts" (1997, 23). These matters are more fully explored in chapter 14.

It is sometimes easy to emphasize the shortcomings of past theoretical schemes in anthropology, but it is important not to overlook the lasting contributions they have made. Despite its excesses, unilineal cultural evolutionism highlights the fact that cultures change over time and that our species has experienced a broad sequence of cultural developments. Structural-functionalist typologies may seem overly rigid and static, but the structural-functionalist ethnographies show just how intricate the social institutions and practices of so-called simple societies can be.

The culture area studies of Boas and his students deemphasize boundaries between separate societies and run the risk of erecting boundaries around culture areas instead. Still, the attention they paid to the movement of cultural objects and practices *across* social boundaries makes clear that indigenous people have never been unthinking slaves to tradition. On the contrary, they have been alert to their surroundings, aware of cultural alternatives, and ready to adopt new ways from other people when it has suited them. Indeed, Boasian attention to forms of social and cultural mixing also highlighted the *biological* mixing that always takes place when human groups meet, providing a context within which biological anthropologists were eventually able to demonstrate the fact that biological races do not exist.

A focus on "underdeveloped" and "developed" societies may have raised more problems than it solved, but it was in the very attempt to explain why those problems existed that new anthropological understandings were achieved. Finally, it is the continuing cultural creativity of all human beings, in all societies, that keeps anthropologists especially busy today: The comparative study of cultural processes highlights the fact that differently situated populations, confronted with similar challenges, are not likely to respond in the same way and indeed may respond in ways that are unexpected and surprising. This is certainly revealed in the work of anthropologists who explore the effects of globalization on different local populations. But these are matters we attend to in the chapters to come.

Chapter Summary

1. Modern Western history has been characterized by the rise of capitalism. The key metaphor of capitalism is that the world is a market and everything within the world—including land, material objects, and human beings—can be bought and sold. Such a view was unknown in noncapitalist societies before Western contact, even in those with highly developed economic institutions. The European capitalist penetration of non-Western societies was frequently followed by political conquest, which then reshaped conquered societies in ways that promoted economic exploitation. Colonial empires drew together economically and politically vast and previously unconnected areas of the world. To function intelligibly within the capitalist world order, colonized peoples had to begin to see the world as a storehouse of potential commodities.

2. The populations anthropologists would later study did not escape the historical processes of colonization and incorporation into a capitalist world economy. Indigenous groups lost their autonomy, and attempts were made to reintegrate them within the new colonial political economy. Many new groups came into existence in the course of commercial and political contacts between indigenous populations and Europeans. The continued existence of descendants of colonized peoples shows that conquered peoples can actively cope to reshape their own social identities despite oppression and exploitation.

3. After anthropology emerged as a formal discipline in the late nineteenth century, the context of European or Euro-American colonialism was an ever-present reality within which anthropologists were obliged to maneuver. Many hoped that the dismantling of colonial empires after World War II would restore sovereignty and dignity to colonized peoples. However, independence did not free former colonies from deeply entangling neocolonial ties with their former masters. In North America and elsewhere, indigenous groups continue to seek social justice for the losses they have sustained as a consequence of colonization.

4. Although the colonial setting within which many anthropologists worked must always be taken into account, there is little evidence to suggest that anthropologists who worked in colonial settings were trying to further colonial domination.

Anthropological findings were often too specialized to be used by colonial administrators, especially compared to the enormous amount of information supplied to them by merchants, missionaries, and other government functionaries. Also, the motives that led anthropologists to carry out work under colonial conditions were complex and variable.

5. A survey of the typologies used by anthropologists over the past century and a half to make sense of human cultural variation is illuminated by the historical circumstances surrounding contact between anthropologists and those with whom they have worked. Depending on an anthropologist's analytical purposes, the same social forms can be classified in different ways. The earliest important anthropological typology of forms of human society was proposed by unilineal cultural evolutionists in the nineteenth century. British anthropologists doing research in colonial settings in the first half of the twentieth century paid attention to the social structural forms of contemporary communities and showed how these structures enabled the communities to function successfully over time. Following Boas, North American anthropologists rejected unilineal cultural evolutionism on the grounds that societies could easily borrow cultural forms from one another, thus skipping supposedly universal evolutionary stages.

6. Boasian attention to forms of social and cultural mixing also highlighted the *biological* mixing that always takes place when human groups meet, providing a context within which biological anthropologists were eventually able to demonstrate the fact that biological races do not exist. Consequently, the aim of much research shifted to making lists of culture traits and mapping the culture areas through which they had spread as a result of cultural borrowing.

7. Since the end of colonialism, new classifications have appeared, such as the Cold War division of nation-states into First, Second, and Third Worlds, and the contrast between "developed" First World societies and "underdeveloped" Third World societies. While some anthropologists were always dissatisfied with these distinctions, they have become increasingly problematic since the end of the Cold War. Although some anthropologists still find some

typologies useful for investigating some issues, classifying forms of human society is not an ultimate goal for most anthropologists today, and this would seem to suggest that the basis for anthropological comparison is also disappearing. But a shift in contemporary ethnography to the study of ongoing social and cultural processes has led to the emergence of work that focuses on comparisions of similar processes as they unfold over time in different social and cultural settings.

For Review

1. In the academic division of labor in the late nineteenth century, when anthropology was born, what was anthropology supposed to be concerned with?
2. Summarize the main elements of capitalism and European colonialism, and their effects on the societies described at the beginning of this chapter.
3. What is "political economy"?
4. Summarize the main points of the argument about the relationship between anthropology and colonialism.
5. What is a typology?
6. Describe the major points of nineteenth-century unilineal evolutionism.
7. Describe how British anthropologists approached the classification of non-Western political structures.
8. How do culture area studies differ from structural-functional studies?
9. Summarize the evidence that led Frank Livingstone to state that there are no human races, only clines.
10. Review the evidence that leads anthropologists to deny that patterns of human diversity can be usefully sorted into a handful of mutually exclusive categories.
11. What is highlighted by the comparative study of processes?

Key Terms

capitalism	unilineal cultural	chiefdom	culture area
colonialism	evolutionism	state	species
political economy	social structure	structural-functional theory	phenotype
neocolonialism	band	culture traits	cline
typology	tribe		

Suggested Readings

Kuklick, Henrika. 2008. *A new history of anthropology*. Malden, MA: Blackwell Publishing. This recent collection includes essays by anthropologists and historians on topics that range across all anthropological subfields, informed by contemporary questions and concerns about the discipline's past, present, and future.

Kuper, Adam. 1996. *Anthropology and anthropologists: The modern British school*, 3rd ed. New York: Routledge. A rich discussion of the heyday of British social anthropology, from the 1920s to the 1970s, carefully tracing developments in theory and method and locating these developments in the personal and political contexts out of which they emerged.

Lewellen, Ted. 1993. *Political anthropology*, 2d ed. South Hadley, MA: Bergin and Garvey. Contains much useful information about the different kinds of societies that different scholars have identified.

Weatherford, Jack. 1988. *Indian givers: How the Indians of the Americas transformed the world*. New York: Fawcett Columbine.

———. 1991. *Native roots: How the Indians enriched America*. New York: Fawcett Columbine.

———. 1994. *Savages and civilization*. New York: Random House. All three of these books are engaging accounts of the consequences of contact between the Old World and New World in the past and in the present.

Whiteley, Peter. 2004. Ethnography. In *A companion to the anthropology of American Indians*, ed. Thomas Biolsi, 435–71. Malden, MA: Blackwell. A thoughtful, thorough, critical account of the history of ethnographic practice in North America, from the arrival of Columbus to the present.

Wolf, Eric. 1982. *Europe and the people without history*. Berkeley: University of California Press. A classic text about the connection of European expansion to the rest of the world. This work also discusses the effect of European contact on indigenous societies.

5

Language

Only human beings have symbolic language, and it is so deeply part of our lives that we rarely even think about how unusual it is. In this chapter, you learn about what makes human symbolic language different from other forms of animal communication, about the building blocks of language, about linguistic inequality, and about the death and revitalization of human languages.

The system of arbitrary symbols human beings use to encode and communicate about their experience of the world and of one another is called **language**. It is a unique faculty that sets human beings apart from other living species. It provides basic tools for human creativity, making possible the cultural achievements that we view as monuments to our species' genius.

The number of languages spoken in the world today is difficult to determine. According to David Crystal, author of *The Cambridge Encyclopedia of Language*, estimates range between 3,000 and 10,000, although he believes that it is unlikely that there are fewer than 4,000. Yet these estimates are problematic because new languages are regularly being identified while old languages continue to disappear (1987, 284–5). Language is a slippery phenomenon, and its tools are double-edged (Figure 5.1). This chapter explores the ambiguity, limitations, and power of human language.

Why Do Anthropologists Study Language?

Human language is a *biocultural* phenomenon. The human brain and the anatomy of our mouth and throat make language a biological possibility for us. At the same time, every human language is clearly a cultural product. It is shared by a group of speakers, encoded in symbols, patterned, and historically transmitted through teaching and learning, thus making communication possible.

Language and Culture

Language is of primary interest to anthropologists for at least three reasons: as a means to communicate in the field, as an object of study in its own right, and for what it reveals about cultures. First, anthropologists often do fieldwork among people whose language is different from theirs. In the past these languages were often unwritten and had to be learned without formal instruction.

Second, anthropologists can transcribe or tape-record speech and thus lift it out of its cultural context to be analyzed on its own. The grammatical intricacies revealed by such analysis suggested to many that what was true about language was true about the rest of culture. Indeed, some schools of anthropological theory have based their theories of culture explicitly on ideas taken from **linguistics**, the scientific study of language.

Third, and most important, all people use language to encode their experience, to structure their understanding of the world and of themselves, and to engage one another interactively. By learning another society's language, we learn something about its culture as well. In fact, learning another language inevitably provides unsuspected insights into the nature of our own language and culture, often making it impossible to take language of any kind for granted ever again.

As with the culture concept, the concept of "language" has regularly involved a distinction between *Language* and *languages*. *Language* with a capital *L* (like *Culture* with a capital *C*) was viewed as an abstract property belonging to the human species as a whole, not to be confused with the specific *languages* of concrete groups of people. This distinction initially enabled the recognition that all human groups possessed fully developed *languages* rather than "primitive," "broken," or otherwise defective forms of vocal communication. Today, however, linguistic anthropologists realize that totalizing views of "languages" can be as problematic as totalizing views of "cultures." The difficulties associated with demarcating the boundaries between one language and another, or with distinguishing between dialects and languages, become particularly obvious in studies of pidgins and creoles, as we will see.

It remains useful, however, to distinguish *language* from *speech* and *communication*. We usually think of spoken language (speech) when we use the term *language*, but English can be communicated in writing, Morse code, or American Sign Language, to name just three nonspoken media. *Human communication* can be defined as the transfer of information from one person to another, which can take place without the use of words, spoken or otherwise. People communicate with one another nonverbally all the time, sending messages with the clothes they wear, the way they walk, or how long they keep other people waiting for them.

In fact, even linguistic communication depends on more than words alone. Native speakers of a language share not just vocabulary and grammar but also a number of assumptions about how to speak that may not be shared by speakers of a different language. Students learning a new language discover early on that word-for-word translation from one language to another does not work. Sometimes there are no equivalent words in the second language; but even when there appear to be such words, a word-for-word translation may not mean in language B what it meant in language A. For example, when English speakers have eaten enough, they say, "I'm full." This may be translated directly into French as *Je suis plein*. To a native speaker of French, this sentence (especially when

---

language The system of arbitrary vocal symbols we use to encode our experience of the world.

linguistics The scientific study of language.

by George Herriman

FIGURE 5.1   In 1918, Krazy Kat asks the question "Why is 'lenguage'?"

uttered at the end of a meal) has the nonsensical meaning "I am a pregnant [male] animal." Alternatively, if uttered by a man who has just consumed a lot of wine, it means "I'm drunk."

Learning a second language is often frustrating and even unsettling; someone who once found the world simple to talk about suddenly turns into a babbling fool. Studying a second language, then, is less a matter of learning new labels for old objects than it is of learning how to identify new objects that go with new labels. The student must also learn the appropriate contexts in which different linguistic forms may be used: A person can be "full" after eating in English, but not in French. Knowledge about context is cultural knowledge. The linguistic system abstracted from its cultural context must be returned to that context if a holistic understanding of language is to be achieved.

Talking about Experience

Language, like the rest of culture, is a product of human attempts to come to terms with experience. Each natural human language is adequate for its speakers' needs, given their particular way of life. Speakers of a particular language tend to develop larger vocabularies to discuss those aspects of life that are of importance to them. The Aymara, who live in the Andes of South America, have invented hundreds of different words for the many varieties of potato they grow (see EthnoProfile 7.1: Aymara). By contrast, speakers of English have created an elaborate vocabulary for discussing computers. However, despite differences in vocabulary and grammar, all natural human languages ever studied by linguists prove to be equally complex. Just as there is no such thing as a "primitive" human culture, there is no such thing as a "primitive" human language.

Traditionally, languages are associated with concrete groups of people called *speech communities*. Nevertheless, because all languages possess alternative ways of speaking, members of particular speech communities do not all possess identical knowledge about the language they share, nor do they all speak the same way. Individuals and subgroups within a speech community make use of linguistic resources in different ways. Consequently, there is a tension in language between diversity and commonality. Individuals and subgroups attempt to use the varied resources of a language to create unique, personal voices. These efforts are countered by the pressure to negotiate a common code for communication within the larger social group. In this way, language is produced and reproduced through the activity of its speakers. Any particular language that we may identify at a given moment is a snapshot of a continuing process.

There are many ways to communicate our experiences, and there is no absolute standard favoring one way over another. Some things that are easy to say in language A may be difficult to say in language B, yet other aspects of language B may appear much simpler than equivalent aspects of language A. For example, English ordinarily requires the use of determiners (*a, an, the*) before nouns, but this rule is not found in all languages. Likewise, the verb *to be*, called the *copula* by linguists, is not found in all languages, although the relationships we convey when we use *to be* in English may still be communicated. In English, we might say "There *are* many people in the market." Translating this sentence into Fulfulde, the language of the Fulbe of northern Cameroon, we get *Him'be boi 'don nder luumo*, which, word-for-word, reads "people-many-there-in-market" (Figure 5.3). No single Fulfulde word corresponds to the English *are* or *the*.

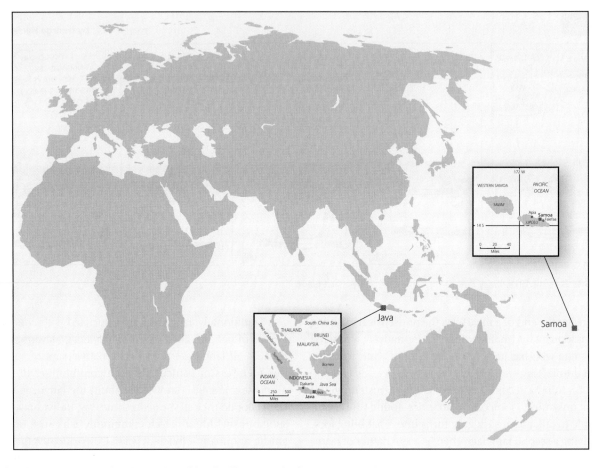

FIGURE 5.2   Locations of societies whose EthnoProfiles appear in chapter 5.

What Makes Human Language Distinctive?

In 1966, anthropological linguist Charles Hockett listed sixteen different **design features** of human language that, in his estimation, set it apart from other forms of animal communication. Six of these design features seem especially helpful in defining what makes human language distinctive: openness, displacement, arbitrariness, duality of patterning, semanticity, and prevarication.

Openness, probably the most important feature, emphasizes the same point that the linguist Noam Chomsky emphasized (1965, 6): Human language is creative. Speakers of any given language not only can create new messages but also can understand new messages created by other speakers. Someone may have never said to you, "Put this Babel fish in your ear," but knowing English, you can understand the message. Openness might also be defined as "the ability to understand the same thing from different points of view" (Ortony 1979, 14). In language, this means being able to talk about the same experiences from different perspectives, to paraphrase using different words and various grammatical constructions. Indeed, it means that the experiences themselves can be differently conceived, labeled, and discussed. In this view, no single perspective would necessarily emerge as more correct in every respect than all others.

The importance of openness for human verbal communication is striking when we compare, for example, spoken human language to the vocal communication systems (or *call systems*) of monkeys and apes. This point is stressed in the work of biological anthropologist Terrence Deacon (1997), who points out that modern human beings still possess a set of six calls: laughing, sobbing, screaming with fright, crying with pain, groaning, and sighing. Linguistic anthropologist Robbins Burling also emphasizes the difference between call systems and symbolic language: "Language . . . is organized in

---

design features Those characteristics of language that, when taken together, differentiate it from other known animal communication systems.

FIGURE 5.3 *Him'be boi 'don nder luumo.*

such utterly different ways from primate or mammalian calls and it conveys such utterly different kinds of meanings, that I find it impossible to imagine a realistic sequence by which natural selection could have converted a call system into a language. . . . We will understand more about the origins of language by considering the ways in which language differs from the cries and gestures of human and nonhuman primates than by looking for ways in which they are alike" (2005, 16). Calls, together with gestures and the changes in speech rhythm, volume, and tonality that linguists call *speech prosody*, all appear to have coevolved alongside symbolic language, which is probably why they integrate with one another so smoothly when we speak. Deacon emphasizes that primate call systems do not map onto any of the elements of human symbolic language and are even controlled by different parts of the brain.

Nonhuman primates can communicate in rather subtle ways using channels of transmission other than voice. However, these channels are far less sophisticated than, say, American Sign Language. The number of calls in a call system range from 15 to 40, depending on the species, and are produced only when the animal finds itself in a situation including such features as the presence of food or danger; friendly interest and the desire for company; or the desire to mark the animal's location or to signal pain, sexual interest, or the need for maternal care. If the animal is not in the appropriate situation, it does not produce the call. At most, it may refrain from uttering a call in a situation that would normally trigger it. In addition, nonhuman primates cannot emit a signal that has some features of one call and some of another. For example, if the animal encounters food and danger at the same time, one of the calls takes precedence. For these reasons, the call systems of nonhuman primates are said to be *closed* when compared to open human languages.

Closed call systems also lack *displacement*, our human ability to talk about absent or nonexistent objects and past or future events as easily as we discuss our immediate situations. Although nonhuman primates clearly have good memories, and some species, such as chimpanzees, seem to be able to plan social action in advance (such as when hunting for meat), they cannot use their call systems to discuss such events.

Closed call systems also lack *arbitrariness*, the absence of any obligatory link between sound and meaning in language. For example, the sound sequence /*boi*/ refers to a "young male human being" in English, but means "more" or "many" in Fulfulde. One aspect of linguistic creativity is the free, creative production of new links between sounds and meanings. Thus, arbitrariness is the flip side of openness: If all links between sound and meaning are open, then the particular link between particular sounds and particular meanings in a particular language must be arbitrary. In primate call systems, by contrast, links between the sounds of calls and their meanings appear to be fixed and under considerable direct biological control.

Arbitrariness is evident in the design feature of language that Hockett called *duality of patterning*. Human language, Hockett claimed, is patterned on two different levels: sound and meaning. On the first level, the small set of meaningless sounds (or *phonemes*) that characterize any particular language are not random but are systematically patterned. On the second level of patterning, however, grammar puts the sound units together according to an entirely different set of rules: The resulting sound clusters are the smallest meaning-bearing units of the language, called *morphemes*.

In Their Own Words

Cultural Translation

Linguistic translation is complicated and beset with pitfalls, as we have seen. Cultural translation, as David Parkin describes, requires knowledge not just of different grammars but also of the various different cultural contexts in which grammatical forms are put to use.

Cultural translation, like translation from one language to another, never produces a rendering that is semantically and stylistically an exact replica of the original. That much we accept. What is not often recognized, perhaps not even by the translators themselves, is that the very act of having to decide how to phrase an event, sentiment, or human character engages the translator in an act of creation. The translator does not simply represent a picture made by an author. He or she creates a new version, and perhaps in some respects a new picture—a matter that is often of some great value.

So it is with anthropologists. But while this act of creation in reporting on "the other" may reasonably be regarded as a self-sustaining pleasure, it is also an entry into the pitfalls and traps of language use itself. One of the most interesting new fields in anthropology is the study of the relationship between language and human knowledge, both among ourselves as professional anthropologists and laypeople, and among peoples of other cultures. The study is at once both reflexive and critical.

The hidden influences at work in language use attract the most interest. For example, systems of greetings have many built-in elaborations that differentiate subtly between those who are old and young, male and female, rich and poor, and powerful and powerless. When physicians discuss a patient in his or her presence and refer to the patient in the third-person singular, they are in effect defining the patient as a passive object unable to enter into the discussion. When anthropologists present elegant accounts of "their" people that fit the demands of a convincing theory admirably, do they not also leave out [of] the description any consideration of the informants' own fears and feelings? Or do we go too far in making such claims, and is it often the anthropologist who is indulged by the people, who give him or her the data they think is sought, either in exchange for something they want or simply because it pleases them to do so? If the latter, how did the anthropologist's account miss this critical part of the dialogue?

Source: Parkin 1990, 90–91.

Since Hockett first wrote, many linguists have suggested that there are more than just two levels of patterning in language. (We will discuss some additional levels later in the chapter.) In all cases, the principle relating levels to each other is the same: Units at one level, patterned in one way (sounds), can be used to create units at a different level, patterned in a different way (morphemes, or units of meaning). The rules governing morphemes, in turn, are different from the rules by which morphemes are combined into sentences, which are different from the rules combining sentences into discourse. Today, linguists recognize many levels of patterning in human language, and the patterns that characterize one level cannot be reduced to the patterns of any other level. By contrast, ape call systems lack multilevel patterning (Wallman 1992).

Arbitrariness shows up again in the design feature of *semanticity*—the association of linguistic signals with aspects of the social, cultural, and physical world of a speech community. People use language to refer to and make sense of objects and processes in the world. Nevertheless, any linguistic description of reality is always

somewhat arbitrary because all linguistic descriptions are selective, highlighting some features of the world and downplaying others. For example, a trained primatologist would distinguish "apes" (like chimpanzees) from "monkeys" (like baboons), and both apes and monkeys from "prosimians" (like lemurs). By contrast, a person with no special knowledge of primates might use the words "monkey" and "ape" interchangeably to refer to chimpanzees, and might never have heard of prosimians. Each speaker links the same words to the world in different ways.

Perhaps the most striking consequence of linguistic openness is the design feature *prevarication*. Hockett's remarks about this design feature deserve particular attention: "Linguistic messages can be false, and they can be meaningless in the logician's sense." In other words, not only can people use language to lie, but in addition, utterances that seem perfectly well formed grammatically may yield semantic nonsense. As an example, Chomsky offered the following sentence: "Colorless green ideas sleep furiously" (1957, 15). This is a grammatical sentence on one level—the right kinds of words are used in the right places—but on another level it contains multiple contradictions. The ability of language users to prevaricate—to make statements or ask questions that violate convention—is a major consequence of open symbolic systems. Apes using their closed call systems can neither lie nor formulate theories.

What Does It Mean to "Learn" a Language?

Years ago, studies of child language amounted to a list of errors that children make when attempting to gain what Chomsky calls **linguistic competence**, or mastery of adult grammar. Today, however, linguists study children's verbal interactions in social and cultural context and draw attention to what children can do very well. "From an early age they appear to communicate very fluently, producing utterances which are not just remarkably well-formed according to the linguist's standards but also appropriate to the social context in which the speakers find themselves. Children are thus learning far more about language than rules of grammar. [They are] acquiring communicative competence" (Elliot 1981, 13).

Communicative competence, or mastery of adult rules for socially and culturally appropriate speech, is a term coined by American anthropological linguist Dell Hymes (1972). As an anthropologist, Hymes objected to Chomsky's notion that linguistic competence consisted only of being able to make correct judgments of sentence grammaticality (Chomsky 1965, 4). Hymes observed that competent adult speakers do more than follow grammatical rules when they speak. They are also able to choose words and topics of conversation appropriate to their social position, the social position of the person they are addressing, and the social context of interaction.

Language and Context

Anthropologists are powerfully aware of the influence of context on what people choose to say. For example, consider the issue of using personal pronouns appropriately when talking to others. For native speakers of English, the problem almost never arises with regard to pronoun choice because we address all people as "you." But any English speaker who has ever tried to learn French has worried about when to address an individual using the second-person plural (*vous*) and when to use the second-person singular (*tu*). To be safe, most students use *vous* for all individuals because it is the more formal term and they want to avoid appearing too familiar with native

EthnoProfile 5.1

Java

Region: Southeastern Asia

Nation: Indonesia

Population: 120,000,000

Environment: Tropical island

Livelihood: Intensive rice cultivation

Political organization: Highly stratified state

For more information: Geertz, Clifford. 1960. *The religion of Java.* New York: Free Press.

speakers whom they do not know well. But if you are dating a French person, at which point in the relationship does the change from *vous* to *tu* occur, and who decides? Moreover, sometimes—for example, among university students—the normal term of address is *tu* (even among strangers); it is used to indicate social solidarity. Native speakers of English who are learning French wrestle with these and other linguistic dilemmas. Rules for the appropriate use of *tu* and *vous* seem to have nothing to do with grammar, yet the choice between one form and the other indicates whether the speaker is someone who does or does not know how to speak French.

But French seems quite straightforward when compared with Javanese, in which all the words in a sentence must be carefully selected to reflect the social relationship between the speaker and the person addressed (see EthnoProfile 5.1: Java). In the 1950s, when Clifford Geertz first did fieldwork in Java, he discovered that it was impossible to say anything in Javanese without also communicating your social position relative to the person to whom you are speaking. Even a simple request like, "Are you going to eat rice and cassava now?" required that speakers know at least five different varieties of the language in order to communicate socially as well as to make the request (Figure 5.4). This example illustrates the range of diversity

linguistic competence A term coined by linguist Noam Chomsky to refer to the mastery of adult grammar.

communicative competence A term coined by anthropological linguist Dell Hymes to refer to the mastery of adult rules for socially and culturally appropriate speech.

Speaking to persons of:	Level	"Are	you	going	to eat	rice	and	cassava	now?"	Complete sentence
Very high position	3a		pandjenengan		dahar		kalijan		samenika	Menapa pandjenengan badé dahar sekul kalijan kaspé samenika?
		menapa		badé						
High position	3					sekul				Menapa sampéjan badé neda sekul kalijan kaspé samenika?
Same position, not close	2	napa	sampéjan	adjéng	neda			kaspé	saniki	Napa sampéjan adjéng neda sekul lan kaspé saniki?
Same position, casual acquaintance	1a						lan			Apa sampéjan arep neda sega lan kaspé saiki?
		apa		arep		sega			saiki	
Close friends of any rank; also to lower status (basic language)	1		kowé		mangan					Apa kowé arep mangan sega lan kaspé saiki?

FIGURE 5.4   The dialect of nonnoble, urbanized, somewhat-educated people in central Java in the 1950s. (From Geertz 1960)

present in a single language and how different varieties of a language are related to different subgroups within the speech community.

Does Language Affect How We See the World?

During the first half of the twentieth century, two American anthropological linguists noted that the grammars of different languages often described the same situation in different ways. Edward Sapir and Benjamin Whorf were impressed enough to conclude that language has the power to shape the way people see the world. This claim has been called the **linguistic relativity principle**, or the Sapir-Whorf hypothesis. This hypothesis has been highly controversial because it is difficult to test and the results of testing have been ambiguous.

linguistic relativity principle A position, associated with Edward Sapir and Benjamin Whorf, that asserts that language has the power to shape the way people see the world.

The so-called strong version of the Sapir-Whorf hypothesis is also known as *linguistic determinism*. It is a totalizing view of language that reduces patterns of thought and culture to the patterns of the grammar of the language we speak. If a grammar classifies nouns in male and female gender categories, for example, linguistic determinism concludes that speakers of that language are forced to think of males and females as radically different kinds of beings. By contrast, a language that makes no grammatical distinctions on the basis of gender presumably trains its speakers to think of males and females as exactly the same. If linguistic determinism is correct, then a change in grammar should change thought patterns: If English speakers replaced *he* and *she* with a new, gender-neutral, third-person singular pronoun, such as *te*, then, linguistic determinists predict, English speakers would begin to treat men and women as equals.

There are a number of problems with linguistic determinism. In the first place, there are languages such as Fulfulde in which only one third-person pronoun is used for males and females (*o*); however, male-dominant social patterns are quite evident among Fulfulde speakers. In the second place, if language determined thought in this way, it would be impossible to translate from one language to another or even to learn another language with

sentence is uttered to find the door and the person standing by the door and thus give a referential meaning to the words *who* and *that* (Figure 5.7). Furthermore, even if we know what a door is in a formal sense, we need the nonlinguistic context to clarify what counts as a door in this instance (for example, it could be a rough opening in the wall).

By forcing analysts to go beyond syntax and semantics, pragmatics directs our attention to **discourse**, which is formally defined as a stretch of speech longer than a sentence united by a common theme. Discourse includes a spoken one-word greeting, a series of sentences uttered by a single individual, a conversation among two or more speakers, or an extended narrative. Many linguistic anthropologists accept the arguments of M. M. Bakhtin and V. N. Voloshinov (see, for example, Voloshinov [1929] 1986) that the series of rejoinders in conversation are the primary form of discourse. In this view, the speech of any single individual, whether a simple *yes* or a book-length dissertation, is only one rejoinder in an ongoing dialogue.

Ethnopragmatics

Linguistic anthropologists analyze the way discourse is produced when people talk to one another. But they go far beyond formal pragmatics, paying attention not only to the immediate context of speech, linguistic and non-linguistic, but also to broader cultural contexts that are shaped by unequal social relationships and rooted in history (Brenneis and Macauley 1996; Hill and Irvine 1992). Alessandro Duranti calls this **ethnopragmatics**, "a study of language use which relies on ethnography to illuminate the ways in which speech is both constituted by and constitutive of social interaction" (Duranti 1994, 11). Such a study focuses on *practice*, human activity in which the rules of grammar, cultural values, and physical action are all conjoined (Hanks 1996, 11). Such a perspective locates the source of meaning in everyday routine social activity, or habitus, rather than in grammar. As a result, phonemes, morphemes, syntax, and semantics are viewed as *linguistic resources* people can make use of, rather than rigid forms that determine what people can and cannot think or say.

If mutual understanding is shaped by shared routine activity and not by grammar, then communication is possible even if the people interacting with one another speak mutually unintelligible languages. All they need is a shared sense of "what is going on here" and the ability to negotiate successfully who will do what (Hanks 1996, 234). Such mutually coengaged people shape *communicative practices* that involve spoken language but also include values and shared habitual knowledge that may

FIGURE 5.7 To answer the question "What is that on the door?" requires that we examine the actual physical context at the moment we are asked the question in order to try to determine what "that" refers to. Is it the locks? the door handles? the studs on the door? Also, what part of the structure is the "door"?

never be put into words. Because most people in most societies regularly engage in a wide range of practical activities with different subgroups, each one will also end up knowledgeable about a variety of different communicative practices and the linguistic habits that go with them. For example, a college student might know the linguistic

discourse A stretch of speech longer than a sentence united by a common theme.

ethnopragmatics A study of language use that relies on ethnography to illuminate the ways in which speech is both constituted by and constitutive of social interaction.

EthnoProfile 5.2

Samoa

Region: Oceania

Nation: Western Samoa

Population: 182,000

Environment: Tropical island

Livelihood: Horticulture, fishing, wage labor in capital

Political organization: Ranked, with linguistic markers for high- and low-status people; now part of a modern nation-state

For more information: Duranti, Alessandro. 1994. *From grammar to politics, Linguistic anthropology in a western Samoan village.* Berkeley: University of California Press.

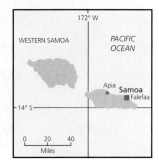

habits appropriate to dinner with her parents, to the classroom, to worship services, to conversations in the dorm with friends, and to her part-time job in a restaurant. Each set of linguistic habits she knows is called a discourse genre. Because our student simultaneously knows a multiplicity of different discourse genres she can use in speech, her linguistic knowledge is characterized by what Bakhtin called *heteroglossia* (Bakhtin 1981).

For Bakhtin, heteroglossia is the normal condition of linguistic knowledge in any society with internal divisions. Heteroglossia describes a coexisting multiplicity of linguistic norms and forms, many of which are anchored in more than one social subgroup. Because we all participate in more than one of these subgroups, our language use is complex, even if the only language we know is English! Our capacity for heteroglossia is another example of Hockett's linguistic openness: It means that our thought and speech are not imprisoned in a single set of grammatical forms, as linguistic determinists argued. Indeed, if our college student reflects on the overlap as well as the contrasts between the language habits used in the dorm and those used in the restaurant, she might well find herself raising questions about what words really mean. To the extent, however, that her habitual ways of speaking are deeply rooted in everyday routine activity, they may guide the way she typically thinks, perceives, and acts. And to that extent, linguistic relativity may be seen to operate on the level of discourse (Hanks 1996, 176, 246; Schultz 1990).

A practice approach to language use aims to show how grammar, human action, and human values are all inextricably intertwined. But this does not mean that formal grammar can be ignored. As William Hanks puts it, "The system of language does have unique properties, and we do better to recognize this than to try to pretend it isn't so" (1996, 232). Each language, as a system, has a particular set of formal possibilities that can be mobilized as resources when people talk to one another. At the same time, "context saturates linguistic forms, right down to the semantic bones" (142). Meaning is the outcome, thus, both of the formal properties of language uttered and the contextual situation in which it is uttered. And context always includes understandings about social relationships and previous history that may never be put into words.

How all this works is best illustrated with an example. One of the most obvious ways that context influences speech is when speakers tailor their words for a particular audience. Advertising agencies, for example, are notorious for slanting their messages to appeal to the people they want to buy their clients' products or services. Alessandro Duranti learned that a sense of audience is highly cultivated among the professional orators who argue cases before the titled people, called *matai*, who meet regularly in the Samoan village council, or *fono* (see EthnoProfile 5.2: Samoa). Orators make use of a discourse genre midway in formality between everyday speech and ceremonial speech. Because the fono renders judgments that assign praise and blame, the main struggle between orators for different sides is "often centered on the ability to frame the reason for the meeting as involving or not involving certain key social actors" (Duranti 1994, 3). Of all the grammatical resources used by Samoan-speaking orators, one particular form, called the *ergative Agent*, most attracted Duranti's attention.

The Samoan ergative Agent indicates who or what has intentionally performed an action that has consequences for others, and it is marked in speech by use of a special morpheme: the preposition *e*. The Samoan language has several morphemes like this one that speakers can choose among to indicate the kind of action (or agency) that they wish to attribute to people or things that are being discussed. For example, the Samoan preposition *i* or *ia* is used to mark a human agent who is understood as transmitting an action that he or she did not initiate. Another example is the Samoan possessive marker *o* or *a*, which is attached to an object belonging to someone; using this possessive marker in speech is an effective way of shifting attention away from the owner of the object in question. For instance, this possessive marker would emphasize the *food* that John had, not the fact that the food belonged *to John*. As linguistic resources, all these features of Samoan grammar offer Samoan speakers a range of ways to talk about who caused what to happen, or who is responsible for what outcome. These ways of framing agency in grammatical terms are common in the fono, as disputants argue over who should be held accountable for some act. Possible agents include God, particular individuals, or groups. It is perhaps not surprising that the speaker who produced the highest number of ergative Agents in his speech was the senior orator, who ran the meetings and often served as prosecutor. "Powerful actors are more likely to define others as ergative Agents when they want to accuse them of something. Less powerful actors can try to resist such accusations by suggesting alternative linguistic definitions of events and people's roles in them" (133). In all cases, final judgments are the outcome of talk, but of talk saturated with sociopolitical awareness and deeply rooted in local historical context.

What Happens When Languages Come into Contact?

The Samoan village fono is a setting in which speakers and listeners are able, for the most part, to draw upon knowledge of overlapping language habits in order to struggle verbally over moral and political issues. In some instances, however, potential parties to a verbal exchange find themselves sharing little more than physical proximity to one another. Such situations arise when members of communities with radically different language traditions and no history of previous contact with one another come face to face and are forced to communicate. There is no way to predict the outcome of such enforced contact on either speech community, yet from these new shared experiences, new forms of practice, including a new form of language—**pidgin**—may develop.

"When the chips are down, meaning is negotiated" (Lakoff and Johnson 1980, 231). The study of pidgin languages is the study of the radical negotiation of new meaning, the production of a new whole (the pidgin language) that is different from and reducible to neither of the languages that gave birth to it. The shape of a pidgin reflects the context in which it arises—generally one of colonial conquest or commercial domination. Vocabulary is usually taken from the language of the dominant group, making it easy for that group to learn. Syntax and phonology may be similar to the subordinate language (or languages), however, making it easier for subordinated speakers to learn. Morphemes that mark the gender or number of nouns or the tenses of verbs tend to disappear (Holm 1988).

Pidgins are traditionally defined as reduced languages that have no native speakers. They develop, in a single generation, between groups of speakers of distinct native languages. When speakers of a pidgin language pass that language on to a new generation, linguists traditionally referred to the language as a *creole*. The creolization of pidgins involves increased complexity in phonology, morphology, syntax, semantics, and pragmatics, such that the pidgin comes to resemble a conventional language.

Pidgins and Creoles

As linguists studied pidgins and creoles more closely, they discovered that the old distinction between pidgins and creoles was more complex than previously thought. In the Pacific, for example, linguists have discovered pidgin dialects, pidgin languages used as main languages of permanently settled groups, and pidgins that have become native languages. Moreover, creolization can take place at any time after a pidgin forms, creoles can exist without having been preceded by pidgins, pidgins can remain pidgins for long periods and undergo linguistic change without acquiring native speakers, and pidgin and creole varieties of the same language can coexist in the same society (Jourdan 1991, 192ff.). In fact, it looks as if heteroglossia is as widespread among speakers of pidgins and creoles as among speakers of other languages.

Negotiating Meaning

More information has been gathered about the historical and sociocultural contexts within which pidgins first formed. Here as elsewhere in linguistic anthropology, the focus has turned to practice. Awareness of heteroglossia in pidgin/creole speech communities has led to redefinition of a pidgin as a shared secondary language in a speech community where speakers also use some other main language in smaller groups, and a creole as a main language in a speech community, whether or not it has native speakers. According to the new view, creolization is likely when pidgin speakers find themselves in new social contexts requiring a new language for *all* the practical activities of everyday life; without such a context, it is unlikely that creoles will emerge (Jourdan 1991, 196).

Viewing pidgin creation as a form of communicative practice means that attention must be paid to the role of pidgin creators as agents in the process (Figure 5.8). As

pidgin A language with no native speakers that develops in a single generation between members of communities that possess distinct native languages.

FIGURE 5.8   Tok Pisin, a pidgin language that developed in New Guinea following colonization by English speakers, has become a major medium of communication in New Guinea. The news in Tok Pisin is available on the Internet at http://www.abc.net.au/ra/tokpisin/.

we negotiate meaning across language barriers, it appears that all humans have intuitions about which parts of our speech carry the most meaning and which parts can be safely dropped. Neither party to the negotiation, moreover, may be trying to learn the other's language; rather, "speakers in the course of negotiating communication use whatever linguistic and sociolinguistic resources they have at their disposal, until the shared meaning is established and conventionalized" (Jourdan 1991, 200).

Linguistic Inequality

Pidgins and creoles turn out to be far more complex and the result of far more active human input than we used to think, which is why they are so attractive to linguists and linguistic anthropologists as objects of study. Where they coexist, however, alongside the language of the dominant group (e.g., Hawaiian Pidgin English and English), they are ordinarily viewed by members of society as defective and inferior languages. Such views can be seen as an outgrowth of the situation that led to the formation of most of the pidgins we know about: European colonial domination. In a colonial or postcolonial setting, the colonizer's language is often considered to be superior to pidgin or creole languages, which the colonizers characterize as broken, imperfect versions of their own language. The situation only worsens when formal education, the key to participation in the European-dominated society, is carried out in the colonial language. Speakers of a pidgin or creole or indigenous language who remain illiterate may never be able to master the colonial tongue and may find

themselves effectively barred from equal participation in the civic life of their societies.

To take one language variety as the standard against which all other varieties are measured might be described as linguistic ethnocentrism, and such a standard may be applied to any language, not just pidgins and creoles. This is one kind of linguistic inequality: making value judgments about other people's speech in a context of dominance and subordination. A powerful example of the effects of linguistic inequality is found in the history and controversies surrounding African American English in the United States.

Language Habits of African Americans

In the 1960s, some psychologists claimed that African American children living in urban areas of the northern United States suffered from linguistic deprivation. They argued that these children started school with a limited vocabulary and no grammar and thus could not perform as well as European American children in the classroom—that their language was unequal to the challenges of communication. Sociolinguist William Labov and his colleagues found such claims incredible and undertook research of their own (Labov 1972), which demonstrated two things. First, they proved that the form of English spoken in the inner city was not defective pseudolanguage. Second, they showed how a change in research context permitted inner-city African American children to display a level of linguistic sophistication that the psychologists had never dreamed they possessed.

When African American children were in the classroom (a European American–dominated context) being interrogated by European American adults about topics of no interest to them, they said little. This did not necessarily mean, Labov argued, that they had no language. Rather, their minimal responses were better understood as defensive attempts to keep threatening European American questioners from learning anything about them. For the African American children, the classroom was only one part of a broader racist culture. The psychologists, due to their ethnocentrism, had been oblivious to the effect this context might have on their research.

Reasoning that reliable samples of African American speech had to be collected in contexts where the racist threat was lessened, Labov and his colleagues conducted fieldwork in the homes and on the streets of the inner city. They recorded enormous amounts of speech in African American English (AAE) produced by the same children who had had nothing to say when questioned in the classroom. Labov's analysis demonstrated that AAE was a variety of English that had certain rules not found in

In Their Own Words

Varieties of African American English

The school board of Oakland, California, gained national attention in December 1996 when its members voted to recognize Ebonics as an official second language. What they called Ebonics is also known as Black English Vernacular (BEV), Black English (BE), African American English Vernacular (AAEV), and African American English (AAE). The school board decision generated controversy both within and outside the African American community because it seemed to be equating Ebonics with other "official second languages," such as Spanish and Chinese. This implied that Standard English was as much a "foreign language" to native speakers of Ebonics as it was to native speakers of Spanish and Chinese and that Oakland school students who were native speakers of Ebonics should be entitled not only to the respect accorded native Spanish- or Chinese-speaking students but also, perhaps, to the same kind of funding for bilingual education. The uproar produced by this dispute caused the school board to amend the resolution a month later. African American linguistic anthropologist Marcyliena Morgan's commentary highlights one issue that many disputants ignored: namely, that the African American community is not monoglot in Ebonics but is in fact characterized by heteroglossia.

After sitting through a string of tasteless jokes about the Oakland school district's approval of a language education policy for African American students, I realize that linguists and educators have failed to inform Americans about varieties of English used throughout the country and the link between these dialects and culture, social class, geographic region and identity. After all, linguists have been a part of language and education debates around AAE and the furor that surrounds them since the late 1970s. Then the Ann Arbor school district received a court order to train teachers on aspects of AAE to properly assess and teach children in their care.

Like any language and dialect, African American varieties of English—ranging from that spoken by children and some adults with limited education to those spoken by adults with advanced degrees—are based on the cultural, social, historical and political experiences shared by many US people of African descent. This experience is one of family, community and love as well as racism, poverty and discrimination. Every African American does not speak AAE. Moreover, some argue that children who speak the vernacular, typically grow up to speak both AAE as well as mainstream varieties of English. It is therefore not surprising that the community separates its views of AAE, ranging from loyalty to abhorrence, from issues surrounding the literacy education of their children. Unfortunately, society's ambivalent attitudes toward African American students' cognitive abilities, like Jensen's 1970s deficit models and the 1990s' *The Bell Curve*, suggest that when it comes to African American kids, intelligence and competence in school can be considered genetic.

African American children who speak the vernacular form of AAE may be the only English-speaking children in this country who attend community schools in which teachers not only are ignorant of their dialect but refuse to accept its existence. This attitude leads to children being marginalized and designated as learning disabled. The educational failure of African American children can, at best, be only partially addressed through teacher training on AAE. When children go to school, they bring not only their homework and textbooks but also their language, culture and identity. Sooner rather than later, the educational system must address its exclusion of cultural and dialect difference in teacher training and school curriculum.

Source: M. Morgan 1997, 8.

Standard English. This is a strictly linguistic difference: Most middle-class speakers of Standard English would not use these rules but most African American speakers of AAE would. However, neither variety of English should be seen as "defective" as a result of this difference. This kind of linguistic difference, apparent when speakers of two varieties converse, marks the speaker's membership in a particular speech community. Such differences can exist in phonology, morphology, syntax, semantics, or pragmatics (Figure 5.9). Indeed, similar linguistic differences distinguish the language habits of most social subgroups in a society, like that of the United States, that is characterized by heteroglossia.

What is distinctive about African American English from a practice perspective, however, are the historical and sociocultural circumstances that led to its creation. For some time, linguists have viewed AAE as one of many creole languages that developed in the New World after Africans were brought there to work as slaves on plantations owned by Europeans. Dominant English-speaking

FIGURE 5.9   The language habits of African Americans are not homogeneous; they vary according to gender, social class, region, and situation.

elites have regarded AAE with the same disdain that European colonial elites have accorded creole languages elsewhere. Because African Americans have always lived in socially and politically charged contexts that questioned their full citizenship, statements about their language habits are inevitably thought to imply something about their intelligence and culture. Those psychologists who claimed that inner-city African American children suffered from linguistic deprivation, for example, seemed to be suggesting either that these children were too stupid to speak or that their cultural surroundings were too meager to allow normal language development.

The work of Labov and his colleagues showed that the children were not linguistically deprived, were not stupid, and participated in a rich linguistic culture. But this work itself became controversial in later decades when it became clear that the rich African American language and culture described was primarily that of adolescent males. These young men saw themselves as bearers of authentic African American language habits and dismissed African Americans who did not speak the way they did as "lames." This implied that everyone else in the African American community was somehow not genuinely African American, a challenge that those excluded could not ignore. Linguists like Labov's team, who thought their work undermined racism, were thus bewildered when middle-class African Americans, who spoke Standard English, refused to accept AAE as representative of "true" African American culture (Morgan 1995, 337).

From the perspective of linguistic anthropology, this debate shows that the African American community is not

homogeneous, linguistically or culturally, but is instead characterized by heteroglossia and a range of attitudes regarding AAE. At a minimum, language habits are shaped by social class, age cohort, and gender. Moreover, members of all of these subgroups use both Standard English and AAE in their speech. Morgan reports, for example, that upper-middle-class African American students at elite colleges who did not grow up speaking AAE regularly adopt many of its features and that hip-hop artists combine the grammar of Standard English with the phonology and morphology of AAE (1995, 338). This situation is not so paradoxical if we recall, once again, the politically charged context of African American life in the United States. African Americans both affirm and deny the significance of AAE for their identity, perhaps because AAE symbolizes both the oppression of slavery and resistance to that oppression (339). Forty years ago, Claudia Mitchell-Kernan described African Americans as "bicultural" and struggling to develop language habits that could reconcile "good" English and AAE (1972, 209). That struggle continues at the beginning of the twenty-first century, while whites continue to adopt words and expressions from AAE as "hip."

Language Ideology

Building on earlier work on linguistic inequality, linguistic anthropologists in recent years have developed a focus on the study of **language ideology:** ways of representing the intersection "between social forms and forms of talk" (Woolard 1998, 3). While the study of language ideology discloses speakers' sense of beauty or morality or basic understandings of the world, it also provides evidence of the ways in which our speech is always embedded in a social world of power differences. Language ideologies are markers of struggles between social groups with different interests, revealed in what people say and how they say it. The way people monitor their speech to bring it into line with a particular language ideology illustrates that language ideologies are "active and effective . . . they transform the material reality they comment on" (Woolard 1998, 11). In settings with a history of colonization, where groups with different power and different languages coexist in tension, the study of language ideologies has long been significant (Woolard 1998, 16). The skills of linguistic anthropologists especially suit them to study language ideologies because their linguistic training allows them to describe precisely the linguistic features (phonological, morphological, or syntactic, for example) that become the focus of ideological attention, and their training in cultural analysis allows them to explain how those linguistic features come to stand symbolically for a particular social group.

language ideology A marker of struggles between social groups with different interests, revealed in what people say and how they say it.

Culture and Individuals

I n this chapter, we explore the way symbolic cultural practices shape your patterns of thought, your sense of self, and even your personality. However, we also consider the active role individuals play in the making of cultural meanings, particularly when challenged by experiences of trauma and social suffering.

If human culture is learned, it is ultimately individual human beings who engage in that learning. They do not all learn the same things, even if they live in the same society, because of socially, culturally, and politically shaped differences in status and experience. But it is because patterns can be detected in learned ways of thinking and ways of acting that anthropologists become interested in cultural learning by individuals. **Psychological anthropology** can be defined as "the study of individuals and their sociocultural communities" (Casey and Edgerton 1998, 1). Historically, psychological anthropology has sought answers for a series of persistent questions: "What characteristics of our species are found in all times and places? What features are limited to specific groups of humans? How can we best take account of individual uniqueness?" (Bock 1994, ix).

Philip Bock notes that "An anthropology that takes account of individuals must make use of ideas from neighboring disciplines" (1994, ix), primarily from different kinds of psychological theories. To some extent this has involved anthropological adoption and cross-cultural evaluation of a series of different theoretical orientations in psychology. For example, some of the first twentieth-century anthropologists to take an interest in psychological matters, such as Margaret Mead and Bronislaw Malinowski, were influenced by the psychoanalytic views of Sigmund Freud, and attempted to test in non-Western settings certain ideas about personality development based on Freud's work in late-nineteenth-century Viennese society.

These early studies initiated a pattern of analysis that has remained central to much psychological anthropology: that of critically examining universal claims about human nature produced by Western psychologists, especially claims that are based on research done in Western societies only. This critical role is especially important in those situations where researchers make extreme claims about all members of the human species. Such claims frequently get a lot of publicity and tend to generate a lot of controversy. Early tests of Freudian theory are a good example. Is the pattern of early childhood development described by Freud universal in all human groups—"found in all times and places"? Or, conversely is it an example of "individual uniqueness," characteristic perhaps of individuals with disturbed childhoods but not of everyone else?

In Euro-American societies claims about universal human psychology compete with assertions of individual uniqueness. One of the most deeply entrenched debates opposes "biology" to "culture" as alternative, mutually exclusive explanations for some particular aspect of human psychological functioning. Such extreme claims and counterclaims seem never to be resolved, perhaps because they are too crude to illuminate much of lasting interest in human psychology.

Most psychological anthropologists would agree that human beings are biocultural organisms. But finding a way to explain the connection between human biology and human culture that avoids an either-or option is often elusive. It is for this reason, as Bock says, that anthropologists have typically concentrated on "the intermediate zone of group differences" where it becomes possible to identify relationships between specific features of a given culture and specific individuals (1994, ix). This sort of demonstration has done a great deal to undermine ethnocentric prejudices, such as the assumption that all people are (or ought to be) "just like us," or that some of us are "rational" while others of us are "irrational."

One of the more promising directions recognized by Bock, and taken by some psychological anthropologists in recent years (e.g., Ingold 2000) has been influenced by the work of developmental psychologist Susan Oyama (1985). Now becoming known as Developmental Systems Theory (DST), this perspective insists that a proper account of development requires taking into account the reciprocal influences of organisms and their environments at every step of this ongoing process. It involves recognizing, furthermore, that environments as well as genes are passed on from parents to offspring, from the cytoplasm of the mother's egg, to the cellular products produced within the developing embryo, to the mother's uterus, to the postnatal setting which provides (or fails to provide) the amounts and kinds of resources the organism needs to continue to develop in one direction or another.

Social, economic, and political environments thus become relevant factors shaping individual development for human beings, and enduring features of socially constructed environments get passed on to subsequent generations as faithfully as genes, thus influencing the developmental trajectory of future life cycles, and potentially, evolutionary selection pressures that impinge on the species itself. This is the case for many kinds of organisms, but is particularly obvious for human beings. Human beings live in social groups that intensively rework their material environments, bequeath social, economic, and political resources to subsequent generations, and so shape in decisive ways the directions of their lives. Much recent work by psychological anthropologists implicitly if not explicitly adopts the DST approach in addressing various issues in human psychology, as we will see below.

Still, the field of psychological anthropology is complex and not easy to summarize because its practitioners have pursued and continue to pursue a wide variety of

psychological anthropology The study of individuals and their sociocultural communities.

research problems and theoretical orientations. According to Bock, however, the work of psychological anthropologists can be grouped into three basic areas of human experience: perception, cognition, and motivation (1994, x). We will look at each area in turn, drawing together classic and more recent work that has demolished stereotypes about the factors responsible for individual thought and action, and that has provided more detailed, nuanced explanations in the intermediate zone.

As we will see, this evidence overwhelmingly sustains the view put forth in our discussion of language: that is, human psychological processes are open to a wide variety of influences. Like language, human psychology is an open system. Human beings not only talk about the world in a variety of ways, but they also think and feel about it in a variety of ways; and if no one way of thinking or feeling is obligatory, then any particular way of thinking or feeling is shaped by factors encountered in the course of development. Human psychology routinely develops in the context of culturally shaped activities that draw our attention to some parts of the world while ignoring others.

Human psychological processes are also heavily influenced by symbols. Language and visual perception, for example, both push human beings to construct symbolic representations of their experiences in order to make sense of them. As a result, the meaning of what we see, touch, smell, taste, or hear depends on context, not only the immediate context of the perception itself, but also the displaced context stored in memory and shaped by culture and history. As with sentences, so too with the objects of perception. The "same" object can mean different things in different contexts. Consider what seeing a butcher knife means (1) lying on a cutting board in your kitchen next to a pile of mushrooms or (2) wielded by an intruder who has cornered you in your kitchen at midnight.

Perception

Perception can be defined as the "processes by which people organize and experience information that is primarily of sensory origin" (Cole and Scribner 1974, 61). Perception as a psychological process has been thought to link people to the world around them or within them: We perceive size, shape, color, pain, and so on. Studies of perception flourished in the 1950s and 1960s, but their results remain significant today as a means of correcting persistent misunderstandings about the way human perception works.

Intellect and emotion have referred to the two principal ways in which perceptions might be dealt with:

rationally and logically on the one hand, passionately and intuitively on the other. Anthropologists and some psychologists suggest, however, that this approach is highly problematic. Particularly troubling is the traditional split between reason and emotion, which has often been accompanied by the overvaluing of one at the expense of the other. But at least as problematic is the assumption, frequently made by psychologists who are not anthropologists, that perception occurs in a culture-free vacuum. Anthropologists have always insisted that, as Bock puts it, "culture enters into every step of the perceptual process, initially by providing patterned material for perception . . . and later, through verbal and nonverbal means, by suggesting (or insisting on) the proper labeling of and responses to perceived patterns" (1994, xi). Although it is not always easy, researchers have been able to identify some of the ways in which meaning is mapped onto our experiences.

Schemas and Prototypes

Chunks of experience that appear to hang together as wholes, exhibiting the same properties in the same configuration whenever they recur, are called **schemas**. As human beings grow up, they gradually become aware of the schemas that their culture (or subculture) recognizes. Such schemas are often embedded in practical activities and labeled linguistically, and they may serve as a focus for discourse. People living in the United States, for example, cannot avoid a schema called *Christmas*, a chunk of experience that recurs once every year. The Christmas schema can include features like cold and snowy weather and activities like baking cookies, singing carols, going to church, putting up a Christmas tree, and buying and wrapping gifts. In the experience of a child, all these elements may appear to be equally relevant parts of a seamless whole. It may take time and conditioning for Christian parents to persuade children what the "true meaning of Christmas" really is. Some adults who celebrate Christmas disagree about its true meaning. Non-Christians living in the United States must also come to terms with this schema and may struggle to explain to their children why the activities associated with it are not appropriate for them.

People take for granted most of the schemas that their culture recognizes, using them as simplified interpretive frameworks for judging new experiences as typical or not, human or not (D'Andrade 1992, 48). That is, they

---

perception The processes by which people organize and experience information that is primarily of sensory origin.

schemas Patterned, repetitive experiences.

FIGURE 6.1   Locations of societies whose EthnoProfiles appear in chapter 6.

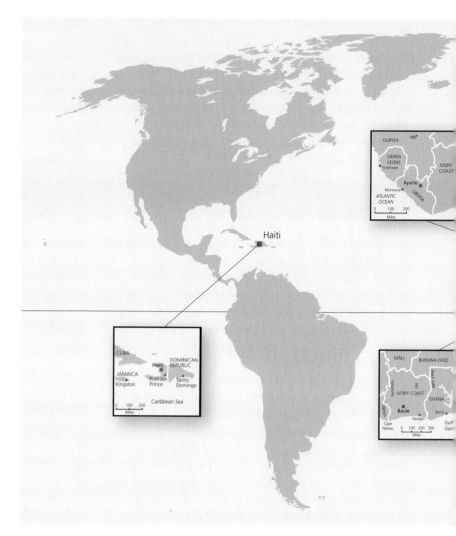

learn to use schemas as **prototypes**. Prototypes of various sorts appear to be central to the way meaning is organized in human language. The words we use refer to typical instances, typical elements or relations, and are embedded, as we saw in chapter 5, in genres of discourse associated with routine cultural practices.

When we organize experience and assign meaning on the basis of prototypes, however, the categories we use have fuzzy boundaries. And because our experiences do not always neatly fit our prototypes, we are often not sure which prototype applies. Is a tossed salad a prototypical tossed salad if in addition to lettuce and tomatoes and onions it also contains raisins and apple slices? Is a library a prototypical library when it contains fewer books than DVDs, videotapes, and electronic databases? In cases like this, suggests linguist R. A. Hudson (1980), a speaker must simply recognize the openness of language and apply linguistic labels creatively.

Similarly, we may be confronted with novel perceptions and experiences with no ready-made cultural interpretation. Thinking and feeling human beings must then extrapolate creatively to make sense of what is going on around them. As we will see, such psychological creativity and resiliency are particularly urgent when people are subjected to extreme social suffering or violent trauma.

Perception and Convention

As we saw in chapter 3, the only evidence recognized by traditional positivist science is the evidence of our five senses. In this view, a suitably objective observer should be able to see and describe the world as it truly is. If other people describe the world differently, then their perceptions must in some way be distorted. Most modern researchers are far less certain about what perception entails. True, our perception is sometimes impaired, either for physical reasons (we aren't wearing our glasses) or because our observations aren't disinterested (our child's forehead feels cool because we are afraid he or she might have a fever). And people do sometimes play jokes on one

prototypes Examples of a typical instance, element, relation, or experience within a culturally relevant semantic domain.

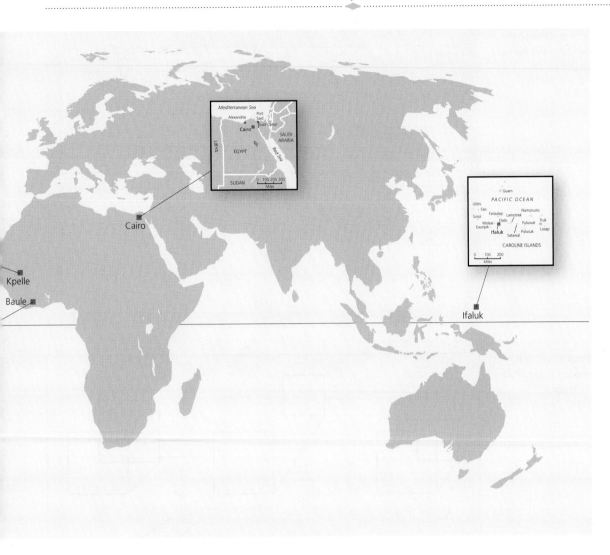

another, insisting that they have seen things they really have not seen. But what about people whose physiological equipment is functioning properly, who have no stake in the outcome, and who are not trying to deceive, and yet who perceive things differently?

In the 1960s, some psychologists began to carry out cross-cultural psychological tests that might provide an answer. For example, psychologist W. Hudson tested non-literate South African mine workers using two-dimensional line drawings of three-dimensional objects (Figure 6.2). The test results indicated that the mine workers consistently interpreted the drawings in two dimensions. When asked at which animal the man was pointing his spear on Card 1, subjects would usually respond, "the elephant." The elephant is, in fact, directly in line with and closest to the spear point in the drawing. However, the elephant ought to be seen as standing on top of the distant hill if the subjects interpret the drawings three-dimensionally. Did their responses mean that these Africans could not perceive in three dimensions?

To find out, J. B. Deregowski soon devised his own test. He presented different African subjects with the same

drawings, asked them to describe what they saw, and got two-dimensional verbal reports. Next, he presented the same subjects with the line drawings in Figure 6.3. This time, he asked his subjects to construct models based on the drawings using materials he provided. His subjects had no difficulty producing three-dimensional models.

Reviewing these results in the 1970s, Michael Cole and Sylvia Scribner concluded that the results "point strongly to the influence of culturally patterned conventions on the perception of pictorial material" (1974, 71). That is, in these tests, the "correct" solution depended on the subject's mastery of a Western convention for interpreting two-dimensional drawings and photographs. For the drawings in Figure 6.2, for example, the Western convention includes assumptions about perspective that relate the size of objects to their distance from the observer. Without such a convention in mind, it is not obvious that the size of a drawn object has any connection with distance. Far from providing us with new insights about the African perceptual abilities, perhaps the most interesting result of such tests is what they teach us about Western perceptual conventions. That is, drawings

FIGURE 6.2 Pictures used for the study of depth perception in Africa.

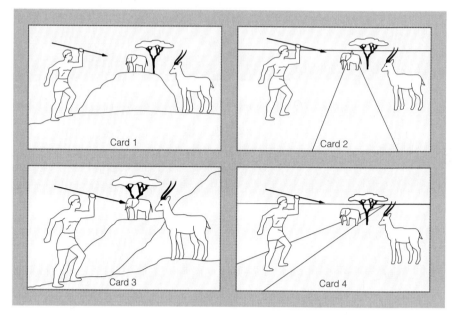

FIGURE 6.3 Drawings used for the construction of models in the depth-perception test in Africa.

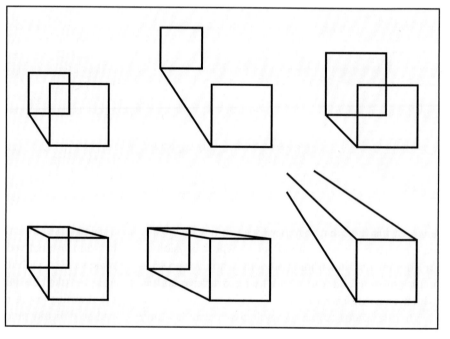

do not necessarily speak for themselves. They can make sense to us only once we accept certain rules for interpreting them.

Illusion

If you examine Figure 6.4, you will see that marks on a piece of paper can be ambiguous. The signals we receive from the outside world tend to be open to more than one interpretation, be they patterns of light and dark striking the retinas of our eyes, or smells, tastes, shapes, or words.

Richard Gregory is a cognitive psychologist who has spent most of his career studying visual illusions. In his

view, illusions are produced by *misplaced procedures:* perfectly normal, ordinary cognitive processes that have somehow been inappropriately selected and applied to a particular set of visual signals. For him, perceptions are symbolic representations of reality, not direct samples of reality. Perceivers must often work very hard to make sense of the visual signals they receive. When they are wrong, they are subject to illusion.

Consider the visual illusion Gregory (R. 1981) calls *distortion:* What you see appears larger or smaller, longer or shorter, and so on, than it really is. Look at the Ponzo illusion in Figure 6.5. Typically, the upper parallel line appears to be longer than the lower one when, in fact,

In Their Own Words

American Premenstrual Syndrome

Anthropologist Alma Gottlieb explores some of the contradictions surrounding the North American bio-cultural construction known as PMS.

To what extent might PMS be seen as an "escape valve," a means whereby American women "let off steam" from the enervating machine of the daily domestic grind? To some extent this explanation is valid, but it tells only part of the story. It ignores the specific contours of PMS and its predictable trajectory; moreover it puts PMS in a place that is peripheral to the American vision of womanhood, whereas my contention is that the current understanding of PMS (and, before its creation, of the menstrual period itself) is integral to how we view femininity. Even if it occupies a small portion of women's lives (although some women may see the paramenstruum as occupying half the month), and even if not all women suffer from it, I contend that the contemporary vision of PMS is so much a part of general cultural consciousness that it constitutes, qualitatively, half the female story. It combines with the other part of the month to produce a bifurcated vision of femininity whose two halves are asymmetrically valued.

Married women who suffer from PMS report that during the "normal" phase of the month they allow their husbands' myriad irritating acts to go uncriticized. But while premenstrual they are hyper-critical of such acts, sometimes "ranting and raving" for hours over trivial annoyances. Unable to act "nice" continually, women break down and are regularly "irritable" and even "hostile." Their protest is recurrent but futile, for they are made to feel guilty about it, or, worse, they are treated condescendingly. "We both know you're going to have your period tomorrow so why don't we just go to bed?" one husband regularly tells his wife at the first sign of an argument, thereby dismissing any claim to legitimate disagreement. Without legitimacy, as Weber taught us long ago, protests are doomed to failure; and so it is with PMS.

I suggest that these women in effect choose, however unconsciously, to voice their complaints at a time that they know those complaints will be rejected as illegitimate. If complaints were made during the non-premenstrual portion of the month, they would have to be taken seriously. But many American women have not found a voice with which to speak such complaints and at the same time retain their feminine allure. They save their complaints for that "time of the month" when they are in effect permitted to voice them yet by means of hormones do not have to claim responsibility for such negative feelings. In knowing when their complaints will not be taken seriously yet voicing them precisely during such a time, perhaps women are punishing themselves for their critical thoughts. In this way, and despite the surface-level aggression they display premenstrually, women continue to enact a model of behavior doomed to failure, as is consistent with what some feminists have argued is a pervasive tendency among American women in other arenas. . . .

So long as American society re-creates its unrealistic expectations of the female personality, it is inevitable that there will be a PMS, or something playing its role: a regular rejection of the stringent expectations of female behavior. But PMS masks the protest even as it embodies it: for, cast in a biological idiom, PMS is made to seem an autonomous force that is often uncontrollable . . . ; or if it can be controlled, it is only by drugs not acts of personal volition. Thus women's authorship of their own states of mind is denied them. As women in contemporary America struggle to find their voices, it is to be hoped that they will be able to reclaim their bodies as vehicles for the creation of their own metaphors, rather than autonomous forces causing them to suffer and needing to be drugged.

Source: Gottlieb 1988.

cultures. Becoming human involves both these processes, for children learn how to act, think, feel, and speak at the same time as they participate in the joint activities carried out by social groups to which they belong. We will use the term *socialization/enculturation* to represent this holistic experience. Socialization/enculturation produces a socially and culturally constructed *self* capable of functioning successfully in society.

Anthropologists and psychologists who seek a theory of cognitive development that is holistic have been attracted to the ideas of George Herbert Mead (1863–1931) and, more recently, to the work of Soviet psychologist Lev Vygotsky (1896–1934). Although both men were contemporaries, Vygotsky's work became influential in the West only recently. Before his early death, Vygotsky had helped to found a major school of Soviet psychology that continues to thrive. The writings of this *sociohistorical school* have inspired some of the most interesting research in cognitive anthropology.

For Mead and Vygotsky alike, human life is social from the outset. As Vygotsky wrote, "The social dimension of consciousness is primary in time and in fact. The individual dimension of consciousness is derivative and secondary" (1978, 30). Like Vygotsky, Mead (1934) believed that human nature is completed and enhanced, not curtailed or damaged, by socialization and enculturation. Indeed, Mead argued that the successful humanization of human beings lies in people's mastery of symbols, which begins when children start to learn language. As children come to control the symbolic systems of their cultures, they gain the ability to distinguish objects and relationships in the world. Most important, they come to see themselves as *objects* as well as *subjects*.

Mead's analysis focused primarily on face-to-face interactions, but anthropologists need a theoretical framework that goes beyond such interactions. Here Vygotsky's work is important because Vygotsky's understanding of context goes beyond Mead's. Vygotsky wanted to create a psychology that was compatible with a marxian analysis of society. His ideas are far from doctrinaire; indeed, during the Stalin years in Russia, his work was censored. At the same time, his marxian orientation directed attention to the social, cultural, and historical context in which face-to-face interaction is embedded.

The Sociohistorical View

The functional cognitive systems employed by adult members of society must be acquired during childhood. For Vygotsky, acquisition takes place in a context of face-to-face interactions between, typically, a child and an adult. When children learn about the world in such a context, they are not working on their own; on the contrary, they are learning about the world as they learn the symbolic forms (usually language) that others use to represent the world.

This learning process creates in the child a new plane of consciousness resting on the dialogue-based, question-and-answer format of social interaction. From this, Vygotsky inferred that our internal thought processes would also take the format of a dialogue. Mead suggested something similar when he spoke of every person as being able to carry on internal conversations between the *I* (the unsocialized self) and the *me* (the socially conditioned self). Only on this basis can an individual's sense of identity develop as the self comes to distinguish itself from the conversational other.

One interesting Vygotskian concept is the *zone of proximal development*, which is the distance between a child's

FIGURE 6.7   The zone of proximal development is the distance between what a child can do on her own and what she can do under adult guidance. Here a woman helps a girl with Chinese calligraphy.

"actual development level as determined by independent problem solving" and the level of "potential development as determined through problem solving under adult guidance or in collaboration with more capable peers" (Vygotsky 1978, 86). Psychologists everywhere have long been aware that children can often achieve more when they are coached than when they work alone (Figure 6.7). Western psychologists, with their individualist bias, have viewed this difference in achievement as contamination of the testing situation or as the result of cheating. Vygotsky and his followers see it as an indispensable measure of potential growth that simultaneously demonstrates how growth is rooted in social interaction, especially in educational settings (Moll 1990).

The concept of the zone of proximal development enables anthropologists and comparative psychologists to link cognitive development to society, culture, and history, because practices of coaching or formal instruction are shaped by social, cultural, and historical factors. To the extent that these factors vary from society to society, we can expect cognitive development to vary as well.

Is Cognitive Development the Same for Everyone?

Most theories, including Mead's, portray cognitive development as a progression through a series of stages. With the exception of Vygotsky's theory, these theories ordinarily assume that the stages are the same for all human beings, or at least all human beings in a particular society. A Vygotskian perspective helps us explain not only cross-cultural differences in development but also differences in the cognitive development of different subgroups in a single society.

For example, from their birth in 1973 through the late 1980s, a sample of 4,299 children were followed by a team of Cuban researchers who periodically collected information on their cognitive, social, economic, physical, and academic development (Gutierrez Muñiz, López Hurtado, and Arias Beatón n.d.). The researchers identified a series of correlations between levels of education, wage employment, living standards, and health of mothers and levels of development and achievement of the children. Put in Vygotskian terms, the data show that the zone of proximal development is greater for children of mothers with higher levels of education and participation in the paid workforce than it is for children of mothers with lower educational levels who do not work outside the home. These findings contradicted popular beliefs that the children of educated working mothers would suffer as a result of their mothers' activities (Arias Beatón, personal communication).

Self/Personality/Subjectivity

As we discussed earlier, the experiences of socialization and enculturation produce a **self**, an individual capable of functioning successfully in society. But what sort of entity is a self? Many Western psychologists have assumed that the mature self was a bounded, independent, self-contained entity with a clear and noncontradictory sense of identity that persisted through time. Anthropologists working in other societies, however, often found that the development of such an independent self was not recognized as the goal of socialization and enculturation. On the contrary, socialization and enculturation were often designed to shape selves that did *not* think of themselves as independent and self-sufficient; the mature individual was one motivated to look out for others, work for the well-being of the family or the lineage rather than in pursuit of his or her own individual self-interest.

Early psychological anthropologists often spoke of individual **personality** rather than the self; this is seen in the name adopted by the early Culture and Personality school of the mid-twentieth century. Bock points out that in such formulations, "personality involves the relative *integration* of an individual's perceptions, motives, cognitions, and behavior within a sociocultural

matrix (The subjective view of this unity is more often referred to as the *self*). The importance of consistent social feedback to individual functioning has been demonstrated. . . . Personality is thus revealed as part of a dynamic interactive system between a human organism and its physical-social environment" (1994, xiv). Many psychological anthropologists, including Bock himself, have argued that an individual's personality, understood in this way, is not merely a reflection of a culturally ideal type, but is regularly shaped by such factors as "the individual's position in the social structure, including his or her social class, gender, occupational role, and even birth order. . . . These quasi-universal structural constraints cut across conventional divisions into 'cultures' and even nations" (1994, xiv).

The notion of an integrated personality, or self, harks back to Enlightenment ideas; as a result, it is hardly surprising that the postmodern critique of Enlightenment ideas questioned the existence of integrated, harmonious personalities or selves. Attention began to be paid to the different dimensions of one's personality or self that were activated (or deactivated) in different contexts, and people began to speak of "decentered" selves as the norm, rather than the exception. The idea of a centered, integrated self was viewed as an illusion or an effect of powerful political ideologies that worked to mask the heterogeneity and contradictory features of individual experience.

Contemporary scholars in many fields continue to disagree about the extent to which anyone's self is integrated or coherent, and few anthropologists would defend an unreflective Enlightenment view of the self. In psychological anthropology, this has led to the shift of focus we see in the work of Lutz, for example: rather than attempt to relate an individual's behavior to internal experiences of the self, attention is focused on social discourse about people's behavior. This suggests that "culture is (largely) created by people in the discourse justifying their behavior as rational and moral" (Bock 1994, xv). But anthropologists who recognize the uneven and contradictory features of individual self-experience also often draw attention to the attempts individuals make, even in the most difficult or bewildering situations, to impose meaning, to make sense of what is happening to them. We struggle to find patterns, strive to achieve ordered, coherent understandings of the world and of ourselves, even if the world is

self The result of the process of socialization/enculturation for an individual.

personality The relative integration of an individual's perceptions, motives, cognitions, and behavior within a sociocultural matrix.

disorderly and even if our understandings are inevitably imperfect and partial.

In recent years, many psychological anthropologists have come to speak not of individual personality or individual self, but of individual **subjectivity**. Veena Das and Arthur Kleinman, for example, define subjectivity as "the felt interior experience of the person that includes his or her positions in a field of relational power" (2000, 1). Where does individual subjectivity come from? Many anthropologists have been influenced by the explanation offered by historian and social theorist Michel Foucault. According to Foucault, human subjects are made, not born. Foucault argued that the kind of subjectivity experienced by individuals in contemporary Western societies, for example, is produced in a field of relational power that began to take shape in the sixteenth century. At this time, following the Protestant Reformation, many individuals were assuming a new responsibility for achieving their own salvation, without the intervention of priests. At the same time, the structures of European states were becoming increasingly concerned with the management of the populations and objects within their borders. State management required accurate information, which spurred the use of *statistics*—the counting and collecting of various kinds of information needed to devise rational policies of government administration. This totalizing form of state power Foucault called *governmentality*, and we will discuss it in chapter 9. But Foucault emphasized that the modern state "is both an individualizing and a totalizing form of power" (1983, 213). The individualizing power of the state he called *pastoral power*, which was deployed not only by the state but by a range of non-state institutions such as hospitals and prisons.

Foucault argued that pastoral power originated in the medieval Catholic Church, and was associated with the priest, a religious expert responsible, like a shepherd, for the welfare of each individual member of his flock. Priests provided for individual welfare by means of the confessional: members of the flock confessed their sins to the priest, who then pronounced both absolution and various forms of penance, intended to discipline individuals and help them avoid sinning again. For Foucault, pastoral power is unusual because, unlike coercion, it "cannot be exercised without knowing the inside of people's minds. . . . It implies a knowledge of the conscience and an ability to direct it" (1983, 214). By the 1700s, pastoral power had spread outside the Church

and was incorporated into state bureaucracies, schools, hospitals, and prisons. In these settings the experts were not priests, but bureaucrats, teachers, doctors, or police; and individuals admitted into their care were expected to reveal, by their own speech, information needed by these experts to manage that care. According to Foucault, however, the "care" provided was often suspect, since the experts were self-appointed, and their goals seemed to have less to do with teaching children or curing the sick or rehabilitating lawbreakers than it did with turning them into submissive, self-monitoring individuals who could take up the roles allotted them by the state with improved efficiency and without the need of supervision (Foucault 1983, 219).

Foucault used the term "technologies of the self" to refer to those methods of self-discipline that do not require constant monitoring by some outside party for compliance. For example, a sick person who reliably "follows doctor's orders" by avoiding certain foods, taking prescribed medicines of the correct dosage every day at the proper hour, and going to bed each night at 9:30 P.M. is engaging in one kind of "technology of the self." People like this can be trusted to do what is required of them by the experts without punishment or supervision. Foucault believed that "Technologies of the self . . . can be found in all cultures in different forms" (1983, 250).

This approach to individual subjectivity has much to recommend it to anthropologists. First, it points to individual agency: each of us is, to some degree, the initiating subject of our actions. Second, however, individual agency is not understood as absolute: We are not free to chart our own destinies unimpeded. Quite the contrary, our agency is circumscribed by various limitations that result from the use of social, economic, and political power in the societies in which we live.

These limitations may be greater or lesser, depending on who we are (remember Bock's urging that we pay attention to the effect of such social variables as class, gender, occupation, or birth order and its impact on our developing sense of self). That is, we are *subject to* the workings of institutionalized power in the various *subject positions* we occupy. The fact that all people in all societies occupy a variety of different subject positions reflects our decentered selves: A particular individual may, in different contexts, be positioned in terms of gender, or ethnicity, or occupation, or class, or some combination of these positions. At the same time, however, all of us can potentially play the insights gained from each subject position off against the others and thus gain a measure of reflexive awareness and understanding of our own situations.

Socialization and enculturation heavily influence individual subjectivity. But social and cultural expectations

---

subjectivity The felt interior experience of the person that includes his or her positions in a field of relational power.

are sometimes overturned by experiences that intrude on predictable daily routines, and these, too, will have a powerful role in shaping the subjectivities of the individuals who are affected.

Avatars, Alts, and the Self in Second Life

As noted in chapter 3, anthropologist Tom Boellstorff carried out fieldwork in the virtual reality computer program Second Life. Second Life participants take on a visual form in the program that is called an avatar. Avatars in Second Life can be customized; residents are able to change almost every aspect of their appearance and can choose to be any age or race, male or female, any species, or even a box or a blue ball. Because people are able to shape their avatars as they wish, residents of Second Life tend to see one another's avatars as fairly obvious representations of how they thought of themselves. As one person put it, "I've come to observe that the outward appearance really does communicate a lot about who you are, because it's made up of conscious choices about how you want to present yourself" (Boellstorff 2008, 130). At the same time, however, residents could also create alternative avatars, know as alts, with which they would sometimes log on. The most common kind of alt was the "social alt," used to try out a different self, or an aspect of the resident's self that was not part of the main avatar. As a consequence of the way Second Life worked, it was impossible to connect alts with avatars, unless the resident who was both of them shared that information with other residents of Second Life. Sometimes, the alts were very different than the main avatar, which was taken by most people as the "default" self in Second Life. Alts might have completely different social networks than the avatar.

Some of the residents Boellstorff knew told him they found it required some time and some mental effort to shift gears from one alt to another. But Boellstorff was struck by the fact that "for most residents, having alts was not cognitively dissonant, despite the lack of any real parallel in the actual world." Here the sense of a single, unified individual self begins to break down in Second Life, becoming what Boellstorff calls a "dividual" self (150). Perhaps the most striking examples of this were people who would log on two or more alts simultaneously from two computers or via multiple copies of the program on one computer. People in Second Life can have multiple selves in a way that is impossible in the real world, and these multiple selves really are discontinuous—"there is a clear gap between where one alt ends and the next begins, even (or perhaps especially) when

people simultaneously log on their distinct alts so that the alts can have company, or so one person's two alts can have sex together." Boellstorff notes that "Such gaps were comprehensible to residents because, as a virtual world, Second Life was already constituted by the gap between actual and virtual" (150). This, perhaps, is one of the surprises of virtual worlds.

How Do Violence and Trauma Alter Our View of Ourselves?

Among the most powerful such experiences are those occasioned by structural violence and social trauma, two areas of social suffering that have unfortunately become all too prevalent in recent times. Processes of globalization, which displace populations or shape the contexts that allow their own governments to oppress or persecute them, have themselves become all too frequent in the late twentieth and early twenty-first centuries. For those who live under such disordered circumstances, orderly, harmonious daily life is not taken for granted. A number of anthropologists have turned explicitly to the investigation of the sources of social suffering and the consequences of such suffering for individual subjectivity. Although the world's attention is usually drawn to large-scale *traumatic violence* that erupts in civil wars or other forms of armed conflict, anthropologists have also pointed to less spectacular forms of *structural violence*, with political and economic causes. Each in its own way is responsible for severe social suffering, and we will look at each in turn.

Structural Violence

Paul Farmer is an anthropologist and medical doctor who has worked since 1983 in Haiti (see EthnoProfile 6.4: Haiti). His activities as a physician have exposed him to extreme forms of human suffering that are part of everyday life for those at the bottom of Haitian society (Figure 6.8). As he points out, "In only three countries in the world was suffering judged to be more extreme than that endured in Haiti; each of these three countries is currently in the midst of an internationally recognized civil war" (Farmer 2002, 424). But if the suffering of poor Haitians is not the outcome of the traumatic violence of war, it can be described as a consequence of another form of violence: structural violence.

EthnoProfile 6.4

Haiti

Region: Caribbean

Nation: Haiti

Population: 7,500,000

Livelihood: Rough, mountainous terrain, tropical to semi-arid climate. About 80 percent of the population lives in extreme poverty

Political organization: Multiparty, nation-state

For more information: Farmer, Paul. 1992. *AIDS and accusation: Haiti and the geography of blame.* Berkeley, University of California Press.

Structural violence is violence that results from the way that political and economic forces structure risk for various forms of suffering within a population. Much of this suffering is in the form of infectious and parasitic disease. But it can also include other forms of extreme suffering, such as hunger, torture, and rape (2002, 424). Farmer's work highlights the effects of structural violence on the production of individual subjectivity. The operations of structural violence create circumscribed spaces in which the poorest and least powerful members of Haitian society are subjected to highly intensified risks of all kinds, increasing the likelihood that sooner or later they will experience one or more varieties of social suffering. The structural aspect of this violence is important to emphasize, since the attention of most Western outside observers, even those who want to alleviate suffering, is often trained on individuals and their personal experiences, with the resulting temptation to blame the victims for their own distress.

Farmer's work as a physician allowed him to see first-hand the suffering of poor Haitians he knew, and his work as an anthropologist allowed him to link that suffering to economic and political structures in Haitian society that are often invisible in local situations, but that can be revealed through careful analysis. Farmer begins by offering the biographies of two young Haitians he treated, one a woman and one a man. Both died young, the woman of AIDS and the man of injuries inflicted on him in the course of a beating by the police. As he says, these two individuals "suffered and died in exemplary fashion," and he shows how the combined forces of racism, sexism, political violence, and poverty conspired "to constrain agency" and "crystallize into the sharp, hard surfaces of individual suffering" (2002, 425).

Acéphie Joseph was the woman who died of AIDS at 25, in 1991. Her parents had been prosperous peasant farmers selling produce in village markets until 1956, when the fertile valley in which they lived was flooded after a dam was built to generate electricity. They lost everything and became "water refugees" forced to try to grow crops on an infertile plot in the village where they were resettled.

Acéphie and her twin brother were born in the village and attended primary school there. Farmer writes that Acéphie's "beauty and her vulnerability may have sealed her fate as early as 1984" (426). She began to help her mother carry produce to the market along a road that went past the local military barracks, where soldiers like to flirt with the passing women, and one soldier in particular approached her. "Such flirtation is seldom unwelcome, at least to all appearances. In rural Haiti, entrenched poverty made the soldiers—the region's only salaried men—ever so much more attractive" (427). Although Acéphie knew he had a wife and children, she nevertheless did not rebuff him; indeed, he visited her family, who approved of their liaison. "'I could tell that the old people were uncomfortable, but they didn't say no . . . I never dreamed he would give me a bad illness . . . it was a way out, that's how I saw it,'" Acéphie explained.

Only a few weeks after the beginning of their sexual relationship, the soldier died. Eventually she found work as a maid and began a relationship with a young man who drove a bus whom she planned to marry. After three years as a maid, Acéphie became pregnant, and went home to her village to give birth, but she had a very difficult delivery, and when she finally sought medical help for a series of infections, she was diagnosed with AIDS. Following her death, her father hanged himself.

Chouchou Louis grew up in a village on the Central Plateau of Haiti. He attended primary school briefly and then worked with his father and older sister to raise produce after his mother died. In the 1980s, times were especially difficult under the repressive dictatorship of Jean-Claude Duvalier. By 1986, a pro-democracy movement had grown powerful enough in Haiti to force Duvalier to leave the country, but he was replaced in power by the military. The U.S. government hoped that this military government would bring democracy, but poor

---

structural violence Violence that results from the way that political and economic forces structure risk for various forms of suffering within a population.

Nothing had happened to Gilsenan's eyes or his other senses, which continued to receive the same signals they had always received, but the meaning of the signals had been altered. Gilsenan's experience in the mosque situated neon light within a new schema, and his growing familiarity with that schema made the neon seem more and more natural. Eventually, Gilsenan was noticing only the color green.

These transformations of perception and understanding remain mysterious, but they seem to occur whenever we have an insight of any kind. Insights, like apt metaphors, reshape the world for us, throwing new aspects into sharp focus and casting other aspects into the background. Our ability to achieve insights remains the most central and most mysterious aspect of human psychological processes.

Chapter Summary

1. Anthropologists have long been interested in cultural learning by individuals. They have tried to find out what all members of our species have in common, what features are limited to specific groups of humans, and how individual uniqueness might be understood. This effort has involved cooperation with other disciplines, such as psychology. Often anthropologists have tested universal assumptions about human psychology in different cultural settings, and have found them to be problematic.

2. The field of psychological anthropology is complex and difficult to summarize, but can be grouped into three basic areas of human experience: perception, cognition, and motivation. Research overwhelmingly sustains the view that human psychological processes are open to a wide variety of influences.

3. Human psychological perception always takes place in a cultural context. Researchers use concepts like schemas and prototypes to describe some of the ways in which meaning is mapped onto our experience. Classic research on cross-cultural variations in perception showed that variation in responses to psychological tests depended on the meanings subjects brought to the testing situation, especially whether they understood the tests the same way Western subjects typically understood them. Alternative understandings are possible because of the ambiguity of many perceptual signals, a phenomenon that is illustrated in the study of visual illusions. In addition, looking and seeing are culturally learned modes of sensory perception, as illustrated in Vogel's study of Baule visuality.

4. Human beings are active meaning-makers, striving to make sense of our experiences, which is a focus of anthropological studies of cognition. Their research has been critical of so-called intelligence tests on which non-Western subjects performed poorly, because outside the laboratory setting the same individuals' intelligence and full humanity were obvious. Today, it is unclear exactly what the results of intelligence tests represent. Consequently, research has shifted its focus to cognitive processes and the way these are organized into culturally shaped functional systems.

5. Several attempts have been made to measure the levels of rational thinking in non-Western populations. The results are problematic. Rational thinking is not the same as logic. Formal Western logic is better understood as a learned reasoning style characteristic of Western culture. Rules of Western logic can be useful, but other logics may be equally valid in other societies—or on other occasions in Western societies—when contextual factors are vital and must be taken into consideration.

6. Our emotions, like our thoughts, are not just something we have; they are culturally constructed of our state of mind, our cultural interpretations, and our levels of bodily arousal. Different cultures recognize different domains of experience and different categories of feeling as being appropriate to these domains. For this reason, it is often difficult to translate the language of emotion from one culture to another.

7. Anthropological approaches to motivation have always embedded the sources of motivation within a cultural matrix. Finding the notion of "instinct" to be unhelpful, anthropologists have had greater success in studying the culturally defined goals which people pursue in different societies.

(continued on next page)

Chapter Summary *(continued)*

8. The mainsprings of motivation are to be uncovered in the study of socialization and enculturation. Humans must learn to pattern and adapt behavior and ways of thinking and feeling to the standards considered appropriate in their respective cultures. Vygotsky's concept of the zone of proximal development stresses that cognitive development results from a dialogue. Children progress through that process at different rates and in different directions, depending on the amount and kind of coaching they receive by others. This concept makes it possible to explain why people in different cultural subgroups are socialized and enculturated in different ways.

9. Anthropologists have been critical of ideas of the individual self that assume it to be a bounded independent entity with a clear and noncontradictory sense of identity that persists through time. Early psychological anthropologists preferred to speak of individual personality, which always assumed that an individual's psychological processes were integrated within a socio-cultural matrix. More recently, anthropologists have shifted from a concern with relating personality to an individual's internal experiences and have paid more attention to attributions about individuals that emerge in social discourse about people's behavior. Some anthropologists prefer to speak not of personality or self, but of individual subjectivity, which focuses on internal experiences of individuals as they are shaped by their positions in a field of power relations.

10. Patterns of socialization and enculturation are sometimes overturned by experiences that intrude on predictable daily routines. Among the most powerful such experiences are those occasioned by structural violence and social trauma, the investigation of which has become a significant topic for some contemporary psychological anthropologists.

For Review

1. Distinguish between schemas and prototypes.
2. What can anthropologists conclude about human perception based on the studies of two-dimensional line drawings among African subjects?
3. What is Susan Vogel's argument about visuality?
4. Describe the differences between European American and African American responses to testing, and explain how these responses can be explained from an anthropological perspective.
5. What was the story of "Spider and Black Deer?" How did Kpelle subjects respond when Cole and Scribner asked them questions about the logical problem embedded in the story? Why? Can you think of logical problems that are difficult for you and your friends to solve?
6. How is emotion culturally constructed?
7. Summarize the key points of the "Emotion in Oceania" case study.

8. Define socialization and enculturation.
9. Explain the zone of proximal development.
10. Explain the differences among self, personality, and subjectivity.
11. What does the phrase "technologies of the self" refer to?
12. Explain how alts in Second Life provide experiences of the self that are impossible in the actual world.
13. What is structural violence? Explain how the Haitian case studies in the text are examples of structural violence.
14. What is trauma? What is "chosen trauma"? Using the case materials in the chapter, explain why these phenomena are important for anthropologists to understand.

Key Terms

psychological anthropology	cognition	emotion	personality
perception	thinking	socialization	subjectivity
schemas	syllogism	enculturation	structural violence
prototypes	reasoning styles	self	trauma
visuality			

Suggested Readings

Bock, Philip K. 1999. *Rethinking psychological anthropology: Continuity and change in the study of human action,* 2d ed. Prospect Heights, IL: Waveland Press. A thorough introduction to psychological anthropology, tracing developments from the early twentieth century to current directions in the field.

Casey, Conerly, and Robert B. Edgertien. 2005. *A companion to psychological anthropology.* Walden, MA: Blackwell. A recent collection of articles by anthropologists who consider the impact of globalization on the traditional concerns of psychological anthropology.

Cole, Michael, and Sylvia Scribner. 1974. *Culture and thought: A psychological introduction.* New York: Wiley. A clear, readable survey of classic literature and case studies on the cultural shaping of cognition.

Farmer, Paul. 2003. *Pathologies of power: Health, human rights, and the new war on the poor.* Berkeley: University of California Press. Paul Farmer, a physician and anthropologist, uses his experiences in several different parts of the world to show how patterns of disease and suffering are shaped by social and political policies that violate human rights, creating landscapes of "structural violence."

Schwartz, Theodore, Geoffrey M. White, and Catherine A. Lutz, eds. 1992. *New directions in psychological anthropology.* Cambridge: Cambridge University Press. A classic survey of psychological anthropology with articles by experts in the fields of cognition, human development, biopsychological studies, and psychiatric and psychoanalytic anthropology.

How Do We Make Meaning?

Human beings are creative, not just in their use of language, but also in their manipulation of a variety of symbolic forms. We look at a range of different kinds of human symbolic creativity in this chapter, including play, art, myth, and ritual.

One of the authors of this book (RHL) was carrying out fieldwork in Caracas, Venezuela, toward the end of October 1974, when excitement about the heavyweight boxing championship featuring George Foreman and Muhammad Ali began to build. Boxing is extremely popular in Venezuela, and the Caracas newspapers devoted a great deal of attention to this bout. They gave Ali little chance of winning. It was late in his career, and he had already lost once to Foreman. Too old, they said, too out of shape, too big a mouth, too strong an opponent.

I (RHL) managed to resist interest in the fight until the last moment. I had other work to do and didn't care for boxing. Besides, I didn't have a television in my apartment. On the night the fight was to be telecast on the national network, I went out to dinner alone. On my way home, I was surprised to see the city almost deserted. Then I remembered that the fight was about to start. I was feeling lonely, and my curiosity got the better of me. I passed a bar that had a television, so I stopped in. The preliminaries, native dancing from Congo where the fight was being held, were just ending. The bar gradually filled up. A couple of people seemed to know each other, but the rest were strangers.

As the fight began, I became aware that we were all Ali fans. As he did better and better, we became increasingly excited, and communication among the patrons increased. When finally, miraculously, Ali won, pandemonium broke loose. The crowd seemed to explode into a paroxysm of *abrazos* ("embraces"), tears, cries of joy, and calls for rounds of beer. Strangers before, all of us were now united in a feeling of oneness and joy. None of us had any idea who the others were or what they did, but it didn't matter—we had witnessed something wonderful and felt a comradeship that transcended our strangerness.

But what was it that we had witnessed and been part of? A sporting event? A ritual? A drama, pitting youth against age? Was there something mythic in that spectacle that so engrossed us? What made it so meaningful to us?

In this chapter, we consider how anthropologists go about trying to make sense of events similar to the event in the bar. We will examine play, art, myth, and ritual—four dimensions of human experience in which the interplay of openness and creativity with rules and constraints enables people to make (and respond to) meanings of many kinds.

play A framing (or orienting context) that is (1) consciously adopted by the players, (2) somehow pleasurable, and (3) systemically related to what is nonplay by alluding to the nonplay world and by transforming the objects, roles, actions, and relations of ends and means characteristic of the nonplay world.

What Is Play?

In the previous two chapters, we explored the concept of *openness* in relation to language and cognition. Openness was defined as the ability to talk or think about the same thing in different ways and different things in the same way. If we expand openness to include all behavior—that is, the ability not just to talk or think about but also to *do* the same thing in different ways or different things in the same way—we begin to define **play**. All mammals play, and humans play the most and throughout their lives.

Robert Fagen (1981, 1992, 2005) looks at play as the product of natural selection. He points out that play gives young animals (including young human beings) the exercise they need to build up their bodies for the rigors of adulthood. Play trains them in activities necessary for physical survival: fighting, hunting, or running away when pursued. During a brief period of neural development, peak brain development associated with motor skills and peak periods of play occur at the same time. Play may be important for the development of cognitive and motor skills and may be connected with the repair of developmental damage caused by either injury or trauma.

It may also communicate the message "all's well," "signaling information about short-term and long-term health, general well-being, and biological fitness to parents, littermates, or other social companions" (1992, 51).

In species with more complex brains, playful exploration of the environment aids learning and allows for the development of behavioral versatility. Fagen (2005) suggests that play reflects natural selection for unpredictability. That is, to be able to produce unpredictable behaviors can be advantageous for an intelligent species faced with unanticipated adaptive challenges.

How Do Anthropologists Think about Play?

Joking, which can be verbal or physical (practical jokes, pranks, horseplay), is a good example of how play operates overall and in its cultural context. Anthropologist Andrew Miracle discusses joking behavior among Aymara people in Bolivia (see EthnoProfile 7.1: Aymara). He notes that ordinarily Aymara do not laugh in the presence of strangers because that is considered disrespectful. They laugh and joke only within a circle of acquaintances and friends. This kind of joking reinforces existing social bonds (1991, 151).

Much of the joking Miracle observed took place on the crowded buses or trucks that transport rural people around the country. Ordinarily, Aymara personal space extends about one arm's length. Where there is any choice, people do not get any closer to one another. They also show respect and honor other people's privacy by not staring. Miracle notes that in everyday situations, "when stared at, the Aymara may yell at the one staring and become quite rude" (1991, 146). On buses or trucks, however, the context changes, and people who are strangers to one another are forced into artificial intimacy. They must sit or stand very close to one another for long periods of time, frequently looking right at one another. Their response, Miracle writes, is often to joke and laugh, behavior normally reserved for intimates. Put another way, they choose to do "different things" (passing time with close friends and passing time with strangers in unusually close quarters) in the "same way," by joking. This altered definition of context gives joking among strangers a new meaning, playfully changing strangers into friends and thus making a socially unpleasant situation more tolerable.

Moving from everyday reality to the reality of play requires a radical transformation of perspective. To an outside observer, the switch from everyday reality to play reality may go undetected. However, sometimes the switch can have serious consequences for other people and their activities. In this case, play and nonplay must be signaled clearly, so that one is not mistaken for the other.

According to Gregory Bateson (1972), shifting into or out of play requires **metacommunication**, or communication about communication. Metacommunication provides information about the relationship between communicative partners. In play there are two kinds of metacommunication. The first, called **framing**, sends a message that marks certain behaviors either as play or as ordinary life. Dogs, for example, have a *play face*, a signal understood by other dogs (and recognizable by some human beings) indicating a willingness to play. If dogs agree to play, they bare their fangs and one animal attacks the other, but bites become nips. Both dogs have agreed to enter the *play frame*, an imaginative world in which bites do not mean bites. Within the play frame, a basic element of Western logic—that A = A—does not apply; the same thing is being treated in different ways. Human beings have many ways of marking the play frame: a smile, a particular tone of voice, a referee's whistle, or the words "Let's pretend." The marker says that "everything from now until we end this activity is set apart from everyday life."

The second kind of metacommunication involves **reflexivity**. Play offers us the opportunity to think about the social and cultural dimensions of the world in which we live. By suggesting that ordinary life can be understood in more than one way, play can be a way of speculating

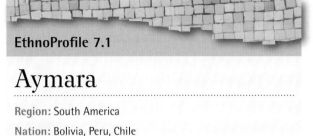

EthnoProfile 7.1

Aymara

Region: South America

Nation: Bolivia, Peru, Chile

Population: 2,000,000

Environment: High mountain lake basin

Livelihood: Peasant farmers

Political organization: Preconquest state societies conquered first by Inkas and later by Spanish; today, part of a modern nation-state

For more information: Miracle, Andrew. 1991. Aymara joking behavior. *Play and Culture* 4:144–52.

about what can be rather than about what should be or what is (Handelman 1977, 186). When we say that jokes keep us from taking ourselves too seriously, for example, we are engaging in reflexive metacommunication. Joking allows us to consider alternative, even ridiculous, explanations for our experience.

What Are Some Effects of Play?

Anthropologist Helen Schwartzman has demonstrated how play may allow children to comment on and criticize the world of adults (1978, 232–45). Some adult play forms, such as the pre-Lenten Carnival or Halloween, also act as a commentary on the "real world." They sanction insults and derision of authority figures, inversions of social status, clowning, parody, satire, stepping outside of everyday life, "trying on" new forms of identity, and the like (124).

A powerful example of this kind of commentary is described by anthropologist Elizabeth Chin, who studied African American girls and their dolls in Newhallville, a working-class and poor neighborhood in New Haven, Connecticut. Although "ethnically correct" dolls

---

metacommunication Communicating about the process of communication itself.

framing A cognitive boundary that marks certain behaviors as "play" or as "ordinary life."

reflexivity Critically thinking about the way one thinks; reflecting on one's own experience.

FIGURE 7.1   Locations of societies whose Ethno-
Profiles appear in chapter 7.

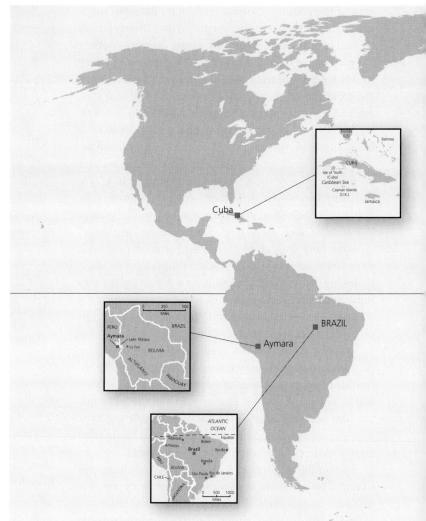

FIGURE 7.1   Locations of societies whose Ethno-Profiles appear in chapter 7.

are on the market, very few of the girls had them, because they cost too much. The poor children Chin knew in Newhallville had white dolls. But in their play these girls transformed their dolls in a powerful way by giving them hairstyles like their own. The designers gave the dolls smooth, flowing hair to be brushed over and over again and put into a ponytail. But the girls' dolls had beads in their hair, braids held at the end with twists of aluminum foil or barrettes, and braids that were themselves braided together (Chin 1999, 315). As Chin observes, "In some sense, by doing this, the girls bring their dolls into their own worlds, and whiteness here is not absolutely defined by skin and hair, but by style and way of life. The complexities of racial references and racial politics have been much discussed in the case of black hair simulating the look of whiteness; what these girls are creating is quite the opposite: white hair that looks black" (315).

It is not that the girls didn't realize that their dolls were white; it is that through their imaginative and material work they were able to integrate the dolls into their own world. The overt physical characteristics of the dolls—skin color, facial features, hair—did not force the girls into treating the dolls in ways that obeyed the boundaries of racial difference. Their transformative play does not make the realities of poverty, discrimination, and racism disappear from the worlds in which they live, but Chin points out that "in making their white dolls live in black worlds, they . . . reconfigure the boundaries of race," and in so doing, "challenge the social construction not only of their own blackness, but of race itself as well" (318).

Societies contain the threat posed by play by defining it as "unserious," "untrue," "pretend," "make-believe," "unreal," and so forth (Handelman 1977, 189). Many political figures recognize that play can undermine the established political order. Repressive political regimes frequently attempt to censor humor critical of the rulers, with the result that such humor becomes an accepted mode of political resistance.

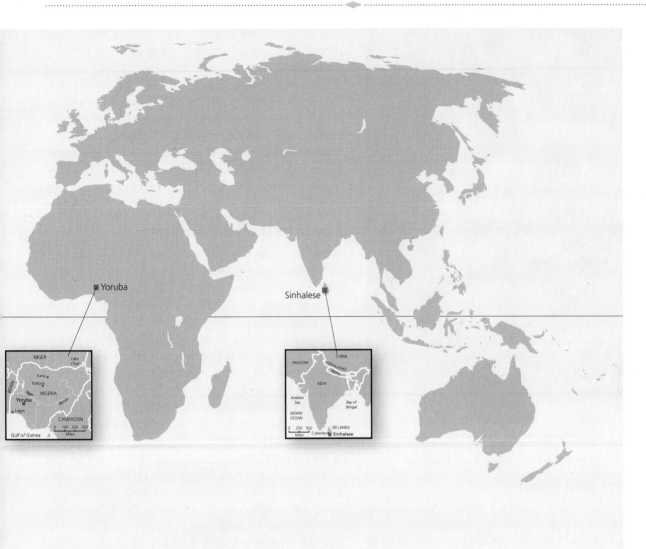

Do People Play by the Rules?

Sport is a kind of physical play that is constrained by rules: "a physically exertive activity that is aggressively competitive within constraints imposed by definitions and rules. A component of culture, it is ritually patterned, gamelike, and of varying amounts of play, work and leisure. In addition, sport can be viewed as having both athletic and nonathletic variations, *athletic* referring to those activities requiring the greater amount of physical exertion" (Blanchard and Cheska 1985, 60).

Play is only one component of sport. Sport can be work for the players and an investment for the owners of professional teams. It is also a form of personal and social identification for fans, who are invited into a make-believe world in which they may playfully identify with their heroes, rage at the opponents, imagine coaching the team, suffer, and rejoice. The play element in sport draws a frame around the activity. Conflict in games and sports is different from conflict in ordinary life. Competitors agree "to strive for an incompatible goal—only one opponent can win—within the constraints of understood rules" (Lever 1983, 3). Conflict becomes the whole point of the activity rather than the means of settling a disagreement.

As with all forms of play, the relationships of means and ends in sport are altered. Sport is struggle for the sake of struggle. "Athletes and teams exist only to be rivals; that is the point of their relationship. In the world of sport, there should be no purpose beyond playing and winning. Unlike rivals in the real world, who have opposing political, economic, or social aims, sports competitors must be protected, not persuaded or eliminated" (4).

---

sport A physically exertive activity that is aggressively competitive within constraints imposed by definitions and rules. Sport is a component of culture that is ritually patterned, gamelike, and consists of varying amounts of play, work, and leisure.

FIGURE 7.2   Play enables this girl in Guider, Cameroon, to incorporate her European doll into the world she knows.

Culture and Sport

Sport is play, but it is embedded in the prevailing social order. "Even a sport that has been introduced from a foreign source is very quickly redefined and adjusted to fit the norms and values of tradition" (Blanchard and Cheska 1985, 55). Sports reflect the basic values of the cultural setting in which they are performed, and they are transformed when they are translated into a new cultural setting.

A striking example of how a sport can transform from one culture to another is found in the Trobriand Islands (see EthnoProfile 3.4: Trobriand Islanders). An English missionary introduced the sport of cricket to the Trobrianders in the very early years of the twentieth century. By the 1970s, in the more rural parts of the islands, it had become a different game. Played between two villages, it became a substitute for warfare and a way of establishing political alliances. If the hosts had 40 men ready to play and the visitors had 36, then there were 36 to a side instead of the "correct" 11. The game was always won by the home team—but not by too many runs because that would shame the visitors. War magic was employed to aid batsmen and bowlers. Teams had dances and chants for taking the field, leaving it, and celebrating outs. These dances and chants were used to comment on current events and became fertile ground for additional competition beyond that of the sporting event itself. The bat was redesigned for greater accuracy, and the entire activity

was associated with the ceremonial exchange of food and other goods. Cricket, the sport of empire, was radically transformed.

From the perspective of some Trobrianders, in fact, their cricket was a way of taking the English colonizers' favorite game—a game that was supposed to teach Trobrianders how to become "civilized"—and using it to express their rejection of the colonial world. As one Trobriand leader says in the film *Trobriand Cricket* (1974), "we rubbished the white man's game; now it's our game."

Sport in the Nation-State

According to Janet Lever, the most important and universal feature of sport in the nation-state is that it helps complex modern societies cohere (1995, 3). In her study of soccer in Brazil, aptly titled *Soccer Madness*, Lever argues that large-scale organized sport presents a mechanism for building political unity and allegiance to the nation (Figure 7.3) (see EthnoProfile 7.2: Brazil). "Sport's paradoxical ability to reinforce societal cleavages while transcending them makes soccer, Brazil's most popular sport, the perfect means of achieving a more perfect union between multiple groups . . . [by giving] dramatic expression to the strain between groups while affirming the solidarity of the whole" (5, 9).

In Brazil, there is at least one professional soccer team in every city. The larger cities have several teams, representing different social groups. In Rio de Janeiro, for example, separate teams tend to be supported by the old rich, the modern middle class, the poor, the blacks, the Portuguese, and a number of neighborhood communities. The teams come to represent these different groups in a concrete, visible fashion. Through these teams, separate groups maintain their identities. At the same time, the teams bring their opposing fans together through a shared enthusiasm for soccer. City and national championships similarly unify the socioeconomically and geographically diverse groups of Brazil.

For many Brazilians—indeed, for many people around the world—the experience of supporting a soccer team may be their first and perhaps only experience of a loyalty beyond the local community. Unity is achieved by demonstrating that different teams, and the groups they represent, are in conflict only at one level. At a higher level, the fans of those teams are really united; for example, fans of all Rio teams support the team that goes on to represent Rio in the national championships. This process reaches a climax in international competition, as the supporters of the many local teams back the national team. At this highest level of integration, soccer provides a way of affirming one's "Brazilianness."

There is one important exception to the global mass culture of sport: It regularly separates women from men.

Soccer is incredibly important to Brazilian men and to many other men in the rest of the world, but it is much less important to women. The gender segregation of the sport has significant consequences for the experience of growing up male or female. It also affects relationships later in life between men and women who do not share the same experiences. There is a fundamental ambiguity in the relation of sports and integration: As sports join people together in one domain, they separate them in another. Sports can maintain and sharpen distinctions that are already significant in many other areas of a culture.

Sport as Metaphor

Why soccer? Why is it so important in Brazil and the rest of the world (outside the U.S.)? French anthropologist Christian Bromberger (1995) has written at length about soccer, based on field research in Marseille, France, and Naples and Turin in Italy. For Bromberger, soccer is fascinating because "it lays bare the major symbolic

EthnoProfile 7.2

Brazil

Region: South America

Nation: Brazil

Population: 157,000,000

Environment: Varied; coastal to tropical rain forest

Livelihood: Industry, farming, mining, manufacturing, and so on

Political organization: Modern nation-state

For more information: Lever, Janet. 1983. *Soccer madness.* Chicago: University of Chicago Press.

horizon of our societies: the course of a match, of a competition, resembles the uncertain fate of people in the contemporary world. Further, the combination of rules that mould the genre give this uncertainty an *acceptable* feel" (197). The outcome of a game, a tournament, even the ups and downs of a team over time can be metaphors for the fragility and the mobility of both individual and collective status.

The complexity and sudden changes of a single game or a tournament offer what Bromberger calls "a shortcut to the joys and dramas that make up a life" (197). A match or a championship season feature not only achievement on the basis of merit, but also uncertainties, introduced by strategy, luck, law and (in)justice in the form of the referee, trickery, and unfairness. It offers the fan the opportunity to compare players, to reflect, to plan, to strategize, and to be surprised. As one of Bromberger's informants put it, "At bottom, what most fascinates me is when a player chooses a solution which I had not thought of . . . and it works!" Remarks Bromberger, "The sprint or the high jump . . . don't offer the same material to reflect on" (199–200). And, as in life, the best team doesn't always win—we suspect that every soccer fan carries memories of amazing matches where a team that was outplayed for the entire game won anyway. These "Cinderella" stories, the uncertainties, the fluctuations, and the possible alternatives that the present offers, lie at the heart of a worldview that is, perhaps, uncomfortable to sports fans in the United States, who are more likely to be optimistic and less likely to embrace the quicksilver turns of fate and chance that characterize soccer.

FIGURE 7.3 In Brazil, soccer provides a mechanism for creating national unity or a sense of "Brazilianness" among fans. Here, the Brazilian national team, draped in Brazilian flags, celebrates its fifth World Cup championship in 2002.

Baseball and Masculinity in Cuba

As we have noted, sport is not just about the people who play; it is also about the spectators and their lives. Anthropologist Thomas Carter has studied baseball fans in Cuba. Baseball has been an important part of life, especially men's lives, in Cuba since the 1860s, and is now the leading sports activity in the country (see EthnoProfile 7.3: Cuba). Prior to Cuban independence, during Spanish colonial rule, baseball was banned because of its "revolutionary potential." The Spanish were not wrong: "To be a baseball fan in nineteenth-century Havana was to adopt a specific political position that asserted the modernity and independence of Cuba as a contrast to its colonial relationship with Spain" (Carter 2001, 122). This position was taken up again by the Fidel Castro government; indeed, Castro himself is a big fan. Today, there are 16 teams that play a 90-game season followed by a championship tournament, as well as a national team that represents Cuba at international baseball tournaments (Cuba took second place at the World Baseball Classic in 2006).

Carter notes that to be a serious baseball fan in Cuba includes being willing and able to *discutir pelota*, to argue about baseball (Figure 7.4). Arguing implies opposition and confrontation, and confrontation is a core aspect of Cuban masculinity (118). Who was the better player? Which was the better team? Which league division is the more demanding? By arguing baseball Cuban men embody and display the values of a Cuban male. These include "discipline (*disciplina*), struggle (*lucha*), and lucidity. Fans' assertive disagreements emphasize their masculinity, as evidenced by their willingness to argue and their ability to maintain self-control in the face of obvious antagonism" (118).

EthnoProfile 7.3

Cuba

Region: Caribbean

Nation: Cuba

Population: 11,380,000 (2006)

Environment: Large tropical island

Livelihood: Natural resource export, especially sugar; agriculture; tourism

Political organization: single-party nation-state

For more information: Carter, Thomas. 2008. *The quality of homeruns: Cuban baseball, identity and the state.* Duke University Press.

Carter goes on to talk about the daily *peña* in the Parque Central in Havana. In Cuban Spanish, a peña is a loose association of people, usually men, who regularly meet for a specific reason (124); in this case, this is a daily gathering of men—some regulars, some attending occasionally—in the middle of Havana's Central Park who come to argue about sports, especially baseball, both Cuban and the U.S. Major Leagues. The men are primarily urban middle class, and their reputations are built on their ability to memorize baseball knowledge, especially statistics, and the speed and accuracy with which

FIGURE 7.4 Cuban men argue about baseball in Havana's Parque Central.

that knowledge can be employed in rapid-fire argument (126). Women never participate in this peña, and very few women know how to (or care to) *discutir pelota*. Carter notes that in nine months of fieldwork in Cuba, he never once observed a woman approach a group of men involved in arguing baseball. One of his informants remarked:

> Women simply do not know anything about baseball. They don't go to the stadium. They might if they know someone there personally, an athlete, security guard, or journalist who is a family member or boy-friend, for example. They might have *antes* ["before" indicating "before the Revolution"]. But even then, they do not grow with it. Their fathers, uncles, or brothers do not teach them. Besides, the language in a *peña* is rough, and it is not meant for a woman. It is not sincere [the insults] but it offends them [women]. So, yes, the sports *peña* has only men, always (126).

Carter's point is that being able to argue about baseball—to be a serious fan—is both to declare and to display one's manliness. One is interested in a male pursuit—baseball—one has the knowledge required to demonstrate that interest, and one has the skill, self-control, and willingness to be confrontational within recognized limits. But "they do not simply declare their masculinity, they demonstrate, through their passion for baseball, that their masculinity is specifically Cuban" (136).

What Is Art?

In Western societies, art includes sculpture, drawing, painting, dance, theater, music, and literature, as well as such similar processes and products as film, photography, mime, mass media production, oral narrative, festivals, and national celebrations. These are the kinds of objects and activities that first caught the attention of anthropologists who wanted to study art in non-Western societies. Whether non-Western peoples refer to such activities or products as "art," however, is a separate question. People everywhere engage in these kinds of playful creativity, yet activities defined as "art" differ from free play because they are circumscribed by rules. Artistic rules direct particular attention to, and provide standards for evaluating, the *form* of the activities or objects that artists produce.

How Can Art Be Defined?

Anthropologist Alexander Alland defines **art** as "play with form producing some aesthetically successful transformation-representation" (1977, 39). For Alland, "form" refers

to the rules of the art game: the culturally appropriate restrictions on the way this kind of play may be organized in time and space.

We can also think about form in terms of style and media. A *style* is a schema (a distinctive patterning of elements) that is recognized within a culture as appropriate to a given medium. The *media* themselves in which art is created and executed are culturally recognized and characterized (R. L. Anderson 1990, 272–75). A "painting" is a form: It is two-dimensional; it is done with paint; it is intentionally made; it represents or symbolizes something in the world outside the canvas, paper, or wood on which it is created. There are different kinds of paintings, as well. There is the painting form called portrait—a portrait depicts a person, it resembles the person in some appropriate way, it is done with paint, it can be displayed, and more.

By "aesthetic," Alland means appreciative of, or responsive to, form in art or nature (1997, xii). "Aesthetically successful" means that the creator of the piece of art (and possibly its audience) responds positively or negatively to it ("I like this," "I hate this"). Indifference is the sign of something that is aesthetically unsuccessful. It is probably the case that the aesthetic response is a universal feature in all human societies.

Aesthetic value judgments guide the artist's choice of form and material; they also guide the observers' evaluations. This implies that art involves more than just objects. V. N. Voloshinov argues that art is a creative "event of living communication" involving the work, the artist, and the artist's audience ([1926] 1987, 107). Artists create their works with an audience in mind, and audiences respond to these works as if the works were addressed to them. Sometimes their response is enthusiastic; sometimes it is highly critical. In addition, if aesthetic creation involves more than the end product, such as a painting or a poem, attention needs to be paid to the *process* through which some product is made. James Vaughan (1973, 186) pointed out, for example, that the Marghi of northeastern Nigeria do not appreciate a folktale as a story per se but rather enjoy the *performance* of it (see EthnoProfile 13.2: Marghi).

To understand what Alland means by **transformation-representation** we can recall that the link between a symbol and what it represents is arbitrary. This means that symbols can be separated from the object or idea represented and appreciated for their own sake. They may also be used to represent a totally different meaning. Because transformation and representation depend on each

---

art Play with form producing some aesthetically successful transformation-representation.

transformation–representation The process in which experience is transformed as it is represented symbolically in a different medium.

other, Alland (1977, 35) suggests that they be referred to together (as *transformation-representation*).

When a Javanese leather puppet maker makes a puppet of the great mythic hero Arjuna, for example, he is representing the traditional form of the hero in his work, but he is also transforming a three-dimensional human form into a two-dimensional flat puppet made of buffalo hide, in which the colors, style, inclination of the head, and adornment stand for the internal state of the hero at a specific moment (Figure 7.5). At the same time, he is carrying out this work more or less skillfully and is representing in his work the meanings that Arjuna has for his Javanese audience (see EthnoProfile 5.1: Java).

Alland's definition of art attempts to capture something universal about human beings and their cultures. Similarly, anthropologist Shelly Errington observes that all human cultures have "'symbolic forms': artifacts, activities, or even aspects of the landscape that humans view as densely meaningful" (1998, 84).

One dramatic example in the United States that demonstrates the power of art as a densely meaningful landscape is the Vietnam Veterans Memorial in Washington, DC (Figure 7.6). This work by architect Maya Lin not only has impressed the art critics but also continues to have a profound aesthetic and emotional impact on hundreds of thousands of people who visit it each year. The memorial continues to draw offerings by visitors, not just wreaths or flowers but also messages of all kinds remembering those memorialized and even communicating with them. Letters from friends and families, a hand-lettered sign from a fortieth high school reunion in a small Indiana town, tracings of names, intensely private grief, and respectful silence in its presence are all testimony to the success of this piece of art.

"But Is It *Art*?"

Many people—anthropologists included—have resisted the notion that art is only what a group of Western experts define as art. To highlight the ethnocentrism of Western art experts, they stressed that the division into categories of art and nonart is not universal. In many societies, there is no word that corresponds to "art," nor is there a category of art distinct from other human activities. On the other hand, convinced that all people were endowed with the same aesthetic capacities, anthropologists felt justified in speaking of art and of artists in non-Western societies. Their goal was to recognize a fully human capacity for art in all societies, but to redefine art until it became broad enough to include on an equal basis aesthetic products and activities that Western art experts would qualify, at best, as "primitive," "ethnic," or "folk" art.

For example, some anthropologists focused on the evaluative standards that artists use for their own work

FIGURE 7.5 One of the great mythic heros of Javanese *wajang* is represented here in a beautifully painted flat leather shadow puppet. The color of the image, the angle of the head, the shape of the eye, the position of the fingers, and the style, color, and amount of clothing all represent the inner state of the hero.

and other work in the same form, and how these may differ from the standards used by people who do not themselves perform such work. Anthony Forge (1967), for example, notes that Abelam carvers in New Guinea discuss carvings in a language that is more incisive than that of noncarvers and other anthropologists pointed out that artists in traditional non-Western societies created objects or engaged in activities that reinforced the central values of their culture. Thus, their work helped to maintain the social order, and the artists did not see themselves as (nor were they understood to be) avant-garde critics of society as they often are in modern Western societies. Forge (1967, 30) tells us that Abelam art works are statements about male violence and warfare, male nurturance, and the combination of the two. These statements about the nature of men and their culture are not made by other means of communication like speech. Moreover, these statements are essential for Abelam social structure.

Recent work in the anthropology of art, however, has prompted many anthropologists to rethink this position.

FIGURE 7.6 The Vietnam Veterans Memorial is a powerfully affecting work of art that speaks directly to central issues in the culture of the United States.

They have turned their attention to the way certain kinds of material objects made by tribal peoples flow into a global art market, where they are transformed into "primitive" or "ethnic" art. Some anthropologists, like Shelly Errington, point out that even in the West most of the objects in fine arts museums today, no matter where they came from, were not intended by their makers to be "art." They were intended to be (for example) masks for ritual use, paintings for religious contemplation, reliquaries for holding the relics of saints, ancestor figures, furniture, jewelry boxes, architectural details, and so on. They are in fine arts museums today because at some point they were claimed to be art by someone with the authority to put them in the museum (Figure 7.7).

For these reasons, Errington distinguishes "art by intention" from "art by appropriation." Art by intention includes objects that were made to be art, such as Impressionist paintings. Art by appropriation, however, consists of all the other objects that "became art" because at a certain moment certain people decided that they belonged to the category of art. Because museums, art dealers, and art collectors are found everywhere in the world today, it is now the case that potentially any material object crafted by human hands can be appropriated by these institutions as "art."

To transform an object into art, Errington argues, it must have *exhibition value*—someone must be willing to display it. Objects that somehow fit into the Western definition of art will be selected for the art market as "art." Looking at the collection of objects that over the years have been defined as "art," Errington sees that the vast majority show certain elements to be embedded rather deeply in the Western definition of art: the objects are "portable (paintings, preferred to murals), durable (bronze preferred to basketry), useless for practical purposes in the secular West (ancestral effigies and Byzantine icons preferred to hoes and grain grinders), representational (human and animal figures preferred to, say, heavily decorated ritual bowls)" (1998, 116–17). In other words, for Errington, art requires that someone *intend* that the objects be art, but that someone does not have to be the object's creator.

She notes that "we humans are amazingly inventive, and we make and have always made things that we imbue with meaning, as befits creatures having both opposable thumbs and consciousness. Human artifacts are admirable. They are ingenious. They are dense with meaning.

FIGURE 7.7 Non-Western sculpture is transformed into art when it is displayed like Western art in a museum and viewed by a public that has the opportunity to look at it intensively (in this case, by then–French president Jacques Chirac).

They are worthy of deep study" (1998, 103). But, she argues, they are not art until someone who carries around a particular definition of art says they are.

This is successful when the artifacts in question can be metaphorically transformed and represented as Western art objects. In their original contexts, most meaningful symbolic forms involve more than one sense: an audience hears drumming while looking at masked dancers as their own bodies respond to the dancers while feeling the warm breeze carrying the smells of palm oil and the shouts of children frightened by the dancers. But some of the sensory experiences—sounds, smells, tastes, muscular exertion, bodily response, and other sensations—that make richly symbolic performances do not last. As masks, audio recordings, and other objects are moved into the international art market, "they slough off their . . . performance contexts, . . . retaining only the durable part that can be set aside in a frame or on a pedestal" (Errington 1998, 84) or can be burned onto a CD and sold in the World Music section of a record store.

It can be fruitful to talk about art as a kind of play. Like play, art presents its creators and participants with alternative realities, a separation of means from ends, and the possibility of commenting on and transforming the everyday world. In today's global art market, however, restrictions of an entirely different order also apply. Shelly Errington observes that the people who make "primitive art" are no longer "tribal" but have become

> modern-day peasants or a new type of proletariat. . . .
> They live in rain forests and deserts and other such
> formerly out-of-the-way places on the peripheries . . .

within national and increasingly global systems of buying and selling, of using natural and human resources, and of marketing images and notions about products. Some lucky few of them make high ethnic art, and sell it for good prices, and obtain a good portion of the proceeds. Others make objects classed as tourist or folk art, usually for much less money, and often through a middleperson. (Errington 1998, 268)

Others fulfill orders from elsewhere, "producing either masses of 'folk art' or expensive handmade items designed by people in touch with world taste and world markets" (269).

Errington points out the bitter irony that international demand for "exotic" objects is growing at the very moment when the makers of these objects are severely threatened by international economic policies and resource extraction projects that impoverish them and undermine the ways of life that give the objects they make their "exotic" allure. It should also be noted that what counts as fashionable decoration this year—"world taste"—may be out of fashion next year, leaving the producers with very little to fall back on.

"She's Fake": Art and Authenticity

Michelle Bigenho is an anthropologist and violinist whose multisited ethnography, mentioned in chapter 3, examines music performance in Bolivia, in part through her experiences performing with *Música de Maestros* (Figure 7.8). This ensemble performs the works of master Bolivian composers of the past and attempts to recreate accurate performances of contemporary original music that they have studied in the countryside (Bigenho 2002, 4). The ensemble included both classically trained and traditionally trained musicians, and three were foreigners: a Japanese who played the Andean flute, a Cuban who played violin, and Bigenho, from the United States, who also played violin. Along with a local dance ensemble, the musicians were invited to represent Bolivia in a folklore festival in France. As the bands were lining up, a member of the Belgian delegation walked over to Bigenho and announced, in French, "She's fake." The Belgian woman then "pointed to one of the Bolivian dancers dressed in her dancing costume with her long fake braids worked into her short brown hair. As she pointed, she said, 'She's real'" (88).

In this way, Bigenho raises the issue of the connection between "authenticity" and so-called folk art. How do the images that people in dominant nations have of "folk" or indigenous people affect the production and circulation of indigenous art? Can a Bolivian band include musicians from Japan, Cuba, and the United States and still be Bolivian? And who gets to decide what is authentic? Bigenho discusses a kind of authenticity that she calls "unique authenticity," which refers to the individual artist's new, innovative, and personal production, such as the original compositions of creative musicians. Unique authenticity is "the founding myth of modern concepts of authorship and copyright" (Bigenho 2002, 20). It concerns who owns cultural products and raises the issue of whether it is possible to talk about collective creation and ownership of the music of a community, a people, an ethnic group.

Bigenho came face-to-face with this issue when she compiled a cassette of music from one of the villages in which she worked. While the villagers recognized that the music they played was composed by individuals, they felt strongly that ownership of the music was collective. In doing so, they moved from uniquely authentic individual compositions—intellectual property—to collective ownership of a "culturally authentic representation"—cultural property (Bigenho 2002, 217). When Bigenho went to La Paz to register the copyright, however, she found that it was impossible to register the cassette under collective authorship or ownership. Ironically, *she* as the compiler could register the work, but the people who created the work could not, unless they were willing to be recognized as individuals. According to Bolivian law, the music on the cassette was legally folklore, "the set of literary and artistic works created in national territory by unknown authors or by authors who do not identify themselves and are presumed to be nationals of the country, or of its ethnic communities, and that are transmitted from generation to generation, constituting one of the fundamental elements of traditional cultural patrimony of the nation" (221). As a result, the music was part of the "National Patrimony," and belonged to the nation-state. Given the context of Bolivian cultural and ethnic politics, Bigenho reports that the villagers decided to gain visibility and connections as a collective indigenous entity, which they believed would provide them with possible economic advantages. Whether this belief was accurate remains to be seen, but this example of the connections of art and authenticity can be found all over the world.

FIGURE 7.8 *Música de Maestros* in costume performing in a folklore festival in France.

Hip-Hop in Japan

An opposite case—where global popular culture is subject to pressures from the local situation into which it is adopted—comes from anthropologist Ian Condry's work on Japanese hip-hop. Starting in mid-1995, Condry spent a year and a half studying hip-hop in Japan, which began there in the 1980s and continues to develop. It seems to be an example of the expansion of a popular culture form from the United States into another part of the world, but Condry shows how Japanese artists and fans have adapted hip-hop so that it is Japanese (Figure 7.9).

On the face of it, the Japanese hip-hop scene looks very similar to that of the United States: "It is more than a little eerie to fly from New York to Tokyo and see teenagers in both places wearing the same kinds of fashion characteristic of rap fans: baggy pants with boxers on display, floppy hats or baseball caps, and immaculate space-age Nike sneakers" (Condry 2001, 373). But the similarities disguise some important differences—most Japanese rappers and fans only speak Japanese, they live at home with their parents, and they are the products of the Japanese educational system. Their day-to-day world is Japanese.

Moreover, to understand hip-hop in Japan requires understanding where the rap scene in Japan is located. For Tokyo, this site (Condry uses the Japanese word *genba* for the "actual site") is the network of all-night clubs, where the show starts at midnight and ends at 5:00 A.M., when the trains start to run again. The largest of these clubs can accommodate over 1,000 people on the weekend. Condry describes one of the bigger clubs, called "Harlem":

> On the wall behind the DJ stage, abstract videos, *anime* clips, or edited Kung Fu movies present a background of violence and mayhem, albeit with an Asian flavor. Strobe lights, steam, and moving spotlights give a strong sense of the space, and compound the crowded, frenetic feeling imposed by the loud music. The drunken revelry gives clubs an atmosphere of excitement that culminates with the live show and the following freestyle session. (376–7)

But it is not only the music that matters. People circulate through the club, sometimes making contact, sometimes doing business (promoters, magazine writers, or record company representatives are also often there), just being part of the scene. Condry notes that he found that the time between 3:00 and 4:00 A.M. was best for his fieldwork because the clubbers had exhausted their supplies of stories and gossip and were open to finding out what he was up to.

One striking experience that Condry observed was of a concert right after the New Year. "I was surprised to see all the clubbers who knew each other going around and saying the traditional New Year's greeting in very formal Japanese: 'Congratulations on the dawn of the New Year. I humbly request your benevolence this year as well.' There was no irony, no joking atmosphere in these statements" (380). As he remarks, "Japanese cultural practices do not disappear" just because people seem to conform to the style of global hip-hop. In the same way, the topics addressed in the lyrics speak in some way to the concerns of the listeners, ridiculing school and television or celebrating video games and young men's verbal play. Most striking, perhaps, is the repeated theme that youth need to speak out for themselves. Rapper MC Shiro of Rhymester remarked, "If I were to say what hip-hop is, it would be a 'culture of the first person singular.' In hip-hop, . . . rappers are always yelling, 'I'm this'" (383). While this may not appear to be the edgy, tough lyrics of U.S. rap,

FIGURE 7.9 A Japanese hip-hop singer performs at 3:30 A.M. at Club Core in Tokyo's Roppongi entertainment district. While the hip-hop scene in Japan may look similar to that in the United States, Ian Condry directs attention to some significant differences.

in the Japanese context, where the dominant ideology is that the harmony of the group should come before individual expression, the idea that people should speak for themselves is powerful. As we will see in chapter 14, this process of localizing the global is one that many anthropologists are now studying.

Sculpture and the Baule Gbagba Dance

The Baule of the Ivory Coast are renowned for their sculpture. Susan Vogel (1997), who has been studying Baule sculpture for over thirty years, identifies four forms of Baule sculpture, which she refers to as art that is watched (performances featuring carved masks), art that is seen without looking (sacred sculpture), art that is glimpsed (private sculptures of personal figures for hunting and sculpture for spirit spouses), and art that is visible to all (the profane; everyday objects that Baule see as beautiful trifles). As we saw in the last chapter, Baule visuality is distinctive; people learn to look in a way different from that of people in the West—"the more important a Baule sculpture is, the less it is displayed" (108).

The Western concept of "art" in the sense that it is used in Western languages does not exist in Baule villages. Rather, "to approach art from a Baule perspective entails speaking of experiences that are not primarily visual, and of art objects that are animate presences, indistinguishable from persons, spirits, and certain prosaic things." The Baule attribute great powers to their artwork—powers that Westerners would consider incredible. The meaning of most art objects, and the emotional responses that these objects have, derive from their ability to act. For the Baule, what Western museum-goers call sculpture contain enormous powers of life and death, and Baule people do not consider their sculpture apart from these powers (85).

We will consider one use of art objects in performance, the Gbagba dance. While anthropologists have often studied dance as an independent art form, we are looking here at the intersection of sculpture and dance. The Gbagba dance is an entertainment performance that lasts much of a day, and may also be performed for the funeral of an important woman. The style of mask that is used in the performance is called *Mblo*, and in the past, a village may have had as many as a dozen or more such masks, some representations of animals, some portraits of people. Portrait masks are usually of a specific woman, and the subject of the portrait always dances alongside the male dancer who dances the mask. Only the best dancers wear these masks, and they appear at the very end of the dance, sometimes right at dusk.

The Gbagba begins with skits that include non-masked performers, young dancers who are just getting started. The skits are supposed to be funny as they present scenes from everyday life from which a moral is drawn. These skits often feature masks of domestic animals—generally sheep and goats. These are followed by masks representing the large wild animals that the Baule hunt. These skits always end with the successful "killing" of the masked animal. Older, more skilled dancers are featured in these skits and there is more actual dancing.

At the same time that the first masks appear, so too does a costumed but not masked figure of a trickster figure, Ambomon, who wears a cloth hood rather than a mask and who dances in a rapid and acrobatic way, including somersaults and tumbling in his movements. Ambomon is a completely ambiguous figure, even to the Baule, who speculate as to whether or not he is a god. He has no respect for possessions, rank, and decent behavior. While comical, he also takes things from people, he sits on the ground, he gets things dirty. He never does any real damage, and people regard him as an amusing nuisance. He stands in direct contrast to the orderly vision of the world, as expressed by the masks; he is the sprit of disorder. Yet at the same time, Ambomon is the only figure in the dance that *must* appear—he can appear without any of the other masks, but the other masks cannot appear without him. When Gbagba is danced for a funeral, only Ambomon enters the courtyard to pay his respects to the deceased and to greet the mourners. Vogel suggests that the obligatory presence of Ambomon suggests that to the Baule the only certainty in life is the threat of disorder and death (167).

Vogel notes that Ambomon's style of dance is quite different from the ideal Baule dance style, which seems to minimize movement. She notes that a female solo dance moves forward very slowly in a curved line, with body and neck held upright, the hands in front, palms up. Sometimes the dancer carries something in her hand. The dancer's facial features are impassive, the eyes are downcast, and the main movement is in the neck, shoulders, and back, often marking two different rhythmic patterns in the polyrhythmic music. A male dancer may be a bit more vigorous, but "Baule dancing in general can be characterized as symmetrically balanced and essentially vertical (the dancer's knees may be flexed but the head and torso are held upright). As in so many other Baule creations, the dancer's body is closed in outline. These qualities are also characteristic of Baule sculpture, and must be recognized as expressing an aesthetic preference, with moral connotations, that is deeply embedded in Baule culture, and is expressed in myriad ways" (156).

Gbagba includes singing, and two of the songs that are repeated from time to time throughout the day refer to death. They are sung both when Gbagba is danced for women's funerals and when it is danced for entertainment. Finally, at the end of the day one or more portrait masks appear, one by one, each accompanied by its human "double." At that moment, the finest skills in the community are on display—the best dancers, the most beautiful masks, the best drummers and singers, and the distinguished women who are represented now take their places (see Figure 7.10).

The term "double" is the term that the Baule themselves use for the portrait mask and its subject. The portrait mask is considered the person's true double; the mask never performs unless the person is there to dance. Vogel tells us that the "relationships between individuals and their portrait masks are close, complex, and lifelong, and become elements of their identities" (166). When the subject of a portrait mask dies or cannot dance any more, a relative becomes the new double, or the mask is never danced again.

In sum, Vogel proposes that a Gbagba performance is a joyous occasion that brings together everyone in the village, of all ages and persuasions, in a happy celebration, the importance of which cannot be underestimated in a world with little entertainment or distractions.

> The performance teaches basic lessons about the Baule world—about hierarchies and mysteries. Each skit has a simple moral lesson, evident even to children: that humans, for example, with skill and supernatural aid, can dominate even the largest and most awesome wild animals, while the portrait masks present a model of human accomplishment and beauty. At the same time, the dance provides deeper insights about blurred boundaries—about the interpenetration of bush and village, and the complexity of gender. The subject of a portrait, most often a woman, sees herself impersonated by a man dancing "like a woman" and wearing a mask that is her double or namesake. A frequent theme of Baule

art is opposite-sex doubling, meaning that two figures appear not as a pair of complementary beings but as manifestations of a single being having qualities of both sexes. The concept is too troubling to articulate openly in words, but in Gbagba it is available to wordless contemplation. (Vogel 1997, 167–68)

The Mass Media: A Television Serial in Egypt

The mass media now include everything from film, radio, and television to comic books and the World Wide Web. As a result of global processes (chapter 14), these are now central to people's lives all over the world. Anthropologists can study the mass media from a variety of perspectives. Our approach in this chapter is to consider mass media as cultural productions. We highlight the creativity of producers and consumers of media in the interpretation and incorporation of these art forms. This is, perhaps, the most important thing anthropology can add to the study of media: the fine-grained ethnographic assessment of the effects and impact of popular media among the people who watch, listen, read, and interpret (cf. Herzfeld 2001, 298), and some of whom also create those media.

In many nations in the world, soap operas or television serials are among the most popular mass entertainments, watched by millions. These programs are seen by their creators in some parts of the world not simply as entertainment, but also as tools useful for teaching certain people in their societies what they need to learn to be modern citizens. But what the intended audience gets from the program is not always the message the creators thought they were transmitting. Anthropologist Lila Abu-Lughod studied an Egyptian television serial called

FIGURE 7.10 Portrait mask of Mya Yanso about to enter the Gbagba dance in the Baule village of Kami in 1972. The mask—an important object—is hidden by the cloths until the last moment, when the mask, its dancer, and its subject will appear dramatically in the performance.

In Their Own Words

Tango

Anthropologist Julie Taylor describes the traditional cultural understandings that inform the contexts in which the Argentine tanguero, or tango-man, dances the tango.

Traditionally, Argentines will not dance to a tango that is sung. If they danced they could not attend properly to the music and lyrics, or hear their own experience and identity revealed in the singer's and musicians' rendering of quintessential Argentine emotions. The singer of the tango shares his personal encounter with experiences common to them all. He does not need bold pronouncement or flamboyant gesture. His audience knows what he means and his feelings are familiar ones. They listen for the nuances—emotional and philosophical subtleties that will tell them something new about their guarded interior worlds.

When they dance to tangos, Argentines contemplate themes akin to those of tango lyrics, stimulating emotions that, despite an apparently contradictory choreography, are the same as those behind the songs. The choreography also reflects the world of the lyrics, but indirectly. The dance portrays an encounter between the powerful and completely dominant male and the passive, docile, completely submissive female. The passive woman and the rigidly controlled but physically aggressive man contrast poignantly with the roles of the sexes depicted in the tango lyrics. This contrast between two statements of relations between the sexes aptly mirrors the insecurities of life and identity.

An Argentine philosophy of bitterness, resentment, and pessimism has the same goal as a danced statement of machismo, confidence, and sexual optimism. The philosopher elaborates his schemes to demonstrate that he is a man of the world—that he is neither stupid nor naive. In the dance, the dancer acts as though he has none of the fears he cannot show—again proving that he is not gil. When an Argentine talks of the way he feels when dancing a tango, he describes an experience of total aggressive dominance over the girl, the situation, the world—an experience in which he vents his resentment and expresses his bitterness against a destiny that denied him this dominance. Beyond this, it gives him a moment behind the protection of this facade to ponder the history and the land that have formed him, the hopes he has treasured and lost. Sábato echoes widespread feeling in Argentina when he says "Only a gringo would make a clown of himself by taking advantage of a tango for a chat or amusement."

While thus dancing a statement of invulnerability, the somber tanguero sees himself, because of his sensitivity, his great capacity to love, and his fidelity to the true ideals of his childhood years, as basically vulnerable. As he protects himself with a facade of steps that demonstrate perfect control, he contemplates his absolute lack of control in the face of history and destiny. The nature of the world has doomed him to disillusionment, to a solitary existence in the face of the impossibility of perfect love and the intimacy this implies. If by chance the girl with whom he dances feels the same sadness, remembering similar disillusion, the partners do not dance sharing the sentiment. They dance together to relive their disillusion alone. In a Buenos Aires dance hall, a young man turned to me from the fiancee he had just relinquished to her chaperoning mother and explained, "In the tango, together with the girl—and it does not matter who she is—a man remembers the bitter moments of his life, and he, she, and all who are dancing contemplate a universal emotion. I do not like the woman to talk to me while I dance tango. And if she speaks I do not answer. Only when she says to me, 'Omar, I am speaking,' I answer, 'And I, I am dancing.'"

Source: Taylor 1987, 484–85.

Hilmiyya Nights that was broadcast during Ramadan (the Islamic holy month) over five successful years. The serial followed the fortunes and relationships of a group of characters from the traditional Cairo neighborhood of Hilmiyya, taking them from the late 1940s, when Egypt was under the rule of King Farouk and the British, up to the early 1990s, even incorporating Egyptian reaction to the first Gulf War.

The central action revolved around the rivalry, financial wheeling-dealing, and love interests of two wealthy men—in many ways it resembles an Egyptian version of *Dallas.* What separated *Hilmiyya Nights* from prime-time serials from the United States, however, was that the Egyptian program attempted to tie the lives of its characters to Egyptian national political events. Above all, it promoted the theme of national unity. With few exceptions, all the characters were shown to be basically good and patriotic.

Abu-Lughod studied two separate groups of Egyptians during the 1990s—poor working-class women in Cairo and villagers in Upper Egypt (see EthnoProfile 6.5: Cairo). When she asked poor women in Cairo what they liked about the show, they volunteered not the serious political or social messages but two women characters: the glamorous, aristocratic femme fatale and the arrogant belly-dancer turned cabaret-owner. Although these two characters were hardly respectable and ended badly, these were nevertheless favorites because they defied the moral system that kept good women quiet. Indeed, Abu-Lughod found that both the urban women and the villagers accepted the moral stances presented in the program only when they resonated with their own worlds and ignored those aspects of the serial that were not part of their experience.

Most interestingly, she argues that television, especially for the villagers, created its own world, one that was part of, but only a small part of, the villagers' daily lives. "What they experienced through television added to, but did not displace, whatever else already existed. They treated the television world not as a fantasy escape but as a sphere unto itself with its familiar time slots and specific attitudes" (Abu-Lughod 1995, 203–4). Moreover, the villagers did not compartmentalize the "modernity" that television serials present in order to preserve a "traditional" community untouched by the outside world. On the contrary, these villagers are deeply affected in a wide variety of ways by the outside world, whether through local government policies or transnationally through the effect of advertising by multinational corporations. "Television is, in this village, one part of a complex jumble of life and the dramatic experiences and visions it offers are surprisingly easily incorporated as discrete—not overwhelming—elements in the jumble" (205).

Television in Egypt, she notes, has had measurable social effects: For example, families prefer to stay home to watch television rather than visit among households in the evenings. Television may also have increased the number of "experiences" shared across generation and gender, as young and old, men and women, now spend time together watching the television.

The intended impact of *Hilmiyya Nights* was not undermined because nobody was watching television: Both villagers and urban poor had their sets on almost constantly. Rather, the positive messages that the creators of *Hilmiyya Nights* and similar serials intended got lost because they are only part of the complex flow of programming in Egypt, which includes many kinds of other information, news, entertainment, advertising, and so on.

More important, all these messages are evaluated in terms of the life experiences of the viewers. Hence they are often neutralized or contradicted by the powerful everyday realities within which poor Egyptian villagers and urban women move. Even soap operas are contested sites, open for multiple interpretations, not simply places for the transmission of messages from the elite to the masses.

What Is Myth?

We have suggested that play lies at the heart of human creativity. However, the openness of play is random and thus just as likely to undermine the social order as to enhance it. Hence societies tend to circumscribe play with cultural rules, channeling it in directions that appear less destructive.

Rules designed to limit artistic expression are one result of this channeling process. As we have seen, artists in various media are permitted a wide range of expression as long as they adhere to rules governing the form that expression takes. Societies differ in how loose or strict the rules of artistic form may be. Artists who challenge the rules, however, are often viewed negatively by those in power, who believe they have the right to restrict artistic expressions that question social, religious, or sexual precepts that ought not to be questioned.

In fact, all societies depend on the willingness of their members *not* to question certain assumptions about the way the world works. Because the regularity and predictability of social life might collapse altogether if people were free to imagine, and act upon, alternatives to the local version of paramount reality, most societies find ways to persuade their members that the local version of reality is the only reality, period. The most venerable way of doing this is through the use of myth.

Myths are stories that recount how various aspects of the world came to be the way they are. The power of myths comes from their ability to make life meaningful for those who accept them. The truth of myths seems self-evident because they do such a good job of integrating personal experiences with a wider set of understandings about how the way the world works.

A conventional definition of myth emphasizes that they are stories about the sacred, as that is defined among a particular group of people. Often these are stories about beginnings—of the natural world, the social world, or the cosmos—or of endings—of time, humanity, the gods, or the cosmos. The term may also be used to refer to "ahistorical stories that are used to validate power relationships, which make the social appear natural and preexistent" (Bowie 2006, 267). As stories that involve a teller and an audience, myths are performances, products of high verbal art (and increasingly of cinematic art). Frequently the

---

myths Stories whose truth seems self-evident because they do such a good job of integrating our personal experiences with a wider set of assumptions about the way society, or the world in general, must operate.

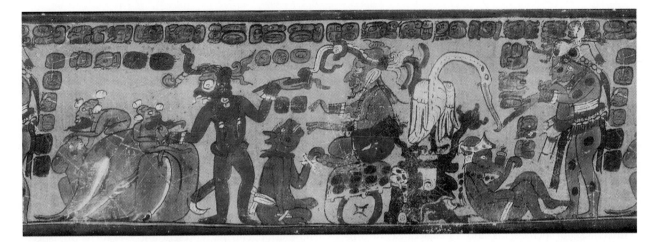

FIGURE 7.11   A vase painting illustrating part of the *Popul Vuh*, the Mayan creation story.

official myth tellers are the ruling groups in society: the elders, the political leaders, the religious specialists. They may also be considered master storytellers. The content of myths usually concerns past events (usually at the beginning of time) or future events (usually at the end of time). Myths are socially important because, if they are taken literally, they tell people where they have come from and where they are going and, thus, how they should live right now (Figure 7.11).

Societies differ in the degree to which they permit speculation about key myths. In complex Western societies, like that of the United States, many different groups, each with its own mythic tradition, often live side by side. Ironically, citizens' rights to do so without state interference are guaranteed in mythic statements from documents crafted at the time of this country's founding. Consider the "self-evident" truths proclaimed in the U.S. Declaration of Independence: "that all men are created equal, that they are endowed by their Creator with certain inalienable rights, that among these rights are life, liberty, and the pursuit of happiness." Despite the imperfect realization of these rights over the centuries, Americans still appeal to the "self-evident" truths enshrined in the Declaration of Independence in ongoing struggles to establish the equality of all citizens under the law. That is, U.S. citizens are striving to bring their lived reality in line with the Declaration's mythic promise, the truth of which remains unquestioned.

Myths and related beliefs that are taken to be self-evident truths are sometimes codified in an explicit manner. When this codification is extreme and deviation from the code is treated harshly, we sometimes speak of **orthodoxy** (or "correct doctrine"). Societies differ in the degree to which they require members to adhere to orthodox interpretations of key myths. But even societies that place little emphasis on orthodoxy are likely to exert some control over the interpretation of key myths,

because myths have implications for action. They may justify past action, explain present action, or generate future action. To be persuasive, myths must offer plausible explanations for our experience of human nature, human society, and human history.

The success of Western science has led many members of Western societies to dismiss nonscientific myths as flawed attempts at science or history. Only recently have some scientists come to recognize the similarities between scientific and nonscientific storytelling about such events as the origin of life on earth. Scientific stories about origins—*origin myths*—must be taken to the *natural* world to be matched against material evidence; the success of this match determines whether they are accepted or rejected. By contrast, nonscientific origin myths get their vitality from how well they match up with the *social* world.

How Does Myth Reflect—and Shape—Social Action?

Early in the twentieth century, anthropologist Bronislaw Malinowski introduced a new approach to myth. He believed that to understand myths, we must understand the social context in which they are embedded. Malinowski argued that myths serve as "charters" or "justifications" for present-day social arrangements. In other words, a myth operates much like the Declaration of Independence. That is, the myth contains some "self-evident" truth that explains why society is as it is and why it cannot be changed. If the social arrangements justified by the myth are challenged, the myth can be used as a weapon against the challengers.

orthodoxy "Correct doctrine"; the prohibition of deviation from approved mythic texts.

Malinowski's famous example is of the origin myths of the Trobriand Islanders ([1926] 1948; see EthnoProfile 3.4: Trobriand Islanders). Members of every significant kinship grouping knew, marked and retold the history of the place from which their group's ancestress and her brother had emerged from the depths of the earth. These origin myths were set in the time before history began. Each ancestress-and-brother pair brought a distinct set of characteristics that included special objects and knowledge, various skills, crafts, spells, and the like. On reaching the surface, the pair took possession of the land. That is why, Malinowski was told, the people on a given piece of land had rights to it. It is also why they possessed a particular set of spells, skills, and crafts. Because the original sacred beings were a woman and her brother, the origin myth could also be used to endorse present-day membership in a Trobriand clan, which depends on a person's ability to trace kinship links through women to that clan's original ancestress. A brother and a sister represent the prototypical members of a clan because they are both descended from the ancestress through female links. Should anyone question the wisdom of organizing society in this way, the myth could be cited as proof that this is indeed the correct way to live.

In Trobriand society, Malinowski found, clans were ranked relative to one another in terms of prestige. To account for this ranking, Trobrianders refer to another myth. In the Trobriand myth that explains rank, one clan's ancestor, the dog, emerged from the earth before another clan's ancestor, the pig, thus justifying ranking the dog clan highest in prestige. To believe in this myth, Malinowski asserted, is to accept a transcendent justification for the ranking of clans. Malinowski made it clear, however, that if social arrangements change, the myth changes too—in order to justify the new arrangements. At some point, the dog clan was replaced in prominence by the pig clan. This social change resulted in a change in the mythic narrative. The dog was said to have eaten food that was taboo. In so doing, the dog gave up its claim to higher rank. Thus, to understand a myth and its transformations, one must understand the social organization of the society that makes use of it.

Do Myths Help Us Think?

Beginning in the mid-1950s, a series of books and articles by the French anthropologist Claude Lévi-Strauss ([1962] 1967) transformed the study of myth. Lévi-Strauss argues that myths have meaningful structures that are worth studying in their own right, quite apart from the uses to which the myths may be put. He suggested that myths should be interpreted the way we interpret musical scores. In a piece of music, the meaning emerges not just from

the melody but also from the harmony. In other words, the structure of the piece of music, the way in which each line of the music contributes to the overall sound and is related to other lines carries the meaning.

For Lévi-Strauss, myths are tools for overcoming logical contradictions that cannot otherwise be overcome. They are put together in an attempt to deal with the oppositions of particular concern to a particular society at a particular moment in time. Using a linguistic metaphor, Lévi-Strauss argues that myths are composed of smaller units—phrases, sentences, words, relationships—that are arranged in ways that give both narrative (or "melodic") coherence and structural (or "harmonic") coherence. These arrangements represent and comment on aspects of social life that are thought to oppose each other. Examples include the opposition of men to women; opposing rules of residence after marriage (living with the groom's father or the bride's mother); the opposition of the natural world to the cultural world, of life to death, of spirit to body, of high to low, and so on.

The complex syntax of myth works to relate those opposed pairs to one another in an attempt to overcome their contradictions. However, these contradictions can never be overcome; for example, the opposition of death to life is incapable of any earthly resolution. But myth can transform an insoluble problem into a more accessible, concrete form. Mythic narrative can then provide the concrete problem with a solution. For example, a culture hero may bridge the opposition between death and life by traveling from the land of the living to the land of the dead and back. Alternatively, a myth might propose that the beings who transcend death are so horrific that death is clearly preferable to eternal life. Perhaps a myth describes the journey of a bird that travels from the earth, the home of the living, to the sky, the home of the dead. This is similar to Christian thought, where the death and resurrection of Jesus may be understood to resolve the opposition between death and life by transcending death.

From this point of view, myths do not just talk about the world as it is, but they also describe the world as it might be. To paraphrase Lévi-Strauss, myths are good to think with; mythic thinking can propose other ways to live our lives. Lévi-Strauss insists, however, that the alternatives myths propose are ordinarily rejected as impossible. Thus, even though myths allow for play with self-evident truths, this play remains under strict control.

Is Lévi-Strauss correct? There has been a great deal of debate on this issue since the publication in 1955 of his article "The Structural Study of Myth" (see Lévi-Strauss [1962] 1967). But even those who are most critical of his analyses of particular myths agree that mythic structures are meaningful because they display the ability of human beings to play with possibilities as they attempt to deal with basic contradictions at the heart of human experience.

For Malinowski, Lévi-Strauss, and their followers, those who believe in myths are not conscious of how their myths are structured or of the functions their myths perform for them. More recent anthropological thinking takes a more reflexive approach. This research recognizes that ordinary members of a society often *are* aware of how their myths structure meaning, allowing them to manipulate the way myths are told or interpreted in order to make an effect, to prove a point, or to buttress a particular referential perspective on human nature, society, or history.

What Is Ritual?

Play allows unlimited consideration of alternative perspectives on reality. Art permits consideration of alternative perspectives, but certain limitations restricting the form and content are imposed. Myth aims to narrow radically the possible perspectives and often promotes a single, orthodox perspective presumed to be valid for everyone. It thus offers a kind of intellectual indoctrination. But because societies aim to shape action as well as thought to orient all human faculties in the approved direction, art, myth, and ritual are often closely associated with one another. In this section, we will look at ritual as it appears as a form of action in a variety of societies.

A Definition of Ritual

For many people in Western societies, rituals are presumed to be "religious"—for example, weddings, Jewish bar mitzvahs, Hmong sacrifices to the ancestors, or the Catholic Mass. For anthropologists, however, rituals also include such practices as scientific experiments, college graduation ceremonies, procedures in a court of law, and children's birthday parties.

In order to capture this range of activities, our definition of **ritual** has four parts. First, ritual is a *repetitive social practice* composed of a sequence of symbolic activities in the form of dance, song, speech, gestures, the manipulation of certain objects, and so forth. Second, it is *set off* from the social routines of everyday life. Third, rituals in any culture adhere to a characteristic, culturally defined *ritual schema*. This means that members of a culture can tell that a certain sequence of activities is a ritual even if they have never seen that particular ritual before. Finally, ritual action is closely connected to a specific set of ideas that are often *encoded in myth*. These ideas might concern the nature of evil, the relationship of human

beings to the spirit world, how people ought to interact with one another, and so forth. The purpose for which a ritual is performed guides how these ideas are selected and symbolically enacted. What gives rituals their power is that the people who perform the rituals assert that the authorization for the ritual comes from outside themselves—from the state, society, a divine being, god, the ancestors, or "tradition." They have not made up the ritual themselves (although they may have contributed to it, as when people create their own wedding vows); rather it connects them to a source of power that they do not control but that controls them.

A Birthday Party as Ritual

Consider a young child's birthday party in the United States. Several children are formally invited to help celebrate the birthday. Each arrives bringing a wrapped gift, which is handed to the birthday child and then set aside. The children often put on birthday hats. They then play group games of some kind, some of which are now *only* played at birthday parties. The games culminate in the appearance of a birthday cake, illuminated by candles (one for each year of the child's life) and accompanied by the singing of "Happy Birthday." The birthday child makes a wish and blows out the candles. Following the cake and ice cream, the birthday child opens the presents. There is much commotion as the guests urge the birthday child to open theirs first. As the birthday child opens each gift, he or she examines it and thanks the guest (often with an adult's prompting). Shortly after the presents are opened, the guests' parents or guardians appear and the guests receive party favors and leave.

The ritual order of these events matters. The central events of the party—the giving of gifts; the events associated with the cake, candles, the wish, and the singing of "Happy Birthday"; and the opening of the gifts—must occur in that order. Additionally, if you, the reader, come from a tradition in which birthday parties are celebrated, it is likely that you cannot remember *learning* how to celebrate a birthday party—it is something you have always known. It's what everyone does. It's just how it is. Its authority comes from "tradition."

In the birthday party, children (both hosts and guests) learn to associate receiving gifts with important moments in life. They discover the importance of exchanging

---

ritual A repetitive social practice composed of a sequence of symbolic activities in the form of dance, song, speech, gestures, or the manipulation of objects, adhering to a culturally defined ritual schema, and closely connected to a specific set of ideas that are often encoded in myth.

material objects in defining significant social relations. They learn to defer gratification (the presents cannot be opened immediately). They live out patterns of sociability and friendship (as anyone knows who has heard the ultimate preschool threat, "I'm not inviting you to my birthday party") while recognizing the centrality of the individual (there are few things worse than sharing your birthday party with someone else!). Finally, the children participate in patterns of sharing, of celebrating the self, and of recognizing relationships with friends and kin that are important in other areas of American life.

What Is Ritual Action?

A ritual has a particular sequential ordering of acts, utterance, and events: That is, ritual has a *text*. Because ritual is action, however, we must pay attention to the way the ritual text is performed. The *performance* of a ritual cannot be separated from its text; text and performance shape each other. Through ritual performance, the ideas of a culture become concrete, take on a form, and, as Bruce Kapferer (1983) puts it, give direction to the gaze of participants. At the same time, ritual performers are not robots but active individuals whose choices are guided by, but not rigidly dictated by, previous ritual texts; ritual performance can serve as a commentary on the text to the extent of transforming it.

For example, Jewish synagogue ritual following the reading of Torah (the Five Books of Moses, the Hebrew Bible) includes lifting the Torah scroll, showing it to the congregation, and then closing it and covering it. In some Conservative synagogues, a man and a woman, often a couple, are called to lift and cover the Torah: The man lifts it and, after he seats himself, the woman rolls the scroll closed, places the tie around it, and covers it with the mantle that protects it. One of the authors (RHL) once observed a performance of this ritual in which the woman lifted the Torah and the man wrapped it; officially, the ritual text was carried out, but the performance became a commentary on the text—on the role of women in Judaism, on the Torah as an appropriate subject of attention for women as well as for men, on the roles of men and women overall, and so on. The performance was noteworthy—indeed, many of the regular members of the congregation seemed quite surprised—precisely because it violated people's expectations, and in so doing, directed people's attention toward the role of men and women in Jewish religious ritual in the United States at the end of the twentieth century as well as toward the Torah as the central symbol of the Jewish people.

rite of passage A ritual that serves to mark the movement and transformation of an individual from one social position to another.

What Are Rites of Passage?

Graduating from college, getting married, joining the military, and other "life-cycle" rituals share certain important features, most notably that people begin the ritual as one kind of person (student, single, recruit, etc.), and by the time the ritual is over, they have been transformed into a different kind of person (graduate, spouse, soldier, etc.). These rituals are called **rites of passage**. At the beginning of the twentieth century, the Belgian anthropologist Arnold Van Gennep noted that certain kinds of rituals around the world had similar structures. These were rituals associated with the movement (or passage) of people from one position in the social structure to another. They included births, initiations, confirmations, weddings, funerals, and the like (Figure 7.12).

Van Gennep (1960) found that all these rituals began with a period of *separation* from the old position and from normal time. During this period, the ritual passenger left behind the symbols and practices of his or her previous position. For example, military recruits leave their families behind and are moved to a new place. They are forced to leave behind the clothing, activities, and even the hair that marked who they were in civilian life.

The second stage in rites of passage involves a period of *transition*, in which the ritual passenger is neither in the old life nor yet in the new one. This period is marked by rolelessness, ambiguity, and perceived danger. Often, the person involved is subjected to ordeal by those who have already passed through. In the military service, this is the period of basic training, in which recruits (not yet soldiers but no longer civilians) are forced to dress and act alike. They are subjected to a grinding-down process, after which they are rebuilt into something new.

During the final stage—*reaggregation*—the ritual passenger is reintroduced into society in his or her new position. In the military, this involves the graduation from basic training and a visit home, but this time as a member of the armed forces, in uniform and on leave—in other words, as a new person. Other familiar rites of passage in youth culture in the United States include high school graduation and the informal, yet significant ceremonies associated with the twenty-first birthday, both of which are understood as movements from one kind of person to another.

The work of Victor Turner has greatly increased our understanding of rites of passage. Turner concentrated on the period of transition, which he saw as important both for the rite of passage and for social life in general. Van Gennep referred to this part of a rite of passage as the liminal period, from the Latin *limen* ("threshold"). During this period, the individual is on the threshold, betwixt and between, neither here nor there, neither in

In Their Own Words

Video in the Villages

Patricia Aufderheide describes how indigenous peoples of the Amazonian rain forest in Brazil have been able to master the video camera and use it for their own purposes.

The social role and impact of video is particularly intriguing among people who are new to mass-communications technologies, such as lowlands Amazonian Indians. One anthropologist has argued persuasively that a naive disdain for commercial media infuses much well-meaning concern over the potential dangers of introducing mass media and that "indigenous media offers a possible means—social, cultural, and political—for reproducing and transforming cultural identity among people who have experienced massive political, geographic, and economic disruption." . . . In two groups of Brazilian Indians, the Nambikwara and the Kayapo, this premise has been tested.

The Nambikwara became involved with video through Video in the Villages, run by Vincent Carelli at the Centro de Trabalho Indigenista in São Paulo. This project is one example of a trend to put media in the hands of people who have long been the subjects of ethnographic film and video. . . . While some anthropologists see this resort as a "solution" to the issue of ethnographic authority, others have focused on it as part of a struggle for indigenous rights and political autonomy. . . . Many of the groups Carelli has worked with have seized on video for its ability to extensively document lengthy rituals that mark the group's cultural uniqueness rather than produce a finished product. . . .

Carelli coproduced a project with a Nambikwara leader, documenting a cultural ritual. After taping, the Nambikwara viewed the ritual and offered criticisms, finding it tainted with modernisms. They then repeated the ritual in traditional regalia and conducted, for the first time in a generation, a male initiation ceremony—taping it all. (This experience is recounted in a short tape, Girls' Puberty Ritual, produced by Carelli with a Nambikwara leader for outsiders.) Using video reinforced an emerging concept of "traditional" in contrast to Brazilian culture—a concept that had not, apparently, been part of the Nambikwara's repertoire before contact but that had practical political utility.

The Kayapo are among the best-known Brazilian Indians internationally, partly because of their video work, promoted as a tool of cultural identification by the anthropologist who works most closely with them. Like other tribes such as the Xavante who had extensive contact with Brazilian authorities and media, the Kayapo early seized on modern media technologies. . . . Besides intimidating authorities with the evidence of recording equipment . . . , the Kayapo quickly grasped the symbolic expectations of Brazilian mass media for Indians. They cannily played on the contrast between their feathers and body paint and their recording devices to get coverage. Even staging public events for the purpose of attracting television crews, they were able to insert, although not ultimately control, their message on Brazilian news by exploiting that contrast. . . . Using these techniques, Kayapo leaders became international symbols of the ironies of the postmodern age and not incidentally also the subjects of international agitation and fundraising that benefited Kayapo over other indigenous groups and some Kayapo over others.

Kayapo have also used video to document internal cultural ceremonies in meticulous detail; to communicate internally between villages; to develop an archive; and to produce clips and short documentaries intended for wide audiences. Their video work, asserts anthropologist Terence Turner, has not merely preserved traditional customs but in fact transformed their understanding of those customs as customs and their culture as a culture. Turner also found that video equipment, expertise, and products often fed into existing factional divisions. Particular Kayapo leaders used the equipment in their own interests, sometimes as a tool to subdue their enemies, sometimes as evidence of personal power. . . .

Source: Aufderheide 1993, 587–89.

nor out. Turner notes that the symbolism accompanying the rite of passage often expresses this ambiguous state. **Liminality**, he tells us, "is frequently likened to death, to being in the womb, to invisibility, to darkness, to bisexuality, to the wilderness, and to an eclipse of the sun or moon" (1969, 95). People in the liminal state tend to develop an intense comradeship with each other in which their nonliminal distinctions disappear or become irrelevant. Turner calls this kind of social relationship **communitas**, which is best understood as an unstructured or minimally structured community of equal individuals.

liminality The ambiguous transitional state in a rite of passage in which the person or persons undergoing the ritual are outside their ordinary social positions.

communitas An unstructured or minimally structured community of equal individuals found frequently in rites of passage.

FIGURE 7.12 Rites of passage are rituals that enable people to move from one position in the social structure to another. Here, in June 2004, an Apache girl, accompanied by her godmother and a helper, moves into adulthood through the Sunrise Dance.

Turner contends that all societies need some kind of communitas as much as they need structure. Communitas gives "recognition to an essential and generic human bond, without which there could be no society" (1969, 97). That bond is the common humanity that underlies all culture and society. However, periods of communitas (often in ritual context) are brief. Communitas is dangerous, not just because it threatens structure but because it threatens survival itself. During the time of communitas, the things that structure ensures—production of food and physical and social reproduction of the society—cannot be provided. Someone always has to take out the garbage and clean up after the party. Thus, communitas gives way to structure, which in turn generates a need for the release of communitas.

The feeling of oneness reported in the earlier anecdote about the Ali-Foreman fight is communitas, and communitas is also possible in play and art. For people in contemporary nation-states the experience of communitas may well come through the climactic winning moments of a sports team, attendance at large-scale rock concerts, or participation in mass public events like Carnival in Rio, the Greenwich Village Halloween parade, or Mardi Gras in New Orleans.

How Are Play and Ritual Complementary?

How does the logic of ritual differ from the logic of play? Play and ritual are complementary forms of metacommunication (Handelman 1977). The movement from nonplay to play is based on the premise of metaphor ("Let's make-believe"); the movement to ritual is based on the premise of literalness ("Let's believe"). From the perspective of the everyday social order, the result of these contrasting premises is the "inauthenticity" of play and the "truth" of ritual.

Because of the connection of ritual with self-evident truth, the metacommunication of the ritual frame ("This is ritual") is associated with an additional metacommunication: "All messages within this frame are true." It is ritual that asserts *what should be* to play's *what can be*. The ritual frame is more rigid than the play frame. Consequently, ritual is the most stable liminal domain, whereas play is the most flexible. Players can move with relative ease into and out of play, but such is not the case with ritual.

Finally, play usually has little effect on the social order of ordinary life. This permits play a wide range of commentary on the social order. Ritual is different: its role is explicitly to maintain the status quo, including the prescribed ritual transformations. Societies differ in the extent to which ritual behavior alternates with everyday, nonritual behavior. When nearly every act of everyday life is ritualized and other forms of behavior are strongly discouraged, we sometimes speak of **orthopraxy** ("correct practice"). Traditionally observant Jews and Muslims, for example, lead a highly ritualized daily life, attempting from the moment they awaken until the moment they fall asleep to carry out even the humblest of activities in a manner that is ritually correct. In their view, ritual correctness is the result of God's law, and it is their duty and joy to conform their every action to God's will.

Ritual may seem overwhelming and all powerful. Yet individuals and groups within a society can sometimes

orthopraxy "Correct practice"; the prohibition of deviation from approved forms of ritual behavior.

EthnoProfile 7.4

Yoruba

Region: Western Africa

Nation: Nigeria

Population: 40,000,000

Environment: Coastal and forest

Livelihood: Farming, commerce, modern professions

Political organization: Traditionally, kingdoms; today, part of a modern nation-state

For more information: Bascom, William. 1969. *The Yoruba of southwestern Nigeria.* New York: Holt, Rinehart and Winston.

manipulate ritual forms to achieve nontraditional ends. This can range from pushing against tradition as far as it can go without actually destroying the ritual (as when a bride and groom have an alternative wedding outdoors, write their own vows, and still have a member of the clergy officiating) to emphasizing the importance of one ritual and ignoring or downplaying another (as when Protestant Baptists downplayed the communion ritual and emphasized the baptism ritual as a way of articulating their challenge to Roman Catholicism) to exchanging one set of rituals for another (as when lone rural migrants to the cities of northern Cameroon convert to Islam shortly after their arrival, abandoning their traditional rituals together with the rural way of life into which they were born).

Margaret Drewal argues that, at least among the Yoruba, play and ritual overlap (see EthnoProfile 7.4: Yoruba). Yoruba rituals combine spectacle, festival, play, sacrifice, and so on and integrate diverse media—music, dance, poetry, theater, sculpture (1992, 198). They are events that require improvisatory, spontaneous individual moves; as a result, the mundane order is not only inverted and reversed but may also be subverted through power play and gender play. For example, gender roles are rigidly structured in Yoruba society. Yoruba rituals, however, allow some crossdressing by both men and women, providing institutionalized opportunities for men and women to cross gender boundaries and to express the traits that Yoruba consider to be characteristic of the opposite sex,

sometimes as parody but sometimes seriously and respectfully (190).

How Do Cultural Practices Combine Play, Art, Myth, and Ritual?

Many anthropologists have suggested that play, art, myth, and ritual may be, and often are, experienced together. Bruce Kapferer has made these connections clear in a study of demon exorcism in Sri Lanka (see EthnoProfile 7.5: Sinhalese). The demon exorcism ceremonies of the Sinhalese Buddhist working class and peasantry last an entire night and are designed to cure disease. The performance combines in "a marvelous spectacle" ritual, comedy, music, and dance. Its goal is "to change the experiential condition of [the] patients and to bring patients back into a normal conception of the world" (1983, 177, 236). In other words, the entire performance is transformative. During the course of the ceremony, a demonic reality is created and then destroyed.

At the beginning of the exorcism, the patient and the audience are in different realities. The audience is in the reality of everyday life; the patient is in the alternative reality of his or her illness. In that reality, demons are central and powerful actors. During the Evening Watch, through music, song, and eventually dance, the audience becomes increasingly engaged in this alternative reality. In this part of the ceremony, the demons are portrayed as figures of horror.

At midnight, the process is complete: The audience has joined the patient's reality. The demons, played by actors, appear. At this point, the Midnight Watch begins. This part of the ceremony is a comic drama that lasts until nearly 3:00 A.M. The eruption of comedy into what had been an intensely serious ceremony transforms the demons into figures of ridicule. Through the comedy, the demonic reality begins to fragment as the gods appear and reassert their dominance. As this occurs, the sick person begins to see that the demons are really subordinate to the gods, not superior to them.

The last part of the exorcism is the Morning Watch, which continues until 6:00 A.M. During this period, the patient and audience become reengaged in the reality of ordinary life. The final comic drama of the performance "confirms the demonic absurdity, and destroys the demonic as powerful and relevant to normal experience in daily life" (Kapferer 1983, 220). Having played on the

EthnoProfile 7.5

Sinhalese

Region: Southern Asia

Nation: Sri Lanka (city: Galle)

Population: 15,000,000 (population of Galle: 95,000)

Environment: Tropical island

Livelihood: Farming, urban life

Political organization: Highly stratified state

For more information: Kapferer, Bruce. 1983. *A celebration of demons.* Bloomington: Indiana University Press.

mind, body, and emotions of the patient and the audience, the performance ends.

To understand the performance as a whole, the interactions of all aspects of the performance must be grasped. Kapferer calls this the ceremony's *aesthetics*. He argues that the ceremony succeeds because it is composed of many different parts that fit together in a way that is satisfying to the Sinhalese. Only in the aesthetic realm are ideas, symbolic objects, and actions brought into the relationship from which their meaning comes.

Play, art, myth, and ritual are different facets of the holistic human capacity to view the world from a variety of perspectives. The human capacity to play is channeled in different directions in different cultures, but it is always present. When the products of this containment process come together in key cultural productions, such as the Sinhalese curing ceremony, they display both the opportunities and dangers that result from open human creativity.

Chapter Summary

1. Play is a generalized form of behavioral openness: the ability to think about, speak about, and do different things in the same way or the same thing in different ways. Play can be thought of as a way of organizing activities, not merely a set of activities. We put a frame that consists of the message "this is play" around certain activities, thereby transforming them into play. Play also permits reflexive consideration of alternative realities by setting up a separate reality and suggesting that the perspective of ordinary life is only one way to make sense of experience.

2. The functions of play include exercise, practice for the real world, increased creativity in children, and commentary on the real world.

3. The fate of national sports teams can come to represent the nation itself, and the devotion of sports fans becomes a way of affirming patriotism. When sports are translated from one culture to another, they are frequently transformed to fit the patterns appropriate to the new culture.

4. Art is a kind of play that is subject to certain culturally appropriate restrictions on form and content. It aims to evoke a holistic, aesthetic response from the artist and the observer. It succeeds when the form is culturally appropriate for the content and is technically perfect in its realization. Aesthetic evaluations are culturally shaped value judgments. We recognize art in other cultures because of its family resemblance to what we call art in our own culture. Although people with other cultural understandings may not have produced art by intention, we can often successfully appreciate what they have created as art by appropriation. These issues are addressed in ethnographic studies that call into question received ideas about what counts as "authentic" art.

5. Myths are stories that recount how various aspects of the world came to be the way they are. Their truth seems self-evident because they do such a good job of integrating personal experiences with a wider set of assumptions about the way the world works. As stories, myths are the products of high verbal art. A full understanding of myth requires ethnographic background information.

6. Ritual is a repetitive social practice composed of sequences of symbolic activities such as speech, singing, dancing, gestures, and the manipulation of certain objects. In studying ritual, we pay attention not just to the symbols but also to how the ritual is performed. Cultural ideas are made concrete through ritual action.

7. Rites of passage are rituals in which members of a culture move from one position in the social structure to another. These rites are marked by periods of separation, transition, and reaggregation. During the period of transition, individuals occupy a liminal position. All those in this position frequently develop an intense comradeship and a feeling of oneness, or communitas.

8. Ritual and play are complementary. Play is based on the premise "Let us make-believe," while ritual is based on the premise "Let us believe." As a result, the ritual frame is far more rigid than the play frame. Although ritual may seem overwhelming and all-powerful, individuals and groups can sometimes manipulate ritual forms to achieve nontraditional ends.

For Review

1. Take the definition of play in the running glossary at the bottom of page 146 and explain the importance of each feature of this complex definition.
2. What are the consequences of play for animals?
3. What is metacommunication?
4. Explain the significance of the case study by Elizabeth Chin about African American girls and their dolls in New Haven, Connecticut.
5. How does sport differ from "pure" play?
6. Discuss how sport is involved with identity.
7. What are the main features of the definition of art offered in the text, and why are they important?
8. Distinguish "art by intention" from "art by appropriation."
9. What major points are made in the text concerning the role of "authenticity" in art? How does the case study illustrate these points?
10. What are myths?
11. Compare Malinowski's view of myth with the view of Claude Lévi-Strauss.
12. Explain the significance of each of the major parts of the definition of ritual given in the text.
13. How may a child's birthday party be understood as a ritual?
14. Describe each stage of a rite of passage.
15. How are play and ritual complementary?

Key Terms

play	sport	myths	liminality
metacommunication	art	orthodoxy	communitas
framing	transformation-	ritual	orthopraxy
reflexivity	representation	rite of passage	

Suggested Readings

Alland, Alexander. 1977. *The artistic animal.* New York: Doubleday Anchor. An introductory look at the biocultural bases for art. This work is very well written, very clear, and fascinating.

Blanchard, Kendall. 1995. *The anthropology of sport.* Rev. ed. Westport, CT: Bergin and Garvey. An excellent introduction to the field.

Carter, Thomas. 2008. *The quality of home runs.* Durham, NC: Duke University Press. An excellent study of baseball in Cuba.

Errington, Shelly. 1998. *The death of authentic primitive art and other tales of progress.* Berkeley: University of California Press. A sharp and witty book about the production, distribution, interpretation, and selling of "primitive art."

Kapferer, Bruce. 1989. *A celebration of demons.* 2d ed. Washington, DC: Smithsonian Institution Press. An advanced text that is well worth reading.

Lever, Janet. 1995. *Soccer madness.* Prospect Heights, IL: Waverland Press. A fascinating study of soccer in Brazil.

Steiner, Christopher. 1994. *African art in transit.* Cambridge: Cambridge University Press. Steiner traces the social life of objects made in rural West African villages from their creation to their resting places in galleries, museums, tourist shops, or private Western art collections, highlighting the role of African merchants who make this transit possible.

Turner, Victor. 1969. *The ritual process.* Chicago: Aldine. An important work in the anthropological study of ritual, this text is an eloquent analysis of rites of passage.

Vogel, Susan. 1997. *Baule: African art/Western eyes.* New Haven: Yale University Press. A book of extraordinary photographs and beautifully clear text, this work explores both Baule and Western views of Baule expressive culture.

CHAPTER

8

Worldview

This chapter explores the encompassing pictures of reality created by members of societies—their *worldviews*. You will learn about metaphors and how they are used to construct worldviews. We focus on one, well-known kind of worldview—religion—as well as a contending worldview—secularism—that originated in western Europe. We also explore some of the ways in which symbolic forms central to different worldviews are shaped by power relations in different social settings.

In 1976, soon after the authors of this book (EAS and RHL) arrived in Guider, Cameroon, we bought a bicycle (see EthnoProfile 8.1: Guider). About a month later, it was stolen. The thief had been seen and was well known. We went directly to the *gendarmerie*, where we swore out a complaint.

A month later, I (RHL) was talking to Amadou, a 19-year-old member of the Ndjegn ethnic group. Amadou mentioned that the Ndjegn were famous for the power of their magic (Figure 8.1). I asked him if he knew any magic. Amadou replied that he was too young but that his older brother was a powerful magician. I asked what kinds of magic his brother was best at. Amadou began to list them—one of the first types of magic was to return stolen property. "Why didn't you mention this when our bike was stolen?" I inquired. "Well, I talked it over with my best friend. We agreed that you white people don't believe in any of that and would laugh at us." But I wanted to know what would happen to the thief if Amadou's brother made the magic against him. "His stomach will begin to hurt," Amadou explained, "and if he doesn't return the bicycle within two weeks, his stomach will swell up until it explodes and he will die." I thought this was a good idea and said I wanted the magic made.

Amadou went home and told his brother, who agreed to cast the spell. Word quickly went around Guider that the two "white visitors" had caused magic to be made against the bicycle thief. The days passed, but the bicycle did not reappear. After three weeks, I asked Amadou what had happened.

"Here's the problem, Monsieur," Amadou explained. "We waited too long after the theft to cast the spell. It works better when the magic is made right after the theft. Also, the thief is in Nigeria now. He's too far away for the magic to reach him."

Why do people believe—or not believe—in magic? Amadou was bright, suspicious of fakery, far from gullible. He had attended primary and secondary school. How could he remain convinced that his brother's magic worked? Why would many Americans be convinced that he was wrong?

Anthropologists are interested in what makes magic work because it occasionally does work: People are cursed, some of them sicken, and some of them die. How can this be? The usual anthropological explanation is that magic works when the people who believe in its power find out that it has been made against them. After all, people do often get stomachaches in northern Cameroon. Many people in Guider knew that the magic had been made and by whom. Only a fool or a desperate person would take the chance of having

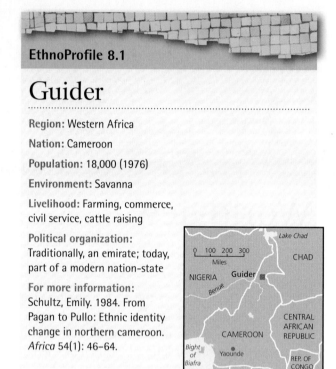

EthnoProfile 8.1

Guider

Region: Western Africa

Nation: Cameroon

Population: 18,000 (1976)

Environment: Savanna

Livelihood: Farming, commerce, civil service, cattle raising

Political organization: Traditionally, an emirate; today, part of a modern nation-state

For more information: Schultz, Emily. 1984. From Pagan to Pullo: Ethnic identity change in northern cameroon. *Africa* 54(1): 46–64.

his or her stomach swell up until it exploded. But in this case, the thief, long gone, did not know that magic had been made, and the magic's effect was neutralized by distance.

Amadou's explanation of why magic succeeds or fails is just as coherent as the traditional anthropological explanation. But each of these explanations is based on a different set of assumptions about what the world is like (see chapter 7). Where do these ideas about the world come from? Why don't all people share the same ideas? This chapter suggests some answers to these questions.

What Is a Worldview?

In our earlier discussions of language and cognition, we looked at some of the ways human beings use culture to construct rich understandings of everyday experiences. In this chapter, we build on those insights and describe how human beings use cultural creativity to make sense of the wider world on a comprehensive scale.

While no set of cultural beliefs or practices is perfectly integrated and without contradiction, anthropologists have good evidence that culture is not just a hodgepodge of unrelated elements. The directions in which cultural creativity goes may differ widely from

FIGURE 8.1 This man from northern Cameroon is believed to know powerful magic.

one group to the next, but in any particular society, culture tends to be patterned, and an individual's everyday attempts to account for experience are not isolated efforts. Members of the same society make use of shared assumptions about how the world works. As they interpret everyday experiences in light of these assumptions, they make sense of their lives and their lives make sense to other members of the society. The encompassing pictures of reality that result are called **worldviews**. Multiple worldviews may coexist in a single society. Anthropologists are interested in how worldviews are constructed and how people use them to make sense of their experiences in the broadest contexts.

How Do Anthropologists Study Worldviews?

People everywhere devise symbols to remind themselves of their significant insights and the connections between them. A **symbol**—be it a word, image, or action—is something that stands for something else. Symbols signal the presence and importance of meaningful domains of experience. Some symbols—what Sherry Ortner (1973) calls *summarizing symbols*—represent a whole semantic domain and invite us to consider the various elements within it. Others—what Ortner calls *elaborating symbols*—represent only one element of a domain and invite us to place that element in its wider semantic context.

Summarizing symbols sum up, express, represent for people "in an emotionally powerful . . . way what the system means to them" (Ortner 1973, 1339). To many people, for example, the American flag stands for the American way. But the American way is a complex collection of ideas and feelings that includes such things as patriotism, democracy, hard work, free enterprise, progress, national superiority, apple pie, and motherhood. As Ortner points out, the flag focuses our attention on all these things at once. It does not encourage us, say, to reflect on how the American way affects non-Americans. But

worldviews Encompassing pictures of reality created by the members of societies.

symbol Something that stands for something else. A symbol signals the presence of an important domain of experience.

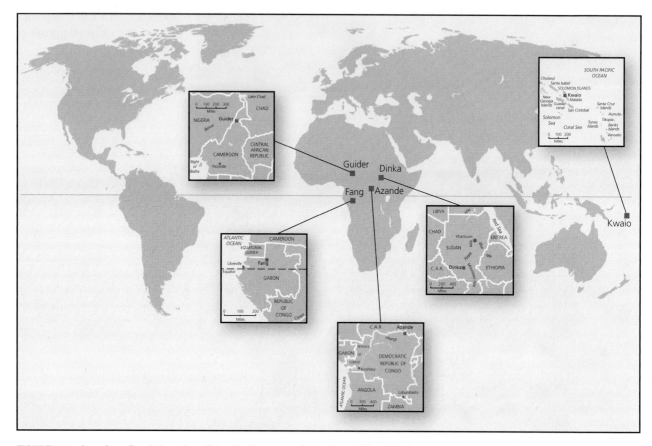

FIGURE 8.2   Location of societies whose EthnoProfiles appear in chapter 8.

the symbolic power of the flag is double-edged. For some people, Americans included, this same flag stands for imperialism, racism, opposition to the legitimate struggle of exploited peoples, and support for right-wing dictatorships. Perhaps stranger still, for many Americans who came of age during the 1960s, the flag sums up all these things at once, contradictory though they are!

Elaborating symbols are essentially analytic. They allow people to sort out and label complex and undifferentiated feelings and ideas into comprehensible and communicable language and action. Elaborating symbols provide people with categories for thinking about how their world is ordered. Consider the Dinka, a cattle-herding people of eastern Africa (Figure 8.3; see Ethno-Profile 8.2: Dinka). According to Godfrey Lienhardt, cattle provide the Dinka with most of the metaphors they use for thinking about and responding to experience. For instance, Dinka perceptions of color, light, and shade are connected to the colors they see in cattle. They even liken how their society is put together to how a bull is put together (Lienhardt 1961; Ortner 1973).

key metaphors   Metaphors that serve as the foundation of a worldview.

What Are Some Key Metaphors for Constructing Worldviews?

Worldviews are comprehensive pictures of reality. They can be regarded as attempts to answer the following question: What must the world be like for my experiences to be what they are? Over the ages, thoughtful people in all cultural traditions have suggested various answers to this question. Often, unfamiliar worldviews become more comprehensible to us if we are able to grasp the **key metaphors** on which they are founded. Anthropologist Robin Horton suggests that people who construct a worldview are "concerned above all to show order, regularity and predictability where primary theory [that is, commonsense experience] has failed to show them." As they search for key metaphors, therefore, they look at those areas of everyday experience that are most associated with order, regularity, and predictability (1982, 237). Some worldviews seem to have tremendous staying power over time and across space, making sense of experience in a variety of circumstances and historical periods. But new worldviews

FIGURE 8.3   For pastoral people such as the Dinka and their neighbors the Nuer, cattle are elaborating symbols of paramount power.

based on different metaphors can emerge under changed circumstances if they provide insight when old understandings fail.

Comparative research suggests that three important images of order and stability have regularly provided key metaphors for worldviews. The first are what we will call **societal metaphors**. In many times and places, human social relations provide great order, regularity, and predictability. In such societies, the model for the world is the social order; or, put another way, the universe (or macrocosm) and one's own society (the microcosm) are understood to operate according to the same principles. Small-scale societies organized on the basis of kinship may relate to powerful cosmic forces as if they were powerful elders; some of those forces may even be understood as the spirits of deceased elders, their ancestors. Complex societies stratified according to differences in wealth, power, and prestige may conceive of a universe in which cosmic powers are similarly stratified, and they may base their ways of dealing with cosmic forces on the skills they use to deal with powerful human beings (Figure 8.4). Societies with well-developed capitalist commercial, industrial, and financial institutions, often liken biological and social processes to operations in a capitalist market (Wolf 1969, 277).

A second image of order and stability has come from **organic metaphors**, which are based on an understanding of living organisms. The advances made by biologists in the nineteenth and early twentieth centuries led social scientists to think of societies and languages as living organisms. Many nineteenth-century theorists of linguistic or cultural evolution used organic metaphors to analyze the life histories of languages or civilizations in terms of birth, youth, maturity, reproduction, old age, and death. In the early twentieth century, by contrast, a different organic metaphor was used to develop the social scientific perspective called **functionalism**. Functionalists drew attention to the way the body of a living organism can be divided into different systems (digestive, reproductive,

societal metaphors Worldview metaphors whose model for the world is the social order.

organic metaphors Worldview metaphors that apply the image of the body to social structures and institutions.

functionalism A social scientific perspective in which a society is likened to a living organism in which different systems carry out specialized tasks; functionalists identify social subsystems into which a society can be divided, identify the tasks each is supposed to perform, and describe a healthy society as one in which all the subsystems are functioning harmoniously.

EthnoProfile 8.2

Dinka

Region: Eastern Africa

Nation: Sudan

Population: 2,000,000

Environment: Savanna

Livelihood: Principally cattle herding, also agriculture

Political organization: Traditionally, egalitarian with noble clans and chiefs; today, part of a modern nation-state

For more information: Deng, Francis Madeng. 1972. *The Dinka of the Sudan.* New York: Holt, Rinehart and Winston.

respiratory, and so on), each carrying out a specialized task. When all these systems are functioning in harmony with one another, the organism is said to be healthy. If society is also a living organism, we should look for the subsystems into which society can be divided, identify the tasks each is supposed to perform, and describe a healthy society as one in which all the subsystems are functioning harmoniously. *Personification* (attributing human characteristics to nonhuman entities) is another organic metaphor. The beliefs that the candy machine down the hall at the office has a personality that is both malevolent and greedy or that you can persuade your car to start on a cold morning by speaking gentle and encouraging words to it both involve personification.

Technological metaphors use machines made by human beings as metaphorical predicates. Technological metaphors became prominent with the rise of western European science, and different machine metaphors have replaced one another over time as Western science and technology have developed and changed. For instance, in the seventeenth-century world of Isaac Newton, models of the universe were based on the most complex artifact of that age: the wind-up mechanical clock. Following the industrial revolution, nineteenth-century psychologists

described human cognitive and emotional processes using a steam engine metaphor (for example, Freud conceived of emotional stress building up inside people like steam in a boiler that would explode unless a social safety valve were available to release the pressure without causing psychic damage). In the second half of the twentieth century, computer metaphors have become popular among some scientists investigating how the mind works (Pinker 1999).

What Is Religion?

For many readers of this text, the most familiar form of worldview is probably **religion**. The anthropological concept of religion, like many analytic terms, began as a description of a certain domain of Western culture. As a result, it has been very difficult for anthropologists to settle on a definition of religion that is applicable in all human societies.

Scholars have often argued that a religion differs from other kinds of worldviews because it assumes the existence of a supernatural domain: an invisible world populated by one or more beings who are more powerful than human beings and are able to influence events in the "natural" human world. The problem with this definition is that the distinction between "natural" and "supernatural" was originally made by nonreligious Western observers in order to distinguish the real "natural" world from what they took to be the imaginary "supernatural" world. Many anthropologists who study different religious traditions believe that it is less distorting to begin with their informants' statements about what exists and what does not. In this way, they are in a better position to understand the range of forces, visible and invisible, that religious believers perceive as active in their world.

For these reasons, John Bowen proposes that anthropologists approach religion in a way that begins broadly but that allows for increasing specificity as we learn more about the details of particular religious traditions. Bowen defines religion as "ideas and practices that postulate reality beyond that which is immediately available to the senses" (2002, 5). In individual societies, this may mean beliefs in spirits and gods, or awareness that ancestors continue to be active in the world of the living. In other cases, people may posit the existence of impersonal cosmic powers that may be compelled to intervene in human affairs following the correct performance of certain rituals. It is important to note that Bowen's definition of religion encompasses both practices and ideas: Religions

---

technological metaphor A worldview metaphor that employs objects made by human beings as metaphorical predicates.

religion Ideas and practices that postulate reality beyond that which is immediately available to the senses.

FIGURE 8.4 In a complex, hierarchically organized society like that of Renaissance Italy, the image of cosmic power was similarly organized.

involve *actions* as well as *beliefs* (Figure 8.5). Indeed, anthropologist A. F. C. Wallace proposed a set of "minimal categories of religious behavior" that describe many of the practices usually associated with religions (1966). Several of the most salient are

1. *Prayer*. Where there are personified cosmic forces, there is a customary way of addressing them, usually by speaking or chanting out loud. Often people pray in public, at a sacred location, and with special apparatus: incense, smoke, objects (such as rosary beads or a prayer wheel), and so on.

2. *Physiological exercise*. Many religious systems have methods for physically manipulating psychological states to induce an ecstatic spiritual state. Wallace suggests four major kinds of manipulation: (1) drugs; (2) sensory deprivation; (3) mortification of the flesh by pain, sleeplessness, and fatigue; and (4) deprivation of food, water, or air. In many societies, the experience of ecstasy, euphoria, dissociation, or hallucination seems to be a goal of religious effort.

3. *Exhortation*. In all religious systems, certain people are believed to have closer relationships with the invisible powers than others, and they are expected to use those relationships in the spiritual interests of others. They give orders, they heal, they threaten, they comfort, and they interpret.

4. *Mana*. Mana refers to an impersonal superhuman power that is sometimes believed to be transferable

from an object that contains it to one that does not. The laying on of hands, in which the power of a healer enters the body of a sick person to remove or destroy an illness, is an example of the transmission of power. In Guider, some people believe that the ink used to copy passages from the Qur'an has power. Washing the ink off the board on which the words are written and drinking the ink transfers the power of the words into the body of the drinker. The principle here is that sacred things are to be touched so that power may be transferred.

5. *Taboo*. Objects or people that may not be touched are taboo. Some people believe that the cosmic power in such objects or people may "drain away" if touched or may injure the toucher. Many religious systems have taboo objects. Traditionally, Catholics were not to touch the Host during communion; Jews may not touch the handwritten text of the biblical scrolls. In ancient Polynesia, commoners could not touch the chief's body; even an accidental touch resulted in the death of the commoner. Food may also be taboo; many societies have elaborate rules concerning the foods that may or may not be eaten at different times or by different kinds of people.

6. *Feasts*. Eating and drinking in a religious context is very common. The Holy Communion of Catholics and Protestants is a meal set apart by its religious context. The Passover Seder for Jews

is another religious feast. For the Huichol of Mexico, the consumption of peyote is set apart by its religious context. Even everyday meals may be seen to have a religious quality if they begin or end with prayer.

7. *Sacrifice.* Giving something of value to the invisible forces or their agents is a feature of many religious systems. This may be an offering of money, goods, or services. It may also be the immolation of animals or, very rarely, human beings. Sacrifices may be made in thanks to the cosmic forces, in hopes of influencing them to act in a certain way, or simply to gain general religious merit.

Religion and Communication

Those who are committed to religious worldviews are convinced of the existence and active involvement in their lives of beings or forces that are ordinarily invisible. Indeed, some of the most highly valued religious practices, such as religious ecstasy or trance, produce outer symptoms that may be perceived by others; but their most powerful effects can be experienced only by the individual who undergoes them personally.

What, then, if you wanted to know what it felt like to experience religious ecstasy? What if you were someone who had had such an experience and wanted to tell others about it? What if you were convinced that the supreme power in the universe had revealed itself to you and you wanted to share this revelation with others? How would you proceed? You might well begin by searching

for metaphors based on experiences already well known to your audience.

Thus, one Hindu Tamil worshiper in Kuala Lumpur who successfully went into trance during the festival of Thaipusam described his experience as being like "floating in the air, followed by the wind" (*Floating in the Air* 1973). And the Hebrew poet who wrote the Twenty-third Psalm tried to express his experience of the power and love of his God by comparing God to his shepherd and himself to a sheep. Many contemporary theologians argue that the language human beings use to talk about God is inevitably full of everyday metaphors (see Gillman 1992, for example). Even those who claim to have had personal experience of the reality of God, or of ancestral spirits, or of witchcraft, will probably still find themselves forced to resort to poetic, metaphorical language if they want to explain that experience to other people—and perhaps even to themselves.

We saw earlier that societal metaphors are often used to gain insight into a complex phenomenon, because in many societies social relations are complex and well understood. Anthropological research suggests that members of many religious traditions apparently conceive of the structure of the universe as being the same as the structure of their society. First, members of the tradition will be likely to conceive of the force or forces at work in the universe as personified beings with many of the attributes of human agents at work in the society they know well. And because societies can be very different from one another, so the way they characterize the universe will also be different. It has long been noted by anthropologists that societies organized in strong groups

FIGURE 8.5   (*a*) The joint pilgrimage by Hindu worshipers to the Ganges River illustrates the social nature of religion. (*b*) Floating on the air, followed by the wind. This participant in the Hindu Thaipusam ritual pilgrimage in Singapore in 2004 has agreed to carry a kavadi for religious benefit. Kavadi can weigh 60 pounds (27 kg).

based on kinship usually conceive of a universe peopled with the spirits of powerful ancestor figures who take an interest in the lives of their living descendants. By contrast, members of societies run by vast and complex bureaucracies, as was the Roman Empire, are apt to picture the universe as being run by an army of hierarchically ordered gods and spirits, all of which may be supervised by a chief god. "The Lord is my shepherd" is not likely to be accepted as an apt description of cosmic reality by people living in a society that lacks class distinctions and has no experience of sheepherding.

Organic metaphors may also figure in the construction of religious understanding. Anthropologist James Fernandez reports that organic metaphors are common in the Bwiti religion of the Fang of Gabon (see EthnoProfile 8.3: Fang). The human heart, for example, is an apt metaphor for Bwiti devotees because "(1) it is the heart which is the most alive of the bloody organs, (2) it is traditionally conceived by the Fang to be the organ of thought, and (3) in its bloodiness it is associated with the female principle. . . . Many meanings are at work in this metaphor, for that bloody organ, the heart, has a congeries of useful associations" (1977, 112).

What about technological metaphors? Their popularity in the Western world accompanied the rise of science. For example, in the seventeenth century, philosopher René Descartes popularized the notion that the human body is a machine, albeit one inhabited by an immortal soul. One of his near contemporaries, Julien La Mettrie, carried this metaphor to its radical conclusion. In his book *L'homme-machine* ("man-machine"), he argued that the concept of the human soul was superfluous because machines do not have souls.

Starting in the Renaissance, machines began to transform the world in unprecedented ways and to stimulate people's imaginations. The increasing complexity of machines, coupled with their builders' intimate knowledge of how they were put together, made them highly suggestive as metaphors. As we saw, the images of human relations suggested by technological metaphors are very different from the images suggested by societal and organic metaphors. When we say that we are only cogs in a machine or talk about social status and roles as interchangeable parts, we are using machine metaphors (Figure 8.6).

What if people should conclude that the structure of the universe is the same as the structure of a machine—say, a clock or a computer? Would the resulting worldview still be a religion? After all, those scholars who originally distinguished the natural from the supernatural associated the supernatural with religion and declared both to be nonsense. At the same time, to view the cosmos as complex, orderly, predictable, and knowable, such that effective intervention into cosmic processes is possible, would

EthnoProfile 8.3

Fang

Region: Central Africa

Nation: Gabon

Population: 400,000 (1978)

Environment: Tropical forest with intense rainfall

Livelihood: Farming, hunting

Political organization: Traditionally, village councils, headmen; today, part of a modern nation-state

For more information: Fernandez, James. 1982. *Bwiti: An ethnography of the religious imagination.* Princeton: Princeton University Press.

certainly qualify as a worldview, even if the cosmos was deaf to human prayer and indifferent to human affairs. Anthropologists and other religious scholars continue to debate the matter.

Religious Organization

The most important entailment that follows from the societal metaphor is that forces in the universe are personalized. Thus, people seeking to influence those forces must handle them as they would handle powerful human beings. Communication is perhaps the central feature of how we deal with human beings: When we address each other, we expect a response. The same is true when we address personalized cosmic forces.

Maintaining contact with invisible cosmic powers is a tremendously complex undertaking. It is not surprising, therefore, that some societies have developed complex social practices to ensure that it is done properly. In other words, religion becomes *institutionalized*. Social positions are created for specialists who supervise or embody correct religious practice.

Anthropologists have identified two broad categories of religious specialists: shamans and priests. A **shaman** is

shaman A part-time religious practitioner who is believed to have the power to travel to or contact supernatural forces directly on behalf of individuals or groups.

FIGURE 8.6   When we say that we are only cogs in a machine or talk about status and roles as interchangeable parts, we are using machine metaphors. Charlie Chaplin made use of technological metaphors in his film *Modern Times* (1936).

a part-time religious practitioner who is believed to have the power to contact invisible powers directly on behalf of individuals or groups. Shamans are often thought to be able to travel to the cosmic realm to communicate with the beings or forces that dwell there. They often plead with those beings or forces to act in favor of their people and may return with messages for them. The Ju/'hoansi, for example, recognize that some people are able to develop an internal power that enables them to travel to the world of the spirits—to enter "half death" (it would be called "trance" in English)—in order to cure those who are sick (see EthnoProfile 11.1: Ju/'hoansi).

In many societies, the training that a shaman receives is long, demanding, and permanent and may involve the use of powerful psychotropic substances. Repeatedly entering altered states of consciousness can produce long-lasting effects on shamans themselves, and shamans may be viewed with suspicion or fear by others in the society. This is because contacting cosmic beings to persuade them to heal embodies dangerous ambiguities: Someone who can contact such beings for positive benefits may also be able to contact them to produce a negative outcome like disease or death. The term *shaman* comes from the Tungus of eastern Siberia, where, at a minimum, it referred to a religious specialist who has the ability to enter a trance through which he or she is believed to enter into direct contact with spiritual beings and guardian spirits for the purposes of healing, fertility, protection, and aggression, in a ritual setting

priest A religious practitioner skilled in the practice of religious rituals, which he or she carries out for the benefit of the group.

(Bowie 2006, 175; Hultkrantz 1992, 10). The healing associated with Siberian shamanism was concerned with the idea that illness was caused by soul loss and healing through recovery of the soul (Figure 8.7). Thus, the shaman was responsible for dealing with spirits that were, at best, neutral and at worst actively hostile to human beings. The shaman could travel to the spirit world to heal someone by finding the missing soul that had been stolen by spirits. But a shaman who was jealous of a hunter, for example, was believed to be able to steal the souls of animals so that the hunter would fail. In these societies, shamans are dangerous.

Shamanic activity takes place in the trance séance, which can be little more than a consultation between shaman and patient, or it can be a major public ritual, rich in drama. Becoming a shaman is not undertaken for personal development—in the societies where shamanism is important, it is said that the shaman has no choice but to take on the role; the spirits demand it. It can take a decade or more to become fully recognized as a shaman, and it is assumed that the shaman will be in service to the society (for good or ill) for the rest of his or her life.

A **priest**, by contrast, is skilled in the practice of religious rituals, which are carried out for the benefit of the group or individual members of the group. Priests do not necessarily have direct contact with cosmic forces. Often their major role is to mediate such contact by ensuring that the required ritual activity has been properly performed. Priests are found in hierarchical societies, and they owe their ability to act as priests to the hierarchy of the religious institution (Figure 8.8). Status differences separating rulers and subjects in such societies are reflected in the unequal relationship between priest and laity.

FIGURE 8.7   Using smoke from a juniper twig, Siberian shaman Vera heals a patient possessed by evil spirits.

Worldviews in Practice: Two Case Studies

We have been discussing how worldviews are constructed, but most of us encounter them fully formed, both in our own society and in other societies. We face a rich tapestry of symbols and rituals and everyday practices linked to one another in what often appears to be a seamless web. Where do we begin to sort things out?

Coping with Misfortune: Witchcraft, Oracles, and Magic among the Azande

Anthropologist E. E. Evans-Pritchard, in his classic work *Witchcraft, Oracles, and Magic Among the Azande* ([1937] 1976), shows how Azande beliefs and practices concerning witchcraft, oracles, and magic are related to one another (see EthnoProfile 8.4: Azande). He describes how Azande use witchcraft beliefs to explain unfortunate things that happen to them and how they employ oracles and magic to exert a measure of control over the actions of other people. Evans-Pritchard was impressed by the intelligence, sophistication, and skepticism of his Azande informants. For this reason, he was all the more struck by their ability to hold a set of beliefs that many Europeans would regard as superstitious.

FIGURE 8.8   The complex organization of the Roman Catholic Church was illustrated at the funeral for Pope John Paul II in 2005.

EthnoProfile 8.4

Azande

Region: Central Africa

Nation: Sudan, Democratic Republic of Congo (Zaire), Central African Republic

Population: 1,100,000

Environment: Sparsely wooded savanna

Livelihood: Farming, hunting, fishing, chicken raising

Political organization:
Traditionally, highly organized, tribal kingdoms; today, part of modern nation-states

For more information:
Evans-Pritchard, E. E. [1937] 1976. *Witchcraft, oracles, and magic among the Azande,* abridged ed. Oxford: Oxford University Press.

Azande Witchcraft Beliefs The Azande believe that *mangu* (translated by Evan-Pritchard as **witchcraft**) is a substance in the body of witches, generally located under the sternum.* Being part of the body, the witchcraft substance grows as the body grows; therefore, the older the witch, the more potent his or her witchcraft. The Azande believe that children inherit witchcraft from their parents. Men and women may both be witches. Men practice witchcraft against other men, women against other women. Witchcraft works when its "soul" removes the soul of a certain organ in the victim's body, usually at night, causing a slow, wasting disease. Suffering such a disease is therefore an indication that an individual has been bewitched.

Witchcraft is a basic concept for the Azande, one that shapes their experience of adversity. All deaths are due to witchcraft and must be avenged by **magic**. Other misfortunes are also commonly attributed to witchcraft unless the victim has broken a taboo, has failed to observe a moral rule, or is believed to be responsible for his own problems. Suppose I am an incompetent potter and my pots break while I am firing them. I may claim that

---

*Beliefs and practices similar to those associated with Azande mangu have been found in many other societies, and it has become traditional in anthropology to refer to them as "witchcraft." This technical usage must not be confused with everyday uses of the word in contemporary Western societies, still less with the practices of followers of movements like Wicca, which are very different.

witchcraft caused them to break, but everyone will laugh at me because they know I lack skill. Witchcraft is believed to be so common that the Azande are neither surprised nor awestruck when they encounter it. Their usual response is anger.

To the Azande, witchcraft is a completely natural explanation for events. Consider the classic case of the collapsing granary. Azandeland is hot, and people seeking shade often sit under traditional raised granaries, which rest on logs. Termites are common in Azandeland, and sometimes they destroy the supporting logs, making a granary collapse. Occasionally, when a granary collapses, people sitting under it are killed. Why does this happen? The Azande are well aware that the termites chew up the wood until the supports give way, but to them that is not answer enough. Why, after all, should that particular granary have collapsed at that particular moment? To skeptical observers, the only connection is coincidence in time and space. Western science does not provide any explanation for why these two chains of causation intersect. But the Azande do: Witchcraft causes the termites to finish chewing up the wood at just that moment, and that witchcraft must be avenged.

Dealing with Witches How to expose the witch? For this task, the Azande employ **oracles** (invisible forces to which people address questions and whose responses they believe to be truthful). Preeminent among these is the poison oracle. The poison is a strychnine-like substance imported into Azandeland. The oracle "speaks" through the effect the poison has on chickens. When witchcraft is suspected, a relative of the afflicted person will take some chickens into the bush along with a specialist in administering the poison oracle. This person will feed poison to one chicken, name a suspect, and ask the oracle to kill the chicken if this person is the witch. If the chicken dies, a second chicken will be fed poison, and the oracle will be asked to spare the chicken if the suspect just named is indeed the witch. Thus, the Azande double-check the oracle carefully; a witchcraft accusation is not made lightly.

People do not consult the oracle with a long list of names. They need only consider those who might wish them or their families ill: people who have quarreled

---

witchcraft The performance of evil by human beings believed to possess an innate, nonhuman power to do evil, whether or not it is intentional or self-aware.

magic A set of beliefs and practices designed to control the visible or invisible world for specific purposes.

oracles Invisible forces to which people address questions and whose responses they believe to be truthful.

with them, who are unpleasant, who are antisocial, and whose behavior is somehow out of line. Indeed, witches are always neighbors, because neighbors are the only people who know you well enough to wish you and your family ill.

Once the oracle has identified the witch, the Azande removes the wing of the chicken and has it taken by messenger to the compound of the accused person. The messenger presents the accused witch with the chicken wing and says that he has been sent concerning the illness of so-and-so's relative. "Almost invariably the witch replies courteously that he is unconscious of injuring anyone, that if it is true that he has injured the man in question he is very sorry, and that if it is he alone who is troubling him then he will surely recover, because from the bottom of his heart he wishes him health and happiness" (Evans-Pritchard [1937] 1976, 42). The accused then calls for a gourd of water, takes some in his mouth, and sprays it out over the wing. He says aloud, so the messenger can hear and repeat what he says, that if he is a witch he is not aware of it and that he is not intentionally causing the sick man to be ill. He addresses the witchcraft in him, asking it to become cool, and concludes by saying that he makes this appeal from his heart, not just from his lips (42).

People accused of witchcraft are usually astounded; no Azande thinks of himself or herself as a witch. However, the Azande strongly believe in witchcraft and in the oracles, and if the oracle says someone is a witch, then that person must be one. The accused witch is grateful to the family of the sick person for letting this be known. Otherwise, if the accused had been allowed to murder the victim, all the while unaware of it, the witch would surely be killed by vengeance magic. The witchcraft accusation carries a further message: The behavior of the accused is sufficiently outside the bounds of acceptable Azande behavior to have marked him or her as a potential witch. Only the names of people you suspect wish you ill are submitted to the oracle. The accused witch, then, is being told to change his or her behavior.

Are There Patterns of Witchcraft Accusation?

Compared with the stereotypes of European American witchcraft—old hags dressed in black, riding on broomsticks, casting spells, causing milk to sour or people to sicken—Azande witchcraft seems quite tame. People whose impression of witchcraft comes from Western European images may believe that witchcraft and witch-hunting tear at the very fabric of society. Yet anthropological accounts like Evans-Pritchard's suggest that practices

such as witchcraft accusation can sometimes keep societies together.

Anthropologist Mary Douglas looked at the range of witchcraft accusations worldwide and discovered that they fall into two basic types (1970, xxvi–xxvii): In some cases, the witch is an evil outsider; in others, the witch is an internal enemy, either the member of a rival faction or a dangerous deviant. These different patterns of accusation perform different functions in a society. If the witch is an outsider, witchcraft accusations can strengthen in-group ties. If the witch is an internal enemy, accusations of witchcraft can weaken in-group ties; factions may have to regroup, communities may split, and the entire social hierarchy may be reordered. If the witch is a dangerous deviant, the accusation of witchcraft can be seen as an attempt to control the deviant in defense of the wider values of the community. Douglas concludes that how people understand witchcraft is based on social relations of their society.

Coping with Misfortune: Seeking Higher Consciousness among the Channelers

Anthropologist Michael F. Brown spent several years studying the beliefs and practices of "alternative spirituality," or "New Age spirituality," focusing particularly on channeling, the use of altered states of consciousness to contact spirits, "or, as many of its practitioners say, to experience spiritual energy captured from other times and dimensions" (Brown 1997, viii). The practitioners of channeling, called channels, believe that they can "use altered states of consciousness to connect to wisdom emanating from the collective unconscious or even from other planets, dimensions, or historical eras" (6). Brown was fascinated to see how channeling brings together several important strands of North American culture: individualism, the personal recovery movement, and women-centered spirituality meld with features of nineteenth-century spiritualism to provide practitioners and followers with meaning, coherence, and a sense of control over events in what Brown refers to as "an anxious age" (Figure 8.9).

If one can speak of a theology of channeling, Brown concludes that it is based on four key assumptions. First, channels and their followers believe that human beings are in essence gods. Individuals are referred to as "fragments of the God-Head" or "Christed beings." These metaphors imply not only that humans share in the divinity that created the universe but also that we are immortal, inherently good, and fully able to create our own reality (47). Second, humans are not all fully developed beings.

FIGURE 8.9   Gerry Bowman channeling John the Baptist at the Harmonic Convergence of the Planets,
celebrated in California in 1987.

Channels and their clients generally believe that human beings undergo a series of reincarnations in order to acquire important learning experiences. This evolutionary process may involve previous lives lived on earth or on different planets or in different dimensions. Third, channels and their clients believe that each of us is responsible for creating our own reality. In their view, thoughts shape reality, and the impact of any thought is magnified when a critical mass of like-minded people share it (47–48). From their perspective, if enough people "Visualize World Peace," it will suddenly happen. Finally, channels and their clients believe in the transcendent value of holism. "The purpose of channeling is to bring together elements of life ripped apart by Western civilization: male and female, reason and intuition, thought and matter. . . . Channels and their clients see the universe as a single interconnected field. Just as the thought patterns of individuals can reshape the cosmos, so shifts in the cosmos affect individuals" (48–49).

What follows from this theology is a moral framework in which the existence of evil is called into question. As we have seen, the Azande explain misfortune in terms of witchcraft. Channels and their clients explain misfortune—illness, poverty, or other forms of suffering—in one of two ways. On the one hand, misfortune occurs because the victims cannot or will not envision the world in ways that protect them from it. "Calamity originates in a failure of individual attitude or thought" (Brown 1997, 65). On the other, channels assert that victims have chosen their own fate, usually at a "deep soul level" that is beyond their own conscious awareness. The logic here is

that the reincarnating soul chooses certain challenges as part of its growth process. Thus, a person who has cancer has, at some level, chosen to have it because the experience is important or necessary to the development of a higher consciousness over the course of the many lives that soul will live.

While some observers regard this as a form of blaming the victim, channels see their position as a way of asserting control. Channels see themselves "explicitly reacting against the contemporary American cult of victimhood. . . . Channeling's theological framework rejects victimhood because of its connotation of powerlessness, arguing instead that everyone suffers indignities on their way to higher consciousness. These painful episodes are important learning experiences, but nothing is gained by dwelling on them" (67).

Thus, people drawn to channeling believe that they are the authors of their own fate. If people are divine actors, then their temporary setbacks and troubles must be part of a master plan that they themselves have designed, and they are inevitably responsible to some degree for their own misfortunes (Brown 1997, 68). Among other things, this way of explaining misfortune totally rejects the social nature of human experience. As opposed to Azande witchcraft beliefs, where misfortune is due to the ill will of others, channeling is a belief system of and for individuals. Although claiming to offer a corrective to the sense of isolation that many people feel, ironically, channeling isolates individuals from one another even more, by making each of us a world unto ourselves.

For All Those Who Were Indian in a Former Life

Andrea Smith challenges members of the New Age movement who, in her view, trivialize the situation of women like herself "who are Indian in this life."

The New Age movement completely trivializes the oppression we as Indian women face: Indian women are suddenly no longer the women who are forcibly sterilized and tested with unsafe drugs such as Depo Provera; we are no longer the women who have a life expectancy of 47 years; and we are no longer the women who generally live below the poverty level and face a 75 percent unemployment rate. No, we're too busy being cool and spiritual.

This trivialization of our oppression is compounded by the fact that nowadays anyone can be Indian if s/he wants to. All that is required is that one be Indian in a former life, or take part in a sweat lodge, or be mentored by a "medicine woman," or read a how-to book.

Since, according to this theory, anyone can now be "Indian," then the term Indians no longer regresses specifically to those people who have survived five hundred years of colonization and genocide. This furthers the goals of white supremacists to abrogate treaty rights and to take away what little we have left. When everyone becomes "Indian," then it is easy to lose sight of the specificity of oppression faced by those who are Indian in this life. It is no wonder we have such a difficult time finding non-Indians to support our struggles when the New Age movement has completely disguised our oppression.

The most disturbing aspect about these racist practices is that they are promoted in the name of feminism. Sometimes it seems that I can't open a feminist periodical without seeing ads promoting white "feminist" practices with little medicine wheel designs. I can't seem to go to a feminist conference without the woman who begins the conference with a ceremony being the only Indian presenter. Participants then feel so "spiritual" after this opening that they fail to notice the absence of Indian women in the rest of the conference or Native American issues in the discussions. And I certainly can't go to a feminist bookstore without seeing books by Lynn Andrews and other people who exploit Indian spirituality all over the place. It seems that, while feminism is supposed to signify the empowerment of all women, it obviously does not include Indian women.

If white feminists are going to act in solidarity with their Indian sisters, they must take a stand against Indian spiritual abuse. Feminist book and record stores should stop selling these products, and feminist periodicals should stop advertising these products. Women who call themselves feminists should denounce exploitative practices wherever they see them.

Source: A. Smith 1994, 71

Maintaining and Changing a Worldview

What makes a worldview stable? Why is a worldview rejected? These questions are related to general questions about persistence and change in human social life. Anthropologists recognize that culture change is a complex phenomenon, and they admit that they do not have all the answers.

Changes in worldview must, first of all, be related to the practical everyday experiences of people in a particular society. Stable, repetitive experiences reinforce the acceptability of any traditional worldview that has successfully accounted for such experiences in the past. When experiences become unpredictable, however, thinking people in any society may become painfully aware that past experiences can no longer be trusted as guides for the future, and traditional worldviews may be undermined (see Horton 1982, 252).

How Do People Cope with Change?

Drastic changes in experience lead people to create new interpretations that will help them cope with the changes. Sometimes the change is an outcome of local or regional struggles. The Protestant Reformation for example, adapted the Christian tradition to changing social circumstances in northern Europe during the Renaissance by breaking ties to the pope, turning church lands over to secular authorities, allowing clergy to marry, and so forth. Protestants continued to identify themselves as Christians even though many of their religious practices had changed.

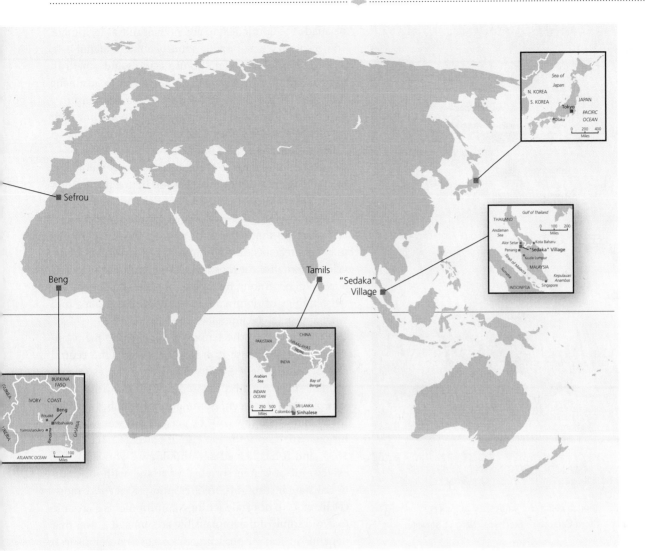

observations were confirmed by later political anthropologists, such as E. E. Evans-Pritchard, based on his work among the Azande. Evans-Pritchard's description of social life among the Azande ([1937] 1976) in no way resembled a war of all against all, even though the Azande lived in a stateless society and held a complex set of beliefs about witchcraft oracles, and magic (see EthnoProfile 8.4: Azande). Evans-Pritchard observed that Azande people discussed witchcraft openly, and if they believed they were bewitched, they were likely to be angry rather than afraid. This kind of attitude made sense because most Azande subscribed to a worldview in which witchcraft had a meaningful place. In addition, they did not feel helpless because their society also supplied them with practical remedies, like vengeance magic, that they could use to defend themselves if they thought they had been bewitched. Here, we see an example of what Wolf called organizational power that does not depend on state coercion. Instead, it depends on *persuasion*. Scaffolded by particular social institutions

and practices, the belief system continues to appear natural and rational to members of the society; this is why ordinary, rational people support it.

Domination and Hegemony

Here we encounter an ambiguity about power in human affairs. Perhaps people do submit to institutionalized power because they have been coerced and fear punishment. But perhaps they submit because they believe that the power structures in their society are legitimate, given their understandings about the way the world works. What could lead people to accept coercion by others as legitimate (Figure 9.3)?

A worldview that justifies the social arrangements under which people live is sometimes called an **ideology**.

ideology A worldview that justifies the social arrangements under which people live.

FIGURE 9.3 Prior to colonial conquest by outsiders, Muslim emirs from northern Cameroon exercised coercive power.

As we saw in chapter 8, an ideology can be defined as a worldview that justifies the social arrangements under which people live. Some Marxian thinkers have emphasized that rulers can consolidate their power by persuading their subjects to accept an ideology that portrays ruling-class domination as legitimate. They argue that groups who accept such a ruling-class ideology suffer from "false consciousness." But the notion of false consciousness is problematic, since it views people as passive and unable to withstand indoctrination. As we discussed in chapter 2, this is not a persuasive view of human nature.

More promising was the approach taken by Antonio Gramsci (1971). Writing in the 1930s, Gramsci pointed out that coercive rule—what he called **domination**—is expensive and unstable. Rulers do better if they can

persuade the dominated to accept their rule as legitimate. To do so, they may provide some genuine material benefits to their subjects and also use schools and other cultural institutions to disseminate an ideology justifying their rule. If they achieve all this—while also ensuring that none of these concessions seriously undermine their privileged position—they have established what Gramsci called **hegemony**.

Hegemony is never absolute, but always vulnerable to challenges: Struggles may develop between rulers trying to justify their domination and subordinate groups who exercise agency by challenging "official" ideologies and practices that devalue or exclude them. Hegemony may be threatened if subordinate groups maintain or develop alternative, or *counterhegemonic*, cultural practices. Successful hegemony, by contrast, involves linking the understandings of dominant and subordinate groups into what appears to be mutual accommodation.

The concept of hegemony is attractive to many anthropologists because it draws attention to the central role of cultural beliefs and symbols in struggles to consolidate social organization and political control. Gramsci's contrast between domination (rule by coercive force) and hegemony (rule by persuasion) was central to his own analysis of the exercise of power (Crehan 2002, 153), and it has helped anthropologists who study the exercise of power in societies with and without traditional state institutions. In attempting to extend Gramsci's insights to nonstate settings, anthropologists are able to avoid some of the implausible accounts of power that depend on fear of punishment or false consciousness. Instead, they draw attention to the verbal skills and personal charisma of leaders who can persuade others to follow them without relying on coercive force. Charismatic leaders must skillfully align shared meanings, values, and goals with a particular interpretation of events or proposed course of action.

Consider, for example, the Zande belief that people use witchcraft only against those they envy. The psychological insight embodied in this belief makes it highly plausible to people who experience daily friction with their neighbors. At the same time, however, this belief makes it impossible to accuse Zande chiefs of using witchcraft against commoners—because, as Zande themselves say, why would chiefs envy their subjects? In this way, hegemonic ideology deflects challenges that might be made against those in power.

In other settings, however, hegemonic ideology may justify social action in some individuals that would be condemned in others. Consider the connection between witchcraft and kingship among the Beng of Ivory Coast (see EthnoProfile 9.1: Beng). The Beng are organized into

domination Coercive rule.

hegemony Persuading subordinates to accept the ideology of the dominant group by mutual accommodations that nevertheless preserve the rulers' privileged position.

EthnoProfile 9.1

Beng

Region: Western Africa

Nation: Ivory Coast

Population: 10,000+

Environment: Savanna and forest

Livelihood: Farming, both subsistence and cash; hunting; gathering

Political organization: Traditionally, a kingdom; today, part of a modern nation-state

For more information:
Gottlieb, Alma. 1989. Witches, kings, and the sacrifices of identity *or* The power of paradox and the paradox of power among the Beng of Ivory Coast. In *Creativity of power: Cosmology and action in African societies*, edited by W. Arens and I. Karp, 245–72. Washington, DC: Smithsonian.

two regions, each ruled by a king and a queen, who come from a specific matrilineal clan. The king is said to be the owner of the Earth, which is the primary focus for worship among the Beng. Violations of taboos concerning the Earth are believed to endanger the entire region and therefore must be dealt with by the king of the region. The king is also said to have the power to foresee those natural calamities that are punishment for sins committed. In general, "the king is responsible not only for the legal but also the moral and spiritual well-being of the people living in this region" (Gottlieb 1989, 249).

The legitimate power of the king is in direct contrast to the power of witches, who are considered to be utterly immoral. Using illegitimate power, working in secret, they kill and "consume" their close matrilineal kin. Nevertheless, when a man becomes king, he has one year to bewitch three close relatives in his matriline. If he fails to do so, he himself will die. Rather than destroying his power, however, this exercise of illegitimate power legitimates his rule. By killing three close matrilineal relatives, the king shows his commitment to the greater public "good." He is demonstrating his control over, and independence from, the narrow interests of his own kinship group. Operating on a plane beyond that of common morality, the king, a man who has sacrificed part of himself, will rule

the kingdom fairly. From the point of view of the Beng, including members of his own matrilineal clan, his actions are not only legitimate but also make it possible for him to rule.

Power and National Identity: A Case Study

Gramsci himself was particularly interested in how hegemony is (or is not) successfully established in state societies. In a postcolonial and globalizing world, where all people are presumed to be citizens of one or another nation-state, understanding the effects of decisions and actions of state authorities becomes crucial for making sense of many events at a local level. Anthropologists have often focused on the processes by which ruling groups in former colonies attempt to build national identity.

For example, the British colony of Ceylon became independent in 1948, later changing its name to Sri Lanka. The residents of Ceylon belonged to two major populations: the Tamils concentrated in the northern part of the island and the larger population of Sinhalese who lived elsewhere (EthnoProfile 9.2: Tamils; see EthnoProfile 7.5: Sinhalese). After independence, however, new Sinhalese rulers worked to forge a national identity rooted in their version of local history, which excluded the Tamils. In 1956, Sinhala was made the only official language; in the 1960s and 1970s, Tamils' access to education was restricted and they were barred from the civil service and the army (Daniel 1997, 316). When some Tamils began to agitate for a separate state of their own, the Sri Lankan government responded in 1979 with severe, violent repression against Tamils, sending many into exile and simulating the growth of the Tamil nationalist Liberation Tigers of Tamil Eelam (LTTE), which grew "into one of the most dreaded militant organizations in the world" (Daniel 1997, 323). By May of 2009, however, the Sri Lankan government army had retaken all territory once controlled by the Tamil Tigers. Since the 1980s, thousands have died in ethnic violence.

The exclusion of the Tamil residents from the Sri Lankan state has thus been pursued by means of violent coercion (Figure 9.4). But violence has also been used by the government against Sinhalese citizens who objected to state policies. Between 1987 and 1990, Indian troops were brought into Sri Lanka to supervise a peace agreement between Tamils and Sinhalese. These troops found themselves fighting the LTTE in the north, but they were also resisted violently in Sinhalese areas:

> the rest of the country was convulsed by a wave of terror as young members of a group called the JVP (Janata Vimukti Peramuna, or People's Liberation Front) attacked

EthnoProfile 9.2

Tamils

Region: South Asia

Nation: Sri Lanka

Population: 3,500,000 (several hundred thousand have fled the country)

Environment: Low plains; tropical monsoon climate

Livelihood: Plantation agriculture, clothing manufacture

Political organization: Modern nation-state. Long-term armed dispute between government and Tamil separatists.

For more information:
Trawick, Margaret. 2002. Reasons for violence: A preliminary ethnographic account of the LTTE. In *Conflict and community in contemporary Sri Lanka*, ed. Siri Gamage and I. B. Watson. Thousand Oaks, CA: Sage.

FIGURE 9.4   The exclusion of Tamil residents of Sri Lanka has included a move to evict Tamils living in the capital as part of a crackdown against the Tamil Liberation Tigers. Sri Lankan activists demonstrated in Colombo in June 2007 in opposition to the eviction. The Sri Lankan Supreme Court halted the eviction and set a date for a hearing on the violation of human rights.

the government not only for betraying the nation by allowing the Indian presence, but also for its own unjust political and economic policies. . . . The government responded with a wave of terror, directed at young males in particular, which reached its climax with the capture and murder of the JVP leadership in late 1989. As far as we can tell, the government won the day by concentrated terror—killing so many young people, whether JVP activists or not, that the opposition ran out of resources and leadership. (Spencer 2000, 124–25)

After 1990, violence directed by the state against Sinhalese lessened, and in 1994, a new government promised to settle the ethnic conflict by peaceful means. But even before then, Sri Lankan government efforts at nation-building had not rested entirely on violence. Leaders also tried to exercise persuasive power to convince Sinhalese citizens that the state had their welfare in mind and was prepared to take steps to improve their lives.

For example, anthropologist Michael Woost (1993) has described how the government of Sri Lanka has used a wide range of cultural media (television, radio, newspapers, the school system, public rituals, and even a lottery) to link the national identity to development. National development strategies are presented as attempts to restore Sinhalese village society to its former glory under the precolonial rule of Sinhalese kings. The ideal village, in

this view, is engaged in rice paddy cultivation carried out according to harmonious principles of Sinhala Buddhist doctrine. The villagers Woost knew could hardly escape this nationalist development discourse, but they did not resist it as an unwelcome imposition from the outside. On the contrary, all of them had incorporated development goals into their own values and had accepted that state-sponsored development would improve their lives. This might suggest that the state's attempt to establish hegemony had succeeded.

But collaboration with the state was undermined as three different village factions selectively manipulated development discourse in their struggle to gain access to government resources. For example, nationalistic rhetoric connected development with "improvement of the land." One village faction claimed it had been the first in the village to "improve the land" by building houses or planting tree crops. A second faction claimed that it had "improved the land" first by introducing paddy cultivation in the village. A third faction claimed it had "improved the land" first since its members had intermarried with other early settlers who had planted a large mango tree, a sign of permanent residence. Each faction made what the other factions interpreted as unjust claims, and each blamed the lack of village unity on the un-Buddhist greed of its opponents. These disagreements eventually led the state to withdraw its offer of resources, ultimately preventing the implementation of a village development scheme that all factions wanted!

Woost argues that the outcome of this political wrangling demonstrates the contradictory and fragile nature of the hegemonic process: Paradoxically, the villagers' active appropriation of nationalist ideology undermined efforts to establish the very social order it was supposed to create. Gramsci himself was well aware that establishing successful hegemony in a nation-state was a difficult process whose outcome was not assured; indeed, it was the very inability of Italians to achieve this goal that stimulated many of his reflections on domination and hegemony. Indeed, Gramsci's own description of a *colonial* state, emphasized by Indian historian Ranajit Guha, as dominance *without* hegemony (Crehan 2002, 125) is brought to mind by the repeated resort of the Sri Lankan state to violent coercion.

By contrast, Fischer and Benson, working in Guatemala after the 1996 peace accords, show how agency can still be exercised under dangerous and ambiguous circumstances (see the opening of this chapter). Mayan farmers they know identify "limit points" beyond which their desire for change must not be allowed to go. Mayan farmers discipline themselves to avoid thinking about all the ways in which the peace accords have failed to live up to their expectations. Instead, farmers identify, work for, and express satisfaction with limited goals they can actually reach, given the uncertain and volatile circumstances under which they must live.

For example, when Mayan farmers who grow broccoli for North American consumers earn less profit than they had hoped for, they often observe that "at least" raising broccoli on your own land is better than having to leave your family to earn cash as a migrant laborer. "At least" statements of this kind "provide a seemingly common-sensical resting place between what 'is' and what 'ought to be'" (2006, 14). By defining satisfaction in terms of limit points they themselves identify, Mayan farmers are able to see themselves as having successfully satisfied at least *some* desires of their own choosing, dissipating their dissatisfaction with and resistance to the circumstances of their lives. And it is precisely their ability to produce such a calming effect that makes the hegemonic process powerful and durable. At the same time, when farmers who hope to use income from broccoli farming to provide "something more" for their families are forced, again and again, to settle for less profit than they feel entitled to, it is difficult for them to avoid the conclusion that they are being shortchanged: "It is precisely this grounding in everyday life . . . that makes the hegemonic process an ambivalent, open-ended, never fully closed field of struggle" (2006, 15).

Biopower and Governmentality

Is there a set of skills that would bring into existence and sustain a peaceful, prosperous nation-state in places like Sri Lanka and Guatemala? This question was addressed by the French philosopher Michel Foucault, who looked at the way European thinkers from the end of the Middle Ages onward had posed (and attempted to answer) similar questions. Together with colleagues, he identified the emergence of a new form of power in the nineteenth century. This form of power he called *biopower* or *biopolitics*, and it was preoccupied with bodies—both the bodies of citizens but also the social body itself (Hacking 1991, 183). As Colin Gordon summarizes, biopower refers to "forms of power exercised over persons specifically insofar as they are thought of as living beings; a politics concerned with subjects as members of a *population*, in which issues of individual sexual and reproductive conduct interconnect with issues of national policy and power" (1991, 4–5).

Before the 1600s, according to Foucault, European states were ruled according to different political understandings. At that time, politics was focused on making sure that an absolute ruler maintained control of the state. Machiavelli's famous guide *The Prince* is the best known of a series of handbooks explaining what such an absolute ruler needed to do to maintain himself in power. But by the seventeenth century, this approach to state rule was proving increasingly inadequate. Machiavelli's critics began to speak instead about *governing* a state, likening such government to the practices that preserved and perpetuated other social institutions.

The example of household management was a preferred model of government. But running a state as if it were a household meant that rulers would need more information about the people, goods, and wealth that needed to be managed. How many citizens were there? What kinds of goods did they produce, and in what quantities? How healthy were they? What could a state do to manage the consequences of misfortunes like famines, epidemics, and death? In the 1700s, state bureaucrats began to count and measure people and things subject to state control, thereby inventing the discipline of *statistics*.

In this way, according to Foucault, European states began to govern in terms of biopolitics, using statistics to manage the people, goods, and wealth within their borders. This, in turn, led to the birth of a new art of governing appropriate to biopolitics, which Foucault calls governmentality. **Governmentality** involves using the information encoded in statistics to govern in a way that promotes the welfare of populations within a state. To exercise governmentality, for example, state bureaucrats might use statistics to determine that a famine was likely, and to calculate how much it might cost the state in the suffering and death of citizens and other losses. They would then come up with a plan of intervention—perhaps a form of insurance—designed to reduce the impact of famine on citizens, protect economic activity within the state, and thereby preserve the stability of the state and its institutions.

Governmentality is a form of power at work in the contemporary world, and institutions that rely on it count and measure their members in a variety of ways (Figure 9.5). Although, as Ian Hacking insists, not all bureaucratic applications of such statistical knowledge are evil (1991, 183), the fact remains that providing the government (or any bureaucratic institution) with detailed vital statistics can be very threatening, especially in cases where people are concerned that the state does not have their best interests at heart. After all, states want to tax citizens, vaccinate and educate their children, restrict their activities to those that benefit the state, control their movements beyond (and sometimes within) state borders, and otherwise manage what citizens do. In a globalizing world full of nation-states, anthropologists are increasingly likely in their fieldwork to encounter both the pressures of governmentality and attempts to evade or manipulate governmentality.

Trying to Elude Governmentality: A Case Study

This was the experience of Aihwa Ong (2002), who carried out research among a dispersed population of wealthy Chinese merchant families. In explaining how

governmentality The art of governing appropriate to promoting the welfare of populations within a state.

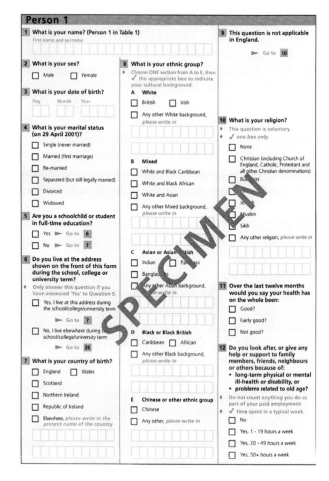

FIGURE 9.5   In order to govern, a state must know whom it is governing. Censuses are one way in which the information a state believes it needs can be collected.

these Chinese became so successful, Ong focused on the different forms of governmentality characteristic of nation-states, the capitalist market, and Chinese kinship and family. All three of these institutional contexts possess rules for disciplining individual conduct in ways that are connected to the exercise of power within the institutions themselves. Ong argues that in the late nineteenth century, some Chinese managed to evade the governmentality of Chinese kinship and family by moving physically out of China and into merchant cities of European imperial possessions in Asia and Southeast Asia.

Under these circumstances, the obligations to one's lineage were effectively severed, and the individual family and its members, under the control of males, became the virtually unique focus of loyalty among kin. But such families have had to deal with two other forms of governmentality in this new setting. One of these was the governmentality of particular states. Moving from one state to the next involved making oneself or one's family subject to different forms of biopower: For example, for

In Their Own Words

Reforming the Crow Constitution

Anthropologist Kelly Branam has worked for many years among the Apsáalooke or Crow Indian nation in central Montana, and she was able to witness complex negotiations as they struggled in 2001 to reform their constitution. In this passage, Branam discusses some of the reasons why the constitutional process has been so complex and difficult for Crow people.

With the turmoil facing the Apsáalooke or Crow Indian nation in central Montana at the turn of the century, including the distrust of their political leaders, a decade of increased chairman decision-making power under "Resolution 90–35," and the lack of large-scale resource development, it is not surprising that the discourse surrounding the 2000 tribal elections included constitutional reform. With the promise of "returning the voice to the tribal council" a new chairman was elected in 2000. In 2001, under this new leadership, the Crow Indian nation accepted a new constitution and a representative democracy. For over 50 years, the Crow Indian nation had been governed under the 1948 Constitution, which maintained a pure democracy system with executive offices of chairman, vice-chairman, secretary, and vice secretary. Why was this system no longer working for the Crow people? Why was a new constitution needed?

For many legal theorists, the importance of constitutions lies in the fact that constitutions outline the relationship the government has to its people. Constitutions restrict governmental power and often ensure citizens' rights. "The theoretical justification for the creation of an independent American nation included, at its center, an assumption that there existed some proper relationship between government and the subjects of government" (Kay 1998, 17). No doubt this is true in other constitutional instances as well. However, when it comes to the unique position of American Indian nations to the U.S. government it is important to contemplate the meaning of their constitutions. American Indian tribal constitutions exist not only to outline the relationship tribal governments have to their people, but to outline

the relationship the tribal government has to the federal government.

In today's global society, having a written form of a polity's rules outlining the ways in which those rules are made, enforced and maintained is quintessential for national survival. Despite and often because of Indian nations' "domestic dependent nation" (*Cherokee Nation v Georgia* 1831) status within the U.S. federal framework, more and more Indian nations are reformulating their tribal governing structures. "If tribal communities want to assert greater control over their economic, political, and cultural lives, they will need more effective forms of government. For many communities there is a growing sense of crisis and movement to remake tribal constitutions" (Champagne 2006, 11). Many Indian nations, including the Apsáalooke, have found constitutions crucial to the maintenance and expansion of their sovereignty.

Analysis of the Crow constitution-making processes reveals the ways in which the Crow Indian nation has resisted federal Indian policies. They have fought to maintain their sovereignty and control their political identity. Through this process, "traditional" notions of governance were redefined, district identity became more important, kinship alliances remained crucial to the political process, and the Crow Indian nation took new steps in defining and asserting their sovereignty in relation to the U.S. government. The ways in which Crows have used constitutions to resist federal assimilationist polices may provide an example for other Indian nations who are also trying to exist under the federal sphere, yet maintain traditional notions of governance.

Source: Branam, 2011.

wealthy residents of Hong Kong, "citizenship becomes an issue of handling the diverse rules or 'governmentality' of host societies where they may be economically correct in terms of human capital, but culturally incorrect in terms of ethnicity" (2002, 340).

Finally, the prosperity of these overseas Chinese families depends on doing business according to the governmentality of the capitalist market. This form of governmentality was least susceptible to evasion or

manipulation, which meant that families would try whenever possible to move family members from country to country, as needed, to take advantage of fresh opportunities for business. Such mobility, in turn, depended on being able to evade or manipulate the bureaucratic rules of state governmentality whenever these threatened to limit mobility. Thanks to their wealth, this sort of evasion was frequently possible: "international managers and professionals have the material and symbolic resources to

Anthropology in Everyday Life

Doing Business in Japan

Anthroplogist Richard Reeves-Ellington (1993) designed and implemented a cross-cultural training program for a North American company doing business in Japan (see EthnoProfile 9.3: Japan). He found that many of the traditional methods of anthropology—cultural understanding, ethnographic data, and participant-observation—helped managers conduct business in Japan. Reeves-Ellington began the training program by having employees first gather general cultural information artifacts ("How are things classified or what are the artifacts of an agreed classification system?"), social knowledge ("What are proper principles for behavior? What are the values that drive the categories and artifacts?"), and cultural logic. Social knowledge or values are based on an underlying, taken-for-granted cultural logic. Coming to understand Japanese cultural logic is of great importance to foreigners wishing to live and work in Japan.

The managers at the company decided to learn how to carry out introductions, meetings, leave-taking, dinner, and drinking in Japan (Figure 9.6). Each practice was analyzed according to the framework of artifacts, social knowledge, and cultural logic and was taught by a combination of methods that included the general observations that the managers collected while visiting Japanese museums, theaters, shrines, baseball games, and business meetings. The managers analyzed these observations and discussed stories that show how badly things can go when cultural knowledge is not sufficient. For example, one thing Reeves-Ellington's students needed to learn about introductions involved the presentation of the business card (*meishi*). The proper presentation and use of the meishi is the central element in the practice of making introductions at business meetings. Reeves-Ellington explained that, to a Japanese businessperson, the meishi is an extension of the self. Damage to the card is damage to the individual. Therefore, mistreatment of a meishi will ruin a relationship. Reeves-Ellington notes that his colleagues did not fully appreciate the consequences of these beliefs until he told them a story:

> A major U.S. company was having problems with one of its distributors, and the parties seemed unable to resolve their differences. The president of the U.S. company decided to visit Japan, meet with his counterpart in the wholesaler organization, and attempt to resolve their differences. The two had not met previously and, upon meeting, each followed proper *meishi* ritual. The American, however, did not put the Japanese counterpart's *meishi* on the table; instead he held on to it. As the conversation became heated, the American rolled up the *meishi* in his hand. Horror was recorded on the

EthnoProfile 9.3

Japan

Region: Northeastern Asia

Nation: Japan

Population: 118,000,000

Environment: Temperate climate

Livelihood: Full range of occupations to be found in a core industrial nation-state

Political organization: Highly urbanized nation-state

For mor information: Kondo, Dorinne, 1990. *Crafting selves.* Chicago: University of Chicago Press.

face of the Japanese businessman. The American then tore the *meishi* into bits. This was more than the Japanese could stand; he excused himself from the meeting. Shortly afterward the two companies stopped doing business with each other. (209)

Table 9.1 shows the information regarding introductions and the use of the meishi that Reeves-Ellington's students derived from their work based on their analytic framework of artifacts, social knowledge, and cultural logic.

On three critical measures—effective working relationships with Japanese executives, shortened project times, and improved financial returns—the anthropologically based training program that Reeves-Ellington designed was a success. Both employees and their Japanese counterparts felt more comfortable in working with each other. Prior to the program, joint projects required an average of fifteen months to complete; projects run by executives applying the methodologies of the program cut completion time to an average of eight months. Financial returns based on contracts negotiated by personnel who had not participated in the program averaged gross income of 6 percent of sales whereas those negotiated by personnel applying the anthropological techniques averaged gross income equal to 18 percent of sales.

FIGURE 9.6 Japanese and North American businesspeople negotiating pickup. Japanese and U.S. business people negotiate better when they understand something of each other's culture.

TABLE 9.1 Introductions at Business Meetings

Artifacts	Social knowledge	Cultural logic
Technology	• Once given, a card is kept—not discarded.	Human relations
• Business cards	• Meishi are not exchanged a second time unless there is a position change.	• Meishi provide understanding of appropriate relations between parties.
• Meishi	• Before the next meeting between parties, the meishi are reviewed for familiarization with the people attending the meeting.	• Meishi take uncertainty out of relationships.
Visual behavior	• The meishi provides status for the owner.	Environment
• Presentation of meishi by presenting card, facing recipient.		• Meishi help establish insider/outsider environment.
• Senior people present meishi first.		• Meishi help establish possible obligations to environment.
• Guest presents first, giving name, company affiliation, and bowing.		Human activity
• Host presents meishi in same sequence.		• Meishi help to establish human activities.
• Upon sitting at conference table, all meishi are placed in front of recipient to assure name use.		

Source: Reeves-Ellington 1993.

manipulate global schemes of cultural difference, racial hierarchy, and citizenship to their own advantage . . . in environments controlled and shaped by nation-states and capitalist markets" Ong (2002, 339).

The Ambiguity of Power

Let us sum up the argument so far. The contrast between domination and hegemony and Foucault's explorations of the machinery of governmentality demonstrate that the exercise of power cannot be equated with physical violence alone. Moreover, the occasional violent outburst of one member of a foraging society against another is not the same thing as the organized violence of one army against another in a conflict between modern nation-states. No one can deny that human beings can be violent with one another. But is this the whole story?

Anthropologist Richard Newbold Adams has said: "It is useful to accept the proposition that, while men have in some sense always been equal (i.e., in that each always has some independent power), they have in another sense never been equal (in that some always have more power than others)" (1979, 409). Political anthropologists who think of power as coercion have traditionally emphasized the universality of human inequality. Others have concentrated on the first part of Adams's observation. Some have focused on power in societies without states, whereas others have taken a more Gramscian approach and reconsidered the nature of independent power available to individuals living in societies with states. The first focus involves looking at power as an independent entity. The second looks at the power of the human imagination to define the nature of social interactions and to persuade other actors to accept these definitions of the situation.

Power as an Independent Entity

In some of the traditionally stateless societies of native North and South America, power is understood to be an entity existing in the universe independent of human beings. As such, it cannot be produced and accumulated

----

resistance The power to refuse being forced against one's will to conform to someone else's wishes.

consensus An agreement to which all parties collectively give their assent.

persuasion Power based on verbal argument.

----

through the interactions of human beings with one another. Strictly speaking, power does not belong to human beings at all. At most, people can hope to *gain access* to power, usually through ritual means. From this point of view, "control over resources is evidence of power, rather than the source of power" (Colson 1977, 382). If people assume that power is part of the natural order of things yet is independent of direct human control, certain consequences seem to follow.

First, they may be able to tap some of that power if they can discover how. Societies that see power as an independent entity usually know, through tradition, how to tap it.

Second, societies that see power as an independent force usually embed this understanding within a larger worldview in which the universe consists of a balance of different forces. Individuals may seek to manipulate those natural forces to their own ends, but only if they can do so without upsetting the universal balance.

For this reason, as a third consequence, coercive means of tapping power sources are ruled out in such societies. Violence threatens to undo the universal balance. Thus, in many native North and South American societies, gentler measures were required. One approached power through prayer and supplication. The Native American vision quest (as among the Lakota) is a good example of such an approach: Through fasting and self-induced suffering, individuals hoped to move the source of power to pity so that the source might then freely bestow on them the power they sought in the form of a vision or a song or a set of ritual formulas. Power freely bestowed would not disrupt the balance of the universe.

This leads to a fourth consequence: in such a worldview, violence and access to power are mutually contradictory. As our discussion of worldview leads us to expect, cultures that conceive of cosmic power in this way also tend to view individual human beings as independent entities who cannot be coerced but must be supplicated. Individuals in such societies are not free agents in the Western sense—free of social ties and responsibilities—but they are free in the sense that they can refuse to be forced against their will to conform to someone else's wishes. They exercise the power of **resistance**.

The power of individuals to resist affects how stateless societies arrive at decisions. A fifth consequence of viewing power as an independent entity is an emphasis on **consensus** as the appropriate means to decide issues affecting the group. In seeking consensus, proponents of a particular course of action must use **persuasion**, rather than coercion, to get other members of the group to support their cause. They resort to verbal argument, not physical intimidation. As a result, the most respected members of stateless societies, those sometimes given the title "chief" by outsiders, are persuasive speakers. Indeed, as Pierre Clastres (1977) pointed out, such respected individuals are often referred to by other members of their society as "those who speak for us." The shamans (or *mara'akate*) of the Huichol Indians of northern Mexico serve this function. By virtue of their verbal ability, they see themselves (and are seen by their fellows) as especially well suited to negotiate for all the Huichol with outsiders, especially representatives of the Mexican state.

This attitude toward power and leadership is also found elsewhere in the world. A classic example comes from the Pacific: the Big Man. Roger Keesing describes his Kwaio friend 'Elota as a *man with influence:* "When he spoke, in his hoarse voice, it was never loudly; he never shouted, never spoke in anger, never dominated conversation. Yet when he spoke people paid attention, deferred to his wisdom or laughed at his wit" (1983, 3; see Ethno-Profile 8.5: Kwaio). He owed part of his influence to an extraordinary memory. Keesing thinks 'Elota could recall genealogical information about some 3,000 to 4,000 people, as well as the details of 50 years' worth of the financial transactions that are at the heart of Kwaio feasts and marriages. In addition, "his wit and wisdom were a continuing guide towards the virtues of the past, towards thinking before rushing into action."

Keesing tells us that 'Elota was "a master gamesman, in a system where prestige derives from manipulating investments and publicly giving away valuables." Finally, 'Elota also realized that the road to prominence lay in hard work devoted to producing goods that other Kwaio wanted. Those goods included taro for feasts, pigs, cane bracelets and anklets, and bark-cloth wrapping for valuables. For 'Elota, and for the Kwaio, prestige and influence come from giving away valued things. A Big Man is a master of this, especially in financing marriages and giving feasts (Figure 9.7).

Pierre Clastres suggested that stateless forms of social organization are strongly resistant to the emergence of hierarchy (1977, 35). Indeed, he argues that members of stateless societies struggle to prevent such authority from emerging. They sense that the rise of state power spells the end of individual autonomy and disrupts beyond repair the harmonious balance between human beings and the forces of the wider world.

Richard Lee agrees, arguing that band societies, and some farmers and herders, have found ways to limit "the accumulation of wealth and power. Such societies operate within the confines of a metaphorical ceiling and floor: a ceiling above which one may not accumulate wealth and a floor below which one may not sink. These

FIGURE 9.7 A Huli man from Papua New Guinea preparing food in an earth oven. The Huli are among the people in Papua New Guinea who recognize that some men are Big Men—men with influence.

limits . . . are maintained by powerful social mechanisms known as leveling devices. . . . Such societies therefore have social and political resources of their own and are not just sitting ducks waiting to adopt the first hierarchical model that comes along" (1992a, 39–40). Leveling devices, such as institutionalized sharing, will be discussed in chapter 10.

The Power of the Imagination

We have considered a variety of attempts to understand power. Finding a focus on coercion alone to be inadequate, we have seen that Gramsci's discussion of the interplay between coercion and persuasion and Foucault's discussions of governmentality and biopolitics all offer more nuanced understandings of the different levels on which social power can operate. Still, no system of social power is ever totally successful in imposing itself. Individual human beings, though not free agents, are nevertheless empowered to resist having another's will imposed on them by force. Many anthropologists would feel that a discussion of social power is incomplete if it does not also pay attention to the way individuals make sense of and use the constraints and opportunities for action open to them, however limited they may be. That is, it is necessary to take into account the imagination—the power of all human beings to invest the world with meaning.

The Power of the Weak

Cynics might argue that the power of the imagination must in the real world be restricted to private opinions; the mind can resist, but the body must conform. From this perspective, for example, the actions of a miner who labors underground daily for a meager wage are clear-cut and unmistakable: He works for money to buy food for his family. However, ethnographic data suggest that this may not be the whole story.

The twentieth-century prototype of the downtrodden and exploited human being was the industrial laborer. In western Europe and the United States, the Industrial Revolution of the eighteenth and nineteenth centuries brought profound social and cultural dislocation. Social scientists at that time observed those changes and tried to describe them. Emile Durkheim used the term **anomie** to refer to the pervasive sense of rootlessness and normlessness that people appeared to be experiencing. Karl Marx used the term **alienation** to describe the deep separation workers seemed to experience between their innermost sense of identity and the labor they were forced to do in order to earn enough money to live.

Do industrial workers in what used to be called the Third World similarly suffer from anomie and alienation? The issue has been hotly debated. Some argue that their condition should be far worse than that of Western workers because the context of non-Western industrialization is so much more backward. This has been called the "scars of bondage" thesis. This thesis predicts that the more complete the political domination and exploitation of a people, the more deeply they will be scarred by the experience, brutalized, and dehumanized. For people

anomie A pervasive sense of rootlessness and normlessness in a society.

alienation A term used by Karl Marx to describe the deep separation that workers seemed to experience between their innermost sense of identity and the labor they were forced to perform in order to earn enough money to live.

suffering the twin exploitations of colonialism and industrialism, the outcome could only be the most bitter, unrelieved tragedy.

Hoyt Alverson (1978) set out to test the "scars of bondage" thesis in the field. He focused on migrant workers and their experiences in the gold mines of South Africa. His informants were Tswana living in the independent nation of Botswana, which forms part of South Africa's northern border (see EthnoProfile 2.1: Tswana). Botswana in the 1960s and 1970s was a poor country, and most of its families were supported only by the wages men received for working in South African mines. Here was a colonized population forced into industrial exploitation in order to survive. If the "scars of bondage" thesis was correct, the Tswana ought to be an alienated, brutalized, dehumanized lot.

Without question, the material standard of living of most of Alverson's Tswana informants was low (Figure 9.8). Without question, life in the South African mines was brutal. Without question, the difficulties families had to face when one or more of their male members was absent for months on a mining contract were considerable. And yet, for most of his informants, there was little evidence of alienation, brutalization, and dehumanization. On the contrary, his informants led coherent, meaningful lives. Despite their bondage to an exploitative system, they remained relatively unscarred. How could this be?

As it turned out, the mine experience simply did not mean to the Tswana what outside observers assumed it meant: "All phenomena, including towns and gold mines, are ambiguous and can therefore be invested with manifold meanings" (Alverson 1978, 215). In most cases, Alverson's informants had managed to come to terms with their experiences in a meaningful way. This was true both for those who were grateful to the mines and for those who hated the mines. Coming to terms with one's experiences involves mental effort. It is largely a question of finding an apt metaphor that links a person's traditional understandings with new experiences. Different people may choose different metaphors. "One Tswana may equate the relations of bosses and workers in the mine to the relationship of parent and child. If he authentically believes this analogy, then the meaning he invests in this 'inequality' will be different from that invested in it by a Tswana who defines the relationship in terms of a set of contractual exchanges made among people bound by the same set of general rights and duties" (1978, 258).

The Tswana encountered brutal inequality and discrimination outside the mines as well. Here again, however, many successfully drew on resources from their traditional culture to make sense of, and thereby

ethnocentric. They pointed out that the capitalist market is a relatively recent cultural invention in human history. Neoclassical economic theory is an equally recent invention, designed to make sense of the capitalist market and its effects, and capitalist market exchange is but one mode of exchange. Western capitalist societies distribute material goods in a manner that is consistent with their basic values, institutions, and assumptions about human nature. So, too, non-Western, noncapitalist societies have devised alternative modes of exchange that distribute material goods in ways that are in accord with their basic values, institutions, and assumptions about the human condition.

In the early twentieth century, for example, French anthropologist Marcel Mauss (2000 [1950]) had contrasted noncapitalist *gift* exchanges (which are deeply embedded in social relations, and always requiring a return gift) with impersonal *commodity* exchanges typical of the capitalist market (in which nothing links exchange partners but cash). Later, Marshall Sahlins (1972) drew on the work of economic historian Karl Polanyi to propose that three **modes of exchange** could be identified historically and cross-culturally: reciprocity, redistribution, and market exchange.

The most ancient mode of exchange was **reciprocity**. Reciprocity is characteristic of egalitarian societies, such as the Ju/'hoansi once were. Sahlins identified three kinds of reciprocity. *Generalized reciprocity* is found when those who exchange do so without expecting an immediate return and without specifying the value of the return. Everyone assumes that the exchanges will eventually balance out. Generalized reciprocity usually characterizes the exchanges that occur between parents and their children. Parents do not keep a running tab on what it costs them to raise their children and then present their children with repayment schedules when they reach the age of 18.

Balanced reciprocity is found when those who exchange expect a return of equal value within a specified time limit (for example, when a brother and sister exchange gifts of equal value with one another at Christmastime). Lee notes that the Ju/'hoansi distinguish between barter, which requires an immediate return of an equivalent, and *hxaro*, which is a kind of generalized reciprocity that encourages social obligations to be extended into the future (1992b, 103).

Finally, *negative reciprocity* is an exchange of goods and services in which at least one party attempts to get something for nothing without suffering any penalties. These attempts can range from haggling over prices to outright seizure.

Redistribution, the second mode of exchange, requires some form of centralized social organization.

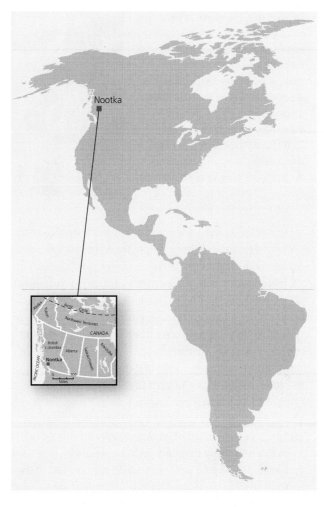

FIGURE 10.4 Locations of societies whose EthnoProfiles appear in chapter 10.

Those who occupy the central position receive economic contributions from all members of the group. It is then their responsibility to redistribute the goods they receive in a way that provides for every member of the group. The Internal Revenue Service is probably the institution of redistribution that Americans know best. A classic anthropological example involves the *potlatch* of the indigenous Americans of the northwest coast of North America (Figure 10.5). In the highly stratified fishing and gathering

---

modes of exchange Patterns according to which distribution takes place: reciprocity, redistribution, and market exchange.

reciprocity The exchange of goods and services of equal value. Anthropologists distinguish three forms of reciprocity: generalized, in which neither the time nor the value of the return are specified; balanced, in which a return of equal value is expected within a specified time limit; and negative, in which parties to the exchange hope to get something for nothing.

redistribution A mode of exchange that requires some form of centralized social organization to receive economic contributions from all members of the group and to redistribute them in such a way that every group member is provided for.

FIGURE 10.5 A classic anthropological case study of redistribution involves the *potlatch* of the Indian people of the northwest coast of North America. Although the potlatch was outlawed in 1904, it continued to be practiced. In 2004, Tlingit clan members, wearing Chilkat and Raven's Tail robes and clan hats, gathered in Sitka, Alaska, for the 100th Anniversary Commemoration of "The Last Potlatch."

society of the Nootka, for example, nobles sought to outdo one another in generosity by giving away vast quantities of objects during the potlatch ceremony (see EthnoProfile 10.1: Nootka). The noble giving the potlatch accumulated goods produced in one village and redistributed them to other nobles attending the ceremony. When the guests returned to their own villages, they, in turn, redistributed the goods among their followers.

Market exchange, invented in capitalist society, is the most recent mode of exchange, according to Polanyi (Figure 10.6). Capitalism involves an exchange of goods (*trade*) calculated in terms of a multipurpose medium of exchange and standard of value (*money*) and carried on by means of a "supply-demand-price mechanism" (the *market*). Polanyi was well aware that trade, money, and market institutions had developed independently of one another historically. He also knew that they could be found in societies outside the West. The uniqueness of capitalism was how all three institutions were linked to one another in the societies of early modern Europe.

According to Polanyi, different modes of exchange often coexist within a single society, although only one functions as the society's mode of economic integration. The United States, for example, is integrated by the market mode of exchange, yet redistribution and reciprocity can still be found. Within the family, parents who obtain income from the market redistribute that income, or goods obtained with that income, to their children. Generalized reciprocity also characterizes much exchange within the family: As noted earlier, parents provide their children with food and clothing without expecting any immediate return.

Some economic anthropologists, however, argued that exchange could not properly be understood without a prior knowledge of production. Like earlier critics of neoclassical economics, such as Karl Marx, they insisted that people who meet to exchange have different kinds and amounts of resources to use in bargaining with one another. Those differences in resources, Marx argued, are not shaped by the market but rooted in the productive process itself.

Does Production Drive Economic Activities?

Some economic anthropologists see production as the driving force behind economic activity. Production creates supplies of goods to which demand must accommodate, and it determines levels of consumption as well. Anthropologists who stress the centrality of production borrow their perspective on economic activity, as well as many key concepts, from the works of Karl Marx. They argue that this perspective is far more insightful than the one taken by neoclassical theorists of market exchange.

Labor

Labor is perhaps the most central Marxian concept these anthropologists have adopted. **Labor** is the activity linking human social groups to the material world around them; human labor is therefore always social labor. Human beings must actively struggle together to transform natural substances into forms they can use. This is clearest in the case of food production but includes the production of clothing and shelter and tools. Marx emphasized the importance of human physical labor in the material world, but he also recognized the importance of mental or cognitive labor. Human intelligence allows us to reflect on and organize productive activities. Mentally and physically,

---

market exchange The exchange of goods (trade) calculated in terms of a multipurpose medium of exchange and standard of value (money) and carried on by means of a supply-demand-price mechanism (the market).

labor The activity linking human social groups to the material world around them; from the point of view of Karl Marx, labor is therefore always social labor.

EthnoProfile 10.1

Nootka

Region: North America

Nation: Canada (Vancouver Island)

Population: 6,000 (1970s)

Environment: Rainy, relatively warm coastal strip

Livelihood: Fishing, hunting, gathering

Political organization: Traditionally, ranked individuals, chiefs; today, part of a modern nation-state

For more information:
Rosman, Abraham, and Paula G. Rubel. 1971. *Feasting with mine enemy: Rank and exchange among northwest coast societies.* New York: Columbia University Press.

human social groups struggle together to ensure their material survival. In so struggling, they reproduce patterns of social organization, production, and thought.

Modes of Production

Marx attempted to classify the ways different human groups carry out production. Each way is called a **mode of production**. Anthropologist Eric Wolf defined a mode of production as "a specific, historically occurring set of social relations through which labor is deployed to wrest energy from nature by means of tools, skills, organization, and knowledge" (1982, 75). Tools, skills, organization, and knowledge constitute what Marx called the **means of production**. The social relations linking human beings who use a given means of production within a particular mode of production are called the **relations of production**. That is, different productive tasks (clearing the bush, planting, harvesting, and so on) are assigned to different social groups, all of which must work together for production to be successful.

The concept of mode of production is holistic, highlighting recurring patterns of human activity in which certain forms of social organization, production practices, and cultural knowledge codetermine one another. Wolf notes that Marx speaks of at least eight different modes of production in his own writings, although he focused mainly on the capitalist mode. Wolf finds the concept of mode of production useful. But like most

anthropologists inspired by Marx's work, he does not feel bound to accept Marx's conclusions as a matter of course (Figure 10.7). He suggests that three modes of production have been particularly important in human history: (1) a *kin-ordered mode*, in which social labor is deployed on the basis of kinship relations (for example, husbands/fathers clear the fields, the whole family plants, mothers/wives weed, children keep animals out of the field); (2) a *tributary mode*, "in which the primary producer, whether cultivator or herdsman, is allowed access to the means of production while tribute is exacted from him by political or military means" (1982, 79); and (3) the *capitalist mode*. The capitalist mode has three main features: The means of production are property owned by the capitalists; workers are denied access to such ownership and must sell their labor to the capitalists in order to survive; and this labor for capitalists produces surpluses of wealth that capitalists may retain or plow back into production to increase output and generate further surpluses.

An overlap exists between this classification of modes of production and the traditional anthropological classification of subsistence strategies. The kin-ordered mode of production is found among foragers and those farmers and herders whose political organization does not involve domination by one group. The tributary mode is found among farmers or herders living in a social system that is divided into classes of rulers and subjects. Subjects produce both for themselves and for their rulers, who take a certain proportion of their subjects' product as tribute. The capitalist mode, the most recent to develop, can be found in the industrial societies of North America and Western Europe beginning in the seventeenth and eighteenth centuries.

Thus, in some ways the mode-of-production concept simply recognizes the same variation in the arts of subsistence recognized in the nineteenth century. Yet the concept of mode of production also highlights certain attributes of subsistence strategies that the unilineal approach tended to downplay. For example, modes of production have as much to do with forms of social and political organization as with material productive activities. That is, the kin-ordered mode of production is distinctive as much for its use of the kinship system to allocate labor to production as for the kind of production undertaken, such as farming.

mode of production A specific, historically occurring set of social relations through which labor is deployed to wrest energy from nature by means of tools, skills, organization, and knowledge.

means of production The tools, skills, organization, and knowledge used to extract energy from nature.

relations of production The social relations linking the people who use a given means of production within a particular mode of production.

In Their Own Words

"So Much Work, So Much Tragedy . . . and for What?"

Angelita P. C. (the author's surnames were initialed to preserve her anonymity) describes traditional labor for farmers' wives in Costa Rica during the 1930s. Her account was included in a volume of peasant autobiographies published in Costa Rica in 1979.

The life of farmers' wives was more difficult than the life of day laborers' wives; what I mean is that we work more. The wife of the day laborer, she gets clean beans with no rubbish, shelled corn, pounded rice, maybe she would have to roast the coffee and grind it. On the other hand, we farm wives had to take the corn out of the husk, shuck it; and if it was rice, generally we'd have to get it out of the sack and spread it out in the sun for someone to pound it in the mortar. Although we had the advantage that we never lacked the staples: tortillas, rice, beans, and sugar-water. When you had to make tortillas, and that was every day, there were mountains of tortillas, because the people who worked in the fields had to eat a lot to regain their strength with all the effort they put out. And the tortilla is the healthiest food that was eaten—still is eaten—in the countryside. Another thing we had to do often was when you'd get the corn together to sell it, you always had to take it off the cob and dry it in the sun: the men spread it out on a tarp, maybe two or three sackfuls, and they would go and bring the corn, still in the husks, up from the cornfield or the shack where it was kept. Well, we women had to guard it from the chickens or the pigs that were always in the house, but the rush we had when it started to rain and the men hadn't gotten back! We had to fill the sacks with corn and then a little later haul it in pots to finish filling them; that's if the rain gave us time. If not, all of us women in the house would have to pick up the tarps—sometimes the neighbor-women would get involved in all the bustle—to carry the corn inside. We looked like ants carrying a big worm! The thing was to keep the corn from getting wet.

It didn't matter if you threw out your spine, or if your uterus dropped, or you started hemorrhaging, or aborted, but since none of that happened immediately, it was the last thing we thought of. So much work, so much tragedy and that was so common that it seemed like just a natural thing, and for what? To sell corn at about 20 colones or at most at 24 colones per fanega [about 3 bushels] of 24 baskets! What thankless times for farm people!

Source: Autobiografías campesinas. 1979, 36 (translation from the original Spanish by Robert H. Lavenda).

In a kin-ordered mode of production, the *relations of kinship* serve as the *relations of production* that enable a particular *mode of production* to be carried out. Compare the differences in the way farm labor is organized in the kin-ordered mode, described here, to the way it is organized in the capitalist mode, where labor is often performed by nonrelatives who are paid a wage.

The Role of Conflict in Material Life

Anthropologists traditionally have emphasized the important links between a society's social organization (kinship groups, chiefdom, state) and the way that society meets its subsistence needs, either to demonstrate the stages of cultural evolution or to display the functional interrelationships between parts of a particular society. In both cases, however, the emphasis of the analysis was on the harmonious fashion in which societies either changed or stayed the same. This implied that social stability should not be tampered with. Social change was possible, but it would take place in an equally orderly fashion, in the fullness of time, according to laws of development beyond the control of individual members of society.

Many anthropologists have not been persuaded that social change is orderly or social organization by nature harmonious. They find the Marxian approach useful precisely because it treats conflict as a natural part of the human condition. The concept of mode of production makes a major contribution to economic anthropology precisely because of the very different interpretation it gives to conflict, imbalance, and disharmony in social life.

Marx pointed out, for example, that the capitalist mode of production incorporates the workers and the owners in different and contradictory ways. These groups, which he called *classes*, have different interests, and what is good for one class may not be good for all classes. The workers' desires (for higher wages with which to purchase more goods) are inevitably opposed to the owners' desires (for lower wages to increase the profits they can keep for themselves or reinvest in tools and raw materials).

FIGURE 10.6 Shirts for sale at the market in Guider, Cameroon. Markets can be found in many societies, but capitalism links markets to trade and money in a unique way.

This does not mean that the different classes engaged in production are always at war; however, it does mean that the potential for conflict is built into the mode of production itself. The more complex and unequal the involvement of different classes in a mode of production, the more intense the struggle between them is likely to be. Such struggle may not always lead to outright rebellion for sound political reasons, as was the case in "Sedaka" Village, Malaysia (see EthnoProfile 9.6: "Sedaka" Village). But we should not be surprised to find the "everyday forms of peasant resistance" that Scott discusses in his analysis of life in "Sedaka." When viewed

from a Marxian perspective, such struggles are clearly not just "healthy competition." Marx was one of the first social analysts, and certainly one of the most eloquent, to document the high level of human suffering generated by certain modes of production, particularly the capitalist mode.

Wolf's three modes of production (kin-ordered, tributary, and capitalist) describe not only a society's subsistence strategy but also that society's social organization. As a result, they accent the lines of cleavage along which tension and conflict may develop—or may have developed historically—between different segments of the society:

FIGURE 10.7 This drawing from 1562 shows Indian men breaking the soil and Indian women planting, a gender-based division of labor.

Producing Sorghum and Millet in Honduras and the Sudan

Applied anthropologists carry out much work in international development, often in agricultural programs. The U.S. Agency for International Development (AID) is the principal instrument of U.S. foreign development assistance. One direction taken by AID in the mid-1970s was to create multidisciplinary research programs to improve food crops in developing countries. An early research program dealt with sorghum and millet, important grains in some of the poorest countries in the world (Figure 10.8). This was the International Sorghum/Millet Research Project (INTSORMIL). Selected American universities investigated one of six areas: plant breeding, agronomy, plant pathology, plant physiology, food chemistry, and socioeconomic studies.

Anthropologists from the University of Kentucky, selected for the socioeconomic study, used ethnographic field research techniques to gain firsthand knowledge of the socioeconomic constraints on the production, distribution, and consumption of sorghum and millet among limited-resource agricultural producers in the western Sudan and in Honduras. They intended to make their findings available to INTSORMIL as well as to scientists and government officials in the host countries. They believed sharing such knowledge could lead to more effective research and development. This task also required ethnographic research and anthropological skill.

The principal investigators from the University of Kentucky were Edward Reeves, Billie DeWalt, and Katherine DeWalt. They took a holistic and comparative approach, called *Farming Systems Research* (FSR). This approach attempts to determine the techniques used by farmers with limited resources to cope with the social, economic, and ecological conditions under which they live. FSR is holistic because it examines how the different crops and livestock are integrated and managed as a system. It also relates farm productivity to household consumption and off-farm sources of family income (Reeves, DeWalt, and DeWalt 1987, 74). This is very different from the traditional methods of agricultural research, which grow and test one crop at a time in an experiment station. The scientists at INTSORMIL are generally acknowledged among the best sorghum and millet researchers in the world, but their expertise comes from traditional agricultural research methods. They have spent little time working on the problems of limited-resource farmers in Third World countries.

The anthropologists saw their job as facilitating "a constant dialog between the farmer, who can tell what works best given the circumstances, and agricultural scientists, who produce potentially useful new solutions to old problems" (Reeves, DeWalt, and DeWalt 1987, 74–75). However, this was easier said than done in the sorghum/millet project. The perspectives of farmers and scientists were very different from one another. The anthropologists found themselves having to learn the languages and the conceptual systems of both the farmers and the scientists for the two groups to be able to communicate.

---

between, say, parents and children or husbands and wives in the kin-ordered mode; between lords and peasants in the tributary mode; and between capitalists and workers in the capitalist mode.

Applying Production Theory to Social and Cultural Life

Economic anthropologists who focus on production as the prime causal force in material life tend to apply the metaphor of production to other areas of social life as well. They see production as involving far more than short-term satisfaction of material survival needs. If a given *mode* of production is to persist over time, the *means* and *relations* of production must also be made to persist.

For example, farmers produce grain and leave behind harvested fields. They exchange some grain with cattle herders for milk and meat, and they permit the herders' cattle to graze in the harvested fields in exchange for manure they need to fertilize their fields. Consequently, farmers and herders alike end up with a mix of foodstuffs to sustain human life (that is, to reproduce the producers). In addition, each group has what it needs in the coming season to renew its means of production. Both groups will want to ensure that similar exchanges are carried out by their children; that is, they must find a way to ensure that the next generation will consist of farmers and cattle herders producing the same goods and willing to exchange them. Therefore, not only the means of production itself must be perpetuated but the relations of production as well. The

FIGURE 10.8 INTSORMIL has been involved in the improvement of the cultivation of sorghum and millet. This is sorghum.

The anthropologists began research in June 1981 in western Sudan and in southern Honduras. They were in the field for 14 months of participant-observation and in-depth interviewing, as well as survey interviewing of limited-resource farmers, merchants, and middlemen. They discovered that the most significant constraints the farmers faced were uncertain rainfall, low soil fertility, and inadequate labor and financial resources (Reeves, DeWalt, and DeWalt 1987, 80). Equally important were the social and cultural systems within which the farmers were embedded. Farmers based their farming decisions on their understanding of who they were and what farming meant in their own cultures.

As a result of the FSR group's research, it became increasingly clear that "real progress in addressing the needs of small farmers in the Third World called for promising innovations to be tested at village sites and on farmers' fields under conditions that closely approximated those which the farmers experience" (Reeves, DeWalt, and DeWalt 1987, 77). Convincing the scientists and bureaucrats of this required the anthropologists to become advocates for the limited-resource farmers. Bill DeWalt and Edward Reeves ended up negotiating INTSORMIL's contracts with the Honduran and Sudanese governments and succeeded in representing the farmers. They had to learn enough about the bureaucracies and the agricultural scientists so they could put the farmers' interests in terms the others could understand.

As a result of the applied anthropologists' work, INTSORMIL scientists learned to understand how small farmers in two countries made agricultural decisions. They also learned that not all limited-resource farmers are alike.

The INTSORMIL staff was so impressed that it began funding long-term research directed at relieving the constraints that limited-resource farmers face. Rather than trying to develop and then introduce hybrids, INTSORMIL research aimed to modify existing varieties of sorghum. The goal is better-yielding local varieties that can be grown together with other crops.

In summary, Reeves, DeWalt, and DeWalt point out that without the anthropological research, fewer development funds would have been allocated to research in Sudan and Honduras. More important, the nature of the development aid would have been different.

result, then, is the reproduction of society from generation to generation.

People also produce and reproduce *interpretations* of the productive process and their roles in that process. As we have seen in earlier chapters, Marx used the term **ideology** to refer to the cultural products of conscious reflection, such as morality, religion, and metaphysics, that are used to explain and justify the social arrangements under which people live. For Marx, ideology was not independent of the productive process itself, and was intended to explain and justify the relations of production to those who engage in them. Anthropologists have been interested in investigating the kinds of ideas, beliefs, and values that are produced and reproduced in societies with different modes of production. As we saw in "Sedaka," the class in power usually holds to an ideology that justifies its domination. Those who are dominated may assent publicly to the ideology of the rulers, but this does not mean that they accept without question the ruling ideology. In private, as Scott demonstrated, they were likely to be highly critical and to offer alternative interpretations.

The production metaphor has yielded some important insights into social and cultural life. First, it highlights processes and relationships that the exchange metaphor tends to downplay or ignore. For example, exchange theorists are less likely to care why the different parties to

ideology Those products of consciousness—such as morality, religion, and metaphysics—that purport to explain to people who they are and to justify to them the kinds of lives they lead.

In Their Own Words

Solidarity Forever

Anthropologist Dorinne Kondo, who worked alongside Japanese women in a Tokyo sweets factory, describes how factory managers, almost despite their best efforts, managed to engender strong bonds among women workers.

Our shared exploitation sometimes provided the basis for commonality and sympathy. The paltry pay was often a subject of discussion. . . . My co-workers and I were especially aware, however, of the toll our jobs took on our bodies. We constantly complained of our sore feet, especially sore heels from standing on the concrete floors. And a company-sponsored trip to the seashore revealed even more occupational hazards. At one point, as we all sat down with our rice balls and our box lunches, the part-timers pulled up the legs of their trousers to compare their varicose veins. In our informal contest, Hamada-san and Iida-san tied for first prize. The demanding pace and the lack of assured work breaks formed another subject of discussion. At most of the factories in the neighborhood where I conducted extensive interviews, work stopped at ten in the morning and at three in the afternoon, so workers could have a cup of tea and perhaps some crackers. Nothing of the sort occurred at the Satō factory, although the artisans were, if the pace of work slackened, able to escape the workroom, sit on their haunches, and have a smoke, or grab a snack if they were out doing deliveries or running up and down the stairs to the other divisions. Informal restrictions on the part-timers' movement and time seemed much greater. Rarely, if ever, was there an appropriate slack period where all of us could take a break. Yet our energy, predictably, slumped in the afternoon. After

my first few months in wagashi, Hamada-san began to bring in small containers of fruit juice, so we could take turns having a five-minute break to drink the juice and eat some seconds from the factory. Informal, mutual support enabled us to keep up our energies, as we each began to bring in juice or snacks for our tea breaks.

The company itself did nothing formally in this regard, but informal gestures of thoughtfulness and friendliness among co-workers surely redounded to the company's benefit, for they fostered our sense of intimacy and obligation to our fellow workers. The tea breaks are one example, but so are the many times we part-timers would stop off at Iris, our favorite coffee house, to sip banana juice or melon juice and trade gossip. We talked about other people in the company, about family, about things to do in the neighborhood. On one memorable occasion, I was sitting with the Western division part-timers in a booth near the window. A car honked as it went by, and Sakada-san grimaced and shouted loudly, "Shitsurei yarō—rude bastard!" The offender turned out to be her husband. In subsequent weeks, Sakada-san would delight in recounting this tale again and again, pronouncing shitsurei yarō with ever greater relish, and somehow, we never failed to dissolve in helpless laughter.

Source: Kondo 1990, 291–92.

---

an exchange have different quantities of resources with which to bargain. Production theorists, by contrast, are interested precisely in this issue. They aim to show that access to resources is determined *before* exchange by the relations of production, which decide who is entitled to how much of what.

In particular, they reject as naive the assumption that access to valued resources is open to anyone with gumption and the spirit of enterprise. Different modes of production stack the deck in favor of some classes of people and against other classes. This is most clear in the capitalist mode, where owners have disproportionate access to wealth, power, and prestige and where the access of workers to these goods is sharply restricted. Thus, the classes who fare poorly do so not because of any inherent inferiority, laziness, or improvidence. They fail to get ahead

because the rules of the game (that is, of the mode of production) were set up in a way that keeps them from winning (Figure 10.9).

Second, a production metaphor provides an especially dynamic perspective on cultural persistence and cultural change. Production theory relates peoples' preferences for different goods to the interests and opportunities of the different classes to which they belong. People buy and sell as they do, not out of idiosyncratic whimsy but because the choices open to them are shaped by the relations of production. From this perspective, poor people do not purchase cheap goods because they have poor taste and cannot recognize quality when they see it; rather, their deprived position within the mode of production provides them with very limited income, and they must make do with the only goods they can afford, however shoddy.

CHAPTER

11

Where Do Our Relatives Come From and Why Do They Matter?

Because human beings need one another to survive and reproduce, they have invented a variety of ways of creating, maintaining, and dissolving social ties with one another. This chapter focuses primarily on a range of forms of face-to-face relatedness that different human groups have imagined and practiced in different times and places.

Martha Macintyre, an Australian anthropologist, did field research on the small island of Tubetube in Papua New Guinea from 1979 to 1983. She writes:

Like many anthropologists, I was initially taken in as "fictive kin." The explanations given to me for this were several. First, as I was going to stay on the island for a long time, I had to live in an appropriate place. I therefore needed to belong to the totemic "clan" that would enable me to live near to the main hamlet. This was a pragmatic decision. Secondly, as the only person who could translate for me was a young married man, I must become his "elder sister" in order to avoid scandal. Later a *post hoc* explanation emerged which drew on a long tradition of incorporating migrants and exiles into the community. My reddish hair, my habit of running my fingers through my hair when nervous, and the way that I hold my head at a slight angle when I listen to people intently, were indicators of my natural connection to Magisubu, the sea eagle clan. This view gained currency as I was "naturalised," and was proved to everybody's satisfaction when an elderly woman from another island pronounced that the lines on my hand proclaimed me as Magisubu.

An equally pressing reason for incorporating me was the need to minimize the disruption I caused by having no rightful place. People found it difficult to use my first name, as first names are used exclusively by spouses, or in intimate contexts. This left them with the honorific "sinabada," a form of address for senior women that was used in the colonial context for white women. It is now redolent of subservience and I hated being addressed in this way. In making me a part of the Magisubu clan, Tubetube leaders lessened my anomalous status and gave everyone on the island a way of speaking to me. Set in a large lineage with two older sisters, a mother and three powerful men as my mother's brothers, as well as numerous younger siblings, I could be managed, instructed, and guided in ways that did not threaten their dignity or mine. Although I was unaware of it at the time, there was a meeting of people who decided my fate in these terms within days of my arrival.

The adoption by Magisubu people carried with it numerous obligations, most of which were unknown to me until I was instructed as to their nature. In retrospect, they were advantageous to my research in the sense that I was given a role in various events affecting my adoptive family and so learned within a defined context. Usually, before any occasion where I might be expected to behave in some role appropriate to my (fictive) status, some senior person would explain to me

what I should do. So, for example, I was told that I must on no account step over people's belongings nor stand so that I looked down on the head of a senior man or woman, nor sit close to any affines [in-laws]. . . . On neighbouring islands I was treated as an honoured guest, unless I was accompanied by a group of Magisubu people, in which case the hosts would treat me in accordance with my fictive status within that clan. (1993, 51–52)

How Do Human Beings Organize Interdependence?

Human life is group life. How we choose to organize ourselves is open to creative variation, as we have seen. But each of us is born into a society that was already established when we arrived. Its political, economic, and cultural practices make some social connections more likely than others. Just knowing the kind of social groups a child is born into tells us much about that child's probable path in life. Such human experiences as sexuality, conception, birth, and nurturance are selectively interpreted and shaped into shared cultural practices that anthropologists call **relatedness**. As we will see in this chapter, relatedness takes many forms—friendship, marriage, parenthood, shared links to a common ancestor, workplace associations, and so on. Furthermore, these intimate everyday relationships are always embedded in and shaped by broader structures of power, wealth, and meaning.

For more than a century, anthropologists have paid particular attention to that form of relatedness believed to be based on shared substance and its transmission (Holy 1996, 171). The shared substance may be a bodily substance, such as blood, semen, genes, or mother's milk. It may be a spiritual substance, such as soul, spirit, nurturance, or love. Sometimes, more than one substance is thought to be shared. Western anthropologists noted that, like themselves, people in many societies believed that those who share a substance were related to each other in systematic ways and that, like the Western societies to which the anthropologists belonged, members of these societies had developed sets of labels for different kinds of relatives, such as *mother* and *cousin*. They also found that people in many parts of the world linked the sharing of substance to conception, the act of sexual intercourse between parents. This collection of similarities was enough to convince early anthropologists that all people base their kinship systems on the biology of reproduction. It was but a short step to conclude that

relatedness The socially recognized ties that connect people in a variety of different ways.

Western beliefs about who counts as relatives are universally valid.

For many decades, kinship studies were based on the assumption that all societies recognize the same basic biological relationships between mothers and fathers, children and parents, and sisters and brothers. But growing ethnographic evidence indicates that quite often people's understanding of their relations to other people is strikingly at odds with these genealogical connections. In other cases, the genealogical connections turn out to form but a small subset of the ways in which people create enduring relationships with one another.

Is there some social glue that ensures social cooperation? In 1968, anthropologist David Schneider argued that North Americans' ideas of kinship generated the feeling of "enduring diffuse solidarity" among all those who understood themselves to be related by ties of blood and sex. In many cases, however, human beings seek to establish (or find themselves belonging to) collectivities organized on regional, national, or global scales. As a result, they come to experience varying degrees of relatedness and solidarity with large numbers of individuals whom they will never meet face to face. As we will see in this chapter, human beings are perfectly capable of establishing and honoring ties of enduring diffuse solidarity that have nothing to do with blood or sex. Sociologist Zygmunt Bauman has argued, in fact, that "all supra-individual groupings are first and foremost processes of collectivization of friends and enemies. . . . More exactly, individuals sharing a common group or category of enemies treat each other as friends" (1989, 152).

Although a common enemy surely has the effect of drawing people together, it is rarely sufficient by itself to produce solidarity that endures. People in all societies have developed patterned social relationships that aim to bind them together for the long term, and some of these reach beyond, and even cut across, ties forged in terms of everyday relatedness. Consider, for example, the way members of Catholic monastic orders, who may neither marry nor bear children, nevertheless refer to one another as *brother*, *sister*, *father*, and *mother*. They also take as the prototype for these interpersonal relationships the formal role obligations of family members. But religious orders in many cases are large, international institutions fitting into the overall global hierarchy of the Catholic Church. Again, the kinds of connections established among members of such institutions reach far beyond the contexts of everyday, face-to-face relatedness.

As we already noted, anthropologists were the first social scientists to recognize that people in different societies classified their relatives into categories that did not correspond to those accepted in European societies.

Coming to understand the complexities of different kinds of formal kin relations helped undermine the ethnocentric assumption that European ways of categorizing relatives were a transparent reflection of natural biological ties. Indeed, beginning anthropology students from many backgrounds regularly assume that the way they grew up classifying their kin reflects the universal truth about human relatedness. For this reason, we devote part of this chapter to introducing some findings from kinship studies in anthropology. Learning to distinguish between cross cousins and parallel cousins, or considering some of the consequences that follow from tracing descent through women rather than men remain useful exercises that help overcome ethnocentric tendencies.

At the same time, it is important to realize that the different classes of relatives identified in a formal kinship system may or may not be considered important in a particular society. Moreover, even when such kin categories remain important, ties of relatedness to people who are not formally kin may be as important as—or more important than—ties to formal kin. Formal kin ties are supplemented by or replaced by other forms of relatedness in many societies, and these forms of relatedness take a variety of patterns and operate at different scales. This chapter pays particular attention to local, face-to-face forms of relatedness, including friendship, kinship, and institutions that anthropologists call *sodalities*.

To recognize the varied forms that institutions of human relatedness can take is to acknowledge fundamental openness in the organization of human interdependence. This openness makes possible the elaboration and extension of ties of relatedness beyond face-to-face contexts. Structures of relatedness with increasingly vast scope tend to emerge when changed historical circumstances draw people's attention to shared aspects of their lives that more intimate forms of relatedness ignore or cannot handle. New shared experiences offer raw material for the invention of new forms of common identity. Recognition of this process led political scientist Benedict Anderson to invent the term **imagined communities** to refer to "all communities larger than primordial villages of face-to-face contact (and perhaps even these)" (1983, 6). Anderson originally applied the concept of "imagined communities" to modern nation-states, but anthropologists were

---

imagined communities Term borrowed from political scientist Benedict Anderson to refer to groups whose members' knowledge of one another does not come from regular face-to-face interactions but is based on shared experiences with national institutions, such as schools and government bureaucracies.

FIGURE 11.1 Locations of societies whose EthnoProfiles appear in chapter 11.

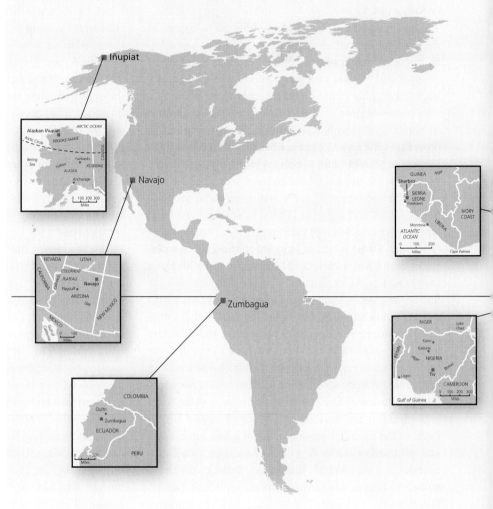

quick to note the range of communities included in his definition and have used the concept successfully to study different forms of human relatedness. The concept of imagined communities is important because it emphasizes that the ties that bind people into *all* supra-individual communities are *contingent*: They have not existed since the beginning of time and they may disappear in the future. Put another way, imagined communities are social, cultural, and historical constructions. They are the joint outcome of shared habitual practices and of symbolic images of common identity promulgated by group members with an interest in making a particular imagined identity endure.

friendship The relatively "unofficial" bonds that people construct with one another that tend to be personal, affective, and often a matter of choice.

What Is Friendship?

Anthropologist Robert Brain cited a dictionary definition of *friend* as "one joined to another in intimacy and mutual benevolence independent of sexual or family love" (1976, 15). He quickly pointed out that the Western belief that friendship and kinship are separate phenomena often breaks down in practice. Today, for example, some husbands and wives in Western societies consider each other "best friends." Similarly, we may become friends with some of our relatives while treating others the same way we treat nonrelatives. Presumably, we can be friends with people over and above any kinship ties we might have with them. Sandra Bell and Simon Coleman suggest that typical "markers" for **friendship** are

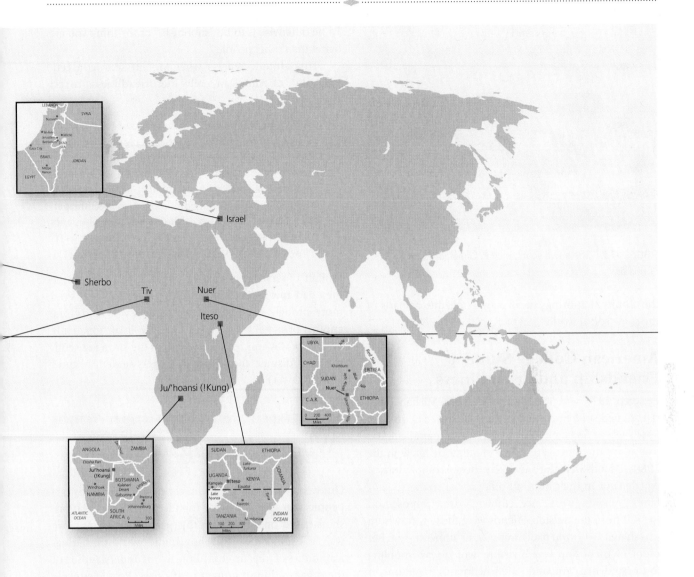

the relatively "unofficial" bonds that people construct with one another (Figure 11.2). These tend to be bonds that are personal, affective, and, to a varying extent from society to society, a matter of choice. In contemporary society, social networking programs like Facebook are taking friendship in new and unprecedented directions: what can it mean to have 900 friends? The line between friendship and kinship is often a very fuzzy one, since there may be an affective quality to kinship relations (we can like our cousins and do the same things with them that we would do with friends), since sometimes friends are seen after a long time as being related, and since some societies have networks of relatedness that can be activated or not for reasons of sentiment, not just for pragmatic reasons. Friendship has been difficult for some anthropologists to study, since in the past they have concentrated on trying to find regular long-

term patterns of social organization in societies with noncentralized forms of political organization (Bell and Coleman 1999, 4). Bell and Coleman also note that the importance of friendship seems to be increasing: "In many shifting social contexts, ties of kinship tend to be transformed and often weakened by complex and often contradictory processes of globalization. At the same time new forms of friendship are emerging" (5). This is illustrated in Rio de Janeiro by Claudia Barcellos Rezende (1999), who observed the ways in which middle-class women and their maids could come to refer to each other as "friends." Within this hierarchical relationship, the distinctions that separated the women were not questioned in themselves, but the "friendship" consisted of affection, care, and consideration that both sets of women valued in their work relationship. It was a way of establishing trust: "What friendship invokes . . . is

FIGURE 11.2 These two young men in Cameroon were the best of friends.

the affinity that brings these people together as parts of the same social world" (93).

American College Student Friendship and Friendliness

Between 1977 and 1987, anthropologist Michael Moffatt studied student culture at Rutgers University in New Jersey, where he taught. Friendship was a central cultural feature for the American college students he knew in the 1980s. Friends were the only freely chosen companions of equal status in their lives; all other social connections—family, religion, work, race, ethnicity—were imposed on the self from the outside. Friends were those with whom you shared "who you really were," your authentic self. But proof of friendship was invisible, which was troubling to the students: "You and I are true friends if and only if both of us consider the other to be a true friend 'in our hearts,' and I am never entirely certain about what you really feel in your heart" (1989, 43). As a result, students spent hours thinking about and discussing the authenticity of their own friendships and those of other people they knew well. Not everyone, of course, could be a friend, but Moffatt found that the students he knew believed that normal Americans should be ready under certain circumstances to extend "real" friendship to any other person.

kinship Social relationships that are prototypically derived from the universal human experiences of mating, birth, and nurturance.

marriage An institution that prototypically involves a man and a woman, transforms the status of the participants, carries implications about sexual access, gives offspring a position in the society, and establishes connections between the kin of the husband and the kin of the wife.

descent The principle based on culturally recognized parent-child connections that define the social categories to which people belong.

adoption Kinship relationships based on nurturance, often in the absence of other connections based on mating or birth.

To be otherwise is to be "snobbish," or to "think you are better than other people."

This attitude reflects what Moffatt sees as a central value of American daily life: friendliness. To act "friendly" is

> to give regular abbreviated performances of the standard behaviors of real friendship—to look pleased and happy when you meet someone, to put on the all-American friendly smile, to acknowledge the person you are meeting by name (preferably by the first name, shortened version), to make casual body contact, to greet the person with one of the two or three conventional queries about the state of their "whole self" ("How are you?" "How's it goin'?" "What's new?") (1989, 43–44).

Moffatt observed that students were friendly to anyone they had met more than once or twice. This was even more strongly required among students who knew one another personally. "To violate 'friendly' in an apparently deliberate way was to arouse some of the strongest sentiments of distrust and dislike in Rutgers student culture" (1989, 43–44).

What Is Kinship?

Our case studies of friendship contrast the relationships people may develop with friends with other relationships based on kin ties. In this part of the chapter, we want to explore more fully how traditional anthropological studies of kinship contribute to our understanding of the organization of human relatedness. People struggle to find ways to preserve certain ties of relatedness over time, reinforcing them with public affirmations and gift exchanges. These practices aim to provide scaffolding for enduring forms of social solidarity that strengthen the agency that group members can exercise jointly in their encounters with other groups. At the same time, as we saw earlier, such publicly acknowledged forms of relatedness can be experienced as a burden from which individuals try to escape.

Anthropologists who study formal systems of **kinship** pay primary attention to those publicly recognized sets of social relations that are prototypically derived from the universal human experiences of mating, birth, and nurturance. Anthropologists call relationships based on mating **marriage** (discussed in chapter 12) and those based on birth **descent**. Although nurturance is ordinarily seen to be closely connected with mating and birth, it need not be, and all societies have ways of acknowledging a relationship based on nurturance alone. In the United States, we call this relationship **adoption**.

Why Do People Get Married and Have Families?

All societies try to find ways not only to organize daily life and social relations among individuals, but also to locate individual groups in space and to sustain and perpetuate those relations over time. The cultural practices discussed in this chapter illustrate both commonalities and variation in the way these goals are achieved in different human groups.

The distinguished Indian novelist R. K. Narayan (1906–2001) writes in his autobiography about falling in love and getting married.

> In July 1933, I had gone to Coimbatore, escorting my elder sister, and then stayed on in her house. There was no reason why I should ever hurry away from one place to another. I was a free-lance writer and I could work wherever I might be at a particular time. One day, I saw a girl drawing water from the street-tap and immediately fell in love with her. Of course, I could not talk to her. I learned later that she had not even noticed me passing and repassing in front of her while she waited to fill the brass vessels. I craved to get a clear, fixed, mental impression of her features, but I was handicapped by the time factor, as she would be available for staring at only until her vessels filled, when she would carry them off, and not come out again until the next water-filling time. I could not really stand and stare; whatever impression I had of her would be through a side-glance while passing the tap. I suffered from a continually melting vision. The only thing I was certain of was that I loved her, and I suffered the agonies of restraint imposed by the social conditions in which I lived. The tall headmaster, her father, was a friend of the family and often dropped in for a chat with the elders at home while on his way to the school, which was at a corner of our street. The headmaster, headmaster's daughter, and the school were all within geographical reach and hailing distance, but the restraint imposed by the social code created barriers. I attempted to overcome them by befriending the headmaster. He was a booklover and interested in literary matters, and we found many common subjects for talk. We got into the habit of meeting at his school after the school-hours and discussing the world, seated comfortably on a cool granite *pyol* in front of a little shrine of Ganesha in the school compound. One memorable evening, when the stars had come out, I interrupted some talk we were having on political matters to make a bold, blunt announcement of my affection for his daughter. He was taken aback, but did not show it. In answer to my proposal, he just turned to the god in the shrine and shut his eyes in prayer. No one in our social condition could dare to proceed in the manner I had done. There were formalities to be observed, and any talk for a marriage proposal could proceed only between the elders of the families. What I had done was unheard of. But the headmaster was sporting enough not to shut me up immediately. Our families were known to each other, and the class, community, and caste requirements were all right. He just said, "if God wills it," and left it at that. He also said, "Marriages are made in Heaven, and who are we to say Yes or No?" After this he explained the difficulties. His wife and womenfolk at home were to be consulted, and my parents had to approve, and so on and so forth, and then the matching of the horoscopes—this last became a great hurdle at the end. . . .
>
> What really mattered was not my economic outlook, but my stars. My father-in-law, himself an adept at the study of horoscopes, had consultations with one or two other experts and came to the conclusion that my horoscope and the girl's were incompatible. My horoscope had the Seventh House occupied by Mars, the Seventh House being the one that indicated . . . nothing but disaster unless the partner's horoscope also contained the same flaw, a case in which two wrongs make one right. . . .
>
> In spite of all these fluctuations and hurdles, my marriage came off in a few months, celebrated with all the pomp, show, festivity, exchange of gifts, and the overcrowding, that my parents desired and expected.
>
> Soon after my marriage, my father became bedridden with a paralytic stroke, and most of my mother's time was spent at his side upstairs. The new entrant into the family, my wife Rajam, was her deputy downstairs, managing my three younger brothers, who were still at school, a cook in the kitchen, a general servant, and a gigantic black-and-white Great Dane acquired by my elder brother, who was a dog-lover. She kept an eye on the stores, replenishing the food-stuffs and guarding them from being squandered or stolen by the cook. Rajam was less than twenty, but managed the housekeeping expertly and earned my mother's praise. She got on excellently with my brothers. This was one advantage of a joint family system—one had plenty of company at home. (1974, 106–10)

Narayan had fallen in love, gotten married, and set up housekeeping with his wife. These are familiar phases in the relationships of many men and women, yet the details of his description may seem extraordinary to many North Americans. Narayan's essay illustrates how the patterns of courtship, marriage, and housekeeping in India engage people in the wider patterns of Indian life. They channel emotion and economic activity. They also link previously unrelated people while binding individuals firmly to groups. One individual, Narayan, fell in love with and married another, Rajam. But they could never have become a married couple without knowing how to maneuver within the cultural patterns that shaped their society. Neither could they have gotten married without the active intervention of the wider social groups to which they belonged—specifically, their families.

Getting married involves more than just living together or having sexual relations, and nowhere in the world is marriage synonymous with *mating*. In most societies, marriage also requires involvement and support from the wider social groups to which the spouses belong—first and foremost from their families. *Marriage* and *family* are two terms anthropologists use to describe how different societies understand and organize mating and its consequences.

How Do Anthropologists Define Marriage?

A prototypical **marriage** (1) transforms the status of the participants; (2) stipulates the degree of sexual access the married partners are expected to have to each other, ranging from exclusive to preferential; (3) perpetuates social patterns through the production or adoption of offspring; (4) creates relationships between the kin of the partners; and (5) is symbolically marked in some way, from an elaborate wedding to simply the appearance of a husband and wife seated one morning outside her hut.

Ordinarily, a prototypical marriage involves a man and a woman. But what are we to make of the following cases? Each offers an alternative way of understanding the combination of features that define appropriate unions in a particular society.

Woman Marriage and Ghost Marriage among the Nuer

Among the Nuer, as E. E. Evans-Pritchard observed during his fieldwork in the 1930s, a woman could marry another woman and become the "father" of the children the wife bore (see EthnoProfile 11.3: Nuer). This practice, which also appears in some other parts of Africa, involves a distinction between *pater* and *genitor* (see chapter 11). The female husband (the pater) had to have some cattle of her own to use for bridewealth payments to the wife's lineage. Once the bridewealth had been paid, the marriage was established. The female husband then got a male kinsman, friend, or neighbor (the genitor) to impregnate the wife and to help with certain tasks around the homestead that the Nuer believed could be done only by men.

Generally, Evans-Pritchard (1951) noted, a female husband was unable to have children herself, "and for this reason counts in some respects as a man." Indeed, she played the social role of a man. She could marry several wives if she was wealthy. She could demand damage payment if those wives engaged in sexual activity without her consent. She was the pater of her wives' children. On the marriage of her daughters, she received

the portion of the bridewealth that traditionally went to the father, and her brothers and sisters received the portions appropriate to the father's side. Her children were named after her, as though she were a man, and they addressed her as *Father*. She administered her compound and her herds as a male head of household would, and she was treated by her wives and children with the same deference shown a male husband and father.

More common in Nuer social life was what Evans-Pritchard called the *ghost marriage*. The Nuer believed that a man who died without male heirs left an unhappy and angry spirit who might trouble his living kin. The spirit was angry because a basic obligation of Nuer kinship was for a man to be remembered through and by his sons: His name had to be continued in his lineage. To appease the angry spirit, a kinsman of the dead man—a brother or a brother's son—would often marry a woman "to his name." Bridewealth cattle were paid in the name of the dead man to the patrilineage of a woman. She was then married to the ghost but lived with one of his surviving kinsmen. In the marriage ceremonies and afterwards, this kinsman acted as though he were the true husband. The children of the union were referred to as though they were the kinsman's—but officially they were not. That is, the ghost husband was their pater, and his kinsman their genitor.

As the children got older, the name of their ghost father became increasingly important to them. The ghost father's name, not his stand-in's name, would be remembered in the history of the lineage. The social union between the ghost and the woman took precedence over the sexual union between the ghost's surrogate and the woman.

Ghost marriage serves to perpetuate social patterns. Although it was common for a man to marry a wife "to his kinsman's name" before he himself married, it became difficult, if not impossible, for him to marry later in his own right. His relatives would tell him he was "already married" and that he should allow his younger brothers to use cattle from the family herd so they could marry. Even if he eventually accumulated enough cattle to afford to marry, he would feel that those cattle should provide the bridewealth for the sons he had raised for his dead kinsman. When he died, he died childless because the children he had raised were legally the children of the ghost. He was then an angry spirit, and someone else (in

marriage An institution that prototypically transforms the status of a man and a woman, carries implications about permitted sexual access, gives the offspring a position in society, and establishes connections between the kin of the husband and the kin of the wife.

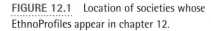

FIGURE 12.1   Location of societies whose EthnoProfiles appear in chapter 12.

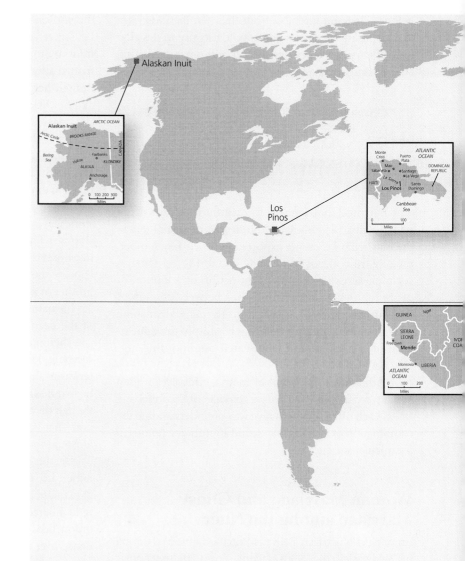

fact, one of the sons he had raised for the ghost) had to marry a wife to *his* name. Thus the pattern continued, as, indeed, it does into the present day.

Marriage as a Social Process

Like all formal definitions, our definition of marriage is somewhat rigid, especially if we think of marriage as a ritual action that accomplishes everything at a single point in time. However, if we think of marriage as a social process that unfolds over time, we find that our definition allows us to account for a wider range of marriage practices (Figure 12.2). For example, a marriage ritual may join spouses together, but their production of offspring who mature into recognized members of a particular social group takes time and cannot be assured in advance. Traditionally in some societies, a couple were not considered fully married until they had a child. Similarly, marriage set up new relations between the kin of both spouses, called **affinal** relationships (based on *affinity*—that is, created through marriage). As we saw in chapter 11, these contrast with descent-based **consanguineal** relationships (from the Latin words for "same blood"). But a married couple's relationships with their affinal kin again develop over time, and whether they get along well and cooperate or become hostile to one another cannot be predicted or controlled when a marriage is first contracted. How successfully the married couple, their children, and their other relatives are able

affinal Kinship connections through marriage, or affinity.
consanguineal Kinship connections based on descent.

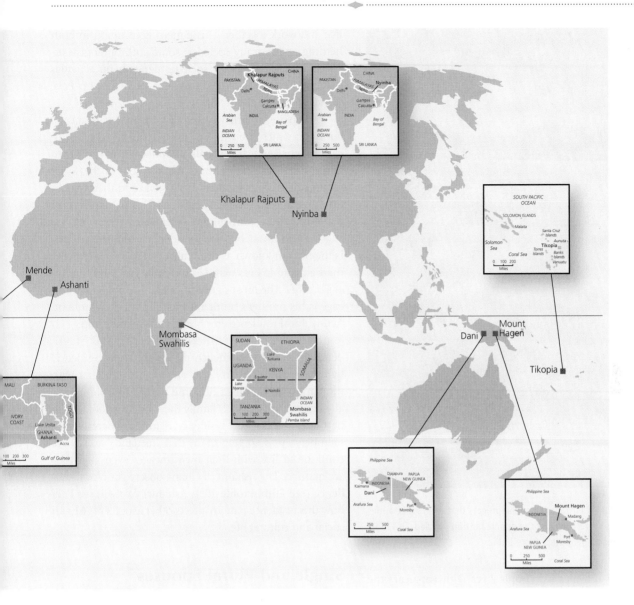

to manage the many challenges that emerge over time (economic transactions such as bridewealth payments, births, deaths, divorces) affects the extent to which they will be able to play important roles in the wider society to which they belong. The lives of all are transformed, though not all at the same time or with the same outcome—shaping the future of the community as a whole.

Sometimes marriages must be contracted within a particular social group, a pattern called **endogamy**. In other cases, marriage partners must be found outside a particular group, a pattern called **exogamy**. In Nuer society, for example, a person had to marry outside his or her lineage. Even in North American society, there is a preference for people to marry within the bounds of certain groups. People are told to marry "their own kind," which usually means their own ethnic or racial group, religious group, or social class. In all societies, some close kin are off limits as spouses or as sexual partners. This exogamous pattern is known as the *incest taboo*.

Patterns of Residence after Marriage

Once married, a couple must live somewhere. There are four major patterns of postmarital residence. Most familiar to North Americans is **neolocal** residence, in which the new couple sets up an independent household at a place of their own choosing. Neolocal residence tends to be found in societies that are more or less individualistic in their social organization.

---

endogamy Marriage within a defined social group.

exogamy Marriage outside a defined social group.

neolocal A postmarital residence pattern in which a married couple sets up an independent household at a place of their own choosing.

FIGURE 12.2 Marriage is a social process that creates social ties and involves more than just the people getting married. This is an elaborate marriage in Rajasthan, India.

When the married couple lives with (or near) the husband's father's family, it is called **patrilocal** residence, which is observed by more societies in the contemporary world than any other residence pattern. It produces a characteristic social grouping of related men: A man, his brothers, and their sons, along with in-marrying wives, all

> **patrilocal** A postmarital residence pattern in which a married couple lives with (or near) the husband's father.
>
> **matrilocal** A postmarital residence pattern in which a married couple lives with (or near) the wife's mother.
>
> **avunculocal** A postmarital residence pattern in which a married couple lives with (or near) the husband's mother's brother (from avuncular, "of uncles").
>
> **monogamy** A marriage pattern in which a person may be married to only one spouse at a time.
>
> **polygamy** A marriage pattern in which a person may be married to more than one spouse at a time.
>
> **polygyny** A marriage pattern in which a man may be married to more than one wife at a time.
>
> **polyandry** A marriage pattern in which a woman may be married to more than one husband at a time.

live and work together. This pattern is common in both herding and farming societies; some anthropologists argue that survival in such societies depends on activities that are best carried out by groups of men who have worked together all their lives.

When the married couple lives with (or near) the family in which the wife was raised, it is called **matrilocal** residence, which is usually found in association with matrilineal kinship systems. Here, the core of the social group consists of a woman, her sisters, and their daughters, together with in-marrying men. This pattern is most common among horticultural groups.

Less common, but also found in matrilineal societies, is the pattern known as **avunculocal** residence. Here, the married couple lives with (or near) the husband's mother's brother. The most significant man in a boy's matrilineage is his mother's brother, from whom he will inherit. Avunculocal residence emphasizes this relationship.

There are other, even less common patterns of residence. In *ambilocal* residence, the couple shifts residence, living first with the family of one spouse and later with the family of the other. At some point, the couple usually has to choose which family they want to affiliate with permanently. *Duolocal* residence is found where lineage membership is so important that husbands and wives continue to live with their own lineages even after they are married. The Ashanti of Ghana observe duolocal residence (see EthnoProfile 12.1: Ashanti). We will see later how this residence pattern affects other aspects of Ashanti social and cultural life.

Single and Plural Spouses

The number of spouses a person may have varies cross-culturally. Anthropologists distinguish forms of marriage in terms of how many spouses a person may have. **Monogamy** is a marriage form in which a person may have only one spouse at a time, whereas **polygamy** is a marriage system that allows a person to have more than one spouse. Within the category of polygamy are two subcategories: **polygyny**, or multiple wives, and **polyandry**, or multiple husbands. Most societies in the world permit polygyny.

Monogamy Monogamy is the only legal spousal pattern of the United States and most industrialized nations. (Indeed, in 1896, a condition of statehood for the territory of Utah was the abolition of polygyny, which had been practiced by Mormon settlers for nearly 50 years.) There are variations in the number of times a monogamous person can be married. Before the twentieth century, people in western European societies generally married only once unless death intervened. Today, some observers suggest that we practice *serial monogamy;* we may be married to several different people but only one at a time.

Polygyny Polygynous societies vary in the number of wives a man may have. Islam permits a man to have as many as four wives but only on the condition that he can support them equally. Some Muslim authorities today argue, however, that equal support must be emotional and affective, not just financial. Convinced that no man can feel the same toward each of his wives, they have concluded that monogamy must be the rule. Other polygynous societies have no limit on the number of wives a man may marry. Nevertheless, not every man can be polygynous. There is a clear demographic problem: For every man with two wives, there is one man without a wife. Men can wait until they are older to marry and women can marry very young, but this imbalance cannot be completely eliminated. Polygyny is also expensive, for a husband must support all his wives as well as their children (Figure 12.3).

Polyandry Polyandry is the rarest of the three marriage forms. In some polyandrous societies, a woman may marry several brothers. In others, she may marry men who are not related to each other and who all will live together in a single household. Sometimes a woman is allowed to marry several men who are not related, but she will live only with the one she most recently married. Studies of polyandry have shed light on the dynamics of polygyny and monogamy.

Polyandry, Sexuality, and the Reproductive Capacity of Women

Different marriage patterns reflect significant variation in the social definition of male and female sexuality. Monogamy and polygyny are in some ways similar because both are concerned with controlling women's sexuality while giving men freer rein. Even in monogamous societies, men (but not women) are often expected to have extramarital sexual adventures. Polyandry is worth a closer look; it differs from polygyny or monogamy in instructive ways.

Polyandry is found in three major regions of the world: Tibet and Nepal, southern India and Sri Lanka, and northern Nigeria and northern Cameroon. The forms of polyandry in these areas are different, but all involve women with several husbands.

Fraternal Polyandry The traditional anthropological prototype of polyandry has been found among some groups in Nepal and Tibet, where a group of brothers marry one woman. This is known as *fraternal polyandry.* During one wedding, one brother, usually the oldest, serves as the

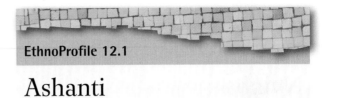

EthnoProfile 12.1

Ashanti

Region: Western Africa

Nation: Ghana

Population: 200,000

Environment: Slightly inland, partly mountainous

Livelihood: Farming, fishing, market trading (women)

Political organization: Traditionally, a kingdom; today, part of a modern nation-state

For more information:
Fortes, Meyer. 1950. Kinship and marriage among the Ashanti. In *African systems of kinship and marriage,* ed. A. R. Radcliffe-Brown and Daryll Forde. Oxford: Oxford University Press.

groom. All brothers (including those yet to be born to the husbands' parents) are married by this wedding, which establishes public recognition of the marriage. The wife and her husbands live together, usually patrilocally. All brothers have equal sexual access to the wife, and all act as fathers to the children. In some cases—notably among the Nyinba of Nepal (Levine 1980, 1988)—each child is recognized as having one particular genitor, who may be a different brother than the genitor of his or her siblings (see EthnoProfile 12.2: Nyinba). In other cases, all the brothers are considered jointly as the father, without distinguishing the identity of the genitor.

There appears to be little sexual jealousy among the men, and the brothers have a strong sense of solidarity with one another. Levine (1988) emphasizes this point for the Nyinba. If the wife proves sterile, the brothers may marry another woman in hopes that she may be fertile. All brothers also have equal sexual access to the new wife and are treated as fathers by her children. In societies that practice fraternal polyandry, marrying sisters (or *sororal polygyny*) may be preferred or permitted. In this system, a group of brothers could marry a group of sisters.

According to Levine, Nyinba polyandry is reinforced by a variety of cultural beliefs and practices (1988, 158ff.). First, it has a special cultural value. Nyinba myth provides a social charter for the practice because Nyinba legendary ancestors are polyandrous, and they are praised for the harmony of their family life. Second, the solidarity of brothers is a central kinship ideal. Third, the corporate,

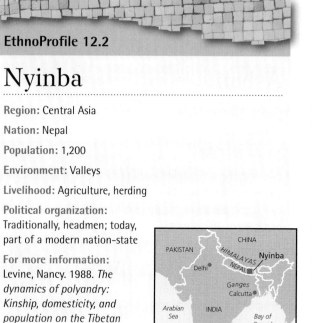

EthnoProfile 12.2

Nyinba

Region: Central Asia

Nation: Nepal

Population: 1,200

Environment: Valleys

Livelihood: Agriculture, herding

Political organization:
Traditionally, headmen; today,
part of a modern nation-state

For more information:
Levine, Nancy. 1988. *The
dynamics of polyandry:
Kinship, domesticity, and
population on the Tibetan
border.* Chicago: University of
Chicago Press.

landholding household, central to Nyinba life, presupposes polyandry. Fourth, the closed corporate structure of Nyinba villages is based on a limited number of households, and polyandry is highly effective in checking the proliferation of households. Finally, a household's political position and economic viability increase when its resources are concentrated.

Associated Polyandry A second form of polyandry, known as *associated polyandry*, refers to any system in

which polyandry is open to men who are not necessarily brothers (Levine and Sangree 1980). There is some evidence that associated polyandry was an acceptable marriage variant in parts of the Pacific and among some indigenous peoples of North and South America. The best-described form of associated polyandry, however, is from Sri Lanka (see EthnoProfile 7.5: Sinhalese). Among the Sinhalese of Sri Lanka, a woman may marry two men, but rarely more than two. Unlike fraternal polyandry, which begins as a joint venture, Sinhalese associated polyandry begins monogamously. The second husband is brought into the union later. Also unlike fraternal polyandry, the first husband is the principal husband in terms of authority. A woman and her husbands live and work together, although economic resources are held independently. Both husbands are considered fathers to any children the wife bears.

This system allows many individual choices. For example, two husbands and their wife may decide to take another woman into the marriage—often the sister of the wife. Thus, their household becomes simultaneously polygynous and polyandrous, a marriage pattern called *polygynandry*. Thus, depending on relative wealth and the availability of economic opportunity, a Sinhalese household may be monogamous, polyandrous, or polygynandrous.

As we mentioned at the beginning of the chapter, one important aspect of marriage is the creation of ties between the bride's and the groom's families. The two forms of polyandry just discussed sharply curtail the potential network of ties created by marriage. This is particularly true where fraternal polyandry occurs with preferred or permitted sororal polygyny. For example, in a Tibetan

FIGURE 12.3 The wives and children of a polygynous family.

Heider points out that Westerners assume that the sex drive is perhaps the most powerful biological drive of all, and that if this drive is not satisfied directly in sexual activity, then some other outlet will be found. In fact, some suggest that the Dani's high levels of outgroup aggression may be connected with their low level of sexual intercourse. The Dani are not celibate, and they certainly have sexual intercourse often enough to reproduce biologically, yet they do not seem very interested in sex (1979, 78–81). The Dani, who are not abnormal physically or mentally, represent an extreme in the cultural construction of sexuality.

Other Sexual Practices

The traditional anthropological focus on what European Americans call heterosexual relationships is understandable. People in every society are concerned about perpetuating themselves, and most have developed complex ideological and ritual structures to ensure that this occurs. The fact that such elaborate cultural constructions seem necessary to encourage heterosexual practices, however, suggests that human sexual expression would resist such confinement if it were not under strict control. As we saw in the previous chapter, anthropological information about supernumerary sexes and genders undermines the "two-sex model" that is hegemonic in European American cultures.

Anthropologists Evelyn Blackwood and Saskia Wieringa have studied cultural shaping of female desires. They examined how female bodies are assigned cultural meanings in different historical and ethnographic settings— and how those meanings affect the way females relate to other females. They found a wide range of "varied and rich cultural identities and same-sex practices between those with female bodies" (Blackwood and Wieringa 1999, ix). This research does not assume that having a male body or a female body necessarily determines any individual's traits, feelings, or experiences (Blackwood and Wieringa 1999, x). As a result, it provides a vital comparative context which can illuminate our understanding of sexual practices that European Americans call *homosexuality* and *bisexuality*.

Female Sexual Practices in Mombasa

Anthropologist Gil Shepherd shows that traditional patterns of male-female interaction among Swahili Muslims in Mombasa, Kenya, make male and female homosexual relationships perfectly intelligible (1987) (see EthnoProfile 12.10: Mombasa Swahilis; Figure 12.10). For one thing, men and women in Muslim Mombasa live

EthnoProfile 12.9

Dani

Region: Oceania (New Guinea)

Nation: Indonesia (Irian Jaya)

Population: 100,000 (1960s)

Environment: Valley in central highlands

Livelihood: Horticulture and pig raising

Political organization: Traditionally, some men with influence but no coercive power; today, part of a modern nation-state

For more information: Heider, Karl. 1979. *Grand Valley Dani*. New York: Holt, Rinehart & Winston.

in very different subcultures. For women, the most enduring relationship is between mothers and daughters, mirrored in the relationship between an older married sister and a younger unmarried sister. By contrast, relationships between mothers and sons and between brothers and sisters are more distant. Except in the case of young, modern, educated couples, the relationship between husband and wife is often emotionally distant as well. Because the worlds of men and women overlap so little, therefore, relationships between the sexes tend to be one-dimensional. Men and women join a variety of sex-segregated groups for leisure-time activities such as dancing or religious study. Within these same-sex groups, individuals compete for social rank.

Of the some 50,000 Swahili in Mombasa, about 5,000 could be called homosexual. The number is misleading, however, because men and women shift between what European Americans call *homosexuality* and *heterosexuality* throughout their lives. Women are allowed to choose other women as sexual partners only after they have been married. Therefore, all such women in Mombasa are married, widowed, or divorced. Both men and women are open about their same-sex relationships, and "nobody would dream of suggesting that their sexual choices had any effect on their work capabilities, reliability, or religious piety" (Shepherd 1987, 241).

Because women in many all-female households do not have sexual relationships with one another, Shepherd uses the term *lesbian* to imply an overt sexual relationship between two women. Lesbian couples in Mombasa are

EthnoProfile 12.10

Mombasa Swahilis

Region: Eastern Africa

Nation: Kenya

Population: 50,000 Swahili among 350,000 total population of city (1970s)

Environment: Island and mainland port city

Livelihood: Various urban occupations

Political organization: Part of a modern nation-state

For more information: Shepherd, Gil. 1987. Rank, gender and homosexuality: Mombasa as a key to understanding sexual options. In *The cultural construction of sexuality*, ed. Pat Caplan, 240–70. London: Tavistock.

far more likely to live together than are male homosexual couples. In addition to having private, sexual relationships with other women, they also form clublike groups that meet regularly in one another's houses. Each group is composed of an inner circle of relatively wealthy older women who are friends. The rule is that younger, lower-status women visit older, higher-status women. Wealthy lesbian women hold court in the afternoons, when Swahili women have the chance to go visiting. Women in the inner circle compete for status by, for example, trying to outdo one another by dressing their lovers as opulently as possible.

Many women were quite clear about the practical reasons that had led them into sexual relationships with other women. Women with little money are unlikely to marry men who can offer them jewelry, shoes, new dresses, status, or financial security, but a wealthy lesbian lover can offer them all these things. Also, a poor young woman in an unhappy marriage may have no way to support herself if she leaves her husband unless she has a lesbian lover. Very occasionally a wealthy lesbian woman will help a girl who has remained single after all her peers have married. Adult status and freedoms come only with marriage, but a woman who is well-educated or from a high-status family may still be unmarried in her late twenties or early thirties due to her parents' intimidation of potential suitors. A wealthy lesbian who wants to help such a woman finds a man willing to make a marriage of convenience and finances his marriage to the woman. The couple are divorced shortly thereafter, and the girl goes to live with her lesbian benefactress.

According to Islamic law, a wealthy, high-ranking Muslim woman can only marry a man who is her equal or superior. A marriage of this kind brings a great deal of seclusion, and her wealth is administered by her husband. The wealthy partner in a lesbian relationship, however, is freed from these constraints. "Thus if she wishes to use her wealth as she likes and has a taste for power, entry into a lesbian relationship, or living alone as a divorced or widowed woman, are virtually her only options" (Shepherd 1987, 257). Financial independence for a woman offers the chance to convert wealth to power. If she pays for the marriages of other people or provides financial support in exchange for loyalty, a woman can create a circle of dependents. Shepherd points out that a few women, some lesbians, have achieved real political power in Mombasa in this way (1987, 257).

Still, it is not necessary to be a lesbian to build a circle of dependents. Why do some women follow this route? The answer, Shepherd tells us, is complicated. It is not entirely respectable for a woman under 45 or 50 to be unmarried. Some women can maintain autonomy by making a marriage of convenience to a man who already lives with a wife and then living apart from him. Many women, however, find this arrangement both lonely and sexually unsatisfying. Living as a lesbian is less respectable than being a second, nonresident wife, but it is more respectable than not being married at all. The lesbian sexual relationship does not reduce the autonomy of the wealthy partner "and indeed takes place in the highly positive context of the fond and supportive relationships women establish among themselves anyway" (1987, 258).

Shepherd suggests that the reason sexual relationships between men or between women are generally not heavily stigmatized in Mombasa is because social rank takes precedence over all other measures of status. Rank is a combination of wealth, the ability to claim Arab ancestry, and the degree of Muslim learning and piety. Rank determines marriage partners, as well as relations of loyalty and subservience, and both men and women expect to rise in rank over a lifetime. Although lesbian couples may violate the prototype for sexual relations, they do not violate relations of rank. Shepherd suggests that a marriage between a poor husband and a rich wife might be more shocking than a lesbian relationship between a dominant rich woman and a dependent poor one. It is less important that a woman's lover be a male than it is for her to be a good Arab, a good Muslim, and a person of wealth and influence.

FIGURE 12.10   View of Mombasa, Kenya.

Anthropologists working in Africa have described a range of relations between females, such as woman marriage, that have been likened to European or American models of lesbian relationships, but disputes have arisen about whether such relationships included an erotic involvement between the female partners. In a survey of this evidence, Blackwood and Wieringa note that woman marriage can take many forms, some of which are more likely than others to have included sexuality between the female partners. Among those where such sexual relations appear more likely are cases like that described by Shepherd, "in which a woman of some means, either married (to a man) or unmarried, pays bride-price for a wife and establishes her own compound" (Blackwood and Wieringa 1999, 5). Such evidence is not merely of academic interest. In the contemporary world of intensified global communication and exchange, Western and non-Western same-sex practices are becoming increasingly entangled with one another, leading to the emergence of local movements for "lesbian" and "gay" rights in Africa and elsewhere. In this context, in the late 1990s, the presidents of Zimbabwe, Kenya, and Namibia declared that homosexuality is "un-African." Based on the ethnographic evidence, however, Blackwood and Wieringa side with those arguing that, on the contrary, it is homophobia that is "un-African:"

"President Mandela from South Africa is a striking exception to the homophobia of his colleagues. The South African constitution specifically condemns discrimination on the basis of sexual orientation" (1999, 27).

Male Sexual Practices in Nicaragua

Anthropologist Roger Lancaster spent many months during the 1980s studying the effects of the Sandinista Revolution on the lives of working people in Managua, Nicaragua. While he was there, he learned about *cochones. Cochón* could be translated into English as *homosexual*, but this would be highly misleading. As Lancaster discovered, working-class Nicaraguans interpret sexual relations between men differently than North Americans do, and their interpretation is central to the traditional Nicaraguan ideas about masculinity that have been called *machismo*.

To begin with, a "real man" (or *macho*) is widely admired as someone who is active, violent, and dominant. In sexual terms, this means that the penis is seen as a weapon used violently to dominate one's sexual partner, who is thereby rendered passive, abused, and subordinate. North Americans typically think of machismo as involving the domination of women by men, but as Lancaster shows, the system is equally defined by the domination of men over other men. Indeed, a "manly man" in working-class Nicaragua is defined as one who is the active, dominant, penetrating sexual partner in encounters with women *and* men. A "passive" male who allows a "manly man" to have sexual intercourse with him in this way is called a cochón.

A North American gay man himself, Lancaster found that Nicaraguan views of male-male sexual encounters differ considerably from contemporary North American ideas about male homosexuality. In Nicaragua, for example, the people Lancaster knew assumed that men "would naturally be aroused by the idea of anally penetrating another male" (1992, 241). Only the "passive" cochón is stigmatized, whereas males who always take the "active" role in sexual intercourse with other males and with females are seen as "normal." Nicaraguans, moreover, find hate crimes such as gay-bashing inconceivable: Cochones may be made fun of, but they are also much admired performers during Carnival. In the United States, by contrast, the active-passive distinction does not exist, and anal intercourse is not the only form that male homosexual expression may take. Both partners in same-sex encounters are considered homosexual and equally stigmatized, and gay-bashing is a sometimes deadly reality, probably because it is *not* assumed that "normal" males will naturally be aroused by the idea of sex with another man.

In Nicaragua, public challenges for dominance are a constant of male-male interaction even when sexual intercourse is not involved. The term *cochón* may be used as an epithet not only for a man who yields publicly to another man, but also for cats that don't catch mice, or indeed anything that somehow fails to perform its proper function. In Lancaster's view, cochones are made, not born: "Those who consistently lose out in the competition for male status . . . discover pleasure in the passive sexual role or its social status: these men are made into cochones. And those who master the rules of conventional masculinity . . . are made into machistas" (1992, 249).

These ideas about gender and sexuality created an unanticipated roadblock for Sandinistas who wanted to improve the lives of Nicaraguan women and children. The Sandinista government passed a series of New Family Laws, which were designed to encourage men to support their families economically and to discourage irresponsible sex, irresponsible parenting, and familial dislocation. When Lancaster interviewed Nicaraguan men to see what they thought of these laws, however, he repeatedly got the following response: "First the interrogative: 'What do the Sandinistas want from us? That we should all become cochones?' And then the tautological: 'A man has to

be a man.' That is, a man is defined by what he is not—a cochón" (1992, 274).

Love, Marriage, and HIV/AIDS in Nigeria

While marriages among the Igbo (the third largest ethnic group in Nigeria) used to be arranged, today ideas about romantic love have become increasingly important, and most young people expect to marry for love. Anthropologist Daniel Smith (2006) explored how changes in Igbo ideas about marriage, romance, intimacy, and premarital sex intersect with older ideas about parenthood, gender inequality; and how male extramarital sexual relationships put married women at serious risk for contracting HIV/AIDS from their husbands.

Historically, Igbo marriage was "an alliance between two families rather than a contract between two individuals" (Uchendu 1965, 50), and regularly took several years to accomplish. After marriage, the couple ordinarily lived in the compound of the husband's father, and (although this was changing by the mid-1960s) the bride was expected to be a virgin at marriage. Uchendu mentioned that among Igbo professionals, the trend was toward living in nuclear, neolocal families, and marrying for love. By the late 1990s, in a sample of 775 Igbo students Daniel Smith found that 95% said they expected to choose their marriage partners by themselves, and all 420 university students he surveyed had that expectation (Smith 2006, 140). Love was frequently mentioned as a criterion for marriage, but was not the only criterion.

Given that men and women are marrying at a later age, that love is becoming an increasingly important criterion for marriage, and that there is a greater value for male–female intimacy in relationships, Smith points out that premarital sexual relationships are increasingly common. "Sex is being socially constructed as an appropriate expression of intimacy, but also as a statement about a particular kind of modern identity" (141). Smith adds that premarital romances also tend to support a more egalitarian gender dynamics with regard to expectations of fidelity. During courtship, the couple's relationship is based on their personal emotional connection to each other, and both parties feel that they should be faithful to each other. If they are not, one or the other is likely to break off the relationship. But once courtship is over and a couple marries, the situation changes: "conjugal relationships are much more deeply embedded in larger kinship structures and relationships to extended family and community than premarital relationships" (143). In large part, this is due to the importance of parenthood— married people are supposed to have children. Once they have children, particularly if there is a son, there are few socially acceptable reasons for a couple to divorce. If their personal relationship is a difficult one, family members will try to mediate, but even a broken relationship between husband and wife is not generally sufficient grounds for divorce.

A second important change after marriage and parenthood is a shift away from the individualistic gender dynamics of courtship toward a more traditional pattern of male infidelity. Wives continue to want a faithful husband, but this is unrealistic; a significant proportion of married men have lovers, sometimes several in sequence. "The sad irony is that even as women continue to deploy ideals of intimacy and love to influence their husbands' sexual behavior, these very ideals prevent the negotiation of safe sex" (145). In the first place, HIV/AIDS has been defined by Igbo people as a disease of immorality spread through reckless sex with prostitutes or other strangers. But married men with lovers do not think they are engaging in reckless or anonymous sex—they know who their lovers are. Even when money changes hands it is not directly for sex; it understood to be for personal or kinship and family matters—it is for school tuition for the lover's siblings or to assist her parents with a problem in the village. Because men's lovers hardly appear to be stereotypical AIDS carriers, men see no reason to use a condom when they are with them, especially since condoms are supposed to inhibit pleasure. At the same time, for a wife who believes in ideals of love and intimacy marked by sexual fidelity, and who expects to have children, to insist that her husband use a condom can be taken by her husband as implying that he (or she!) is unfaithful. Thus, for a wife to try to protect herself undermines exactly what she wants to preserve. "Rather than protecting women, love marriages may contribute to the risk of contracting HIV from their husbands" (153).

Sexuality and Power

The physical activity that we call sexual intercourse is not just doing what comes naturally. Like so much else in human life, sex does not speak for itself, nor does it have only one meaning. Sexual practices can be used to give concrete form to more abstract notions we have about the place of men and women in the world. They may serve as a metaphor for expressing differential power within a society. This is particularly clear in the sexual practices that embody Nicaraguan machismo or North American date rape and family violence. That is, sexual practices can be used to enact, in unmistakable physical terms, the reality of differential power. This is equally clear in the arguments over "gay marriage" in the United States, since marriage in a nation-state has legal consequences and protections, as well as embodying the legitimacy of the couple's commitment to each other. This reminds us that marriages, families, and sexual practices never occur in a vacuum but are embedded in other social practices such as food production, political organization, and kinship.

Chapter Summary

1. Marriage is a social process that transforms the status of a man and woman, stipulates the degree of sexual access the married partners may have to each other, establishes the legitimacy of children born to the wife, and creates relationships between the kin of the wife and the kin of the husband.

2. Woman marriage and ghost marriage highlight several defining features of marriage and also demonstrate that the roles of husband and father may not be dependent on the gender of the person who fills it.

3. There are four major patterns of postmarital residence: neolocal, patrilocal, matrilocal, and avunculocal.

4. A person may be married to only one person at a time (monogamy) or to several (polygamy). Polygamy can be further subdivided into polygyny, in which a man is married to two or more wives, and polyandry, in which a woman is married to two or more husbands.

5. The study of polyandry reveals the separation of a woman's sexuality and her reproductive capacity, something not found in monogamous or polygynous societies. There are three main forms of polyandry: fraternal polyandry, associated polyandry, and secondary marriage.

(continued on next page)

Chapter Summary (continued)

6. Bridewealth is a payment of symbolically important goods by the husband's lineage to the wife's lineage. Anthropologists see this as compensation to the wife's family for the loss of her productive and reproductive capacities. A woman's bridewealth payment may enable her brother to pay bridewealth to get a wife.

7. Dowry is typically a transfer of family wealth from parents to their daughter at the time of her marriage. Dowries are often considered the wife's contribution to the establishment of a new household.

8. In some cultures, the most important relationships a man and a woman have are with their opposite-sex siblings. Adult brothers and sisters may see one another often and jointly control lineage affairs.

9. Different family structures produce different internal patterns and tensions. There are three basic family types: nuclear, extended, and joint. Families may change from one type to another over time and with the birth, growth, and marriage of children.

10. Most human societies permit marriages to end by divorce, although it is not always easy. In most societies, childlessness is grounds for divorce. Sometimes nagging, quarreling, adultery, cruelty, and stinginess are causes. In some societies, only men may initiate a divorce. In very few societies is divorce impossible.

11. Families have developed ingenious ways of keeping together even when some members live abroad for extended periods. Gays and lesbians in North America have created families by choice, based on nurturance, which they believe are as enduring as families based on marriage and birth.

12. Marriage rules are subject to negotiation, even when they appear rigid. This is illustrated by Iteso marriage. The Iteso depend upon women from the outside to perpetuate their patrilineages, and the women express their ironic awareness of this fact through ritualized laughter at marriage.

13. Sexual practices vary greatly worldwide, from the puritanical and fearful to the casual and pleasurable. In some societies, young men and women begin having free sexual relations from an early age until they are married. Sexual practices that North Americans call *homosexuality* or *bisexuality* may be understood very differently in different societies. In the contemporary globalizing world, Western and non-Western same-sex practices are becoming increasingly entangled with one another, leading to the emergence of local movements for "lesbian" and "gay" rights on many continents.

For Review

1. Define marriage and explain each of the five points of the definition given in the text.
2. Explain woman marriage and ghost marriage among the Nuer. Why is it important to distinguish *pater* and *genitor*?
3. What are affinal relationships? What are consanguineal relationships?
4. Distinguish between endogamy and exogamy.
5. Summarize the different kinds of residence human groups adopt after marriage.
6. Describe monogamy, polygyny, and polyandry.
7. Discuss how different marriage patterns reflect variation in social understandings of male and female sexuality.
8. What are the differences between bridewealth and dowry?
9. What is a family?
10. Summarize the major forms of the family that are discussed in the text.
11. Discuss the ways in which families change, as discussed in the text.
12. Describe the effects of international migration on families.
13. Using the case studies in the text, discuss how anthropologists understand human sexual practices.

Key Terms

marriage	patrilocal	polyandry	nuclear family
affinal	matrilocal	bridewealth	extended family
consanguineal	avunculocal	dowry	joint family
endogamy	monogamy	family	blended family
exogamy	polygamy	conjugal family	
neolocal	polygyny	nonconjugal family	

Suggested Readings

Bohannan, Paul, and John Middleton. 1968. *Marriage, family, and residence*. New York: Natural History Press. A classic collection, with important and readable articles.

Hirsh, Jennifer and Holly Wardlow, eds. 2006. *Modern loves: The anthroplogy of romantic courtship and companionate marriage*. Ann Arbor: University of Michigan Press. This collection of essays explores the many ways in which love, marriage, and desire are changing in societies around the world.

Lancaster, Roger. 1992. *Life is hard*. Berkeley: University of California Press. A stunning analysis of machismo in Nicaragua, in which sexual practices North Americans consider homosexual are interpreted very differently.

Sacks, Karen. 1979. *Sisters and wives*. Urbana: University of Illinois Press. A Marxian analysis of the notion of sexual equality. This book includes very important data and analysis on sister-brother relations.

Shostak, Marjorie. 1981. *Nisa: The life and words of a !Kung woman*. New York: Vintage. A wonderful book. The story of a Ju/'hoansi (!Kung) woman's life in her own words. Shostak provides background for each chapter. There is much here on marriage and everyday life.

Suggs, David, and Andrew Miracle, eds. 1993. *Culture and human sexuality*. Pacific Grove, CA: Brooks/Cole. A collection of important articles from a variety of theoretical perspectives on the nature and culture of human sexuality.

CHAPTER
13

What Can Anthropology Tell Us about Social Inequality?

The ethnographic and historical records show that societies in which people enjoy relatively equal relations with one another have flourished in different times and places. But cultural constructions of human differences and the use of such cultural constructions to build societies based on unequal social relations also have a long history. This chapter discusses some key forms of social and cultural inequality in the contemporary world to which anthropologists have devoted attention.

Chapter Outline

In the previous chapter, we described some of the distinctive forms of face-to-face social organization invented by societies that, at one time, were relatively egalitarian in political organization. But anthropologists have also long been interested in documenting the various forms of social stratification that human beings have invented. **Stratified societies**, you will recall, are societies made up of permanently ranked subgroups, in which the higher-ranking groups have disproportionately greater access to wealth, power, and prestige than do lower-ranking groups.

All people in the world today, even refugees, must deal with the authority of one or another nation-state, and all nation-states are socially stratified. But inequality within nation-states may be constructed out of multiple categories arranged in different, and sometimes contradictory, hierarchies of stratification. In this chapter we discuss six such categories: gender, class, caste, race, ethnicity, and nationality. It is important to emphasize from the outset that *every one of these categories is a cultural invention* designed to create boundaries around one or another imagined community. *None* of these categories maps onto unambiguous biological subdivisions within the human species, although members of societies that employ these categories often will invoke "nature" to shore up their legitimacy.

Some of these patterns (i.e., gender, class, caste) reach back thousands of years into human history. Others (i.e., race, ethnicity, and nationality) are far more recent in origin and are closely associated with changes that began in Europe some 500 years ago. The spread of capitalism and colonialism introduced new forms of stratification into formerly autonomous, egalitarian societies, and these also reshaped forms of stratification that predated their arrival.

Gender

Anthropological research on issues involving sex and gender increased enormously in the last third of the twentieth century, especially in the work of feminist anthropologists. As we saw in chapter 11, anthropologists initially defined **gender** as the cultural construction of beliefs and behaviors considered appropriate for each

---

stratified societies Societies in which there is a permanent hierarchy that accords some members privileged access to wealth, power, and prestige.

gender The cultural construction of beliefs and behaviors considered appropriate for each sex.

---

sex. Research focused not only on reproductive roles and sexuality, but also on the question of gender inequality. Beginning in the 1970s, feminist anthropologists dissatisfied with gender inequality in their own societies closely examined the ethnographic record to determine whether male dominance is a feature of all human societies.

Early work seemed to suggest that male dominance is in fact universal. For example, Sherry Ortner suggested that male dominance was rooted in a form of binary cultural thinking that opposed male to female. Males were then ranked higher than females because females were universally seen as "closer to nature," by virtue of the fact that they gave birth and nursed their young (Ortner 1974). Yet Jane Collier, Michelle Rosaldo, and Sylvia Yanagisako (1997) were able to show that the roles of men and women within families—even the very idea of what constituted a "family"—varied enormously, cross-culturally and historically. They concluded that the "nuclear family" of father, mother, and children was far from universal and was in fact best understood as a relatively recent historical consequence of the rise of industrial capitalism in western European societies. Attention to history also led anthropologist Eleanor Leacock to argue that women's subordination to men was not inevitable but could be connected explicitly to the rise of private property and the emergence of the state. She used ethnographic and historical evidence from North and South America, Melanesia, and Africa to show how Western capitalist colonization had transformed egalitarian precolonial indigenous gender relations into unequal, male-dominated gender relations (Leacock 1983).

More recently, anthropologists like Marilyn Strathern (1988) have argued that the particular relations between males and females in society need to be recognized as just one example of gender *symbolism*. Strathern defines gender as "those categorizations of persons, artifacts, events sequences, and so on which draw upon sexual imagery—upon the ways in which the distinctiveness of male and female characteristics make concrete people's ideas about the nature of social relations" (1988, ix). Thinking of gender in this way helps explain why people in some societies not only apply gendered forms of inequality to phenotypic males and females but may also use gender categories to structure relations between hierarchically ranked categories of men, as in the Nicaraguan contrast between "manly men" and *cochones* described in chapter 12. Similarly, Roy Richard Grinker found that male village-dwelling Lese householders of the Democratic Republic of Congo distinguished themselves from their forest-dwelling Efe pygmy trading partners using the same unequal gender categories that they used to distinguish themselves from their wives. From

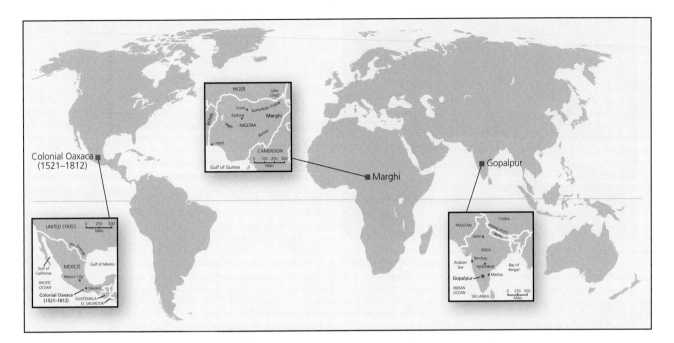

the point of view of Lese men, both Efe partners and Lese wives were subordinate to them because both had been incorporated within the households of Lese men (Grinker 1994).

Anthropologist Ann Stoler has compared Dutch colonialism in Indonesia with colonialism elsewhere. She found that white European colonizers conceived of their relationship to indigenous males in terms of both "racial" and gender inequality. The colonizers constructed a "racial" divide between colonizer and colonized, ranking "white" colonial males above the "nonwhite" indigenous males whom they had conquered. At the same time, they violently punished any hint of sexual involvement between indigenous males and "white" women while allowing themselves unrestricted sexual access to indigenous women. In this way, white male colonizers "feminized" indigenous males, constructing them as less than fully male because they had been unable to defend their land or "their women" against more powerful white outsiders. Stoler points out that white male colonizers struggled to shore up these racialized and gendered colonial hierarchies whenever indigenous males organized politically and threatened colonial rule.

Haiti began as a colony of France and achieved its independence following a successful revolt of black slaves against their white colonial masters. As Nina Glick Schiller and Georges Fouron argue, however, "Haiti has its own particular and mixed messages about gender that give to women and men both rights and responsibilities to family and nation" (2002, 133). Women appear in official stories about the Haitian revolution, some even portrayed as

heroines. Yet most are portrayed as silent wives and mothers. Moreover, the founders of the Haitian state borrowed from their former French masters "a patriarchal idea of family as well as a civil code that gave men control of family life, wealth, and property" (134). Women belonged to the Haitian nation, but "state officials and the literate elite envisioned women as able to reproduce the nation only in conjunction with a Haitian man" (134). Until recently, Haitian women who married foreigners lost their Haitian citizenship. High-status Haitian women are those who are supported economically by their Haitian husbands and who stay home with their children. Schiller and Fouron argue that many Haitians "still believe that to live by these values is to uphold not only family but also national honor" (135) (Figure 13.2).

By contrast, Haitian women who cannot live by these values are accorded low status. On the one hand, this means that they are not confined to the domestic sphere. On the other hand, for this very reason they are assumed to be always sexually available. "Men in Haiti see women alone or in the workplace as willing and able to trade their sexuality for other things they need. Men may ask rather than take, but often they are making an offer that women cannot afford to refuse" (139–40). This well describes the structural constraints with which Acéphie Joseph had to contend in our discussion of structural violence in chapter 6; options open to women of higher social class position were not available to her. To understand why, however, we need to look more closely at what anthropologists have to say about the connections between social class and social inequality.

FIGURE 13.2   The founders of the Haitian state borrowed from their former French masters an idea of gender that gave men control of family life. Women belonged to the Haitian nation, but until recently Haitian women who married foreigners lost their Haitian citizenship and their children would not be Haitians.

Class

In general, **classes** are hierarchically arranged social groups defined on economic grounds. That is, higher-ranked social classes have disproportionate access to sources of wealth in the society, whereas the members of low-ranked classes have much more limited access to wealth (Figure 13.3).

The concept of class has a double heritage in modern anthropology, one stemming from Europe, the other from the United States. European social scientists lived in states with a long history of social class divisions reaching back into the Middle Ages and, in some cases, even into Roman times. In their experience, social classes are well entrenched and relatively closed groups. The Industrial Revolution and the French Revolution promised to end the oppressive privileges of the ruling class and to equalize everyone's access to wealth. However, class divisions did not wither away in Europe during the nineteenth century; they just changed their contours. At best, an old ruling class had been displaced by a new one: feudal aristocrats by bourgeois capitalists. The lowest level in European societies—rural peasants—were partially displaced as well, with the appearance of the urban working class. But the

barriers separating those at the top of the class hierarchy from those on the bottom seemed just as rigid as ever.

As we saw in an earlier chapter, Marx defines classes in terms of their members' different relations to the means of production. This means that as long as a particular set of unequal productive relations flourishes in a society, the classes defined by these unequal roles in the division of labor will also persist. The French Revolution had triggered the displacement of aristocrats and peasants who had played the key roles in European feudalism. They were replaced by new key classes—industrial entrepreneurs and the industrial working class—who were linked together within the capitalist mode of production. In time, Marx predicted, these industrial workers would become the new "leading class," rising up to oust capitalists when the socialist revolution came.

As Marx was well aware, all those who are linked to the means of production in the same way (e.g., as workers) often do not recognize what they have in common and may therefore fail to develop the kind of solidarity among themselves—the "class consciousness"—that could, in Marx's view, lead to revolution. Indeed, the possibility of peasant- or working-class solidarity in many of the stratified societies studied by anthropologists is actively undercut by institutions of **clientage**. According to anthropologist M. G. Smith, clientage "designates a variety of relationships, which all have inequality of status of the associated persons as a common characteristic" ([1954] 1981, 31). Clientage is a relationship between individuals rather than groups. The party of superior status is the patron, and the party of inferior status is the client. Stratified societies united by links of clientage can be very stable. Low-status clients believe their security depends on finding a high-status individual who can protect them. For example, clientage is characteristic of *compadrazgo* relationships, especially when the ritual parents are of higher social status than the biological parents. In fact, the Latin American societies in which compadrazgo flourishes are class societies, and parents who are peasants or workers often seek landowners or factory owners as *compadres*.

Marx's view of class is clearly different from the view of class hegemonic in the United States. For generations the "American dream" has been that in the United States individuals may pursue wealth, power, and prestige unhampered by the unyielding class barriers characteristic of "Old World" societies. As a result, many social scientists trained in the United States (including cultural anthropologists) have tended to define social classes primarily in terms of income level and to argue that such social classes are open, porous, and permeable, rather than rigid and exclusionary. Upward class mobility is supposed to be, in principle, attainable by all people, regardless of how low their social origins are. Even poor boys like Abraham

class A ranked group within a hierarchically stratified society whose membership is defined primarily in terms of wealth, occupation, or other economic criteria.

clientage The institution linking individuals from upper and lower levels in a stratified society.

FIGURE 13.3 Social classes often live within easy sight of one another. Here, luxury apartments and squatter settlements rub shoulders in Caracas, Venezuela.

Lincoln, born in a log cabin on the frontier, can grow up to be president.

But the promise of the American Dream of equal opportunity for upward class mobility has not been realized by all those living in the United States. In the early twentieth century, both black and white social scientists concluded that an unyielding "color bar" prevented upward class mobility for U.S. citizens with African ancestry. One participant in these studies, an anthropologist named W. Lloyd Warner, argued in 1936 that the color bar looked more like the rigid barrier reported to exist between castes in India than the supposedly permeable boundary separating American social classes. That is to say, membership in a **caste** is ascribed at birth and each ranked caste is closed, such that individuals are not allowed to move from one caste into another. Membership in social classes is also ascribed at birth, according to Warner, but unlike castes, classes are not closed and individual social mobility from one class into another is possible (Harrison 1995, 1998; Sharma 1999, 15; Warner 1936). Warner's distinction between caste and class became standard for decades in American cultural anthropology.

Is this a plausible contrast? The aspect of caste that impressed Warner was the reported rigidity of the barrier between castes, which seemed much like the barrier separating blacks and whites in the United States. But in 1948, an African American sociologist named Oliver Cromwell Cox rejected an equation between caste and race. Cox pointed out that many authorities on caste in India claimed that Hindu castes were harmoniously integrated within a *caste system* shaped by Hindu religious beliefs about purity and pollution. Most importantly, it appeared that members of low-ranked "impure" castes did

not challenge the caste system even though it oppressed them. If this were true, Cox concluded, caste relations were *unlike* race relations in the United States, because whites had imposed the color bar by force and only by force had they been able to repress black resistance to the injustice of the system. Ursula Sharma (1999) points out, however, that both Warner and Cox were relying on an understanding of Hindu castes that today is considered highly misleading.

Caste

The word *caste* comes from the Portuguese word *casta*, meaning "chaste." Portuguese explorers applied it to the stratification systems they encountered in South Asia in the fifteenth century. They understood that these societies were divided into a hierarchy of ranked subgroups, each of which was "chaste" in the sense that sexual and marital links across group boundaries were forbidden. That is, in anthropological terms, castes were *endogamous*, and many anthropologists agree that caste is fundamentally a form of kinship (Guneratne 2002).

Most Western scholars have taken the stratification system of India as the prototype of caste stratification, and some insist that caste cannot properly be said to exist outside India. Others, however, do find value in applying the term to forms of social stratification developed elsewhere

---

caste A ranked group within a hierarchically stratified society that is closed, prohibiting individuals to move from one caste to another.

that bear a family resemblance to the South Asian pattern. One important example, which we examine later in this chapter, comes from Nigeria.

Caste in India

The term *caste*, as most Western observers use it, collapses two different South Asian concepts. The first term, *varna*, refers to the widespread notion that Indian society is ideally divided into priests, warriors, farmers, and merchants—four functional subdivisions analogous to the estates of medieval and early modern Europe (Guneratne 2002; Sharma 1999). The second term, *jati*, refers to localized, named, endogamous groups. Although jati names are frequently the names of occupations (e.g., farmer, saltmaker), there is no agreed upon way to group the many local jatis within one or the other of the four varnas, which is why jati members can disagree with others about where their own jati ought to belong. In any case, varna divisions are more theoretical in nature, whereas jati is the more significant term in most of the local village settings where anthropologists have traditionally conducted fieldwork.

Villagers in the southern Indian town of Gopalpur defined a jati for anthropologist Alan Beals (see Ethno-Profile 13.1: Gopalpur). They said it was "a category of men thought to be related, to occupy a particular position within a hierarchy of jatis, to marry among themselves, and to follow particular practices and occupations" (Beals 1962, 25). Beals's informants compared the relationship between jatis of different rank to the relationship between brothers. Ideally, they said, members of low-ranking jatis respect and obey members of high-ranking jatis, just as younger brothers respect and obey older brothers.

Villagers in Gopalpur were aware of at least 50 different jatis, although not all were represented in the village. Because jatis have different occupational specialties that they alone can perform, villagers were sometimes dependent on the services of outsiders. For example, there was no member of the Washerman jati in Gopalpur. As a result, a member of that jati from another village had to be employed when people in Gopalpur wanted their clothes cleaned ritually or required clean cloth for ceremonies.

Jatis are distinguished in terms of the foods they eat as well as their traditional occupations. These features have a ritual significance that affects interactions between members of different jatis. In Hindu belief, certain foods and occupations are classed as pure and others as polluting. In theory, all jatis are ranked on a scale from purest to most polluted (Figure 13.4). Ranked highest of all are the vegetarian Brahmins, who are pure enough to approach the gods. Carpenters and Blacksmiths, who also eat a vegetarian diet, are also assigned a high rank. Below the vegetarians are those who eat "clean," or "pure," meat. In

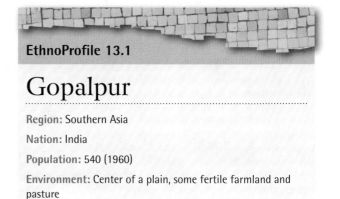

EthnoProfile 13.1

Gopalpur

Region: Southern Asia

Nation: India

Population: 540 (1960)

Environment: Center of a plain, some fertile farmland and pasture

Livelihood: Intensive millet farming, some cattle and sheep herding

Political organization: Caste system in a modern nation-state

For more information: Beals, Alan. 1962. *Gopalpur, a south Indian village*. New York: Holt, Rinehart, & Winston.

Gopalpur, this group of jatis included Saltmakers, Farmers, and Shepherds, who eat sheep, goats, chicken, and fish but not pork or beef. The lowest-ranking jatis are "unclean" meat eaters, who include Stoneworkers and Basketweavers (who eat pork) and Leatherworkers (who eat pork and beef). Occupations that involve slaughtering animals or touching polluted things are themselves polluting. Jatis that traditionally carry out such activities as butchering and washing dirty clothing are ranked below jatis whose traditional work does not involve polluting activities.

Hindu dietary rules deal not only with the kinds of food that may be eaten by different jatis but also with the circumstances in which members of one jati may accept food prepared by members of another. Members of a lower-ranking jati may accept any food prepared by members of a higher-ranking jati. Members of a higher-ranking jati may accept only certain foods prepared by a lower-ranking jati. In addition, members of different jatis should not eat together.

In practice, these rules are not as confining as they appear. In Gopalpur, "'food' referred to particular kinds of food, principally rice. 'Eating together' means eating from the same dish or sitting on the same line. . . . Members of quite different jatis may eat together if they eat out of separate bowls and if they are facing each other or turned slightly away from each other" (Beals 1962, 41). Members of jatis that are close in rank and neither at the top nor at the bottom of the scale often share food and eat together

FIGURE 13.4 Gautam Ganu Jadhao, a city worker, removes a cart full of sewage waste from a Bombay neighborhood in July 2005. People like him, whose occupations are characterized as polluting, are ranked at the bottom of Hindu caste society.

Although the interdependence of jatis is explained in theory by their occupational specialties, the social reality is a bit different. For example, Saltmakers in Gopalpur are farmers and actually produce little salt, which can be bought in shops by those who need it. It is primarily in the context of ritual that jati interdependence is given full play. Recall that Gopalpur villagers required the services of a Washerman when they needed *ritually* clean garments or cloth; otherwise, most villagers washed their own clothing. "To arrange a marriage, to set up the doorway of a new house, to stage a drama, or to hold an entertainment, the householder must call on a wide range of jatis. The entertainment of even a modest number of guests requires the presence of the Singer. The Potter must provide new pots in which to cook the food; the Boin from the Farmer jati must carry the pot; the Shepherd must sacrifice the goat; the Crier, a Saltmaker, must invite the guests. To survive, one requires the cooperation of only a few jatis; to enjoy life and do things in the proper manner requires the cooperation of many" (Beals 1962, 41).

Caste Struggle in Contemporary India

Beals's study of Gopalpur documented three dimensions of caste relations in India that have become increasingly significant over time. First, Beals describes a rural village in which jati membership mattered most on ritual occasions. In the last 30 years, cultural practices associated with caste in village India have become even more attenuated or have disappeared as increasingly large numbers of Indians have moved to large cities where they are surrounded by strangers whose caste membership they do not know (Sharma 1999, 37). They still use the idiom of purity and pollution to debate the status of particular castes, but otherwise their understanding of caste usually has nothing to do with ritual status.

Second, Beals describes members of middle-ranking jatis in Gopalpur who treated one another as equals outside of ritual contexts. Subrata Mitra points out that "By the 1960s, electoral mobilization had led to a new phenomenon called horizontal mobilization whereby people situated at comparable levels within the local caste hierarchy came together in caste associations," many of which formed new political parties to support their own interests (1994, 61). Moreover, increased involvement of Indians in capitalist market practices has led to "a proliferation of modern associations that use traditional ties of *jati* and *varna* to promote collective economic well-being" (65). For example, a housing trust set up for Brahmins in the Indian state of Karnataka recruits Brahmins from throughout the Karnataka region, in an effort to overcome "*jati*-based division into quarrelling sects of Brahmins"

on a daily basis. Strict observance of the rules is saved for ceremonial occasions.

The way in which non-Hindus were incorporated into the jati system in Gopalpur illuminates the logic of the system. For example, Muslims have long ruled the region surrounding Gopalpur; thus, political power has been a salient attribute of Muslim identity. In addition, Muslims do not eat pork or the meat of animals that have not been ritually slaughtered. These attributes, taken together, led the villagers in Gopalpur to rank Muslims above the Stoneworkers and Basketweavers, who eat pork. All three groups were considered to be eaters of unclean meat because Muslims do eat beef.

There is no direct correlation between the status of a jati on the scale of purity and pollution and the class status of members of that jati. Beals noted, for example, that the high status of Brahmins meant that "there are a relatively large number of ways in which a poor Brahmin may become wealthy" (1962, 37). Similarly, members of low-status jatis may find their attempts to amass wealth curtailed by the opposition of their status superiors. In Gopalpur, a group of Farmers and Shepherds attacked a group of Stoneworkers who had purchased good rice land in the village. Those Stoneworkers were eventually forced to buy inferior land elsewhere in the village. In general, however, regardless of jati, a person who wishes to advance economically "must be prepared to defend his gains against jealous neighbors. Anyone who buys land is limiting his neighbor's opportunities to buy land. Most people safeguard themselves by tying themselves through indebtedness to a powerful landlord who will give them support when difficulties are encountered" (Beals 1962, 39).

(66). The interests that draw jatis into coalitions of this kind "often turn out to be class interests. . . . This does not mean that caste and class are the same, since commentators note caste as blurring class divisions as often as they express them. Rather it tells us that class and caste are not 'inimical' or antithetical" (Sharma 1999, 68).

Third, Beals showed that middle-ranking jatis in Gopalpur in the 1960s were willing to use violence to block the upward economic mobility of members of a low-ranking jati. Similar behavior was reported in the work of other anthropologists like Gerald Berreman, who did fieldwork in the late 1950s in the peasant village of Sirkanda in the lower Himalayas of North India. Berreman observed that low-caste people in Sirkanda "do not share, or are not heavily committed to, the 'common official values' which high-caste people affect before outsiders. . . . Low-caste people resent their inferior position and the disadvantages which inhere in it" while "high castes rely heavily on threats of economic and physical sanctions to keep their subordinates in line," such that when low-caste people do publicly endorse "common official values," they do so only out of fear of these sanctions (1962, 15–16).

In recent years, a number of low-caste groups in urban India have undertaken collective efforts to lift themselves off the bottom of society, either by imitating the ritual practices of higher castes (a process called "Sanskritization") or by converting to a non-Hindu religion (such as Buddhism or Christianity) in which caste plays no role. According to Dipankar Gupta, this should not surprise us. His research has shown that "castes are, first and foremost, discrete entities with deep pockets of ideological heritage" and that "the element of caste competition is, therefore, a characteristic of the caste order and not a later addition. . . . This implies that the caste system, as a system, worked primarily because it was enforced by power and not by ideological acquiescence" (2005, 412–13).

These challenges have had little effect in changing the negative stereotypes of so-called untouchables held by the so-called clean castes. However, the constitution of India prohibits the practice of untouchability, and the national government has acted to improve the lot of the low castes by regularly passing legislation designed to improve their economic and educational opportunities. In some cases, these measures seem to have succeeded, but violent reprisals have been common. In rural areas many disputes continue to be over land, as in Gopalpur. However, even worse violence has been seen in urban India, as in 1990, when unrest was triggered by publication of a report recommending increases in the numbers of government jobs and reserved college places set aside for members of low castes. At the end of the twentieth century, relations between low-caste and high-caste Hindus were described as "conflictual rather than competitive in some localities"

with "caste violence . . . recognized as a serious problem in contemporary India" (Sharma 1999, 67).

Caste in Western Africa

Anthropologists often use the term *caste* to describe societies outside India when they encounter one of two features: (1) endogamous occupational groupings, whose members are looked down on by other groups in the society or (2) an endogamous ruling elite who set themselves above those over whom they rule. Anthropologist James Vaughan (1970; see also Tamari 1991) reviewed the data on western African caste systems. The presence of endogamous, stigmatized occupational groupings was common in all societies of the Sahara and in the western Sudan (the band of territory between Senegal and Lake Chad that lies south of the Sahara and north of the coastal rain forest). Vaughan also found castes in a second culture area located in the mountain ranges that lie along the modern border between Nigeria and Cameroon. In this region, many societies had endogamous groups of "blacksmiths" whose status was distinct from that of other members of society. These "blacksmiths" were not despised, however; if anything, they were feared or regarded with awe.

Vaughan studied such a caste of blacksmiths in a kingdom of the Marghi, whose traditional territory was in the mountains and nearby plains south of Lake Chad in present-day Nigeria (see EthnoProfile 13.2: Marghi; see also http://www.indiana.edu/margi). Members of the caste, who were called *ingkyagu*, were traditional craft specialists whose major occupation was the smithing of iron. They made a variety of iron tools for ordinary Marghi, the most important of which were the hoes used for farming. They also made weapons and iron ornaments of various kinds. They worked leather, fashioning traditional items of apparel, leather-covered charms, and slings in which infants were carried. They worked wood, making beds and carving stools. They were barbers, incising traditional tribal markings on Marghi women, and were responsible in some Marghi kingdoms for shaving the head of a newly installed king. They were morticians, responsible for assisting in the preparation of a body for burial, digging the grave, and carrying the corpse from the household to the grave. They were musicians, playing a distinctive drum played by no one else. Some were diviners and "doctors." And female caste members were the potters of Marghi society.

Vaughan stressed that although regular Marghi and ingkyagu both recognized that ingkyagu were different, in most ways the ingkyagu did not stand out from other Marghi. All the same, Marghi and ingkyagu did not intermarry and would not share the same food. In an interesting parallel to the Indian case described earlier, ingkyagu could drink beer brewed by Marghi women as long as

EthnoProfile 13.2

Marghi

Region: Western Africa

Nation: Nigeria

Population: 100,000 to 200,000 (1960s)

Environment: Mountains and plains

Livelihood: Farming, selling surplus in local markets

Political organization:
Traditionally, kingdoms; today,
part of a modern nation-state

For more information:
Vaughan, James. 1970. Caste
systems in the western Sudan.
In *Social stratification in
Africa*, ed. Arthur Tuden and
Leonard Plotnikov, 59–92. New
York: Free Press.

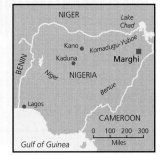

they provided their own drinking vessel. Marghi, however, would not drink beer brewed by female ingkyagu.

When Marghi described the differences between themselves and ingkyagu to Vaughan, they said that caste members were "different" and "strange." In Vaughan's opinion, this had to do in large part with the fact that ingkyagu did not farm: "To be a Marghi means to be a farmer. . . . A person who does not farm cannot in the Marghi idiom be considered an altogether normal person" (1970, 71). By contrast, ingkyagu attributed the difference between themselves and other Marghi to the division of labor and pointed out that both groups depended on one another. Marghi did their own smelting, but they required ingkyagu to use their skills as smiths to turn the smelted ore into implements. Thus, Marghi relied on members of the caste for their farming tools, but ingkyagu relied on Marghi for food.

Vaughan suggested that this division of labor and interdependence was not only practical but also part of the Marghi worldview, revealed in the domains of politics and ritual. For example, a curious relationship linked ingkyagu to Marghi kings. The most remarkable feature of this relationship was that Marghi kings traditionally took a female member of the caste as a bride, thereby violating the rule of endogamy. Recall the role a member of the caste plays during the investiture of a new king; it was even more common for ingkyagu to bury deceased Marghi kings seated on an iron stool, surrounded by charcoal, which is the way ingkyagu themselves were buried. In addition, of all Marghi clans, only the ingkyagu clans were

exempt from participating in the choice of a new Marghi king. Indeed, traditionally they had their own "king," the *ptil ingkyagu*, who decided disputes among ingkyagu without recourse to the legal advisers of the Marghi king.

All this suggests that the two categories Marghi and ingkyagu formed the foundation of Marghi society. They were mutually interdependent. The ritual prohibitions that divided them, however, suggest that this interdependence carried symbolic overtones. According to Vaughan, the caste distinction allowed the Marghi to resolve a paradox. They were a society of farmers who needed to support full-time toolmaking nonfarmers in order to farm. Marghi disliked being dependent on others, yet their way of life required them to depend on ingkyagu. The ritual prohibitions that separated ingkyagu from other Marghi also seemed designed to ensure that there would always be some caste specialists around to provide Marghi with the goods they could not make themselves.

The Value of Caste as an Analytic Category

Vaughan's study is but one example of how a generalized concept of caste can illuminate anthropological understanding of social systems with no historical connections to India. The concept of caste was also applied by anthropologist Jacques Maquet (1970) to describe the closed, endogamous ranked strata Tutsi, Hutu, and Twa in the central African kingdom of Rwanda prior to 1959. Pierre van den Berghe (1970) documented the history of caste-like relationships dating from the beginnings of white settlement in southern Africa that culminated in the twentieth-century "color caste" system distinguishing Whites, Asians, Coloreds, and Bantu that was enforced in apartheid South Africa. De Vos and Wagatsuma (1966) used the term *caste* to describe the *burakumin* of Japan, low-ranking endogamous groups traditionally associated with polluting occupations, who have been subject to dehumanizing stereotypes and residential segregation from other Japanese (Figure 13.5). Ursula Sharma suggests that the concept of caste might be fruitfully used to characterize the relations between the Rom (or Gypsies) of Europe and their non-Rom neighbors, who for centuries have subjected the Rom to stigmatization, social segregation, and economic exclusion (1999, 85–86).

A key element recognized by all anthropologists who use the concept of caste is the endogamy that is enforced, at least in theory, on the members of each ranked group. As van den Berghe put it, membership in such groups is "determined by birth and for life" (1970, 351). Sharma notes the significance of this link between descent and caste, observing that "in societies where descent is regarded as a crucial and persistent principle (however reckoned, and whatever ideological value it is given) almost

In Their Own Words

As Economic Turmoil Mounts, So Do Attacks on Hungary's Gypsies

Ethnic conflict in Europe takes a variety of forms, but one that has a long history is prejudice against Roma, the Gypsies. In April 2009, reporter Nicholas Kulish filed this story with the New York Times.

Tiszalok, Hungary—Jeno Koka was a doting grandfather and dedicated worker on his way to his night-shift job at a chemical plant last week when he was shot dead at his doorstep. To his killer, he was just a Gypsy, and that seems to have been reason enough.

Prejudice against Roma—widely known as Gypsies and long among Europe's most oppressed minority groups—has swelled into a wave of violence. Over the past year, at least seven Roma have been killed in Hungary, and Roma leaders have counted some 30 Molotov cocktail attacks against Roma homes, often accompanied by sprays of gunfire.

But the police have focused their attention on three fatal attacks since November that they say are linked. The authorities say the attacks may have been carried out by police officers or military personnel, based on the stealth and accuracy with which the victims were killed.

In addition to Mr. Koka's death, there were the slayings of a Roma man and woman, who were shot after their house was set ablaze last November in Nagycsecs, a town about an hour's drive from Tiszalok in northeastern Hungary. And in February, a Roma man and his 4-year-old son were gunned down as they tried to escape from their home, which was set on fire in Tatarszentgyorgy, a small town south of Budapest.

Jozsef Bencze, Hungary's national police chief, said in an interview on Friday with the daily newspaper *Nepszabadsag* that the perpetrators, believed to be a group of four or more men in their 40s, were killing "with hands that are too confident." Military counterintelligence is taking part in the investigation, Hungarian radio reported, and Mr. Bencze said the pool of suspects included veterans of the Balkan wars and Hungarian members of the French Foreign Legion.

Experts on Roma issues describe an ever more aggressive atmosphere toward Roma in Hungary and elsewhere in Central and Eastern Europe, led by extreme right-wing parties, whose leaders are playing on old stereotypes of Roma as petty criminals and drains on social welfare systems at a time of rising economic and political turmoil. As unemployment rises, officials and Roma experts fear the attacks will only intensify.

"One thing to remember, the Holocaust did not start at the gas chambers," said Lajos Korozs, senior state secretary in the Ministry of Social Affairs and Labor, who works on Roma issues for the government. . . .

"In the past five years, attitudes toward Roma in many parts of Eastern Europe have hardened, and new extremists have started to use the Roma issue in a way that either they didn't dare to or didn't get an airing before," said Michael Stewart, coordinator of the Europe-wide Roma Research Network.

The extreme-right party Jobbik has used the issue of what its leaders call "Gypsy crime" to rise in the polls to near the 5 percent threshold for seats in Hungary's Parliament in next year's election, which would be a first for the party. Opponents accuse the Hungarian Guard, the paramilitary group associated with the party, of staging marches and public meetings to stir up anti-Roma sentiment and to intimidate the local Roma population.

The group held a rally last year in Tiszalok and in 2007 in Tatarszentgyorgy, the town where the father and son were killed in February, an act that some residents deplored while in the same breath complaining about a spate of break-ins in town that they blamed on Roma.

"The situation is bad because of the many Roma," said Eva, 45, a non-Roma Hungarian in Tatarszentgyorgy who declined to give her last name, out of what she said was fear of reprisals. "When the guard was here, for a while they weren't so loud. It helped."

Since the attacks in Tatarszentgyorgy, some local residents have joined their terrified Roma neighbors in nighttime patrols, looking for strange cars armed with nothing but searchlights.

"We are living in fear, all the Roma people are," said Csaba Csorba, 48, whose son Robert, 27, and grandson, also named Robert, were killed by a blast from a shotgun shortly after midnight in the February attack. They were buried together in one coffin, the little boy laid to rest on his father's chest.

The child's death in particular shook Roma here. "It proved to us it doesn't matter whether we are good people or bad people," said Agnes Koka, 32, the niece and goddaughter of Mr. Koka, who relatives said loved to bring candy and fruit to his grandchildren. "It only matters that we are Gypsy," Ms. Koka said.

Source: Kulish 2009.

FIGURE 13.5   A burakumin man in Japan. De Vos and Wagat-suma argue that the term *caste* is an accurate term to apply to the burakumin.

any social cleavage can become stabilized in a caste-like form" (1999, 85). She suggests the term *castification* to describe a political process by which ethnic or other groups become part of a rank order of some kind, probably orchestrated from the top, but which need not result in the construction of a caste system (92–93).

But the principle of descent has also played a central role in the identification and persistence of race, ethnicity, and nation. As noted above, these three categories are all closely bound up with historical developments over the past 500 years that built the modern world. Indeed, these categories are particularly significant in nation-states, and many contemporary nation-states are of very recent, postcolonial origin. To make sense of contemporary postcolonial forms of social stratification, we will also need some understanding of the categories of race, ethnicity, and nation.

Race

As we saw in chapter 4, the concept of **race** developed in the context of European exploration and conquest, beginning in the fifteenth century. Europeans conquered indigenous peoples in the Americas and established colonial political economies that soon depended on the labor of Africans imported as slaves. By the end of the nineteenth century, light-skinned Europeans had established colonial rule over large territories inhabited by darker-skinned peoples, marking the beginnings of a global racial order (see Harrison 1995; Köhler 1978; Smedley 1995, 1998; Sanjek 1994; Trouillot 1994). European intellectuals wished both to explain the existence of the human diversity they had encountered and to justify the domination of indigenous peoples and the enslavement of Africans. They argued that the human species was subdivided into "natural kinds" of human beings called "races" that could be sharply distinguished from one another on the basis of physical (or *phenotypic*) appearance. Biological anthropologists contrast an organism's genetic inheritance, or *genotype*, with its observable external appearance, or *phenotype*, which is shaped by environmental as well as genetic influences. All individuals assigned to the same race were assumed to share many common features, of which phenotype was only the outward index.

Race as a Social Category

In the latter half of the nineteenth century, European thinkers, including many early anthropologists, devised schemes for ranking the "races of Mankind" from lowest to highest. Not surprisingly, the "white" Northern Europeans at the apex of imperial power were placed at the top of this global hierarchy. Darker-skinned peoples like the indigenous inhabitants of the Americas or of Asia, were ranked somewhere in the middle. But Africans, whom Europeans had bought and sold as slaves and whose homelands in Africa were later conquered and incorporated into European empires, ranked lowest of all.

In this way, the identification of races was transformed into **racism**: the systematic oppression of one or more socially defined "races" by another socially defined "race" that is justified in terms of the supposedly inherent biological superiority of the rulers and the supposed inherent biological inferiority of those they rule.

It is important to emphasize once again that all the so-called races of human beings are *imagined communities*. The racial boundaries that nineteenth-century European observers thought they had discovered do *not* correspond to major biological discontinuities within the human species. Although our species as a whole does exhibit variation in phenotypic attributes such as skin color, hair texture, or stature, these variations do *not* naturally clump into separate populations with stable boundaries that can be sharply distinguished from one another. Put another way, *the traditional concept of race in Western society is biologically and genetically meaningless.*

Nevertheless, racial thinking persists at the beginning of the twenty-first century. This can only mean that

race A human population category whose boundaries allegedly correspond to a distinct set of biological attributes.

racism The systematic oppression of one or more socially defined "races" by another socially defined "race" that is justified in terms of the supposedly inherent biological superiority of the rulers and the supposed inherent biological inferiority of those they rule.

In Their Own Words

On the Butt Size of Barbie and Shani

Dolls and Race in the United States

Anthropologist Elizabeth Chin writes about race and Barbie dolls, based on some hands-on research.

The Shani line of dolls introduced by Mattel in 1991 reduces race to a simulacrum consisting of phenotypical features: skin color, hair, and butt. Ann DuCille . . . has discussed much of their complex and contradictory nature, highlighting two central issues: derriere and hair. According to DuCille's interviews with Shani designers, the dolls have been remanufactured to give the illusion of a higher, rounder butt than other Barbies. This has been accomplished, they told her, by pitching Shani's back at a different angle and changing some of the proportions of her hips. I had heard these and other rumors from students at the college where I teach: "Shani's butt is bigger than the other Barbies' butts," "Shani dolls have bigger breasts than Barbie," "Shani dolls have bigger thighs than Barbie." DuCille rightly wonders why a bigger butt is necessarily an attribute of blackness, tying this obsession to turn-of-the-century strains of scientific racism.

Deciding I had to see for myself, I pulled my Shani doll off my office bookshelf, stripped her naked, and placed her on my desk next to a naked Barbie doll that had been cruelly mutilated by a colleague's dog (her arms were chewed off and her head had puncture wounds, but the rest was unharmed). Try as I might, manipulating the dolls in ways both painful and obscene, I could find no difference between them, even after prying their legs off and smashing their bodies apart. As far as I have been able to determine, Shani's bigger butt is an illusion (see photo). The faces of Shani and Barbie dolls are more visibly different than their behinds, yet still, why these differences could be considered natural indicators of race is perplexing. As a friend of mine remarked acidly, "They still look like they've had plastic surgery." The most telling difference between Shani and Barbie is at the base of the cranium, where Shani bears a raised mark similar to a branding iron scar: © 1990 MATTEL INC. Barbie's head reads simply © MATTEL INC. Despite claims of redesign, both Barbie and Shani's torsos bear a 1966 copyright, and

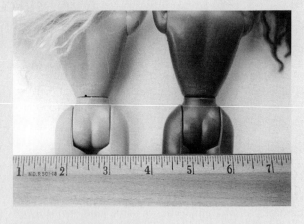

Barbie and Shani from behind.

although DuCille asserts that Shani's legs are shaped differently than Barbie's, their legs are imprinted with the same part numbers. This all strongly suggests that despite claims and rumors to the contrary, Shani and Barbie are the same from the neck down.

These ethnically correct dolls demonstrate one of the abiding aspects of racism: that a stolid belief in racial difference can shape people's perceptions so profoundly that they will find difference and make something of it, no matter how imperceptible or irrelevant its physical manifestation might be. If I had to smash two dolls to bits in order to see if their butts were different sizes, the differences must be small indeed: holding them next to each other revealed no difference whatsoever—except color—regardless of the positioning (crack to crack or cheek to cheek). With the butt index so excruciatingly small, its meaning as a racial signifier becomes frighteningly problematic. Like the notion of race itself, Shani's derriere has a social meaning that is out of all proportion to its scientific measurement.

Source: Chin 1999, 311–13.

racial categories have their origins not in biology but in society. And in fact, anthropologists have long argued that race is a culturally constructed social category whose members are identified on the basis of certain selected phenotypic features (such as skin color) that all of them are said to share. The end result is a highly distorted but more or less coherent set of criteria that members of a society can use to assign people they see to one or another culturally

defined racial category. Once this happens, members of society can treat racial categories *as if* they reflect biological reality, using them to build institutions that include or exclude particular culturally defined races. In this way, race can become "real" in its consequences, even if it has no reality in biology.

The social category of race is a relatively recent invention. Audrey Smedley reminds us that in the worlds

untouched. The outcomes of these processes are often portrayed as unambiguously positive. As we will see, however, anthropologists who study globalization have shown that its outcomes are not positive for everyone. Finding ways to cope with these processes is an ongoing challenge for anthropologists and the people with whom they work.

What Happened to the Global Economy after the Cold War?

In 1989, the Cold War came to an end. The Soviet Union and its satellite states collapsed, and China began to encourage some capitalist economic practices. These radical changes in the global political economy left no part of the world unaffected. For some, this period of uncertainty offered a chance to challenge long-unquestioned truths about development and underdevelopment that had guided government policies throughout the Cold War. New social movements questioned both the importance of market capitalism and the need for socialist revolution. From vigilante movements such as the *rondas campesinas* of Peru to squatter movements in cities, to movements defending the rights of women and homosexuals and movements to preserve rain forests, people attempted to construct entirely new social institutions that often bypassed national governments or

development agencies (see Figure 14.3; EthnoProfile 9.7: Northern Peru [Rondas Campesinas]). Anthropologist Arturo Escobar (1992) argued that the new social movements in Latin America were struggles over meanings as well as over material conditions.

This work offered the hope that new social movements might promote less exploitative forms of society in generations to come. But such a world was already disappearing. The breakdown of communism led to a crisis of confidence among many who had been inspired by key tenets of Marxian thought. At the same time, the apparent triumph of capitalism reanimated the traditional Cold War supporters of modernization theory. Under the new conditions of an emerging global capitalism, they now began to offer a new view of the future, called *neoliberalism*. Modernization theory had urged nation-states to seek self-sufficient prosperity while avoiding communist revolution. Neoliberalism, by contrast, relied on international institutions like the World Bank and the International Monetary Fund to encourage nation-states to achieve prosperity by finding a niche in the growing global capitalist market. Market discipline would force state bureaucrats to support economic enterprises that would bring them income. However, it would also eliminate expensive state institutions and subsidies that had provided a safety net for the poor. Western leaders embraced with enthusiasm the beckoning opportunity to bring the entire world within the compass of the capitalist economy. Less enthusiastic observers began to suspect that forces unleashed at the end of the Cold War were remaking the global political economy in unprecedented new ways, with outcomes that no one could predict or control.

FIGURE 14.3 Following the Cold War, a number of "new social movements" developed around the world, including Wangari Maathai's Green Belt Movement, a tree-planting project in Kenya, run mostly by women.

Cultural Processes in a Global World

Cold War–era economic and political theories presupposed a world with relatively clear-cut geographic and cultural boundaries. Only if this is the case does it make sense to distinguish developed from underdeveloped nations, cores from peripheries, or local cultures from global social processes. The worldwide political, economic, and technological changes of recent decades, however, have challenged the utility of these distinctions. The cybernetics revolution led to advances in manufacturing, transportation, and communications technology that removed the seemingly insuperable barriers to long-distance communication and contact, a phenomenon called "space-time compression" (Harvey 1990). These changes made it easier, cheaper, and faster to move people and things around the world than ever before; they also made it possible to stretch social relationships of all kinds over huge distances that previously would have been unbridgeable (Giddens 1990). With the end of the Cold War, all parts of the world were drawn into these processes of **globalization**: the reshaping of local conditions by powerful global forces on an ever-intensifying scale. Globalization suggests a world full of movement and mixture, contacts and linkages, and persistent cultural interaction and exchange (Inda and Rosaldo 2002, 2).

Globalization is understood and evaluated differently by different observers. Anthropologists ordinarily approach globalization from the perspective of those among whom they do their research. From this point of view, it has been apparent for some time that the effects of globalization are *uneven*: "There are large expanses of the planet only tangentially tied to the webs of interconnection that encompass the globe" (Inda and Rosaldo 2002, 4). As a result, global processes are interpreted and experienced in contradictory ways by different groups and actors.

Faye Ginsburg and Rayna Rapp, for example, describe the global process of *stratified reproduction*, in which some categories of people are empowered to nurture and reproduce, while others are not: "Low-income African American mothers, for example, often are stereotyped as undisciplined 'breeders' who sap the resources of the state through incessant demands on welfare. But historically and in the present, they were 'good enough' nurturers to work as childcare providers for other, more privileged

class and ethnic groups" (1995, 3). Globalization has created new opportunities for some groups, like the Kayapó of Brazil and other indigenous peoples, to build worldwide organizations to defend their interests (Niezen 2003; Kearney 1995). At the same time, global forces can also reinforce old constraints. Evaluating the record of new social movements in Latin America, for example, John Gledhill writes that "to date the challenge that popular forces have been able to mount to the remorseless progress of the neoliberal, neomodernization agenda, has remained limited" (1994, 198).

It would be difficult to find any research project in contemporary cultural anthropology that does not in some way acknowledge the ways in which global forces affect the local societies in which they work. In this respect, globalization studies emphasize the ways in which *the global articulates with the local*: anthropological studies of globalization aim to show "how globalizing processes exist in the context of, and must come to terms with, the realities of particular societies" (Inda and Rosaldo 2002, 4). In other words, "while everyone might continue to live local lives, their phenomenal worlds have to some extent become global" (Inda and Rosaldo 2002, 9).

Globalization is seen in the growth of transnational corporations that relocate their manufacturing operations from core to periphery or that appropriate local cultural forms and turn them into images and commodities to be marketed throughout the world (Figure 14.4). It is seen in tourism, which has grown into the world's largest industry, and in migration from

FIGURE 14.4 One dimension of globalization involves the appropriation of local cultural forms and their use on a variety of widely sold commodities. For example, the image of "Kokopelli," taken from ancient rock art of the southwestern United States, has been reproduced on many items with no connection to its region or culture of origin, including this mailbox flag from Albuquerque, New Mexico. Such items are readily available on the Internet.

---

globalization Reshaping of local conditions by powerful global forces on an ever-intensifying scale.

In Their Own Words

The Ethnographer's Responsibility

French ethnographers Jacques Meunier and A. M. Savarin reflect on the role they can play in Europe to affect the policies of Latin American governments toward the indigenous peoples living within their borders.

At the most fundamental level, the history of thought about primitive people—are they human, overgrown children, or replicas of early stages of Western civilization?—provides a summary of the changes that have taken place in our own culture: the West knows that it can no longer hold exclusive power, but it still considers itself the dominant power. Western ignorance follows from this error. Our taste for exoticism and our morality stem from it, as does the deadly intolerance that seems lodged in our hearts. Centuries of culture and well-intentioned unreasonableness, centuries of humanism have led to the most heinous of all crimes: genocide.

Entire communities forced to abandon their lands, children kidnapped, people treated barbarously, degraded mentally and physically, punitive expeditions launched against them. . . . With genocide, with racism, we confront horror itself. We have spoken of the fragility of traditional societies, of the blind intolerance of our civilization toward the Indians, of the lack of understanding that has led the Amazonians—white, creole, and mestizo—to the organized extermination of the Indians. But there is one question that haunts us, that emerges through the pages of this case like the recurring notes of a flute, forcing us to weigh an unpleasant possibility: aren't we just as guilty of exploiting the Indians, aren't we indulging in a lot of useless discussion? But when we use the word genocide, we have no intention of turning ourselves into defenders of a lost cause; we do not see our roles as charity and moralism. We are not writing off the Indians; we do not believe that genocide should be considered an inevitable calamity.

Ethnographers must organize; they must enact plans to safeguard the threatened minorities—this is important. But if they do not capture public opinion, their projects will not produce results. More than anything, ethnographers need to launch an information campaign, a sound and systematic campaign. The general public has the right to know. The right and the duty. To accept this atrocity, to allow these terrible crimes to be committed, is to become an accomplice in them.

Do not misjudge us: our indignation is not mere posturing. We are convinced that it is possible to affect the policy of Latin American governments. Especially since these countries, while dependent on the United States economically, still turn toward Europe culturally. We can say to them without paternalism: the sense Latin Americans have of their countries still comes from Europe. Why shouldn't they learn a respect for their indigenous populations from Europe, just as they have acquired a taste for pre-Columbian antiquities and folklore? In our view, the salvation of the Indian must begin here and now.

Source: Meunier and Savarin 1994, 128–29.

---

periphery to the core on such a massive scale that observers now speak of the "deterritorialization" of peoples and cultures that, in the past, were presumed to be firmly attached to specific geographical locations. Not only that: Deterritorialized people always "reterritorialize" in a new location. Such reterritorialization regularly sparks social conflicts and generates new forms of cultural identity, as nation-states try to retain control over citizens living beyond their borders and as relocated populations struggle both for recognition in their new homes and for influence in their places of origin. Globalization has drawn the attention of many anthropologists to regions such as the borderland between northern Mexico and the southwestern United States, where struggles with contradictory social practices and ambiguous identities have long been the rule, rather than the exception. Such contexts exhibit a "diffusion of culture traits gone wild, far beyond that imagined by the Boasians" (Kearney 1995, 557). Since borderland conditions are now becoming worldwide, they undermine views of culture that depend upon settled peoples with distinct cultural attributes.

Such heterogeneous and unstable cultural spaces also call into question views like that of sociologist Immanuel Wallerstein, which portrays global processes as part of a world *system*. Anthropologist Arjun Appadurai claims, to the contrary, that ever-intensifying global flows of people, technology, wealth, images, and ideologies are highly contradictory, generating global processes that are fundamentally disorganized and unpredictable (1990).

Jonathan Friedman, by contrast, argues that the disorder may be real but is also a predictable consequence of the breakdown of Western global hegemony. As European colonial empires dissolved, capitalist economic

In Their Own Words

Slumdog Tourism

This and the following In Their Own Words *box offer two different understandings of tourism from the perspectives of the people whom the tourists go to see. In August 2010, the* New York Times *published an op-ed essay by Kennedy Odede, a junior at Wesleyan University and the executive director of Shining Hope for Communities, a social services organization he co-founded to work in the Kibera slum. Shining Hope for Communities can be found at www.hopetoshine.org.*

Nairobi, Kenya—Slum tourism has a long history—during the late 1800s, lines of wealthy New Yorkers snaked along the Bowery and through the Lower East Side to see "how the other half lives."

But with urban populations in the developing world expanding rapidly, the opportunity and demand to observe poverty firsthand have never been greater. The hot spots are Rio de Janeiro, Mumbai—thanks to "Slumdog Millionaire," the film that started a thousand tours—and my home, Kibera, a Nairobi slum that is perhaps the largest in Africa.

Slum tourism has its advocates, who say it promotes social awareness. And it's good money, which helps the local economy.

But it's not worth it. Slum tourism turns poverty into entertainment, something that can be momentarily experienced and then escaped from. People think they've really "seen" something—and then go back to their lives and leave me, my family and my community right where we were before.

I was 16 when I first saw a slum tour. I was outside my 100-square-foot house washing dishes, looking at the utensils with longing because I hadn't eaten in two days. Suddenly a white woman was taking my picture. I felt like a tiger in a cage. Before I could say anything, she had moved on.

When I was 18, I founded an organization that provides education, health and economic services for Kibera residents. A documentary filmmaker from Greece was interviewing me about my work. As we made our way through the streets, we passed an old man defecating in public. The woman took out her video camera and said to her assistant, "Oh, look at that."

For a moment I saw my home through her eyes: feces, rats, starvation, houses so close together that no one can breathe. I realized I didn't want her to see it, didn't want to give her the opportunity to judge my community for its poverty—a condition that few tourists, no matter how well intentioned, could ever understand.

Other Kibera residents have taken a different path. A former schoolmate of mine started a tourism business. I once saw him take a group into the home of a young woman giving birth. They stood and watched as she screamed. Eventually the group continued on its tour, cameras loaded with images of a woman in pain. What did they learn? And did the woman gain anything from the experience?

To be fair, many foreigners come to the slums wanting to understand poverty, and they leave with what they believe is a better grasp of our desperately poor conditions. The expectation, among the visitors and the tour organizers, is that the experience may lead the tourists to action once they get home.

But it's just as likely that a tour will come to nothing. After all, looking at conditions like those in Kibera is overwhelming, and I imagine many visitors think that merely bearing witness to such poverty is enough.

Nor do the visitors really interact with us. Aside from the occasional comment, there is no dialogue established, no conversation begun. Slum tourism is a one-way street: They get photos; we lose a piece of our dignity.

Slums will not go away because a few dozen Americans or Europeans spent a morning walking around them. There are solutions to our problems—but they won't come about through tours.

Source: New York Times*, August 9, 2010.*

accumulation has decentralized, from Europe and North America to parts of the world such as the Pacific Rim (1994). In his view, these developments exemplify a pattern of commercial expansion and contraction that began at least 5,000 years ago with the rise of the first commercial civilizations—world systems in Wallerstein's sense—each of which was characterized by its own form of "modernity." Recognition of this pattern makes Friedman even more pessimistic than Wallerstein about possibilities for the future.

Not all anthropologists accept Friedman's conclusions. But even if Friedman's overall schema of civilizational cycles seems plausible, it cannot by itself account for the "local structures" and "autonomous cultural schemes" that appear at any point in the cycle. It is this historically specific local detail—what Inda and Rosaldo

(2002, 27) call "the conjunctural and situated character of globalization"—that anthropologists aim to document and analyze. In the rest of the chapter, we examine three important areas of study in the anthropology of globalization: the effect of global forces on nation-states, human rights as the emerging discourse of globalization, and debates about cultural hybridization, cosmopolitanism, and the emergence of new global assemblages.

Globalization and the Nation-State

Are Global Flows Undermining Nation-States?

In the second half of the twentieth century, one of the fundamental suppositions about global social organization was that it consisted of an international order of independent nation-states. This assumption has roots that can be traced back to nineteenth-century nationalist struggles in Europe, but it seems to have come fully into its own after World War II, with the final dissolution of European empires, as former colonies achieved independence. The United Nations (UN), created in 1945, presupposed a world of nation-states. Social theorists and activists alike assumed that the world was a mosaic of nations that, one way or another, were entitled to self-determination and a state of their own (Figure 14.5).

The flows of wealth, images, people, things, and ideologies unleashed by globalization have undermined

FIGURE 14.5   Queen Elizabeth II at Nigerian Independence ceremonies, January 1956.

the ability of nation-states to police their boundaries effectively, and have seemed to suggest that the conventional ideas about nation-states require revision. Many observers have suggested that globalization inevitably undermines the power and sovereignty of nation-states. National governments are virtually powerless to control what their citizens read or watch in the media: Satellite services and telecommunications and the Internet elude state-ordered censorship. Nation-states allow migrants or students or tourists to cross their borders because they need their labor or tuition or vacation expenditures, but in so doing states must contend with the political values or religious commitments or families that these outsiders bring with them. Some people have argued that to weaken boundaries between states is a good thing, since border restrictions and censorship need to be overcome. Since 1989, however, as we witness the ways that forces of globalization have made weakened states vulnerable to chaos and violence, the ability of the nation-state to protect its citizens from such destruction has led some to ask whether stronger nation-states might not have at least some points in their favor.

Massive global displacements of people have characterized Western modernity, starting with the slave trade and the movement of indentured labor to the colonies. In the nineteenth century, developing capitalist markets pushed and pulled waves of European and Asian emigrants out of their homelands and installed them in different parts of the globe. At the same time, colonial authorities revived the institution of indentured labor to rearrange population within their dominions. A hundred years ago, when volumes of immigration were lower and moved at a slower pace and jobs were plentiful, the possibility of assimilation into the society of reterritorialization was often possible. Today, however, desperate economic and political situations in migrants' home territories plus ease of transportation have increased the volume and speed of migration. Meanwhile, market crises in the countries where migrants have settled have sharply reduced the economic opportunities available once they arrive.

Migrants often find themselves caught. On the one hand, they now form a sizeable and highly visible minority in the countries of settlement, often in the poorer areas of cities. There they find opportunities for economic survival and political security, encouraging them to stay. On the other hand, hostility and sometimes violence is directed against them whenever there is a local economic downturn. Many migrants conclude that the possibility of permanent assimilation is unrealistic, which encourages them to maintain ties to the homeland or to migrant communities elsewhere.

In Their Own Words

Cofan

Story of the Forest People and the Outsiders

Randy Borman is president of the Centro Cofan Zabalo. He was born to missionary parents and grew up in Cofan culture in the Ecuadorian Amazon. Borman briefly attended school in North America and then returned to Ecuador to become a leader in the Cofan fight for economic and cultural survival. He has written in Cultural Survival Quarterly *about the development of ecotourism in the Cofan area of Ecuador. The results of tourism elsewhere in the world are not always as positive as they have been for the Cofan people, in part because tourism is often imposed from the outside. To find out more about the Cofan people, visit www.cofan.org.*

I had the fortune to grow up as a forest person, enjoying the clean rivers and unlimited forests, learning the arts and skills of living comfortably in a wonderland of the marvelous, beautiful, and deadly. I experienced first hand both the good and the bad of a world, which will never again be possible, at least in the foreseeable future. And I also experienced the crushing physical, psychological, and spiritual impact of the invasion of the outside that erased our world.

In 1955, the Cofan people were the sole inhabitants of more than 1,000,000 hectares of pristine forest in northeastern Ecuador. By 1965, oil exploration and exploitation had begun. And by 1975, the forest was fast disappearing before a massive mestizo colonization, which was brought in by roads created to access vast quantities of oil. The rivers were fouled with chemicals and raw crude; the animals disappeared; boom towns sprung up all over; and the Cofan struggled to survive on less than 15,000 hectares of badly degraded forest. The old life was gone forever, and my companions and I faced the numbing prospect of discarding our culture and way of life, and becoming peasant farmers like so many others, trying to eke out a living from crops and animals which were never meant to grow in this environment. We had been powerless to maintain our forests in the face of outsider pressures to make every given piece of land profitable. If we were to save anything from the wreckage we needed alternatives, and quickly. . . .

[As the only member of his community with an outsider education, Borman worked with the community in trying to develop strategies for community survival, including those associated with marketing forest products. These strategies did not work.]

As we were wrestling with these possible alternatives, we were also acting as boatmen for the slowly increasing economy on the river. Several of us had managed to buy outboard motors with carefully saved returns from corn fields, animal skins, and short stints as trail makers with the oil companies. We had a long tradition of carving dugouts, and soon our canoes were traveling up and down the rivers with loads of lumber, corn, and coffee; occasional trips carrying cattle provided excitement and variety. This was not an alternative for the entire community, and it was only viable until roads were built, but it worked as a stop-gap measure for some of us. And unexpectedly, it led us directly into the alternative, which we have adopted as our own in the years since.

Travelers were coming to our region. The roads made it easier than at any previous time, and people from First World countries—the USA, Canada, England, Germany, Israel, Italy—began to come, searching for the vanishing rain forest. Most of them were primarily interested in seeing wildlife. This fit with our view of the situation precisely. We had our motorboats. There was still a lot of good forest out there, but it was hard to access with regular paddling and poling expeditions. So when these travelers arrived and wanted to go to "wild jungle," we were delighted to take them. They paid the transportation cost, and we took our shotguns and spears along to go hunting. Our attitude was that if the traveler wanted to go along with us, and didn't mind that we were hunting, why, we were happy to have them along to help carry the game home! From such a pragmatic beginning, we slowly developed our concept of tourism.

There were changes. We soon learned that the traveler had a lot more fun if we modified our normal hunting pattern a bit, and we even got paid extra for it. We found out that the average tourist didn't mind if we shot birds that looked like chickens, even if they were rare. But if we shot a toucan they were outraged, despite the fact that toucans are very common. Tourists preferred a board to a stick as a seat in the canoe, and a pad made them even happier. Tourists' food needed to be somewhat recognizable, such as rice, rather than the lumpy, thick manioc beer we normally eat and drink. But the community as a whole decided early that our role would be that of guides and service providers for tourists interested in the forest. We would not dress up and

In Their Own Words

do dances, or stage fake festivals, or in any way try to sell our traditions and dress. We would not accept becoming the objects of tourism—rather, we would provide the skills and knowledge for the tourist to understand our environment. We would sell our education, at a price that was in line with the importance to the outsiders who wanted to buy it, such as lawyers, biologists, doctors, teachers, and other professionals the world over do.

Being guides for the tourism experience, not the objects of it, has provided both a very real economic alternative and a very solid incentive for the younger generation to learn the vast body of traditional knowledge, which lies at the heart of our culture. A deep conservation ethic—the roots of which lie at the hearts of most cultures who maintain a viable relation with their environments—has helped the Cofan community to create a number of projects which combine outsider science with our traditional knowledge. Interestingly enough, this has also turned out to be an economic success, as many of our projects began to receive funding in recognition of their innovation and replicability in other communities throughout Amazonia. . . .

Tourism is not for everyone. Some of our experiences have been negative. One of our biggest and most constant headaches is effective commercialization. To operate a community-based tourism business while maintaining our cultural heritage is not possible using the outsider formula of a tour operator. The implied hierarchy of manager, finance department, buyers, transport specialists, etc., all working eight hours a day, five days a week, with an office and a fax machine is clearly not applicable. Instead, we rely on teams, which rotate in their work, leaving time for farms, family duties, crafts, fishing, hunting and the garden. But the lack of a full-time office makes it difficult to commercialize effectively, and we walk the precarious line between too much tourism (no time left over to live a normal life, and possible loss of our cultural way of life) and too little (not enough jobs, not enough income, lack of attraction for a forest-based life and education for our young people). If we commercialize effectively, we run the risk of the operation snowballing, with more and more tourists arriving, and eventually, we are all wealthy in outsider goods and income but without our culture's wealth of time and interpersonal relationships that we all value so much now. If we don't commercialize effectively, we will wake up tomorrow back at the beginning, with the need to destroy our forest for short-term survival.

But in the overall scheme of things, our experiment with tourism has been overwhelmingly positive. Contact with people who wish to know what we can teach, who value our forests and are willing to pay to help us maintain them has been very important. Our increased awareness of the conservation imperatives facing us has led to many changes in our way of life, all aimed at preserving core values for future generations.

Source: Borman 1999, 48–50.

Migration, Transborder Identities, and Long-Distance Nationalism

The term *diaspora* is commonly used to refer to migrant populations with a shared identity who live in a variety of different locales around the world, but Nina Glick Schiller and Georges Fouron point out that not all such populations see themselves in the same way. Schiller and Fouron describe different types of "transborder identities" that characterize different groups of migrants. They prefer to use the term **diaspora** to identify a form of trans-border identity that does not focus on nation-building. Should members of a diaspora begin to organize in support of nationalist struggles in their homeland, or to agitate for a state of their own, they become **long-distance nationalists** (Schiller and Fouron 2002, 360–61). "Long-distance nationalism" was coined by political scientist Benedict Anderson to describe the efforts of émigrés to offer moral, economic, and political support to the nationalist struggles of their countries of origin. In his original discussion, Anderson emphasized the dangerous irresponsibility of the "citizenshipless participation" of the long-distance nationalists: "while technically a citizen of the state in which he comfortably lives, but to which he may feel little attachment, he finds it tempting to play identity politics by participating (via propaganda, money, weapons, any

diaspora Migrant populations with a shared identity who live in a variety of different locales around the world; a form of trans-border identity that does not focus on nation building.

long-distance nationalists Members of a diaspora organized in support of nationalist struggles in their homeland, or to agitate for a state of their own.

way but voting) in the conflicts of his imagined *Heimat* [homeland]" (2002, 269–70).

Schiller and Fouron argue, however, that the conditions of globalization have led to new forms of long-distance nationalism that do not correspond to Anderson's original description. They point to the emergence of the **trans-border state**: a form of state "claiming that its emigrants and their descendants remain an integral and intimate part of their ancestral homeland, even if they are legal citizens of another state" (Schiller and Fouron 2002, 357).

Trans-border states did not characterize periods of mass emigration in the nineteenth and twentieth centuries. At that time, nations sending emigrants abroad regarded permanent settlement elsewhere as national betrayal. They encouraged emigrants to think of migration as temporary, expecting them eventually to return home with new wealth and skills to build the nation. But in today's global world, political leaders of many states sending emigrants accept the likelihood that those emigrants will settle permanently elsewhere. They may even insist that émigrés retain full membership in the nation-state from which they came. This form of long-distance nationalism creates what Schiller and Fouron call a **trans-border citizenry**: "Citizens residing within the territorial homeland and new emigrants and their descendants are part of the nation, whatever legal citizenship the émigrés may have" (Schiller and Fouron 2002, 358).

Trans-border states and trans-border citizenries are more than symbolic identities: They have become concretized in law. For example, several Latin American countries, including Mexico, Colombia, the Dominican Republic, Ecuador, and Brazil, permit emigrants who have become naturalized citizens in countries such as the United States to retain dual nationality and even voting rights in their country of origin (Figure 14.6). Special government ministries are set up to address the needs of citizens living abroad. This is very different from Anderson's notion of "citizenshipless participation." Schiller and Fouron stress that trans-border states and citizenries spring "from the life experiences of migrants of different classes" and are "rooted in the day to day efforts of people in the homeland to live lives of dignity and self-respect that compel them to include those who have migrated" (Schiller and Fouron 2002, 359).

FIGURE 14.6   The Dominican Republic permits emigrants who have become naturalized citizens of the United States to vote in Dominican elections. Here, a Dominican woman in New York campaigns in 2004 for a second term for President Hipólito Mejía.

But some trans-border citizenries face difficulties. First, their efforts at nation-building are sometimes blocked by political forces in the homeland who do not welcome their contributions. This has been the case for Haitians living abroad while Haiti was ruled by the Duvalier family dictatorship and for Cubans living abroad whose efforts are blocked by the Castro revolutionary government. Second, the states in which immigrants have settled may not welcome the continued involvement of trans-border citizens in the affairs of another state. Such involvement has often been seen as even more threatening since terrorists destroyed the World Trade Center and attacked the Pentagon on September 11, 2001. Yet in an era of globalization, attempts to control migration threaten to block the flows of people that keep the global economy going. Moreover, the vulnerability of trans-border citizens in these circumstances often increases the appeal of long-distance nationalism (Schiller and Fouron 2002, 359–60).

The globalizing forces that produce long-distance nationalism and trans-border states and citizens have undermined previous understandings of what a world made up of nation-states should look like. In addition, unacknowledged contradictions and weaknesses of actual nation-states are revealed. For example, the existence and strength of trans-border states and citizenries show that some nation-states—especially those sending migrants—are actually what Schiller and Fouron call *apparent states:* They have all the outward attributes of nation-states (government bureaucracies, armies, a seat in the United Nations), but in fact they are unable to meet the needs of their people (Schiller and Fouron 2002, 363). The strength of long-distance nationalism and trans-border

---

trans–border state   A form of state in which it is claimed that those people who left the country and their descendents remain part of their ancestral state, even if they are citizens of another state.

trans–border citizenry   A group made up of citizens of a country who continue to live in the homeland plus the people who have emigrated from the country and their descendents, regardless of their current citizenship.

citizenries also exposes inconsistencies and paradoxes in the meaning of citizenship in the nation-states where migrants settle.

Schiller and Fouron contrast legal citizenship with what they call substantive citizenship, and point out that, for trans-border citizens, the two often do not coincide. As we saw, **legal citizenship** is accorded by state laws and can be difficult for migrants to obtain. But even those trans-border citizens who obtain legal citizenship often experience a gap between what the legal citizenship promises and the way they are treated by the state. For example, people of color and women who are United States citizens are not treated by the state the same way white male citizens are treated. By contrast, **substantive citizenship** is defined by the actions people take, regardless of their legal citizenship status, to assert their membership in a state and to bring about political changes that will improve their lives. Some trans-border citizenries call for the establishment of full-fledged **transnational nation-states**. That is, "they challenge the notion that relationships between citizens and their state are confined within that territory" and work for the recognition of a new political form that contradicts the understandings of political theory, but which reflects the realities of their experiences of national identity (Schiller and Fouron 2002, 359).

Anthropology and Multicultural Politics in the New Europe

One of the more interesting things about the early twenty-first century is that Europe—the continent that gave birth to the Enlightenment and colonial empires and (along with North America) to anthropology itself—has become a living laboratory for the study of some of the most complex social and cultural processes to be found anywhere in the world.

During the last half of the twentieth century, the countries of Europe, including Italy, were the target of large waves of migration from all over the world. Visitors to Rome regularly make stops at the ancient ruins in the center of the city. One venerable working-class Roman neighborhood, only a short walk from the Colosseum, is Rione Monti, which has a fascinating history of its own (EthnoProfile 14.2). In 1999 anthropologist Michael Herzfeld (2003) moved into Rione Monti to explore social change in the uses of the past. Longtime residents of Monti share a common local culture, which includes use of the *romanesco* dialect rather than standard Italian, and a strong sense of local identity that distinguishes them from "foreigners," including diplomats and non-Roman Italians. Their identity survived Mussolini's demolition of part of the neighborhood in the early twentieth century. They successfully dealt

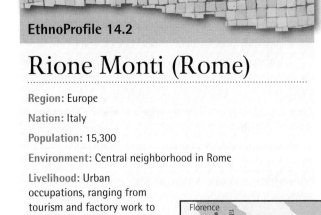

EthnoProfile 14.2

Rione Monti (Rome)

Region: Europe

Nation: Italy

Population: 15,300

Environment: Central neighborhood in Rome

Livelihood: Urban occupations, ranging from tourism and factory work to restaurants, small businesses, bureaucratic, executive

Political organization: Urban neighborhood in a modern nation-state

For more information: http://www.rionemonti.net/

with a local criminal underworld by mastering a refined urbane code of politeness. The underworld had faded away by the 1970s, but beginning in the 1980s, residents began to face two new challenges to their community. First, historic Roman neighborhoods became fashionable, and well-to-do Italians began to move into Rione Monti, pushing many workers into cheaper housing elsewhere. Second, in the 1990s, another group of newcomers arrived: immigrants from Eastern Europe.

Italy is one of the more recent destinations of immigration into Europe, reversing the country's historical experience as a source, rather than a target, of immigration. However, after Germany, France, and Britain passed laws curtailing immigration in the 1970s, Italy became an increasingly popular destination for immigrants from Africa, Asia, and Latin America; after the end of the Cold War came immigrants from outside the European Union (EU), including Eastern Europe. Until recently, laws regulating immigration were few, and the country appeared welcoming. But this is changing. "Italy has not historically been a racist country, but intolerant attitudes towards immigrants have increased. To a large extent, this seems to

---

legal citizenship The rights and obligations of citizenship accorded by the laws of a state.

substantive citizenship The actions people take, regardless of their legal citizenship status, to assert their membership in a state and to bring about political changes that will improve their lives.

transnational nation-state A nation-state in which the relationships between citizens and their states extend to wherever citizens reside.

be the result of a long-standing underestimation of the magnitude of the changes and thus poor policy implementation for a lengthy period, in spite of the best intentions officially proclaimed" (Melotti 1997, 91).

Umberto Melotti contrasts the distinctive ways in which immigration is understood by the governments of France, Britain, and Germany. According to Melotti, the French project is *ethnocentric assimilationism:* Since early in the nineteenth century, when French society experienced a falling birthrate, immigration was encouraged and immigrants were promised all the rights and privileges of native-born citizens as long as they adopted French culture completely, dropping other ethnic or cultural attachments and assimilating the French language, culture, and character (1997, 75). The British project, by contrast, is *uneven pluralism:* that is, the pragmatic British expect immigrants to be loyal and law-abiding citizens, but they do not expect immigrants to "become British" and they tolerate private cultivation of cultural differences as long as these do not threaten the British way of life (1997, 79–80). Finally, Melotti describes the German project as *the institutionalization of precariousness,* by which he means that despite the fact that Germany has within its borders more immigrants than any other European country, and began receiving immigrants at the end of the nineteenth century, its government continues to insist that Germany is not a country of immigrants. Immigrants were always considered "guest workers," children born to guest workers are considered citizens of the country from which the worker came, and it remains very difficult for guest workers or their children born in Germany to obtain German citizenship. (This contrasts with France, for example, where children of immigrants born on French soil automatically become French citizens.)

Coming to terms with increasing numbers of Muslims living in countries where Christianity has historically been dominant is a central theme in multicultural debates within Europe. Although all European states consider themselves secular in orientation (see Asad 2003), the relation between religion and state is far from uniform. France is unusual because of its strict legal separation between religion and state. In Britain, the combination of a secular outlook with state funding of the established Anglican Church has allowed citizens to support forms of religious inclusion that first involved state funding of Catholic schools for Irish immigrants and now involve state funding of Muslim schools for Muslim immigrants (Lewis 1997; Modood 1997). In Germany, where a secular outlook also combines with state-subsidized religious institutions, the state has devised curricula for elementary schools designed to teach all students about different religious traditions, including Islam, in ways that emphasize the possibility of harmonizing one's religious faith with one's obligations as a citizen. Although this approach may be seen as presumptuous or paternalistic, its supporters counter that its advantages outweigh its costs. Perhaps as a result of their own history, many contemporary Germans have less faith than the British that a civic culture of religious tolerance will automatically lead to harmony without state intervention, and less faith than the French in the existence of a separate secular sphere of society from which religion can be safely excluded (Schiffauer 1997).

These are, of course, thumbnail sketches of more complex attitudes and practices. But they illustrate the fact that there is no single "European" approach to the challenges posed by immigration. In a way, each European state, with its own history and own institutions, is experimenting with different ways of coping with the challenges of multiculturalism, and their failures and successes will influence the kinds of multicultural relations and institutions that develop in the twenty-first century. This is particularly significant in light of the fact that European nation-states have joined together in the EU, a continent-wide super-state with 25 members. Reconciling the diverse interests and needs of member states poses enormous challenges for EU members, and multicultural issues are among them.

Many scholars and activists hope that solutions can be found that will involve extensions of social justice throughout the EU (e.g., Ben-Tovim 1997; Brewin 1997). But there is still a lot of work to be done, and no guarantees about the outcome. Tariq Modood points out, for example, that European multiculturalism requires supporting conceptions of citizenship that allow the "right to assimilate" as well as the "right to have one's 'difference' . . . recognized and supported in the public and the private spheres"; multiculturalism must recognize that "participation in the public or national culture is necessary for the effective exercise of citizenship" while at the same time defending the "right to widen and adapt the national culture" (1997, 20). The potential and actual contradictions among some of these goals are apparent, but insofar as they are seen as necessary, the challenge becomes one of finding ways to move forward. And here, with no blueprint to follow, all parties find themselves involved in creating new cultural practices. Based on her experience in France, Dembour is convinced that "we need to accept the discomfort of moving in-between, as a pendulum" (Dembour 2001, 71–72). Modood agrees: "There is indeed a tension here, and perhaps it can only be resolved in practice through finding and cultivating points of common ground between dominant and subordinate cultures, as well as new syntheses and hybridities. The important thing is that the burdens of change . . . are not all dependent on one party to this encounter" (1997, 20).

Anthropologist John Bowen's recent fieldwork in France documents the process Modood describes. Bowen has worked among the many French Muslims who are not interested in terrorism, but who "who wish to live fulfilling *and* religious lives in France" (2010, 4). He has paid particular attention to the work of a number of French Muslim religious teachers and scholars, whom he calls "Islamic public actors." Other French Muslims come to them for religious instruction, and for advice about how to cope with the difficulties of living in a non-Muslim country. In turn, the Islamic public actors Bowen knew are working to craft solutions that, in their view, are true both to the laws of the French republic and to the norms and traditions of Islam.

For example, many French Muslims are concerned about how to contract a valid marriage in France. Ever since the French Revolution, France has refused to accept the legality of religious marriages and recognizes only civil marriages contracted at city hall. Yet Muslims who want to marry are often confused about whether a "secular" marriage at city hall is appropriate or necessary. Indeed, some Muslims have argued that city hall marriages are un-Islamic because they did not exist at the time of the Prophet Muhammad. But other Muslims, including some of Bowen's consultants, disagree with this position. They argue that there was no need for civil marriages at the time of the Prophet, because in those days, tribal life made it impossible to avoid the obligations of the marriage contract. But things are different today for Muslims in urban France: Bowen's consultants have seen many tragic outcomes when young women who thought they had a valid Muslim marriage were left by their husbands, only to discover that the French state did not recognize their marriage and could offer them no legal redress.

Because this was not the outcome that Islamic marriage was intended to produce, the scholars Bowen knew looked beyond traditional Islamic marriage practices in order to clarify the larger purposes that Islamic marriage was supposed to achieve. Then they asked if these purposes could be achieved using the French institution of civil marriage. One scholar told Bowen: "I say that if you marry at the city hall, you have already made an Islamic marriage, because all the conditions for that marriage have been fulfilled" (2010, 167). Those conditions include the fact that both Islamic marriages and French civil marriages are contracts; that both require the consent of the spouses; and that the legal requirements imposed on the spouses by French civil marriage further the Islamic goal of keeping the spouses together. When this kind of reasoning is strengthened by appealing to opinions on marriage drawn from the four traditional Sunni schools of Islamic law, many Islamic public intellectuals believe that a way can be found to craft acceptable practices for French Muslims in many areas of daily life.

Because Bowen agrees with Modood that accommodation has to go in both directions, he also shows how some French legal scholars are working to craft solutions to the challenges Muslim marriage practices present to French law. Most French judges agree, for example, that Islamic marriages or divorces contracted outside France remain valid when the parties involved move to France. But French judges can refuse to accept international rules for resolving legal conflicts if they decide that the solution would violate French "public order." Bowen found that the concept of "public order" is basic to the French legal system, referring "both to the conditions of social order and to basic values, and it limits the range of laws that a legislator may pass and the decisions that a judge may make" (2010, 173).

Violations of public order may include customs from outside France that are judged to "offend the morality and values" of French law. Some French jurists argue that consequences following from Muslim practices of marriage and divorce should not be recognized in France if they violate French and European commitments to the equality of women and men. Other French jurists, however, point to the practical problems that this argument creates: not recognizing the validity of Islamic divorces in France, for example, would mean that a woman divorced according to Islamic law abroad could not remarry if she came to France. Similarly, refusing to recognize polygamous marriage in France would deprive the children of all but a man's first wife of their rights under French and European law. In recent years, Bowen reports, French judges have devised two ways of crafting a solution to these unwelcome consequences. One has been to modify the concept of "public order" by making so-called "practical exceptions" for Muslims who emigrate to France. The other is to be more flexible with Muslim marriage and family practices as long as these arrangements involve individuals who are not French citizens. These pragmatic solutions are an improvement over what Bowen calls the "more blunt-instrument approach" associated with the older understanding of public order. Bowen concludes that in France today, Muslim and French jurists alike are both struggling to craft "the legal conditions for common life that are capacious enough to `reasonably accommodate' people living in differing conditions and with differing beliefs, yet unitary enough to retain the hope that such a common life is conceivable" (2010, 178).

Thus, the struggles and dilemmas facing residents of Rione Monti are widespread across the new Europe. But the specifics of their situation, and the cultural resources at their disposal, have their own particularity. Thus, the traditionally left-wing Monti residents have

FIGURE 14.7 Rione Monti is a neighborhood in central Rome where longtime residents and new immigrants are negotiating new forms of relationship.

resisted attempts by neofascist politicians to get them to turn against immigrant families in the neighborhood. Still, they are unhappy with the location of the Ukranian church in a building that overlooks the neighborhood's central square, because church-goers gather there twice a week, invading "their" space (Herzfeld 2003, 4) (Figure 14.7). Herzfeld reports that the residents of Monti, like other Romans, claim not to be racist (which accords with Melotti's views of Italians in general), and that they seem less hostile to immigrants of color than to Ukranians. But Ukranians are more numerous in Monti, and more threatening, because they look like local people but in fact are competing with local people for work and space in the neighborhood (5). At the same time, the Monti code of politeness "underlies the facility with which democratically inclined residents today construct a popular street democracy, a system of neighbourhood associations" (2). Currently, immigrants are not able to deploy this code, a fact that signals their outsider status and can lead to misunderstandings and bad feelings. If they could learn to use the code, however, fresh opportunities for political cooperation might be forged. This could be decisive, for the code of politeness is the foundation of local democratic processes and "may also eventually be the only generally available means of denying access to manipulative party politics and land speculation alike" (6).

flexible citizenship The strategies and effects employed by managers, technocrats, and professionals who move regularly across state boundaries who seek both to circumvent and benefit from different nation-state regimes.

Flexible Citizenship

Schiller and Fouron's observations about the way globalization has undermined the stability of conventional nation-states exposes contradictory and ambiguous practices associated with such basic concepts as "national identity" and "citizenship." Their contrast between formal and substantive citizenship suggests that conventional notions of citizenship that previously seemed straightforward begin to break down in the context of globalization. Another way of addressing these contradictions and ambiguities is suggested by anthropologist Aihwa Ong, who speaks of **flexible citizenship**: "the strategies and effects of mobile managers, technocrats, and professionals seeking both to circumvent *and* benefit from different nation-state regimes by selecting different sites for investment, work, and family relocation" (2002, 174). Ong's research concerns diaspora communities of elite Chinese families who have played key roles in the economic successes of the Pacific Rim in recent years. Although their success is often attributed by outsiders to "Chinese culture," Ong's research calls this simplistic explanation into question. Ong documents the ways in which Chinese families have responded creatively to opportunities and challenges they have encountered since the end of the nineteenth century, as they found ways to evade or exploit the governmentality of three different kinds of institutions: Chinese kinship and family, the nation-state, and the marketplace.

The break from mainland Chinese ideas of kinship and Confucian filial piety came when Chinese first moved into the capitalist commercial circuits of European empires. Money could be made in these settings, but success required Chinese merchant families to cut themselves off from ties to mainland China and to reinforce bonds among family members and business partners in terms of *guanxi* ("relationships of social connections built primarily upon shared identities such as native place, kinship or attending the same school" [Smart 1999, 120]).

The family discipline of overseas Chinese enabled them to become wealthy, and provided the resources to subvert the governmentality of the nation-state. The orientation of these wealthy families toward national identity and citizenship, Ong explains, is "market-driven." In Hong Kong, for example, in the years leading up to its return to mainland China in 1997, many wealthy Chinese thought of citizenship "not as the right to demand full democratic representation, but as the right to promote familial interests apart from the well-being of society" (Ong 2002, 178). None of the overseas Chinese she knew expressed any commitment to nationalism, either local or long-distance. This understanding of citizenship could not be more different from the committed transborder citizenship of long-distance nationalists described by Schiller and Fouron.

Quite the contrary. Relying on family discipline and loyalty, and buttressed by considerable wealth and strong interpersonal ties, they actively worked to evade the governmentality of nation-states. For example, Chinese from Hong Kong who wanted to migrate to Britain in the 1960s were able to evade racial barriers that blocked other "colored" immigrants because of their experience with capitalism and their reputation for peaceful acquiescence to British rule. When the British decided to award citizenship to some Hong Kong residents in the 1990s, they used a point system that favored applicants with education, fluency in English, and training in professions of value to the economy, such as accountancy and law. These attributes fitted well the criteria for citizenship valued under the government of Margaret Thatcher, while other applicants for citizenship who lacked such attributes were excluded. Citizenship, or at least a passport, could be purchased by those who had the money: "well-off families accumulated passports not only from Canada, Australia, Singapore and the United States but also from revenue poor Fiji, the Philippines, Panama and Tonga (which required in return for a passport a down payment of U.S. $200,000 and an equal amount in installments" (2002, 183) (Figure 14.8).

Although wealthy overseas Chinese families had thus managed to evade or subvert both the governmentality of Chinese kinship and of nation-states, they remained vulnerable to the discipline of the capitalist market. To be sure, market discipline under globalization was very different from the market discipline typical in the 1950s and 1960s. Making money in the context of globalization required the flexibility to take advantage of economic opportunities wherever and whenever they appeared. Ong describes one family in which the eldest son remained in Hong Kong to run part of the family hotel chain located in the Pacific region while his brother lived in San Francisco and managed the hotels located in North America and Europe. Children can be separated from their parents when they are, for example, installed in one country to be educated while their parents manage businesses in other countries on different continents.

The Postnational Ethos

These flexible business arrangements are not without costs. "Familial regimes of dispersal and localization . . . discipline family members to make do with very

FIGURE 14.8 Overseas Chinese are to be found in many parts of the world, as here in Tahiti. They are not always millionaire businesspeople but are shopkeepers and small businesspeople as well.

little emotional support; disrupted parental responsibility, strained marital relations, and abandoned children are such common circumstances that they have special terms." At the same time, individual family members truly do seem to live comfortably as citizens of the world. A Chinese banker in San Francisco told Ong that he could live in Asia, Canada, or Europe: "I can live anywhere in the world, but it must be near an airport" (2002, 190).

The values and practices to which overseas Chinese adhere, and which seem responsible for their tremendous achievements in a globalized capitalist economy, suggest to Ong that, for these elite Chinese, the concept of nationalism has lost its meaning. Instead, she says, they seem to subscribe to a **postnational ethos** in which they submit to the governmentality of the capitalist market while trying to evade the governmentality of nation-states, ultimately because their only true loyalty is to the family business (2002, 190). Ong notes, however, that flexible citizenship informed by a postnational ethos is not an option for nonelite migrants: "whereas for bankers, boundaries are always flexible, for migrant workers, boat people, persecuted intellectuals and artists, and other kinds of less well-heeled refugees, this . . . is a harder act to follow" (2002, 190).

She also points out that, on the way to their success, contemporary Chinese merchants "have also revived premodern forms of child, gender, and class oppression, as well as strengthened authoritarianist regimes in Asia" (2002, 190). Yet neither the positives nor the negatives should, she insists, be attributed to any "Chinese" essence; instead, she thinks these strategies are better understood as "the expressions of a habitus that is finely tuned to the turbulence of late capitalism" (2002, 191).

Are Human Rights Universal?

Globalization has stimulated discussions about **human rights**: powers, privileges, or material resources to which people everywhere are justly entitled by virtue of being human. Rapidly circulating capital, images, people, things, and ideologies juxtapose different understandings about what it means to be human, or what kinds

---

postnational ethos An attitude toward the world in which people submit to the governmentality of the capitalist market while trying to evade the governmentality of nation-states.

human rights A set of rights that should be accorded to all human beings everywhere in the world.

---

of rights people are entitled to. It is in multicultural settings—found everywhere in today's globalized world—that questions of rights become salient, and different cultural understandings of what it means to be human and what rights humans are entitled to become the focus of contention (issues that we talked about in chapter 2, on cultural relativism).

Human Rights Discourse as the Global Language of Social Justice

Discourses about human rights have proliferated in recent decades, stimulated by the original United Nations Declaration on Human Rights in 1948, and followed by numerous subsequent declarations. For example, in 1992, the Committee for the Elimination of Discrimination against Women (CEDAW) declared that violence against women was a form of gender discrimination that violated the human rights of women. This declaration was adopted by the UN General Assembly in 1993 and became part of the rights platform at the Fourth World Conference on Women in Beijing, China, in 1995 (Figure 14.9). Anthropologist Sally Merry observes that this declaration "dramatically demonstrates the creation of new rights—rights which depend on the state's failure to protect women rather than its active violation of rights. . . . The emergence of violence against women as a distinct human rights violation depends on redefining the family so that it is no longer shielded from legal scrutiny" (Merry 2001, 36–37).

Although CEDAW has proved particularly contentious, other human rights documents have been signed without controversy by many national governments. Signing a human rights declaration ostensibly binds governments to take official action to implement changes in local practices that might be seen to violate the rights asserted in the declarations. Human rights discourses are common currency in all societies, at all levels. As Jane Cowan, Marie-Bénédicte Dembour, and Richard Wilson write, it is "no use imagining a 'primitive' tribe which has not yet heard of human rights. . . . What it means to be 'indigenous' is itself transformed through interaction with human rights discourses and institutions" (2001, 5).

Because of the wide adoption of human rights discourses throughout the world, some people have come to speak of an emerging "culture of human rights" which has now become "the preeminent global language of social justice" (Merry 2001, 38). These developments mean that anthropologists need to take note of the important influence this discourse is having in the various settings where they do their research.

What counts as "human rights" has changed over time, due not only to the action of international bodies

FIGURE 14.9   Women marching against violence at the Fourth World Conference on Women in Beijing, 1995.

like the UN, but also to the efforts of an increasing number of nongovernmental organizations (NGOs) that have become involved in various countries of the world, many of them deeply committed to projects designed to improve people's lives and protect their rights (Figure 14.10). As Merry says, these developments "have created a new legal order" that has given birth to new possibilities throughout the world for the elaboration and discussion of what human rights are all about (Merry 2001, 35).

In addition, because the "culture of human rights" is increasingly regarded, in one way or another, as the "culture of globalization," it would seem to be a topic well suited to anthropological analysis in itself. This is because, as we shall see, human rights discourse is not as straightforward as it seems. On the face of things, defending human rights for all people would seem unproblematic. Few

FIGURE 14.10   Women's shelters run by NGOs in Afghanistan provide a variety of services. Classmates applaud a fellow student after she stood up to read in a literacy class at one such shelter.

people who are aware of the devastation wrought by colonial exploitation, for example, would want to suggest that the victims of that exploitation did not have rights that needed to be protected at all costs. Yet, when we look closely at particular disputes about human rights, the concept no longer seems so simple.

Cowan and her colleagues have noted that there are two major arguments that have developed for talking about the way human rights and culture are related. The first involves the idea that *human rights are opposed to culture*, and that the two cannot be reconciled. The second involves the idea that a key universal human right is precisely one's *right to culture*. We will consider each in turn.

Rights versus Culture

Arguments that pit human rights against culture depend on the assumption that "cultures" are homogeneous, bounded, and unchanging sets of ideas and practices, and that each society has only one culture, which its members are obligated to follow. As we saw in chapter 2, this view of culture has been severely criticized by cultural anthropologists. But it is a view of culture that is very much alive in many human rights disputes. For if people have no choice but to follow the rules of the culture into which they were born, international interference with customs said to violate human rights would seem itself to constitute a human rights violation. Outsiders would be disrupting a supposedly harmonious way of life and preventing those who are committed to such a way of life from observing their own culturally specific understandings about rights. Thus, it is concluded, cultures should be allowed to enjoy absolute, inviolable protection from interference by outsiders.

This has been the position adopted, for example, by some national governments that have refused to sign the CEDAW declaration that violence against women violates women's human rights. "Many states have opposed this conception of human rights on cultural or religious grounds, and have refused to ratify treaties" (Merry 2001, 37). Nevertheless, by 2009, 186 countries had ratified CEDAW (http://www.unifern.org/cedaw30/).

Sometimes representatives of non-Western nation-states may feel free to dismiss rights talk as an unwelcome colonial imposition of ideas that, far from being universal, reflect ethnocentric European preoccupations. But such dismissal of human rights discourse needs to be closely examined.

In the case of the right of women to protection from violence, for example, Merry points out that although some forms of violence against women may be culturally sanctioned in some societies, violence against women can take many forms even in those societies, and not all of these are accorded the same amount of cultural support. Practices like female genital cutting could be justified in the past in some circumstances as an appropriate cultural action, but it is now being questioned and even outlawed in the societies where it was traditional. This suggests "culture values" cannot be held responsible for everything that people do in any society, and that members of the same society can disagree about these matters, and sometimes change their minds.

As talk about human rights has become incorporated into local cultural discussions in recent decades, anthropologists are not surprised to discover that the notion undergoes transformation as people try to make sense of what it means in their own local contexts (Cowan et al. 2001, 8). Being forced to choose between rights *or* culture, however, seems increasingly unviable in a globalizing, multicultural world. In their own anthropological work on these matters, Cowan and her colleagues are convinced that the rights-versus-culture debate exaggerates cultural differences. Like many cultural anthropologists today, they find that "it is more illuminating to think of culture as a field of creative interchange and contestation" (2001, 4). Such a view of culture makes it possibile to find points of connection between the defense of certain human rights and the defense of particular cultural values.

Finally, it is worth asking if "culture" is sometimes used as a scapegoat to mask the unwillingness of a government to extend certain rights to its citizens for reasons that have nothing to do with culture. Cowan, Dembour, and Wilson observe that states like Indonesia and Singapore, which position themselves as stout defenders of "Asian values," have welcomed Western industrial capitalism. To reject human rights discourse because it contradicts "Asian values" would, at the very least, suggest

"an inconsistent attitude toward westernization," which, in turn, feeds suspicions that the defense of "Asian values" may be a political tactic designed "to bolster state sovereignty and resist international denunciations of internal repression and political dissent" (Cowan et al. 2001, 6–7).

Rights to Culture

A second popular argument about the relationship between rights and culture begins from very different premises. This argument does not view universal "human rights" as alien and opposed to "cultures." Instead, it says that all peoples have a universal human right to maintain their own distinct cultures. The *right to culture* has already been explicit in a number of international rights documents.

This argument is interesting because it seems to concede that such things as universal human rights do exist after all. The list of universal rights is simply amended to include the right to one's culture. It draws strength from the idea that cultural diversity is intrinsically valuable, and people should be able to observe their own cultural practices free from outside interference. However, it calls into question the common understanding that people frequently cannot enjoy their full human rights until they are *freed* from the constraints of local cultures. A right to culture therefore shows how the very idea of rights and culture is transformed and contested by globalization.

One key issue in the struggle to protect the right to culture is shared by *any* claim to human rights. It concerns the kinds of legal mechanisms needed to ensure protection. The great promise of international documents like the UN Declaration of Human Rights seems to be that people are now free to bring allegations of human rights abuses to an international forum to seek redress. But in fact this is not the case. As human rights activists have discovered, human rights are legally interpreted as *individual* rights, not group rights. This means that people must demand that the *governments of the nation-states in which they are citizens* recognize and enforce the individual rights defended in international documents. International institutions like the United Nations have been unwilling to challenge the sovereignty of individual nation-states.

The defense of all human rights, including a right to culture, thus depends on the policies of national governments. Some activists see this reliance as a serious contradiction in human rights discourse that undermines its effectiveness. Talal Asad recounts, for example, how Malcolm X argued in the 1960s that African Americans who wanted redress for abuses of their human rights should go

EthnoProfile 14.3

Hawaii

Region: Polynesia

Nation: United States

Population: 1,244,000 (2002 census)

Environment: Tropical Pacific island

Livelihood: Agriculture, industry, tourism, service, state and local government

Political organization: Modern state within United States

For more information: Merry, Sally Engle. 1999. *Colonizing Hawai'i.* Princeton: Princeton University Press.

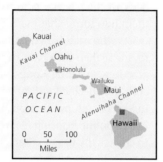

Over the course of the century, Hawaiian law went through two important periods of "legal transplantation." The first, between 1820 and 1844, involved the adoption of a Christianized Hawaiian law. The second, between 1845 and 1852, involved the adoption of a secularized Western law. Although these legal transformations involved colonial imposition, they also depended upon active collaboration by Hawaiian elites (2001, 43–44). Indeed, Merry says that these legal changes are best understood as a process of *transculturation* in which subjugated Hawaiians received and adopted forms of self-understanding imposed by the Christian West, even as the Christian West was modified in response to this reception and adoption.

Because the Hawaiians were not passive in this process, and tried to make use of Christianity and Western ideas for purposes of their own, the process, Merry argues, was fraught with frustration and failure. Missionaries and rulers who wanted to turn Hawaii into a "civilized" place were forced to try to impose their will in stages, rather than all at once, and the end result still bore many Hawaiian traces that, to their dismay, seemed to evade the civilizing process (Figure 14.14).

FIGURE 14.14   The Hawaiian Sovereignty Movement has emphasized Hawaii's traditional culture and has taken action more broadly. Here members lead a march protesting the Asian Development Bank.

In this uncertain process of cultural appropriation, change comes in fits and starts, and it requires constant adjustment as circumstances change. It is very similar, Merry argues, to how contemporary Hawaiians are claiming human rights (2001, 46–47). For the past decade she has studied a feminist program in Hilo, Hawaii, that "endeavors to support women victims of violence and retrain male batterers" (48). This program is based on one originally created in Duluth, Minnesota, and it works closely with the courts. In 1985, the courts adopted the language of rights in dealing with violence against women. This means that the law supports the notion of gender equality, and when husbands are found guilty of battering their wives, calls for separation of the couple. By contrast, Hawaiian couples who participate in the program are often conservative Christians who do not believe in divorce.

It might seem that this is a classic example of the conflict between "rights" and "culture," but in fact "local adaptations of the rights model do take place" (2001, 47). This was done by tailoring the program's curriculum to local circumstances by using Hawaiian images and examples. Particularly interesting was the way the part of the program designed to teach anger management to batterers was made locally relevant by combining Christian ideas with ideas from Hawaiian activists that connected male anger to the losses they have suffered as a consequence of conquest. Merry visited a similar kind of program in New Zealand, based on the same Minnesota model, that had been locally modified for Maori men in a way that linked their anger to Maori experiences of racism and loss.

Merry has since completed a study investigating the ways local activists in India, China, Hong Kong, Fiji, and the United States have appropriated international human rights discourse concerning violence against women and translated that discourse into local cultural terms. Two major findings emerged from this study. First, Merry found that many activists often refused to indigenize international women's rights discourse completely, even though they did dress it in local cultural forms: "To blend completely . . . is to lose the radical possibilities of human rights. It is the unfamiliarity of these ideas that makes them effective in breaking old modes of thought, for example, denaturalizing male privilege to use violence against women as a form of discipline" (2009, 296). Second, she found that activists promoted very similar practices in all five settings to prevent violence against women: either they followed a social service approach offering shelters for victims of violence, training for the perpetrators, support groups, and legal aid; or they adopted a human rights advocacy approach that worked to raise local awareness of global human rights standards and to bring local laws into conformity with these standards.

What was responsible for these similarities? Merry found that these "programs are tailored to local contexts but arrive through paths of global circulation" (2009, 265). That is, social service activists and human rights advocates had often attended the same international conferences, many sponsored by the UN, at which they learned about successful programs used elsewhere in the world. The activists and advocates who participated in these conferences (usually middle-class professionals, lawyers, or members of the political elite) gained valuable skills and experience working with government officials on issues of gender violence. Then they brought what they learned back to their home countries and set about translating them into forms that made sense locally. For example, activists who established battered women's shelters needed to adapt their advocacy to the realities of local housing practices. In Hong Kong, where public housing is available, they decided to lobby to get battered women placed higher on the public housing list. In India, by contrast, where public housing is rarely available, activists worked to change the laws so that a battered woman might safely remain in her husband's house (2009, 267). Merry also found that the work of social service advocates and legal advocates were complementary: women who made use of social services and came to understand themselves as individuals with rights to equality, autonomy, and bodily protection were more likely to support the legal reforms promoted by the human rights advocates, and vice versa. Nevertheless, the possibilities for such changes were shaped by global inequalities of wealth and power: "In countries with few social service resources, the provision of services is shaped . . . more by international definitions of problems and solutions since these are the principal funders" (2009, 296).

Child Prostitution in Thailand

Reaching successful accommodations between human rights discourse and local cultural practices is not always easy. A particularly difficult set of issues must be confronted when attempting to enforce the rights of children. Anthropologist Heather Montgomery did field research in a slum settlement in Thailand that was located near a prosperous seaside resort catering to foreign tourists (2001; see EthnoProfile 14.4: Thailand). Those who lived in this settlement had broken all ties to other kin and other places from which they had migrated, which meant, Montgomery tells us, that the bonds linking parents and children in the settlement had become especially strong. Of overriding importance among these families was the duty of children to work to help support their families. Children did their best to fulfill this duty as soon as they were able, trying many different jobs, including begging.

EthnoProfile 14.4

Thailand

Region: Southeast Asia

Nation: Thailand

Population: 64,265,000

Environment: Tropical monsoon climate

Livelihood: Agriculture, industry, tourism, service

Political organization: Constitutional monarchy; modern state

For more information: van Esterik, Penny. 2000. *Materializing Thailand.* Oxford: Berg.

But none of these options earned very much. And so, sooner or later, children began working as prostitutes for wealthy foreign tourists who visited the resort. At the time of her research, 65 children in the community were working as prostitutes.

Children could earn as much as five times the money working as prostitutes as they could get from begging, plus they were able to visit fancy hotels and were well fed. Many of the clients, moreover, developed long-term relationships with the families of the child prostitutes, often lending them large sums of money—in one case, enough to rebuild the family home of one girl. It was friends and neighbors of the children, not their mothers, who recruited children into prostitution. When faced with the reality of the nature of their children's employment, mothers were able to claim that they had not found out until it was too late, and they interpreted the children's acts as evidence of their strong sense of filial duty in fulfilling obligations to help support the family.

"Both adult and child were aware of the child's duties, but there was a degree of unease about how far a child had to go to fulfill them" (Montgomery 2001, 90). The children claimed not to hate the men whom they worked for, especially those who kept in touch even when not in Thailand and who continued to send money to the children. Because of the financial generosity and long-term involvement of these men with their children, mothers said they felt the men were trustworthy. The actual sexual acts for which the children are paid take place outside the settlement and are never publicly discussed, and the bleeding and tearing the children experience is ignored.

Commercial sex and even child prostitution are not new in Thailand, but in recent years many Thais working in the media and for NGOs have denounced child sex tourism and have tried to force the national government to put a stop to it. Human rights discourse—particularly discourse about the rights of the child—have played a prominent role in this campaign (Figure 14.15). Montgomery points out that, since 1924, international bodies have issued nine separate documents dealing with human rights and the rights of the child.

Children's rights, like human rights in general, are based on Western middle-class ideas about what constitutes an acceptable human childhood, and on Western ideas of when childhood begins and ends. For example,

FIGURE 14.15 Doctors Without Borders runs a rehabilitation center for child prostitutes in Thailand.

the 1989 Convention on the Rights of the Child defines a child as anyone under 18 years of age, and AntiSlavery International has claimed that child-marriage is a form of slavery and therefore violates human rights. But as Montgomery observes, "it does not take an anthropologist to recognize that a child marrying at 15 in full accordance with traditional norms and local custom in India is very different from a child marrying at 15 in the UK" (2001, 82). In common with other forms of human rights discourse, declarations on the rights of the child normally emphasize the importance of rights over duties, although this is not universal. But this is the issue that needs to be emphasized, Montgomery argues, in order to talk meaningfully about the rights of the children working as prostitutes in the Baan Nua slum.

The model of ideal Western childhood contained in the UN Convention on the Rights of the Child includes the idea that, as Montgomery puts it, "every child has a right to a childhood that is free from the responsibilities of work, money and sex" (2001, 83). The problem with this standard is that it fits so poorly with understandings of childhood in which, for example, children are expected (or needed) to work for money to support the family, and it seems unable to imagine situations in which the entire support of a family depends on a child's earnings from prostitution. Yet that is an accurate description for many families and children in Baan Nua.

Local Thai activists have been particularly interested in enforcing Article 34 of the Convention which aims to protect children "from all forms of sexual exploitation and sexual abuse" (2001, 86). But the Convention also recognizes many other children's rights, including the notion that the child's best interests must always be kept uppermost and that they have a right to live with their families. The problem is that "how these rights are prioritized is not culturally neutral. . . . Too often . . . Article 34 is quoted in isolation, decontextualizing sexual abuse and presenting it as the paramount difficulty that poor children face, without linking it to global issues of poverty, cultural background, and discrimination" (2001, 85–87). The child's best interests are certainly compromised through prostitution, but they are also compromised when children are removed from their families and communities, or when they have nothing to eat.

This is particularly poignant in the case of the children of Baan Nua, many of whom claimed that they were

not exploited, and all of whom were strongly motivated to engage in prostitution based on the cultural belief that children are obliged to support their parents. Montgomery concludes:

> By ensuring that their families could stay together and have a sustainable income, it would be possible to eradicate child prostitution without enforcing punitive measures against their parents. . . . Thailand's positions in globalized political and economic relations are as important as cultural specificities in perpetuating that sexual exploitation. . . . Article 34 would be redundant if the other rights enshrined in the convention . . . could be reliably enforced." (2001, 97–98)

These and other examples suggest two important conclusions. First, it is possible to find ways of accommodating the universal discourse of human rights to the particularities of local conditions. Second, no single model of the relationship between rights and culture will fit all cases. Moreover, as the culture of human rights becomes better established, it increasingly becomes enmeshed in political and legal institutions that go beyond the local level. As activists become more experienced operating in globalized circumstances, they are likely to become more sophisticated about making use of these different settings as they plan their human rights strategies (Cowan et al. 2001, 21). Struggles over human rights are hardly likely to go away; indeed, along with struggles over global citizenship, they can be seen as the prime struggles of our time (Mignolo 2002). Anthropologists are well positioned to help make sense of these complex developments as they unfold.

Cultural Imperialism or Cultural Hybridization?

The *impact* of the global spread of images, ideas, people, things, and ideologies in local social settings has clearly been profound, as illustrated by the preceding examples. But how should anthropologists characterize the processes by which these changes have come about?

Cultural Imperialism

One explanation, formulated during the Cold War, was **cultural imperialism**. Cultural imperialism is based on two notions. First, it says some cultures dominate other cultures. In recent history, the culture(s) of Europe or the United States or "the West" have come to dominate all other cultures of the world, owing to the spread of

cultural imperialism The idea that some cultures dominate other cultures, and that cultural domination by one culture leads inevitably to the destruction of subordinated cultures and their replacement by the culture of those in power.

colonialism and capitalism. Second, cultural domination by one culture is said to lead inevitably to the destruction of subordinated cultures and their replacement by the culture of those in power. Thus, Western cultural imperialism is seen as responsible for destroying, for example, local music, technology, dress, and food traditions and replacing them with rock and roll, radios, flashlights, cell phones, T-shirts, blue jeans, McDonald's hamburgers, and Coca-Cola (Figure 14.16). The inevitable outcome of Western cultural imperialism is seen as "the cultural homogenization of the world," with the unwelcome consequence of "dooming the world to uniformity" (Inda and Rosaldo 2002, 13, 14).

The idea of cultural imperialism developed primarily outside anthropology, but anthropologists could not ignore it, because it purported to describe what was happening to the people they studied. Anthropologists, too, were aware that Western music, fashion, food, and technology had spread among those they worked with. But cultural imperialism did not seem to explain this spread, for at least three reasons (Inda and Rosaldo 2002, 22–24). First, cultural imperialism denies *agency* to non-Western peoples who make use of Western cultural forms. It assumes that they are passive and without the resources to resist anything of Western origin that is marketed to them. Second, cultural imperialism assumes that non-Western cultural forms never move "from the rest to the West." But this is clearly false. Non-Western music and food and material culture have large and eager followings in Western Europe and the United States. Third, cultural imperialism ignores that cultural forms and practices sometimes move from one part of the non-Western world to other parts of the non-Western world, bypassing the West entirely. Movies made in India have been popular for decades in northern Nigeria (Larkin 2002), Mexican soap operas have large followings in the Philippines, and karaoke is popular all over the world.

Cultural Hybridity

Dissatisfied with the discourse of cultural imperialism, anthropologists began to search for alternative ways of understanding global cultural flows. From the days of Franz Boas and his students, anthropologists had recognized the significance of cultural borrowing. They had also emphasized that borrowing cultural forms or practices from elsewhere always involves *borrowing-with-modification*. That is, people never adopt blindly, but always adapt what they borrow for local purposes. Put another way, people rarely accept ideas or practices or objects from elsewhere without *domesticating* or *indigenizing* them—finding a way of reconciling them with local practices in order to serve local purposes.

In the 1980s, for example, weavers in Otavalo, Ecuador, were making a lot of money selling textiles to tourists. They could then organize small production firms and purchase television sets to entertain their employees while they worked at their looms. In addition, some men had so much business that they encouraged their wives to take up weaving, even though women were not traditionally weavers. In order to spend more time weaving, women started to use indoor cookstoves, which relieved them from the time-consuming labor of traditional meal preparation over an open fire (Colloredo-Mansfeld 1999). From the perspective of anthropologist Rudi Colloredo-Mansfeld, these uses of Western technology could not be understood as the consequences of Western cultural imperialism, because they clearly had nothing to do with trying to imitate a Western lifestyle. It made more sense to interpret these changes as Otavalan *domestication* or *indigenization* of televisions and cookstoves, since these items from elsewhere were adopted precisely in order to promote indigenous Otavalan weaving. Put yet another way, borrowing-with-modification always involves *customizing* that which is borrowed to meet the purposes of the borrowers, which may be quite remote from the

FIGURE 14.16   People line up outside a McDonald's in Cairo.

In Their Own Words

How Sushi Went Global

Talk of "global flows" can seem abstract and divorced from everyday life, but one of the strengths of anthropology is its ability to capture the articulation of the local with the global. As sushi swept the United States, anthropologist Theodore Bestor looked at the trade in tuna.

A 40-minute drive from Bath, Maine, down a winding two-lane highway, the last mile on a dirt road, a ramshackle wooden fish pier stands beside an empty parking lot. At 6:00 P.M. nothing much is happening. Three bluefin tuna sit in a huge tub of ice on the loading dock.

Between 6:45 and 7:00, the parking lot fills up with cars and trucks with license plates from New Jersey, New York, Massachusetts, New Hampshire, and Maine. Twenty tuna buyers clamber out, half of them Japanese. The three bluefin, ranging from 270 to 610 pounds, are winched out of the tub, and buyers crowd around them, extracting tiny core samples to examine their color, fingering the flesh to assess the fat content, sizing up the curve of the body.

After about 20 minutes of eyeing the goods, many of the buyers return to their trucks to call Japan by cellphone and get the morning prices from Tokyo's Tsukiji market—the fishing industry's answer to Wall Street where the daily tuna auctions have just concluded. The buyers look over the tuna one last time and give written bids to the dock manager, who passes the top bid for each fish to the crew that landed it.

The auction bids are secret. Each bid is examined anxiously by a cluster of young men, some with a father or uncle looking on to give advice, others with a young woman and a couple of toddlers trying to see Daddy's fish. Fragments of concerned conversation float above the parking lot: "That's all?" "Couldn't we do better if we shipped it ourselves?" "Yeah, but my pickup needs a new transmission now!" After a few minutes, deals are closed and the fish are quickly loaded onto the backs of trucks in crates of crushed ice, known in the trade as "tuna coffins." As rapidly as they arrived, the flotilla of buyers sails out of the parking lot—three bound for New York's John F. Kennedy Airport, where their tuna will be airfreighted to Tokyo for sale the day after next.

Bluefin tuna may seem at first an unlikely case study in globalization. But as the world rearranges itself—around silicon chips, Starbucks coffee, or sashimi-grade tuna—new channels for global flows of capital and commodities link far-flung individuals and communities in unexpected new relationships. The tuna trade is a prime example of the globalization of a regional industry, with intense international competition and thorny environmental regulations; centuries-old practices combined with high technology; realignments of labor and capital in response to international regulation; shifting markets; and the diffusion of culinary culture as tastes for sushi, and bluefin tuna, spread worldwide. . . .

Culture Splash

Just because sushi is available, in some form or another, in exclusive Fifth Avenue restaurants, in baseball stadiums in Los Angeles, at airport snack carts in Amsterdam, at an apartment in Madrid (delivered by motorcycle), or in Buenos Aires, Tel Aviv, or Moscow, doesn't mean that sushi has lost its status as Japanese cultural property. Globalization doesn't necessarily homogenize cultural differences nor erase the salience of cultural labels. Quite the contrary, it grows the franchise. In the global economy of consumption, the brand equity of sushi as Japanese cultural property adds to the cachet of both the country and the cuisine. A Texan Chinese-American restauranteur told me, for example, that he had converted his chain of restaurants from Chinese to Japanese cuisine because the prestige factor of the latter meant he could charge a premium; his clients couldn't distinguish between Chinese and Japanese employees (and often failed to notice that some of the chefs behind his sushi bars were Latinos).

The brand equity is sustained by complicated flows of labor and ethnic biases. Outside of Japan, having Japanese hands (or a reasonable facsimile) is sufficient warrant for sushi competence. Guidebooks for the current generation of Japanese global *wandervogel* sometimes advise young Japanese looking for a job in a distant city to work as a sushi chef; U.S. consular offices in Japan grant more than 1,000 visas a year to sushi chefs, tuna buyers, and other workers in the global sushi business. A trade school in Tokyo, operating under the name Sushi Daigaku (Sushi University), offers short courses in sushi preparation so "students" can impress prospective employers with an imposing certificate. Even without papers, however, sushi remains firmly linked in the minds of Japanese and foreigners alike with Japanese cultural

In Their Own Words

identity. Throughout the world, sushi restaurants operated by Koreans, Chinese, or Vietnamese maintain Japanese identities. In sushi bars from Boston to Valencia, a customer's simple greeting in Japanese can throw chefs into a panic (or drive them to the far end of the counter).

On the docks, too, Japanese cultural control of sushi remains unquestioned. Japanese buyers and "tuna techs" sent from Tsukiji to work seasonally on the docks of New England laboriously instruct foreign fishers on the proper techniques for catching, handling, and packing tuna for export. A bluefin tuna must approximate the appropriate *kata*, or "ideal form," of color, texture, fat content, body shape, and so forth, all prescribed by Japanese specifications. Processing requires proper attention as well. Special paper is sent from Japan for wrapping the fish before burying them in crushed ice. Despite high shipping costs and the fact that 50 percent of the gross weight of a tuna is unusable, tuna is sent to Japan whole, not sliced into salable portions. Spoilage is one reason for this, but form

is another. Everyone in the trade agrees that Japanese workers are much more skilled in cutting and trimming tuna than Americans, and no one would want to risk sending botched cuts to Japan.

Not to impugn the quality of the fish sold in the United States, but on the New England docks, the first determination of tuna buyers is whether they are looking at a "domestic" fish or an "export" fish. On that judgment hangs several dollars a pound for the fisher, and the supply of sashimi-grade tuna for fishmongers, sushi bars, and seafood restaurants up and down the Eastern seaboard. Some of the best tuna from New England may make it to New York or Los Angeles, but by way of Tokyo—validated as top quality (and top price) by the decision to ship it to Japan by air for sale at Tsukiji, where it may be purchased by one of the handful of Tsukiji sushi exporters who supply premier expatriate sushi chefs in the world's leading cities.

Source: Bestor 2000.

---

purposes of those among whom the form or practice originated (Inda and Rosaldo 2002, 16). This form of cultural change is very different from having something from elsewhere forced upon you, against your will (Figure 14.17).

At the same time, the consequences of borrowing-with-modification can never be fully controlled. Thus, Otavalan weavers may start watching television because local reruns of old American television series relieve the tedium of weaving. However, once television watching becomes a habitual practice, it also exposes them to advertising and news broadcasts, which may stimulate other local changes that nobody can predict. The domestication or indigenization of cultural forms from elsewhere *both* makes it possible to do old things in new ways *and* leaves open the possibility of doing new things as well. Put another way, cultural borrowing is double-edged; borrowed cultural practices are both amenable to domestication and yet able to escape it. No wonder that cultural borrowing is often viewed with ambivalence.

The challenges are particularly acute in globalizing conditions, colonial or postcolonial, where borrowed ideas, objects, or practices remain entangled in relationships with donors even as they are made to serve new goals by recipients (Thomas 1991). People in multicultural settings must deal on a daily basis with tempting cultural alternatives emanating from more powerful groups.

It is therefore not surprising that they regularly struggle to control processes of cultural borrowing and to contain domesticated cultural practices within certain contexts, or in the hands of certain people only.

Many social scientists have borrowed a metaphor from biology to describe this complex process of globalized cultural exchange and speak of *cultural hybridization* or *hybridity*. Both these concepts were meant to highlight forms of cultural borrowing that produced something new that could not be collapsed or subsumed, either within the culture of the donor or within the culture of the recipient. In addition, both terms stressed the positive side of cultural mixing: Rather than indicating a regrettable loss of original purity, hybridity and creolization draw attention to positive processes of cultural creativity. Furthermore, if hybridity is a normal part of all human social experience, then the idea that "authentic" traditions never change can legitimately be challenged. For members of a social group who wish to revise or discard cultural practices that they find outmoded or oppressive, hybridity talk is liberating. Choosing to revise or discard, borrow or invent *on terms of one's own choosing* also means that one possesses agency, the capacity to exercise at least some control over one's life. And exercising agency calls into question charges that one is succumbing to cultural imperialism or losing one's cultural "authenticity."

FIGURE 14.17 Musical performance has become an important part of the Otavalo Indian economy, as musicians from Otavalo travel throughout the world performing and selling woven goods. They have domesticated CD production as well and have been quite successful in selling CDs of their music to tourists in Otavalo and to listeners abroad.

The Limits of Cultural Hybridity

However, as anthropologist Nicholas Thomas puts it, "hybridity is almost a good idea, but not quite" (1996, 9). Close examination of talk about cultural hybridization reveals at least three problems. First, it is not clear that this concept actually frees anthropologists from the modernist commitment to the existence of bounded, homogeneous, unchanging "cultures." That is, the idea of **cultural hybridity** is based on the notion of cultural mixing. But what is it that is mixed? Two or more non-hybridized, original, "pure" cultures! But such "pure" homogeneous, bounded, unchanging cultures are not supposed to exist.

Thus we are caught in a paradox. For this reason Jonathan Friedman, among others, is highly critical of

cultural hybridity Cultural mixing.

discussions of cultural hybridity; in his view, cultures have *always* been hybrid and it is the existence of *boundaries*, not cultural borrowing, that anthropologists need to explain. Besides, hybrid cultural mixtures often get transformed into new, unitary cultural identities. This process can be seen, he argues, in the way in which the "mixed race" category in the United States has been transformed into a "new, unitary group of mixtures for those who feel 'disenfranchised' by the current single-race categories" (1997, 83). Friedman also points out that hybrid identities are not liberating when they are thrust upon people rather than being adopted freely. He draws attention to cases in Latin America where the "mestizo" identity has been used "as a middle-/upper-class tool" against indigenous groups. "We are all part-Indian, say members of the elite who have much to lose in the face of minority claims" (1997, 81–82).

These examples highlight a second difficulty with hybridity talk: Those who celebrate cultural hybridization often ignore the fact that its effects are experienced differently by those with power and those without power. As Friedman says, "the question of class becomes crucial" (1997, 81). The complexity of this issue is seen in many popular discussions of "multiculturalism" that celebrate cultural hybridization and that, in the context of globalizing capitalism, turn hybridity into a marketable commodity. The commodification of hybridity is problematic because it smooths over differences in the experience of cultural hybridization, offering multiculturalism as an array of tempting consumables for outsiders. "Multiculturalism is aimed at nourishing and perpetuating the kind of differences which do not [threaten]," writes Nira Yuval-Davis (1997, 197). International Folk Festivals, Festivals of Nations, and the like—events that emphasize costume, cuisine, music, and dance—spring to mind. But the troubling fact is that cultural hybridity is experienced as both nonthreatening and very threatening, depending on the terms on which it is available.

Because of power differences among groups challenged by cultural hybridization, any globalized "multicultural" setting reveals active processes of cultural hybridization *together with* the defense of discrete cultural identities that seem to *resist* hybridization (Werbner 1997, 3). Cultural hybridization is unobjectionable when actors perceive it to be under their own control, but cultural hybridization is resisted when it is "perceived by actors themselves to be potentially threatening to their sense of moral integrity" (Werbner 1997, 12). The threat is greatest for those with the least power who feel unable to control forms of cultural hybridization that threaten to undermine the fragile survival structures on which they depend in an unwelcoming multicultural setting.

And this leads to a third problem with the concept of cultural hybridization. Fashionable hybridity talk hides the differences between elite and nonelite experiences of multiculturalism. Anthropologist John Hutnyk, for example, deplores the way "world music" is marketed to middle-class consumers, because such sales strategies divert attention "from the urgency of anti-racist politics" (1997, 122). That is, when cultural hybridization becomes fashionable, it easily turns the experiences of hybridized elites into a hegemonic standard suggesting that class exploitation and racial oppression are easily overcome or no longer exist. But to dismiss or ignore continuing nonelite struggles with cultural hybridization can spark dangerous confrontations that can quickly spiral out of control.

Anthropologist Peter van der Veer argues that such a dynamic ignited the furor in Britain that followed the publication of Salman Rushdie's novel *The Satanic Verses*. Rushdie is an elite, highly educated South Asian migrant to Britain who experienced cultural hybridity as a form of emancipation from oppressive religious and cultural restrictions. His novel contained passages describing Islam and the Prophet Muhammad that, from this elite point of view, embodied "transgression" that was liberating. But migrants from South Asia in Britain are not all members of the elite. Most South Asian Muslim immigrants in Britain are workers, and they saw *The Satanic Verses* not as a work of artistic liberation but as a deliberate attempt to mock their beliefs and practices. "These immigrants, who are already socially and culturally marginalized, are thus doubly marginalized in the name of an attack on 'purity' and Islamic 'fundamentalism'" (1997, 101–2).

Even more important, however, may be the way popular interpretations of their objections in the press and among Western intellectuals ignored these immigrants' own, very different but very real, *nonelite* experiences of cultural hybridization.

Put simply, elites experience cultural hybridization in ways that are often very different from the way nonelites experience cultural hybridization. We all ignore this fact at our peril.

Can We Be at Home in a Global World?

The era of globalization in which we live is an era of uncertainty and insecurity. Possibilities for emancipatory new ways of living are undercut by sharpening economic and political differences and the looming threat of violence. Is it possible, in the midst of all this confusion and conflict, to devise ways of coping with our circumstances that would provide guidance in the confusion, moderation to

the conflict? No one expects such efforts to be easy. But anthropologists and other concerned scholars are currently struggling to come up with concepts and practices that might be helpful.

Cosmopolitanism

Our era is not the first to have faced such challenges. Walter Mignolo argues that multiculturalism was born in the sixteenth century when Iberian conquest in the New World first raised troubling issues among Western thinkers about the kinds of relationships that were possible and desirable between the conquerors and the indigenous peoples whom they had conquered. During the ensuing centuries, the challenges posed by a multicultural world did not disappear. In the context of eighteenth-century Enlightenment promises of human emancipation based on *The Rights of Man and the Citizen*, philosopher Immanuel Kant concluded that the achievements of the Enlightenment offered individuals new opportunities for developing ways of being at home in the world wherever they were.

To identify this orientation, he revived a concept that was first coined by the Stoic philosophers of ancient Rome: **cosmopolitanism** (Mignolo 2002). Kantian cosmopolitanism "by and large meant being versed in Western ways and the vision of 'one world' culture was only a sometimes unconscious, sometimes unconscionable, euphemism for 'First World' culture" (Abbas 2002, 210). But is it possible to rework our understandings of cultural hybridity to stretch the notion of cosmopolitanism beyond its traditional association with privileged Western elites (Figure 14.18)? Many anthropologists have become comfortable talking about "alternative" or "minority modernities" that depart from the Western European norm. In a similar fashion, any new anthropological understanding of cosmopolitanism would have to be plural, not singular, and it would have to include nonelite experiences of cultural hybridization.

Friction

Anthropologist Anna Lowenhaupt Tsing has worked in Indonesia for many years, investigating what she calls **friction**, "the awkward, unequal, unstable aspects of interconnection across difference" (2005, 4).

She seeks to understand how capitalist interests brought about the destruction of the Indonesian rain forests in the 1980s and 1990s as well as how environmental

---

cosmopolitanism Being at ease in more than one cultural setting.
friction The awkward, unequal, unstable aspects of interconnection across difference.

In Their Own Words

Destructive Logging and Deforestation in Indonesia

WALHI, Wahana Lingkungan Hidup Indonesia, Friends of the Earth Indonesia, is an Indonesian umbrella organization for nongovernment and community-based organizations. It is represented in 25 provinces and has over 438 member organizations (as of June 2004). According to their website (http://www.eng .walhi.or.id/) it "stands for social transformation, people's sovereignty, and sustainability of life and livelihoods. WALHI works to defend Indonesia's natural world and local communities from injustice carried out in the name of economic development." In late March 2007, they issued the following release.

The deforestation problem in Indonesia is spreading. Illegal and destructive logging is a major cause. In addition, conversion of forest areas for the development of oil palm and the pulp and paper industry has been substantial. Since the beginning of this decade, as much as 2.8 million ha of Indonesia's forests have been lost each year to illegal and destructive logging. This has led to US $4 billion or 40 trillion rupiah in losses to the State per year.

If we put two and two together, forest conversion and the pulp and paper industry are also causal factors in the rising rate of deforestation. We know that some 15.9 million ha of natural tropical forest has been cleared for forest conversion. The conversion of forests for oil palm development is a contributing factor to the increase in deforestation in Indonesia. From being prime land, 15.9 million ha of natural tropical forests have been cleared. On the contrary, there has been no meaningful increase in planted land area. Plantation area has only increased to 5.5 million ha in 2004, from 3.17 million ha in 2000. More than 10 million ha of forest have been abandoned after the harvest of the wood crop growing there.

Similarly, the pulp and paper industry have also brought problems. This industry needs at least 27 million cubic meters of timber each year (Department of Forestry, 2006). Since plantation forests can only supply 30 percent of the total demand for pulp, this industry continues logging activities in natural forests, harvesting some 21.8 million cubic meters in order to fulfill its annual requirement. The timber obtained from natural forests is owned by company affiliates or taken from the concessions of its partners. This is not mentioning plywood or other trades, for which only 25% of timber requirements are supplied by plantation forests.

The negative impacts of forestry crime in Indonesia are described above. Economic losses from forestry crimes such as illegal logging, conversion of natural forests, and so on are calculated to reach 200 trillion rupiah. This loss does not include ecological disasters caused by illegal logging activities, such as floods and landslides, which now occur frequently in all corners of the Archipelago.

WALHI deduces that the ecological degradation caused by forestry crimes is caused, at least, by two major factors: (1) differences in the outlooks and value systems upheld by the community, the forestry department, and the government (both local and central); and (2) erosion of the judicial process due to corruption, collusion and nepotism. At this point, enforcement of the law is inconsistent.

Inconsistency in the judicial process is caused by the viruses of corruption, collusion and nepotism, which intricately bind the immediate interests of law enforcers (and even bureaucratic officers) throughout the judicial process, starting with the police, attorneys and the judiciary. The result is that anti-illegal logging operations in Papua Province (March 2005) failed to catch top-rung criminals or their protectors in the police force and military. From this operation, 186 suspects were arrested. But, until January 2007, only 13 suspects had been successfully prosecuted and not one syndicate leader has been caught. From the 18 major cases that have reached court, all accused have been released.

Furthermore, differences in the outlooks and value systems upheld by the community, the forestry department and the government (both local and central) have been a major factor in the increasing rate of forestry crime. From the community's perspective, forests function to protect people from high winds, drought and erosion. The forestry department also recognises the ecological functions of the forests; however, illegal clearing and logging are allowed to continue in accordance with the economic calculations maintained by the forestry department. Similarly, the government's stance also draws from economic aspects of forests rather than its ecological functions. For them, the forests are a resource with abundant natural resource wealth that must be extracted for the national income. Unfortunately, the development policies that are implemented do not favour forest sustainability.

As we track the rate of forestry crime (illegal logging, conversion of forests without replanting, the unlimited thirst of the pulp and paper industry for wood), it is clear that the government needs to halt several

In Their Own Words

forms of forestry crime that have the potential to trigger a series of ecological disasters, such as floods, landslides, and drought. In addition, community involvement (especially the traditional community) in securing forest conservation is highly necessary. Moreover, the seriousness of all law enforcers (starting with the police force, attorneys, and judges) is crucial to stopping deforestation associated with forestry crimes. Without the serious involvement of all parties in carrying out surveillance, it is quite possible that Indonesia's forests will be completely cleared in the not-too-distant future.

Finally, deforestation as a consequence of illegal logging is caused, at least, by three major factors, that is, the lack of acknowledgement by the government of people's rights to manage their forest resources, widespread corruption in various sectors of forest resource management, and the large gap between supply and demand. If these three factors are not immediately overcome—make no mistake—Indonesia's forests will be rapidly cleared within a short timeframe.

Source: WALHI, 2007

movements emerged to defend the forests and the people who live in them. Discussions of cultural imperialism assume that processes of global change will be smooth and unstoppable, that "globalization can be predicted in advance" (2005, 3). After the Cold War, for example, a number of politicians and social theorists predicted "an inevitable, peaceful transition" to global integration of the capitalist market (2005, 11). On the contrary, her research showed that the encounters between Japanese lumber traders and Indonesia government officials that turned Indonesia into the world's largest tropical lumber producer by 1973 were "messy and surprising" (2005, 3). She points out that "Indonesian tropical rain forests were not harvested as industrial timber until the 1970s" because "large-scale loggers prefer forests in which one valuable species predominates; tropical rain forests are just too biologically diverse" (2005, 14). However, in the 1970s

the Japanese trading companies that began negotiations with the Indonesian New Order regime of President Suharto did not want access to valuable hardwoods; instead, they wanted "large quantities of cheaply produced logs," which they intended to turn into plywood.

The Japanese traders did not get what they wanted right away, however. Rather, as Tsing points out, this could not happen until three specific transformations had occurred. First, the forest had to be "simplified." Japanese lumber traders and Indonesian officials ignored species diversity, recognizing as valuable only those species that could be turned into plywood and regarding everything else—"the rest of the trees, fungi, and fauna . . . the fruit orchards, rattans, and other human-tended plants of forest dwellers"—as waste (2005, 16). Second, to make such forest simplification politically palatable, forests were reconfigured as a "sustainable

FIGURE 14.18 Cosmopolitanism is no longer only for Western elites. Otavalo Indian tourist José María Cotachaci, visiting the San Francisco Bay Area, November 2000. Otavalos have created their own form of modernity.

resource" that could be replaced later by industrial tree plantations. However, once the Japanese traders were successful, Indonesian businessmen built their own plywood industry, based on the Japanese model. This led to the development of links between destruction of the forest and nation-building, as the state came to depend on income from selling forest concessions to favored political cronies. Once this alliance was forged, legal and illegal forms of forest exploitation could no longer be distinguished from one another, and it became impossible for forest dwellers to defend their own, preexisting property rights. "Either official or unofficial alone could be challenged, but together they overwhelmed local residents. . . . Together they transform the countryside into a free-for-all frontier" (2005, 17). But the production of such a frontier was not inevitable. It was the outcome of contingent encounters that people reworked in order to produce desired outcomes, along with additional, unintended consequences.

In response to rain forest destruction, a strong Indonesian environmental movement came into existence (Figure 14.19). Once again, however, this cannot be understood as a simple, predictable extension of Western environmentalist practices into Indonesia. On the contrary, "the movement was an amalgam of odd parts: engineers, nature lovers, reformers, technocrats" (2005, 17). In fact, activists who were dissatisfied with other features of President Suharto's New Order regime decided to focus on environmental issues, because these seemed to be issues less likely to trigger government censorship and repression. In any case, as Tsing says, "the movement was organized around difference" (2005, 17). It was not centralized, but "imagined itself as coordinating already existing but scattered and disorganized rural complaints. Activists' jobs, as they imagined it, involved translating subaltern demands into the languages of the powerful" and "translating back to let people know their rights" (2005, 18). It was messy, but this did not deter activists. "Within the links of awkwardly transcended difference, the environmental movement has tried to offer an alternative to forest destruction and the erosion of indigenous rights."

Like the alliance between businessmen and New Order government officials, the environmental movement emerged out of relationships forged by unlikely parties who struggled to find ways of working together to achieve overlapping but nonidentical goals. Thus, friction in the struggle to bridge differences makes new things possible: "Rubbing two sticks together produces heat and light; one stick alone is just a stick. As a metaphorical image, friction reminds us that heterogeneous and unequal encounters can lead to new arrangements of culture and power" (2005, 3–5). And these arrangements, while potentially dangerous, may also be seen as a source of hope: "Just as the encounter of Japanese trading companies and Indonesian politicians produced simplified dipterocarp forests, these activist-inspired encounters may yet produce different kinds of forests" (2005, 18).

Border Thinking

Tsing's understanding of "friction" as an unavoidable and productive feature of the process of cultural hybridization has much in common with what Walter Mignolo calls *border thinking*. For Mignolo, in a globalized world, concepts like "democracy" and "justice" can no longer be defined

FIGURE 14.19 Heavy logging activity has led to destruction of the rain forest in Kalimantan and to the emergence of a strong Indonesian environmental movement.

within a single Western logic—or, for that matter, from the perspective of the political left or the political right. Border thinking involves detaching these concepts from their hegemonic "Western" meanings and practices. It means using them as "connectors," tools for imagining and negotiating new, cosmopolitan forms of democracy or justice informed by the ethical and political judgments of nonelites (Mignolo 2002, 179, 181).

Finally, in reimagining what cosmopolitanism might mean, it is important not only to go beyond Kantian limitations, but also to go beyond standard anthropological orientations to other ways of life. The hope is that border thinking can produce a *critical cosmopolitanism* capable of negotiating new understandings of human rights and global citizenship in ways that can dismantle barriers of gender and race that are the historical legacies of colonialism (Mignolo 2002, 161, 180). In many cases this may require seriously revising Western modernist ideas and practices, if that is the only honorable way of overcoming power differentials and threats to moral integrity experienced by nonelites. But because cosmopolitanism involves border thinking, ideals and practices with Enlightenment credentials may also turn out to be valuable counterweights to extremism and violence.

This is apparent in the stance taken by those citizens of Bombay (Mumbai), India, who resist attempts by radical Hindus to banish Muslims from the city and to turn India into a Hindu state. Relationships between Hindus and Muslims in India took a severe turn for the worse after Hindu vandals destroyed a mosque in the city of Ayodhya in 1992. Arjun Appadurai, who followed these developments closely, noted that the brutal Hindutva movement pushing to turn India into a Hindu state "violates the ideals of secularism and interreligious harmony enshrined in the constitution" (Appadurai 2002, 73–74). Appadurai writes of Indians from many walks of life, rich and poor, Muslim and Hindu, who have shown "extraordinary displays of courage and critical imagination in Mumbai," who have "held up powerful images of a cosmopolitan, secular, multicultural Bombay." Their "radical moderation" in resisting violent religious polarization is, he argues, neither naïve nor nostalgic: "These utopian visions and critical practices are resolutely modernist in their visions of equity, justice, and cultural cosmopolitanism" (Appadurai 2002, 79). Secularism, as we saw in chapter 8, is a notion with impeccable Enlightenment credentials that arrived in India with British colonialism. And yet it is this "situated secularism"—indigenized, customized, domesticated, *Indian* secularism, opposed to *Indian* interreligious violence—that Appadurai and many other Indian citizens see as a key element of a form of local Indian cosmopolitanism that have been effective in preventing religious strife in the past and may be able to do so again.

Many of the cases in this chapter demonstrate the human ability to cope creatively with changed life circumstances. They remind us that human beings are not passive in the face of the new, that they actively and resiliently respond to life's challenges. Nevertheless, the example of the Panará reminds us that successful outcomes are never ensured. Modes of livelihood that may benefit some human groups can overwhelm and destroy others. Western capitalism and modern technology have exploded into a vortex of global forces that resist control. A critical cosmopolitanism involving concerted practical action to lessen violence and exploitation may be all that can prevent these forces from destroying us all.

Why Study Anthropology?

First, studying cultural anthropology brings students into contact with different ways of life. It makes them aware of just how arbitrary their own understanding of the world is as they learn how other people have developed satisfying but different ways of living. In addition, if they are from Western countries that were responsible for colonialism and its consequences, it makes them painfully aware of just how much their own tradition has to answer for in the modern world.

We may start to doubt assumptions about the right way to live that we had previously taken for granted. We doubt because a familiarity with alternative ways of living can make the rightness of any action, or the meaning of any object, a highly ambiguous matter. Ambiguity is part and parcel of the human condition. Human beings have coped with ambiguity from time immemorial by means of culture, which places objects and actions in contexts and thereby makes their meanings plain. This doubt can lead to anxiety, but it can also be liberating.

All human beings, ourselves included, live in culturally shaped worlds, entangled in threads of interpretation and meaning that we have spun. It has been the particular task of anthropology and its practitioners to go out into the world to bear witness to and record the vast creative diversity in world-making that has been the history of our species. In our lifetimes, we will witness the transformation of many of those ways of life, loss that is tragic, for as these worlds disappear, so too does something special about humanity: variety, creativity, and awareness of alternatives.

Our survival as a species and our viability as individuals depend on the possibility of choice, of perceiving and being able to act on alternatives in the various situations we encounter during our lives. If, as a colleague has suggested, human life is a minefield, then the more paths we can see and imagine through that minefield, the more likely we are to get further—or at least to have an interesting time trying. As alternatives are destroyed, wantonly smashed, or thoughtlessly crushed, *our* own human possibilities are reduced. A small group of men and women have for the last century labored in corners of the world, both remote and nearby, to write the record of human accomplishment and bring it back and teach it to others.

Surely our greatest human accomplishment is the creation of the sometimes austerely beautiful worlds in which we all live. Anthropologists have rarely given in to the romantic notion that these other worlds are all good, all life-enhancing, all fine or beautiful. They are not.

Ambiguity and ambivalence are, as we have seen, hallmarks of the human experience. There are no guarantees that human cultures will be compassionate rather than cruel or that people will agree they are one or the other. There are not even any guarantees that our species will survive. But all anthropologists have believed that these are *human* worlds that have given those who have lived in them the ability to make sense out of their experiences and to derive meaning for their lives, that we are a species at once bound by our culture and free to change it.

This is a perilous and fearsome freedom, a difficult freedom to grasp and to wield. Nevertheless, the freedom is there, and in this interplay of freedom and constraint lies our future. It is up to us to create it.

Chapter Summary

1. Anthropologists have made use of a variety of theoretical perspectives to explain the relationship between the West and the rest of the world. During the Cold War, anthropologists debated the relative merits of modernization theory and dependency theory. Later, they were influenced by world system theory, which divided the territories controlled by capitalism into core, periphery and semiperiphery, and argued that the relationships between these regions had been established during the years when capitalism first was introduced outside Europe.

2. The end of the Cold War and the fall of communism led to a crisis in Marxian thought, and many of the tenets of modernization theory were revived in neoliberal economic theory, which promised to bring prosperity to any nation-state to find its niche in the globalizing capitalist market.

3. Globalization is understood and evaluated differently by different observers, but most anthropologists agree that the effects of globalization are uneven. In a globalizing world, wealth, images, people, things, and ideologies are deterritorialized. Some groups in some parts of the world benefit from global flows, contacts, and exchanges, whereas others are bypassed entirely.

4. Anthropologists and others disagree about whether these global processes are or are not systemic, or whether they are only the latest in a series of expansions and contractions that can be traced back to the rise of the first commercial civilizations several

thousand years ago. But none of these overall schemas can by itself account for the historically specific local details of the effects of global forces in local settings, which is what most anthropologists aim to document and analyze.

5. The flows unleashed by globalization have undermined the ability of nation-states to police their boundaries effectively, suggesting that conventional ideas about nation-states require revision. Contemporary migrants across national borders have developed a variety of trans-border identities. Some become involved in long-distance nationalism that leads to the emergence of trans-border states claiming emigrants as trans-border citizens of their ancestral homelands even if they are legal citizens of another state. Some trans-border citizenries call for the establishment of fully fledged transnational nation-states.

6. The contrasts between formal and substantive citizenship suggest that conventional notions of citizenship are breaking down in the context of globalization. Diaspora communities of elite Chinese families have developed a strategy of flexible citizenship that allows them both to circumvent and benefit from different nation-state regimes by investing, working, and settling their families in different sites. For these elite Chinese, the concept of nationalism has lost its meaning, and they seem to subscribe instead to a postnational ethos in which their only true loyalty is to the family business.

7. Discussions of human rights have intensified as global flows juxtapose and at least implicitly challenge different understandings of what it means to be human, or what kinds of rights people may be entitled to under radically changed conditions of everyday life. But different participants in this discourse have different ideas about the relationship that human rights and culture have with one another. As talk about human rights becomes incorporated into local cultural discussions, the notion is transformed to make sense in local contexts. Sometimes, "culture" may be used as a scapegoat for a government unwilling to extend certain rights to its citizens.

8. Some arguments about human rights include the right to one's culture. One of the key issues involved concerns the kinds of legal mechanisms needed to ensure such protection. But most international human rights documents only protect individual human rights, not group rights. And even those who seek to protect their individual rights are supposed to appeal to the governments of their own nation-states to enforce rights defended in international documents. Many activists and others view this factor as a serious contradiction in human rights discourse that undermines its effectiveness.

9. Some anthropologists argue that a "culture of human rights" has emerged in recent years that is based on certain ideas about human beings, their needs, and their abilities that originated in the West. Some consider this culture of human rights to be the culture of a globalizing world that emphasizes individual rights over duties or needs, and that proposes only technical rather than ethical solutions to human suffering. Anthropologists disagree about the value of such a culture of human rights in contemporary circumstances.

10. Groups and individuals who assert that their human rights have been violated regularly take their cases to courts of law. But because human rights law only recognizes certain kinds of rights violations, groups with grievances must tailor those grievances to fit the violations that human rights law recognizes. Groups that enter into the human rights process are entering into ethically ambiguous territory that is both enabling and constraining.

11. Debates about women's rights in Hawaii and children's rights in Thailand show both that it is possible to accommodate the universal discourse of human rights to local conditions and that no single model of the relationship between rights and culture will fit all cases. Struggles over human rights, along with struggles over global citizenship, can be seen as the prime struggles of our time.

12. The discourse of cultural imperialism, which developed primarily outside anthropology, tried to explain the spread of Western cultural forms outside the West. But anthropologists reject cultural imperialism as an explanation because it denies agency to non-Western peoples, because it assumes that cultural forms never move "from the rest to the West," and because it ignores flows of cultural forms that bypass the West entirely.

13. Anthropologists have developed alternatives to the discourse of cultural imperialism. They speak about borrowing-with-modification, domestication, indigenization, or customization of practices or objects imported from elsewhere. Many anthropologists describe these processes as examples of cultural hybridization or hybridity.

14. Talk of cultural hybridization has been criticized because the very attempt to talk about cultural mixtures assumes that "pure" cultures existed prior to mixing. Others object to discussions of cultural hybridization that fail to recognize that its effects are experienced differently by those with power and those without power. Cultural hybridization is unobjectionable when actors perceive it to be under their own control, but is resisted when they see it threatening their moral integrity.

15. Some anthropologists are working to devise ways of coping with the uncertainties and insecurities of globalization. Some would like to revive the notion of cosmopolitanism originally associated with Western elite forms of cultural hybridization and rework it in order to be able to speak about alternative or discrepant cosmopolitanisms that reflect the experiences of those who have been the victims of modernity. The ideal end result would be a critical cosmopolitanism capable of negotiating new understandings of human rights and global citizenship in ways that can dismantle barriers of gender and race that are the historical legacies of colonialism.

For Review

1. How is globalization defined in the textbook? What are the key features of the anthropological approach to the study of globalization?
2. Discuss the effects of migration on the nation-state.
3. What does it mean to talk about a trans-border citizenry?
4. Summarize the key points concerning multicultural politics in contemporary Europe, with particular attention to the different ways in which the UK, France, and Germany deal with immigration.
5. Summarize the issues surrounding Muslim marriage in France.
6. What is "flexible citizenship" and how is it used in Chinese diaspora communities?
7. How do anthropologists study human rights?
8. What is the "rights versus culture" debate?
9. What does it mean to defend "rights to culture"?
10. Explain how the anthropological concept of culture can help clarify issues in discussions of human rights.
11. Describe how programs to deal with violence against women in Hawaii and elsewhere in the world are related to globalization.
12. What are the key points in the case study of child prostitution in Thailand?
13. What is cultural imperialism? What are the three difficulties that anthropologists have found with this concept?
14. Discuss cultural hybridity, paying particular attention to the idea of borrowing-with-modification.
15. What are the difficulties associated with the concept of cultural hybridity?
16. What does it mean to be cosmopolitan?
17. Summarize Anna Tsing's discussion of "friction."
18. Describe border thinking.

Key Terms

globalization	legal citizenship	human rights
diaspora	substantive citizenship	cultural imperialism
long-distance nationalism	transnational nation-states	cultural hybridity
trans-border state	flexible citizenship	cosmopolitanism
trans-border citizenry	postnational ethos	friction

Suggested Readings

Hobart, Mark, ed. 1993. *An anthropological critique of development*. London: Routledge. Anthropologists from Britain, Holland, and Germany challenge the notion that Western approaches to development have been successful. They use ethnographic case studies to demonstrate how Western experts who disregard indigenous knowledge contribute to the growth of ignorance.

Inda, Jonathan Xavier and Renato Rosaldo, eds. 2002. *The anthropology of globalization: A reader*. Malden, MA: Blackwell.

A recent, comprehensive collection of articles by anthropologists who address the process of globalization from varied points of view and different ethnographic situations.

Merry, Sally Engle. 2009. *Gender violence: A cultural perspective*. Malden, MA: Wiley-Blackwell. An innovative and insightful book about the many forms gender violence takes around the world, and major efforts being made to diminish it.

Bibliography

Abbas, Akhbar. 2002. Cosmopolitan description: Shanghai and Hong Kong. In *Cosmopolitanism*, ed. Carol Breckenridge, Sheldon Pollock, Homi Bhaba, and Dipeesh Chakrabarty, 209–28. Durham, NC: Duke University Press.

Abu-Lughod, Lila. 1995. The objects of soap opera: Egyptian television and the cultural politics of modernity. In *Worlds apart: Modernity through the prism of the local*, ed. Daniel Miller, 190–210. London: Routledge.

Abusharaf, Rogaia Mustafa. 2000. Female circumcision goes beyond feminism. *Anthropology News* 41(March): 17–18.

Abwunza, Judith M. 1997. *Women's voices, women's power: Dialogues of resistance from East Africa*. Peterborough, ON: Broadview Press.

Adams, Richard Newbold. 1979. *Energy and structure: A theory of social power*. Austin: University of Texas Press.

Advocates for Indigenous California Language Survival. 2010. Master Apprentice Program. http://www.aicls .org/. Accessed April 15, 2010.

Agar, Michael. 1996. *The professional stranger*, 2d ed. San Diego: Academic Press.

Alland, Alexander. 1977. *The artistic animal*. New York: Doubleday Anchor.

Allen, Catherine J. 1988. *The hold life has: Coca and cultural identity in an Andean community*. Washington, DC: Smithsonian Institution Press.

Allen, Theodore. 1994–1997. *The invention of the white race*, 2 vols. London: Verso.

Alonso, Ana María. 1994. The politics of space, time, and substance: State formation, nationalism, and ethnicity. *Annual Review of Anthropology* 23: 379–405.

Alverson, Hoyt. 1977. Peace Corps volunteers in rural Botswana. *Human Organization* 36(3): 274–81.

Alverson, Hoyt. 1978. *Mind in the heart of darkness*. New Haven, CT: Yale University Press.

Alverson, Hoyt. 1990. Guest editorial. In *Cultural anthropology: A perspective on the human condition*, Emily Schultz and Robert Lavenda. St. Paul, MN: West.

Anderson, Benedict. 1983. *Imagined communities*. London: Verso.

Anderson, Richard L. 1990. *Calliope's sisters: A comparative study of philosophies of art*. Englewood Cliffs, NJ: Prentice Hall.

Apfel, Roberta, and Bennett Simon. 2000. Mitigating discontents with children in war: An ongoing psychological inquiry. In *Cultures under siege: Collective violence and trauma*, ed. Antonius C. G. M. Robben and Marcelo M. Suárez-Orozco, 271–84. Cambridge: Cambridge University Press.

Appadurai, Arjun. 1990. Disjuncture and difference in the global cultural economy. In *Global culture*, ed. Mike Featherstone, 295–310. London: Sage.

Appadurai, Arjun. 2002. Grassroots globalization and the research imagination. In *The anthropology of politics*, ed. Joan Vincent, 271–84. Malden, MA: Blackwell.

Asad Talal. 1973. *Anthropology and the colonial encounter*. New York: Humanities Press.

Asad, Talal. 2002. From the history of colonial anthropology to the anthropology of Western hegemony. In *The anthropology of politics*, ed. Joan Vincent, 133–42. Malden, MA: Blackwell.

Asad, Talal. 2003. *Formations of the secular: Christianity, Islam, modernity*. Stanford, CA: Stanford University Press.

Aufderheide, Patricia. 1993. Beyond television. *Public Culture* 5: 579–92.

Autobiografías Campesinas. 1979. Heredia, Costa Rica: Editorial de la Universidad Nacional.

Baer, Hans, Merrill Singer, and Ida Susser. 2003. *Medical anthropology and the world system*, 2d ed. Westport, CT: Praeger.

Bakhtin, M. M. 1981. *The dialogic imagination: Four essays*. Ed. Michael Holquist. Trans. Michael Holquist and Caryl Emerson. Austin: University of Texas Press.

Barad, Karen. 1999. Agential realism: Feminist interventions in understanding scientific practices. In *The science studies reader*, ed. Mario Biagioli, 1–11. New York: Routledge.

Barrionuevo, Alexei. 2010. "Bypassing resistance Brazil prepares to build a dam." *The New York Times*. August 15.

Basham, Richard. 1978. *Urban anthropology*. Palo Alto, CA: Mayfield.

Bateson, Gregory. 1972. A theory of play and fantasy. In *Steps to an ecology of mind*, ed. Gregory Bateson. 1955, 177–93. New York: Ballantine Books.

Bauman, Zygmunt. 1989. *Modernity and the Holocaust.* Ithaca, NY: Cornell University Press.

Beals, Alan. 1962. *Gopalpur, a south Indian village.* New York: Holt, Rinehart & Winston.

Behrendt, Larissa. 2007. The emergency we had to have. In *Coercive reconciliation: Stabilise, normalise, exit Aboriginal Australia*, eds. Jon Altman and Melinda Hinkson, 15–20. North Carlton, Australia: Arena Publications Association.

Beidelman, Thomas. 1982. *Colonial evangelism.* Bloomington: Indiana University Press.

Bell, Sandra, and Simon Coleman. 1999. The anthropology of friendship: Enduring themes and future possibilities. In *The anthropology of friendship*, ed. Sandra Bell and Simon Coleman, 1–19. Oxford: Berg.

Bellman, Beryl. 1984. *The language of secrecy.* New Brunswick, NJ: Rutgers University Press.

Ben-Tovim, Gideon. 1997. Why "positive action" is "politically correct." In *The politics of multiculturalism in the new Europe: Racism, identity, and community*, ed. Tariq Modood and Pnina Werbner, 209–22. London: Zed Books.

Bernard, H. Russell. 2006. *Research methods in anthropology.* 4th ed. Thousand Oaks, CA: Sage.

Berreman, Gerald. 1962. *Behind many masks: Ethnography and impression management in a Himalayan village.* Lexington, KY: Society for Applied Anthropology.

Bestor, Theodore. 2000. How sushi went global. *Foreign Policy* (November-December): 54–63.

Bigenho, Michelle. 2002. *Sounding indigenous: Authenticity in Bolivian music performance.* New York: Palgrave Macmillan.

Blackwood, Evelyn, and Saskia E. Wieringa. 1999. Preface. In *Female desires: Same-sex relations and transgender practices across cultures*, ed. Evelyn Blackwood and Saskia E. Wieringa, ix–xiii. New York: Columbia University Press.

Blanchard, Kendall, and Alyce Cheska. 1985. *The anthropology of sport.* South Hadley, MA: Bergin & Garvey.

Bledsoe, Caroline. 1993. The politics of polygyny in Mende education and child fosterage transactions. In *Sex and gender hierarchies*, ed. Barbara Diane Miller, 170–92. Cambridge: Cambridge University Press.

Boaz, Noel T., and Linda Wolfe, eds. 1995. *Biological anthropology: The state of the science.* Bend, OR: International Institute for Human Evolutionary Research.

Bock, Philip. 1994. *Rethinking psychological anthropology: Continuity and change in the study of human action.* 2d ed. Prospect Heights, IL: Waveland.

Boddy, Janice. 1997. Womb as oasis: The symbolic context of pharaonic circumcision in rural northern Sudan. In *The Gender/Sexuality Reader*, edited by Roger Lancaster and Micaela De Leonardo, 309–24. New York: Routledge.

Bodenhorn, Barbara. 2000. "He used to be my relative": Exploring the bases of relatedness among Iñupiat of northern Alaska. In *Cultures of relatedness: New approaches to the study of kinship*, ed. Janet Carsten, 128–48. Cambridge: Cambridge University Press.

Boellstorff, Tom. 2008. *Coming of age in Second Life. An anthropologist explores the virtually human.* Princeton, NJ: Princeton University Press.

Boesch-Ackermann, H., and C. Boesch. 1994. Hominization in the rainforest: The chimpanzee's piece of the puzzle. *Evolutionary Anthropology* 3(1): 9–16.

Borman, Randy. 1999. Cofan: Story of the forest people and the outsiders. *Cultural Survival Quarterly* 23(2): 48–50.

Bourgois, Philippe. 1995. *In search of respect: Selling crack in El Barrio.* New York: Cambridge University Press.

Bowen, John, ed. 1998. *Religion in culture and society.* Needham Heights, MA: Allyn & Bacon.

Bowen, John. 2002. *Religions in practice: An approach to the anthropology of religion.* 2d ed. Needham Heights, MA: Allyn & Bacon.

Bowen, John. 2010. *Can Islam be French? Pluralism and pragmatism in a secularist state.* Princeton, NJ: Princeton University Press.

Bowie, Fiona. 2006. *The anthropology of religion: An introduction.* 2d ed. Malden, MA: Blackwell.

Bowie, Katherine. 2008. Standing in the shadows: Of matrilocality and the role of women in a village election in Northern Thailand. *American Ethnologist* 35(1):136–53.

Bradburd, Daniel. 1998. *Being there: The necessity of fieldwork.* Washington, DC: Smithsonian Institution Press.

Brain, Robert. 1976. *Friends and lovers.* New York: Basic Books.

Branam, Kelly M. 2011 [forthcoming]. *Constitution making: Law, power and kinship in Crow Country.* Albany, NY: SUNY Press.

Brenneis, Donald, and Ronald Macaulay, eds. 1996. *The matrix of language: Contemporary linguistic anthropology.* Boulder, CO: Westview Press.

Brewin, Christopher. 1997. Society as a kind of community: Communitarian voting with equal rights for individuals in the European Union. In *The politics of multiculturalism in the new Europe: Racism, identity, and community*, ed. Tariq Modood and Pnina Werbner, 223–39. London: Zed Books.

Briggs, Jean. 1980. Kapluna daughter: Adopted by the Eskimo. In *Conformity and conflict.* 7th ed., ed. by James Spradley and David McCurdy, 44–62. Boston: Little, Brown.

Weinker, Curtis. 1995. Biological anthropology: The current state of the discipline. In *Biological anthropology: The state of the science*, ed. Noel T. Boaz and Linda Wolfe. Bend, OR: International Institute for Human Evolutionary Research.

Weismantel, Mary. 1995. Making kin: Kinship theory and Zumbagua adoptions. *American Ethnologist* 22(4): 685–709.

Werbner, Pnina. 1997. Aferword: Writing multiculturalism and politics in the new Europe. In *The politics of multiculturalism in the new Europe: Racism, identity, and community*, ed. Tariq Modood and Pnina Werbner, 261–67. London: Zed Books.

Weston, Kath. 1991. *Families we choose: Lesbians, gays, kinship.* New York: Columbia University Press.

Weston, Kath. 1995. Forever is a long time: Romancing the real in gay kinship ideologies. In *Naturalizing power*, ed. Sylvia Yanagisako and Carol Delaney, 87–110. New York: Routledge.

Whiteley, Peter. 2004. Ethnography. In *A companion to the anthropology of American Indians*, ed. Thomas Biolsi, 435–71. Malden, MA: Blackwell.

Whorf, Benjamin Lee. 1956. *Language, thought, and reality.* Ed. John B. Carroll. Cambridge, MA: M.I.T. Press.

Wilk, Richard. 1996. *Economies and cultures: Foundations of economic anthropology.* Boulder, CO: Westview Press.

Wilk, Richard, and Lisa Cliggett. 2007. *Economies and cultures: Foundations of economic anthropology.* Boulder, CO: Westview Press.

Williams, Brackette F. 1989. A class act: Anthropology and the race to nation across ethnic terrain. *Annual Review of Anthropology* 18: 401–44.

Wilmsen, Edwin. 1989. *Land filled with flies: A political economy of the Kalahari.* Chicago: University of Chicago Press.

Wilmsen, Edwin. 1991. Pastoro-foragers to "Bushmen": Transformation in Kalahari relations of property, production and labor. In *Herders, warriors, and traders: Pastoralism in Africa*, ed. John G. Galaty and Pierre Bonte, 248–63. Boulder, CO: Westview Press.

Wilson, R. A., ed. 1997. *Human rights, culture and context.* London: Pluto Press.

Witherspoon, Gary. 1975. *Navajo kinship and marriage.* Chicago: University of Chicago Press.

Wolcott, Harry F. 1999. *Ethnography: A way of seeing.* Walnut Creek, CA: AltaMira Press.

Wolf, Eric. 1969. *Peasant wars of the twentieth century.* New York: Harper and Row.

Wolf, Eric. 1982. *Europe and the people without history.* Berkeley: University of California Press.

Wolf, Eric. 1994. Facing power: Old insights, new questions. In *Assessing cultural anthropology*, ed. Robert Borofsky, 218–28. New York: McGraw-Hill.

Wolf, Eric. 1999. *Envisioning power: Ideologies of dominance and resistance.* Berkeley: University of California Press.

Wolfe, Linda. 1995. Current research in field primatology. In *Biological anthropology: The state of the science*, ed. Noel T. Boaz and Linda Wolfe, 149–67. Bend, OR: International Institute for Human Evolutionary Research.

Woolard, Kathryn A. 1998. Introduction: Language ideology as a field of inquiry. In *Language ideologies: Practice and theory*, ed. Bambi Schieffelin, Kathryn Woolard, and Paul V. Kroskrity, 3–47. New York: Oxford University Press.

Woost, Michael D. 1993. Nationalizing the local past in Sri Lanka: Histories of nation and development in a Sinhalese village. *American Ethnologist* 20(3): 502–21.

Yanagisako, Sylvia, and Jane Collier. 1987. Towards a unified analysis of gender and kinship. In *Gender and kinship: Essays toward a unified analysis*, ed. Jane Collier and Sylvia Yanagisako, 14–50. Stanford, CA: Stanford University Press.

Yuval-Davis, Nira. 1997. Ethnicity, gender relations, and multiculturalism. In *Debating cultural hybridity: Multicultural identities and the politics of anti-racism*, ed. Pnina Werbner and Tariq Modood. London: Zed Books.

Credits

Photography and Illustration

Chapter 1 1.2a, © Karl Ammann/CORBIS; 1.2b, courtesy Robert Lavenda; 1.3, © Macduff Everton/CORBIS; 1.4, © Irven DeVore/AnthroPhoto; 1.5, © Reuters/CORBIS; 1.6, courtesy Andrea Wiley. **Chapter 2** 2.2, reprinted by permission of Basic Books, a member of Perseus Book Group; 2.3, courtesy Daniel Lavenda; 2.4, © Anthony Bannister/Gallo Images/CORBIS; 2.5, © Anthony Bannister/Gallo Images/CORBIS; 2.6, courtesy Daniel Lavenda; 2.7, © CORBIS. **Chapter 3** 3.1, © Shepard Sherbell/CORBIS SABA; 3.3, © Rudi Von Briel/PhotoEdit; 3.4, © Mary Evans Picture Library/Alamy; 3.5, courtesy Ryan Cook; 3.6, courtesy Michelle Bigenho; 3.7, courtesy Luke Eric Lassiter; 3.8, courtesy Daniel Bradburd; 3.9, © Lawrence Manning/CORBIS. **Chapter 4** 4.2, © The Granger Collection/New York; 4.3, © Stefan Zaklin/Getty Images; 4.4, © Bettmann/CORBIS; 4.5, courtesy of the Peabody Essex Museum, Salem MA; 4.6, from *Political Anthropology: An Introduction*, Second Edition, by Ted Lewellen, © 1983 by Ted Lewellen, reproduced with permission of Greenwood Publishing Group, Inc., Westport, CT; 4.9, courtesy Arjun Guneratne. **Chapter 5** 5.1, © KING FEATURES SYNDICATE; 5.4, reprinted with permission of the Free Press, a division of Simon & Schuster, from *The Religion of Java* by Clifford Geertz, © 1960 by The Free Press; 5.5, © Robert Estall/CORBIS; 5.7, courtesy Robert Lavenda; 5.8, courtesy of the Australian Broadcasting Corporation; 5.9, © Chuck Savage/CORBIS; 5.10, © Ed Kashi/CORBIS; 5.11, courtesy Advocates for Indigenous California Language Survival. **Chapter 6** 6.2, from Michael Cole and Sylvia Scribner, *Culture and Thought: A Psychological Introduction*. With permission of the authors; 6.3, from Michael Cole and Sylvia Scribner, *Culture and Thought: A Psychological Introduction*. With permission of the authors; 6.6, © Anders Ryman/CORBIS; 6.7, © Randy Faris/CORBIS; 6.8, Gilles Peress/Magnum Photos; 6.9, © STOCKE/SUN SENTINEL/CORBIS SYGMA. **Chapter 7** 7.2, courtesy Robert Lavenda; 7.3, © Tim De Waele/CORBIS; 7.4, © REUTERS/Claudia Daut; 7.5, © Owen Franken/CORBIS; 7.6, © Gregg Newton/CORBIS; 7.7, © BISSON BERNARD/CORBIS SYGMA; 7.8, courtesy Michelle Bigenho; 7.9, © Everett Kennedy Brown/epa/CORBIS; 7.10, courtesy Susan Vogel; 7.11, courtesy Justin Kerr/Kerr Associates; 7.12, © Anders Ryman/CORBIS. **Chapter 8** 8.1, courtesy Robert Lavenda; 8.3, © Kazuyoshi Nomachi/CORBIS; 8.4, © Alinari Archives/CORBIS; 8.5a, © Reuters/CORBIS; 8.5b, © Bazuki MuhammadReuters/CORBIS; 8.6, © Motion Picture & Television Photo Archive; 8.7, © Abbas/Magnum Photos; 8.8, © AlessandroBianchi/Reuter/CORBIS; 8.9, © Roger Ressmeyer/CORBIS; 8.10, © Desirey Minkoh/Getty Images; 8.11, © Bryan & Cherry Alexander Photography/Alamy; 8.12, © Jean-Philippe Ksiazek/Getty Images. **Chapter 9** 9.1, © Jorge Uzon/Getty Images; 9.4, © Lakruwan Wannirachchi/Getty Images; 9.6, © Larry Dale Gordon/CORBIS; 9.7, Glen Allison, Getty Images; 9.8, Dave Saunders, Getty Images; 9.9, Stuart Franklin/Magnum Photos; 9.10, courtesy Orin Starn. **Chapter 10** 10.2, © Irven DeVore/AnthroPhoto; 10.3a, from Guaman Poma de Ayala, Nueva Coronica, c. 1610. With permission from Thames & Hudson Ltd.; 10.3b, map from Richard W. Keatinge, Peruvian Prehistory, 1988. Reprinted with permission from Cambridge University Press; 10.5, © AP Photo/Daily Sitka Sentinel, James Poulson; 10.6, courtesy Robert Lavenda; 10.7, © Bettman/CORBIS; 10.8, © Philip Gould/CORBIS; 10.9, © Georges Gobet/Getty Images; 10.10, © Marjorie Shostack/AnthroPhoto; 10.11, © Caroline Penn/Corbis. **Chapter 11** 11.2, courtesy Robert Lavenda; 11.3a, © Owen Franken/CORBIS; 11.3b, © Pete Saloutos/CORBIS; 11.7, © Alison Wright/CORBIS; 11.9, © Luciana Whitaker/Getty Images; 11.10, © AP Photo/Alastair Grant; 11.11, © AP Photo/Mike Wintroath; 11.12, © Reuters/CORBIS; 11.13, © Kambou Sia/Getty Images. **Chapter 12** 12.2, © Galen Rowell/CORBIS; 12.3, courtesy Robert Lavenda; 12.4, © Irven DeVore/AnthroPhoto; p. 299 © Amit Bhargava/CORBIS; 12.5, © Fred Mayer/Getty Images; 12.6, courtesy Robert Lavenda; 12.7, © Raghu Rai/Magnum Photos; 12.8, © Stephen Ferry/Getty Images; 12.9, © AP Photo/Radu Sigheti, Pool; 12.10, © Jan Buchofsky-Houser/CORBIS. **Chapter 13** 13.2, © David Turnley/CORBIS; 13.3, © Pablo Corral/CORBIS; 13.4, © Shawn Baldwin/CORBIS; 13.5, © The Cover Story/CORBIS; p. 334, from Elizabeth Chin, "Ethnically Correct Dolls: Toying with the Race Industry," *American Anthropologist 101*(2), 1999, reprinted by permission of the American Anthropological Association, not for further reproduction; 13.6, © Schalkwijk/Art Resource, NY; 13.7, © Stephanie Maze/CORBIS; 13.9, © Nik Wheeler/CORBIS; 13.10, © Matthew Mckee, Eye Ubiquitous/CORBIS; 13.12, © Reuters/CORBIS; 13.13, © Reuters/CORBIS. **Chapter 14** 14.1, © Reuters/CORBIS;

14.3, © Wendy Stone/CORBIS; 14.4, © Richard Cummins/ CORBIS; 14.5, © Bettmann/CORBIS; 14.6, © Chip East/ Reuters/CORBIS; 14.8, Giraud Philippe/CORBIS SYGMA; 14.9, © Attar Maher/CORBIS SYGMA; 14.10, © Stephanie Sinclair/CORBIS; 14.11, © AP Photo/Henry Griffin; 14.12, © Crawford/AnthroPhoto; 14.13, © UN Photo; 14.14, © Reuters/CORBIS; 14.15, © Micheline Pelletier/CORBIS SYMA; 14.16, © Reuters/CORBIS; 14.17, courtesy Lynn Meisch; 14.19, © Kazuyoshi Nomachi/CORBIS.

Text

Chapter 1 p. 8, courtesy of James W. Fernandez; p. 14, courtesy of John Omohundro, SUNY Plattsburgh. **Chapter 2** p. 21, courtesy Ivan Karp; p. 23, courtesy Hoyt Alverson; p. 25, Courtesy Sally Engle Merry. **Chapter 3** p. 51, © University of Illinois Press; p. 53, from Sawa Kurotani, *Home away from home: Japanese corporate wives in the United States.* Durham, NC: University of North Carolina Press. Reprinted with permission; p. 61, excerpt from *Yuquí: Forest Nomads in a Changing World* by Allyn M. Stearman. Copyright © 1989 by Holt, Rinehart and Winston. Reprinted by permission of the publisher; p. 63, courtesy Stephen Gudeman. **Chapter 4** p. 73, courtesy Annette Weiner; p. 75, excerpt from Ken Redford, "The Ecologically Noble Savage," *Cultural Survival Quarterly,* Vol. 15, No. 1, Spring 1991. Used with permission of the publisher. **Chapter 5** p. 94, courtesy David Parkin; p. 105, "Race and Language" (editorial), Marcyliena Morgan, *AAA Newsletter,* 1997, reprinted with permission of the American Anthropological Association. **Chapter 6** p. 127, from Robert Borofsky (ed), *Assessing Cultural Anthropology,* Copyright © 1993, McGraw-Hill, Inc. Reprinted with permission of the publisher; p. 131, from Alma Gottlieb, "American Premenstrual Syndrome," *Anthropology Today* 4(6), 1988. Reprinted by permission of the Royal Anthropological Institute. **Chapter 7** p. 161, from Julie Taylor, "Tango," *Cultural Anthropology* 2:4, 1987. Reprinted by permission of the American Anthropological Association; p. 167, from Patricia Aufderheide, "Latin American Grassroots Video: Beyond Television," *Public Culture* 5:3, Spring 1993. Copyright © 1993 by Duke University Press. All rights reserved. Reprinted by permission of Duke University Press. **Chapter 8** p. 187, from Andrea Smith, "For All Those Who Were Indian in a Former Life," *Cultural Survival Quarterly,* Vol. 17, No. 4, Winter 1994. Used with permission of the publisher; p. 191, from Roger M. Keesing, *Custom and Confrontation.* Copyright © 1992 by the University of Chicago Press. Reprinted by permission of the publisher. **Chapter 9** p. 209, courtesy of Kelly Branam; p. 218, from *The New York Times,* © 6/12/2009 The New York Times All Rights Reserved. Used by permission and protected by the Copyright Laws of the United States. The printing, copying, redistribution, or retransmission of the material without express written permission is prohibited. **Chapter 10** p. 236, from

Autobiographias campesinas, 1979, Vol. 1, Heredia, Costa Rica: Editorial della Universidad Nacional, translated from Spanish by Robert H. Lavenda; p. 240, from *Crafting Selves* by Dorinne Kondo. Copyright 1990 by The University of Chicago Press. Reprinted with permission of the publisher; p. 247, from *African Art in Transit* by Christopher Steiner, 1994, Cambridge University Press. Reprinted with permission from the publisher. **Chapter 12** p. 296, from Judith Abwunza, *Women's Voices, Women's Power: Dialogues of Resistance from East Africa.* Copyright © 1997 by Judith Abwunza. Reprinted by permission of Broadview Press; p. 299, from "Dowry Too High. Lose Bride and Go to Jail," by James Brooke. Copyright © 2003 by The New York Times Co. Reprinted with permission; p. 305, from John van Willigen and V. C. Channa, "Law, Custom, and Crimes against Women," *Human Organization* 50(4) 1991, 369–370. Reproduced by permission of the Society for Applied Anthropology; p. 310, Courtesy Brett Williams; p. 312, reproduced by permission of the American Anthropological Association from *Anthropology News,* Volume 45, Issue #6, pp. 21–24, 2004. Not for sale or further reproduction. **Chapter 13** p. 332, from *The New York Times,* © 4/272009 The New York Times All Rights Reserved. Used by permission and protected by the Copyright Laws of the United States. The printing, copying, redistribution, or retransmission of the material without express written permission is prohibited; p. 334, from Elizabeth Chin, "Ethnically Correct Dolls: Toying with the Race Industry," *American Anthropologist* 101(2), 1999. Reprinted by permission of the American Anthropological Association; p. 340, from Stanley Tambiah, "The Politics of Ethnicity," *American Ethnologist,* 16(2), 1989. Reprinted by permission of the American Anthropological Association; p. 341, from Mathiasson, J. "Living on the Land", pp. 161–62, from *Women's Voices, Women's Power: Dialogues of Resistance from East Africa* by J. Abwunza, © University of Toronto Press, Higher Education Division, 1997. Reprinted with permission of the Publisher. **Chapter 14** p. 355, from Larry Rohter, "Amazon Indians Honor an Intrepid Spirit." Copyright © 2003 by the New York Times Co. Reprinted with permission; p. 359, from *The Amazonian Chronicles* by Jacques Meunier and A. M. Savarin, San Francisco: Mercury House. Translation copyright 1994 by Carol Christiansen. Reprinted by permission; p. 360, from *The New York Times,* © 8/10/2010 The New York Times All Rights Reserved. Used by permission and protected by the Copyright Laws of the United States. The printing, copying, redistribution, or retransmission of the material without express written permission is prohibited; p. 362, from Randy Borman, "Cofan: Story of the Forest People and the Outsiders," *Cultural Survival Quarterly,* Summer 1999, 48–50. Reprinted by Permission of the Publisher; p. 382, from "How Sushi Went Global," by Theodore Bestor, *Foreign Policy,* November 2000; p. 386, from WALHI, http://www.eng.walhi.or.id/, March 2007.

Index